REDISCOVERING GANDHI

VOLUME 9 : Conflict Resolution and Peace Building: The Gandhian Way

Series Editor: ***Prof. R.P. Misra***

Vol. 1. Hind Swaraj: *Gandhi's Challenge to Modern Civilization*—***R.P. Misra***
2. Ahimsa: *The Way to Peace*—***Jonathan K. Crane & Jordi Agusti-Panareda***
3. Satyagraha: *Gandhian Approach to Conflict Resolution*—***Jainarain Sharma***
4. Consensual Democracy: *Gandhi on State, Power, and Politics*—***Ashu Pasricha***
5. Humanizing Science and Technology: *Some Case Studies*
—***Vinnie Jauhari*** and ***Parul Goyal***
6. Gandhi and Jesus : The End of Fundamentalism—***Wolfgang Sternstein***
7. How Relevant is Gandhi Today? A Japanese View—***Yamaguchi Hiroichi***
8. Gandhian Economics and Its Contemporary Relevance
—***R.P. Misra*** and ***D. Gopal***
9. Conflict Resolution and Peace Building: The Gandhian Way
—***R.P. Misra*** and ***D. Gopal***
10. Mahatma Gandhi: The Man, His Vision and Mission—***R.P. Misra***

About the Editors

Prof. R.P. Misra. Born in 1930, Prof. Misra did his BA (1952) and MA (1954) at the University of Allahabad, and Ph.D. at the University of Maryland, College Park, Md., USA in 1964. Author of 15 books and editor of over 30 volumes on Gandhian thought, local and regional planning, environment, and human development, Prof. Misra specializes in economic geography, urban and regional planning, sustainable development, Gandhian studies and peace research. After joining the University of Mysore, Department of Gegraphy in 1965 as its head, he launched an interdisciplinary Institute of Development Studies (IDS) in 1968 and took over as its founder Director (1968-79).

He made a name in the field of Geography and local and regional planning both in India and abroad and was invited as Vice-Director of the United Nations Centre for Regional Development (UNCRD), Nagoya, Japan (1979-83). Earlier, he was consultant/advisor at the United Nations Research Institute for Social Development (UNRISD), Geneva, and UNDP, Teheran, Iran. Prof. Misra was Vice-Chancellor of Allahabad University (1984-87) and Professor of Regional Planning at Delhi School of Economics, Delhi University (1987-95). He was honoured with prestigious Bhoogol Ratna award by the Bhoovigyan Vikas Foundation, India.

Prof. D. Gopal, Prof. Darvesh Gopal hails from Gulburga, Karnataka. At present, he is Professor of Political Science, Director of School of Social Sciences, and Coordinator of Gandhi and Peace Studies Programme in Indira Gandhi National Open University (IGNOU), New Delhi. He has been serving IGNOU for the last 25 years and has more than 30 years experience in teaching and research. Prof. Gopal earned his M.Phil. and Ph.D. degrees in International Relations from JNU, New Delhi and M.A. (Political Science) from Karnataka University, Dharwar. He developed MA degree course in Peace Studies and Conflict Resolution and brought out course material to suit learners of the subject on ODL (Open and Distance Learning) Mode.

Prof. Gopal is involved in the development of curriculum on "Gandhian Approach to Conflict Resolution and Peace building" in selected Colombian universities. He is a Visiting Professor or Fellow at several reputed Universities in India and abroad, including Hawke Research Institute, University of South Australia, Adelaide; and Malviya Centre for Peace Research, BHU, Varanasi, India. He has authored and edited 10 books and published more than thirty research papers in various journals and books.

REDISCOVERING GANDHI

Series Editor
Prof. R.P. Misra

Volume 9
Conflict Resolution and Peace Building: The Gandhian Way

Edited by
R.P. Misra
and
D. Gopal

CONCEPT PUBLISHING COMPANY PVT. LTD.
NEW DELHI-110059

ISBN-13: 978-81-8069-374-8 (Series)
ISBN-13: 978-93-5125-237-5 (Vol. 9)

First Published 2018

Published and Printed by

Concept
Since 1974

Concept Publishing Company Pvt. Ltd.
A/15-16, Commercial Block, Mohan Garden,
New Delhi-110059 (INDIA)
T: 91 11 25351460, 91 11 25351794
E: publishing@conceptpub.com; *W*: www.conceptpub.com

Cataloging in Publication Data--Courtesy: D.K. Agencies (P) Ltd. <docinfo@dkagencies.com>

Conflict resolution and peace building : the Gandhian way / edited by R.P. Misra and D. Gopal.
pages cm. — (Rediscovering Gandhi ; volume 9)
Contributed articles.
Includes bibliographical references and index.
ISBN 9788180693748 (series)
ISBN 9789351252375 (vol. 9)

1. Conflict management—India. 2. Peace-building—India. 3. India—Foreign relations. 4. India—Politics and government. 5. Gandhi, Mahatma, 1869-1948. I. Misra, R. P., 1930- editor. II. Gopal, D. (Darvesh), editor. III. Series: Rediscovering Gandhi ; volume 9.

JZ5584.I4C66 2018 DDC 327.1720954 23

Preface

Conflict is undesirable and the main source of unhappiness in the world, so think the people. It spoils relations among individuals, families, groups, societies and nations and generates tension, hatred and war. Everyone loves peace but those who do not have conflicting interests are rare. Even though the great religions of the world call for peace and harmony, there is hardly a religious group which has not waged wars to extend the domain of peace. Millions of children of God have been butchered in God's name and even today killing of innocent people in the name of God is continuing. Today conflict is more pervading than peace; and if people are not engaged in hot wars, it is because there is fear of a mightier enemy or mutual destruction.

Conflict is inherent to human psyche. Each individual is unique in physical built, emotional stability, mental capability and like and dislikes; and each is born in a different geographical and temporal setting and hence has different perceptions of the past, present and the future. What is right for one becomes wrong for others and what is good for some becomes bad for many others. Conflicts takes place when differently made and brought up individuals try to create a space for themselves and compete for scarce resources — material and non-material. When competition among the contending parties becomes deliberate and tense the mutual relations are marred by dislike and hatred. All this gives rise to conflicts. "Conflict is the deliberate attempt to oppose, resist or coerce the will of others."[1] It is these externally similar, but internally disparate individuals who constitute the building blocks of collectivities like families, communities, groups, classes, and nations. They infect these collectivities too with the viruses of dislike, hatred, superiority complex and ultimately violence in various forms.

Yet and at the same time, each individual is so desirous of peace that his whole life is spent in search of it often through conflict. All cultural traditions as expressed through religions are nothing but search for eternal peace. Those who sacrifice their own interests for the sake of the interests and good of their fellow beings are not rare. It is natural for humans, nay even animals to sacrifice everything for the good of their young offspring. Each individual is thus a bundle of love and hate, sacrifice and lust, non-violence and violence, and conflict and peace. Which of the two contradictory tendencies prevail at a particular time depends partly on the circumstances and partly on the tendencies; and partly inherent and partly acquired from early childhood.

Psychologists assert that the character (*samskaras*) of a person is shaped during the first 8-10 years of his birth. Thus, the parents especially the mother plays a very crucial role in shaping the character of a person. Superimposed on these *samskaras* is the education the young get in schools, colleges and universities as they grow to become adults. The external environment in which a person is born and live is also plays an important role in shaping the character of an individual. The children copy the adults. An environment of peace at home and in the society at large makes a person peace loving; while an environment of conflict and violence trains him to be self-centered and violent. That is the general rule.

The human history and even prehistory is nothing but a record of clash between love and hate; violence and non-violence, creation and destruction. Tired of violence and conflict man turns to spirituality and follows the great peace builders of the world like Rama, Krishna, Mahavira, Buddha, Christ and Mohammad, and Gandhi. All these great souls tried hard to take humanity away from avarice, hatred, violence, and conflict. They were branded as incarnations of God, Messengers of God, Sons of God, and so on. But the teachings of even these great souls fell foul on many a human mind. Millions of people have been killed and are being killed even today in the name of religion.

Differences of opinion on everything concerning human life are but to emerge from time to time. In the past, such differences have led to differences in traditions, cultures and histories and in dealing with the differences as and when they arise. One of the approaches followed was to fight the issues out violently, if need be to defeat the opponent. A parallel and most sought after approach has been sort out the differences peacefully and create conditions in which all could live together in peace and harmony. Love and hate, non-violence and violence and conflict and peace are thus a part and parcel of human nature. Individual initiatives, societal norms and traditions and formal rules and laws have evolved to ensure that conflicts and the psychic, economic and social factors that promote them are subdued and humanity moves towards an era of peace.

How strange it is that most wars have been fought for justice and peace and many peace treaties have led to newer and more devastating wars? No peace formula has so far been effective in killing the germs of wars. Eternal peace has thus remained a dream. And if there is any possibility of living in peace, it is only in the life after death and even for that man has to be a good human being to ensure a place in the heaven, *swarga*, or *behist*. If there is no apparent war at a given time and place, it is not because there is peace. Similarly, if there is a semblance of peace at a given time and place, it does not mean that the germs of conflict are dead. When conflict is promoted by those who command wealth, arms, and manpower, war breaks out; and when peace is promoted by a spiritual leader, who rules over the hearts of the people, peace rules supreme. Each conflict is thus followed by peace which in turn is followed by conflict as if peace is an eternal need and conflict an eternal means to break peace. Human beings ever since their emergence as *Homo sapiens* have tried to limit conflicts and to extend the domain of peace. But alas, they have not succeeded so far.

We can learn some lessons from the animal world. The love they bestow on their minors and fellow members of the herd is well known. Yet, they fight to override the interests of others in matters of sex, food, and space. Once the fight is over, they throw the love net on the opponent and become friends again. Human beings are at a far higher pedestal in matters of evolution. They have been bestowed with larger brain and more advanced physiology and hence, they behave differently. Their relationship with the world around them is not limited to their toddlers; it extends to the whole life span and many generations. In fact the Vedics over 5,000 years ago envisioned the whole human race as a single family (*vasudhaiva kutumbakam*) bound by love, affection, sacrifice, and sharing.

How can the 8 billion people of the world together with the animal and plant life and the inanimate world constitute a family unless there is give and take among them; unless there is a craving to live together, work together and love each other? Peace is thus an eternal craving of man and he translates this craving through family, community, religion, group, national, and international ties. These ties work for some time and then fissures develop because of contrasting visions, desires and needs. Love is then overtaken by hate and peace by conflict. This happens because man's evolutionary journey has not yet crossed the milestone where rights are overtaken by duties; hatred by love; untruth by truth; and violence by non-violence.

Knowing that permanent peace in any society is just not possible unless the nature of man changes and the factors that promote conflict are subdued, efforts have been made from times immemorial to resolve conflicts as and when they surfaced peacefully and by advancing the evolutionary process further following the footsteps of Rama, Krishna, Mahavira, Buddha, Christ, Mohammad in days bygone and Gandhi in our own times. They demonstrated peace can reign in an environment of love and thus left behind enduring legacies to make human beings better humans and to live in peace and harmony.

Conflicts and wars have claimed millions of lives in the past. In twentieth century the casualties during I and II World Wars amounted to over 100 million people. The WW I was fought to end all wars but it was followed by WW II. Although, there was no World War since 1945, international, intra-national, regional and local conflicts have continued unabated. If the WW III has not yet taken place, it is only because of the fear of the Atom Bomb and Mutual Destruction. Between 1945 and 1987 about 76 million people 'have been murdered in cold blood by one regime or the other, around thirteen times the number of Jews who became victims of the Holocaust. Much of this genocide was carried out for political reasons (reasons of state or power), but it has also been outright genocide (the killing of people by virtue of their ethnicity, race, religion, or nationality, says R.J. Rummel in his book *Death by Government*.

Mahatma Gandhi was the foremost peace builders of the twentieth century. He liberated India using Truth and Non-violence as the means to win over the mighty British Raj. He tried first to clean the minds of the people of India of hatred towards the British people. "Hate the sin not the sinner", said he. And he further elaborated this statement by saying that India's fight was against the British Raj, not against the British people. Thus Gandhi revived the spiritual path of winning hatred by love and thereby minimizing the sphere of conflict and maximizing the sphere of peace. Many a people followed Gandhi to secure their freedom and human rights. In the USA, the blacks followed him under the leadership of Martin Luther King Jr. to stop racial discrimination and ensure their human rights. Under Nelson Mandela, South Africa won its national freedom peacefully. And in East Europe, the Polish trade union leader Lech Walesa lighted a lamp of democracy that enlightened the whole of the then communist world.

Gandhi's approach to building peace has been used in many other places with considerable success. Today, it has become part of the general theory of conflict resolution and peace. Yet, conflicts have not ceased. They have rather become more widespread as new factors like control over natural resources; super-power rivalry, ethnic identities, economic competition and religious fundamentalism have overtaken the age-old tradition of sharing, human brotherhood, cooperation, and non-violence. If the conflicts do not escalate to become major wars, it is because of the fear of mutual destruction or the fear of super powers imposing their will directly or through the United Nations. How strange, it is that the whole of the Islamic world is burning because dictators have taken over the reigns of the government.

It is in this context that peace building has become an expanding field of study and practice all over the world. Many researchers, scholars and men and women in public life are engaged in analyzing the causes and consequences of conflicts and in finding ways and means of resolving them peacefully. Top universities of the world have established institutions/centres of peace studies to train conflict resolution specialists at all levels: local to international. And the number of NGIs and NGOs engaged in mediation and arbitration to help the contending parties to arrive at a win-win point has increased manifold.

The Indira Gandhi National Open University (IGNOU) has taken a lead in India in launching a series of courses ranging from certificate to doctorate levels in Gandhian Studies and Peace Research in association with Gandhi Smriti and Darshan Samiti (GS&DS), Ministry of Culture, Government of India, New Delhi. It has also built a Gandhi Centre at the Gandhi Darshan Complex of the GS&DS at Rajghat.

The Centre organized a number of expert group meetings to prepare the courses of studies and seminars and conferences to get feedback from scholars engaged in Gandhian studies in general and peace research in particular. One of these conferences focused on Conflict Resolution and Peace Building: The Gandhian Way. This volume is a compendium of chapters presented and discussed in this conference. In order to fill some important gaps, a few more papers were invited and included in the volume.

We are grateful to the participants of the conference and other scholars for contributing quality papers and extending further the scope of peace research in India. But for their contributions, a volume that is comprehensive in coverage and highly relevant to present socio-political and economic situation in the world, in general, and India in particular, would not have become a reality. We also appreciate the Concept Publishing Company Pvt. Ltd., New Delhi for bringing out the book so professionally and beautifully.

New Delhi
February 12, 2016

R.P. Misra
D. Gopal

Contents

List of Contributors

Amrutkar, Prasant, is a Professor of Political Science in Bhimarao Ambedkar University, Marathwada, Aurangabad, Maharashtra.

Basu, Swaraj, is a Professor of History in Indira Gandhi National Open University, New Delhi. He can be contacted at *basuswaraj@gmail.com*, 011-29535737, 29572716.

Das, Samir Kumar, is presently the Vice-Chancellor of the University of North Bengal. A Professor of Political Science at the University of Calcutta, Kolkata (now on lien), he was a Post-Doctoral Fellow (2005) of the Social Science Research Council (South Asia Programme) based in New York. He specializes in and writes on ethnicity, security, migration, rights, justice and democracy.

Kamath, P.M., Formerly Professor of Political Science, Mumbai University, the author is Honorary Director, VPM's Centre for International Studies, Mumbai. His latest book is: India's Policy of "No First Use of Nuclear Weapons: Relevance to Peace and Security in South Asia", (2009), New Delhi: Anamika Publishers.

Malviya, Gopalji, is a Professor in the Department of Defence and Strategic Studies, University of Madras Chepauk Campus, Chennai-600 005. He specializes in Sino-Indian Relations: Strategic Dimension. Author of five books and a number of papers, he can be contacted at his office telephone number 044-25399633, and email: *gopalji.malviya2000@unom.ac.in; gopalji_malviya2000@yahoo.com*

Misra, R.P., is a well-known Gandhian Scholar, rural, urban and regional development specialist. A Ph.D. from University of Maryland, USA. Prof. Misra was Director, Institute of Development Studies, University of Mysore, Vice Director, UNCRD, Nagoya Japan and Vice-Chancellor of Allahabad University. Mobile: 9450869688; 8860502161; e-mail: *sdf.misra@gmail.com*

Nair, Yogesh, Lieutenant Colonel Yogesh Nair is currently posted as GSO1 (Operations) in Indian Army. He often writes on water security, a topic of contemporary relevance across the world. The issue of availability of fresh water has always been central to sustainable development, economic growth, social stability and poverty alleviation across the globe. Among the various papers he has authored is one titled "Threat from China's River Diversion Project."

Narayanan, R., Former Dean, School International Studies, Jawahar Lal Nehru University (JNU), Prof. Narayanan is currently Adjunct Professor, School of Social Sciences, Indira Gandhi National Open University (IGNOU), New Delhi.

Premasekhara, L., Senior Lecturer, Department of Politics and International Studies, Pondicherry University, Puducherry.

Raju, A. Subramanyam, An Associate Professor at the Centre for South Asian Studies, University of Pondicherry, Puducherry-605014, Dr. Raju has published over forty papers in reputed journals and books. He can be contacted at e-mail: *asraju.sas@pondiuni.edu.in*

Ramaswamy, Susheela, is a Professor of Political Science; She is currently employed as Professor of Political Science, Jesus and Mary College, University of Delhi.

Samraj, P. Lazarus, Department of Political & International Studies, Pondicherry University, Puducherry-605014.
e-mail: *lazarus.pol@pondiuni.edu.in*

Savitri, K., Associate Professor, Department of Political Science, Jamia Millia Islamia, New Delhi. She holds Ph. D. degree from JNU; M.A. in Human Rights from Leicester, U.K. e-mail: *savi_kad@yahoo.co.in*

Sharma, Jai Narain, Professor in Department of Gandhian and Peace Studies, Punjab University, Chandigarh, Prof. is the author several books and papers on Gandhian thought. He can be contacted at mobile number 9417192372 and *e-mail: gps@pu.ac.in*

Shri Krishan, is Professor of History at Indira Gandhi University, Meerpur (Rewari), Haryana. His area of interest is Modern Indian History. He can be contacted at Mobile: 8800520040 or e-mail: *iguhistory@gmail.com*.

Sundaram, S.K.G., Professor of Economics at the S.N.D.T. Women's University, Badodara, Gujarat, he obtained his Ph.D. in Social Sciences from the Tata Institute of Social Sciences, Mumbai-88. His special field of interest is "labour and industry" with focus on informal sector, trade unions, industrial relations, Gandhian studies, entrepreneurship, consumer protection, NGOs, and higher education. He has acted as Vice-Chancellor on several occasions. Presently he is a free lance teacher and researcher and can be contacted by email: *skg_sundaram@rediffmail.com*

Talpadi, Rajaram, The author is Reader, Department of Political Science, Mangalore University, Mangala, Gangothri-574199, Karnataka.

Upadhyay, Shashi Bhushan, is a Professor with the Faculty of History of JNU, New Delhi. Specialist in fields of Labour History, Dalit Studies and Literary studies. He has authored and edited here books and published over 20 articles. He can be contacted at 91-011-29533845, 29572739 and
e-mail: *sbu11@hotmail.com*

Wancho, Rohit, did his M.A. in History at Jawaharlal Nehru University, New Delhi, and his Ph. D. from Cambridge University, U.K. He has been teaching history at St. Stephen's College, Delhi University, Delhi-110007 since 1985. At present he is a Fellow at the Nehru Memorial Museum and Library, New Delhi. He has co-authored a book entitled Representing India published by OUP in 2007.

1
Introduction

"When the Power of Love overcomes the Love of Power,
the World will Know Peace."

–James Marshall "Jimi" Hendrix
(November 27, 1942 – September 18, 1970):
American guitarist and singer-songwriter

Peace and conflict are opposite to each other but they go together. Peace is eternal craving of man and conflict is his eternal character. He is different from the animals because he has progressed far beyond the animal stage of evolution. He is so built physiologically and mentally that he is different from the rest of his species. He has no true copies. And he is so greatly influenced by his past experiences and the present circumstances that he cannot remain his true self. The differences turn into disparities and disparities lead to conflicts. When conflicts arise, man tries to resolve them and by establishing a new set of human relationships wherein misunderstanding is subdued by understanding, hatred by love; disparity by unity; and enmity by friendship. That is called peace.

Peace thus established does not last long. As new generation take charge of the society and new natural and social circumstances develop, new challenges before the individuals, groups and nations emerge. To meet these challenges new strategies are developed. Moreoftenthannot these strategies clash with those others. And new conflicts take over the otherwise peaceful relations. Whether an individual or society or nation would be in peace or will be torn by conflicts depends on a number of factors.

This chapter tries to introduce this volume by defining peace and conflict, and deliberating on the causes and consequences of each. Lastly, it introduces the Gandhian approach to building peace.

UNDERSTANDING PEACE

> To enjoy inner peace, to keep one's family and community in peace and to spread peace all around, one must first discipline and control one's own mind. If a man can control his mind he can find the way to Enlightenment, and all wisdom and virtue will naturally come to him. *–Buddha*
>
> Peace cannot be kept by force; it can only be achieved by understanding. *–Albert Einstein*
>
> Each one has to find his peace from within. And peace to be real must be unaffected by outside circumstances.
> *–Mahatma Gandhi*
>
> If we are to teach real peace in this world, and if we are to carry on a real war against war, we shall have to begin with the children.
> *–Mahatma Gandhi*

Peace is usually defined as absence of war. This definition, however, hides more than it reveals. If we consider the word war as coterminous with conflict, then the above definition gets closer to the reality. Wars are few but conflicts widespread. Today, each individual is torn by conflicts within; and there is hardly a family, community, group, society and nation, which is not conflict-ridden. The conflicts have now emerged between man and nature. The result is global warming and climate change. So, there is man himself has become a torn personality, and the institutions and relations that he built have also become conflict ridden. No wonder then that the search for peace has become one of the pre-occupations of thinkers especially the social scientists. Each culture, therefore, has its own definition of peace. The followers of different religions see peace differently and so do ideologues like pacifists, socialists, libertarians or idealistic theorists.

RELIGION AND PEACE

Hinduism: *Shanti* in Sanskrit denotes tranquillity, calm and bliss; it also denotes absence of isolation (*vigrahabhava*) and hostility, strife or war (*yuddhabhava*). The *Vedas* and *Upanishads*, (*c*. 6000 to 500 BC) the ancient most religious books of the world, linked *Shanti* to *Nirvana* and considered former as the means to escape from rebirth. It could be achieved through meditation and *sadkarma* (good deeds). It was also linked to *ahimsa* or non-violence towards all life forms because all souls

(*Atma*) have a common source, i.e., *paramatma* or God. All life is one and even an insect could harbour the soul of a close relative after his rebirth. Harm to any living creature is, therefore, a bad deed (*dushkarma*). The non-violence of Mahatma Gandhi (1869-1948) owed a great deal to this concept of peace.

In *Bhagavad Gita*, Krishna tells Arjuna that death is not to be feared because all souls return to new bodies after the old ones die. To get freedom from rebirth, one must reject all greed and anger and once an individual is on the path of self-denial, he would have peace within even in the midst of war.

Peace is thus an inner state that leads to peace in the society at large. Much before *Bhagavad Gita*, the *Rig Veda* had said:

"Come together, talk together
Let our minds be in harmony.
Common be our prayer
Common be our end,
Common be our purpose
Common be our deliberations,
Common be our desires
United be our hearts,
United be our intentions
Perfect be the union among us."

The *Rig Veda* also laid down the right conduct of war. Vedic rules maintain that it is unjust to strike someone from behind, cowardly to poison the tip of the arrow and heinous to attack the sick or old, children and women. To quote Swami Bhaskarananda of the Vedanta Society of Western Washington, "The rulers think that punishing the peace-breakers will bring peace. The oppressed think that eliminating the oppressors will ensure peace. The nations think that destroying or subduing the enemy nations will create peace. But the wise say that ever-enduring peace can never be obtained through external means."

"One who has found inner peace has indeed found peace that abides forever. Through spiritual discipline alone this inner peace can be acquired.

One who has found peace within transmits peace to others by one's own life's example, though one be not aware of it."

"Therefore, say the wise, may all try to create peace within, before trying to create any temporary or superficial peace in the world through external means."

Thus, Hinduism lays great emphasis of peace within. A person in peace within would not be violent nor would he try to bring any one down emotionally, physically, socio-politically or economically. A world shaped in Hindu thought would be a peaceful world.

Buddhism: The Buddhist ideas of peace is based on early Hindu notion that self-denial was the key to inner peace as well peace with the universe around. True peace and happiness can come only when desires are eradicated and life becomes need based. Non-violence (*Ahimsa*) is the way to peace with the world around. And through meditation, selfish desire can be eliminated and once this happens one reaches the stage of absolute peace (*Nirvana*). At that stage one loses his identity and merges in the whole. Once this happens, all sensory awareness and feeling is shut down, in what is known as *sannavedayitanirodha*. This being a temporary phenomenon, Buddha believed that eternal peace (*shanti*), both internal and external can only be achieved when it is merged in one's conception of the world and the people inhabiting it. Buddha considered peace to be conditional and related to time and space. Insistence on permanence led to inflexibility, and thus conflict. So, the path to enlightenment was not fixed once for all; there was scope for change and newness in seeking peace within, as well as without.

Buddhism like Jainism and to a great extent Hinduism lay emphasis on self-control. By conquering one's own self, one attains internal peace; to attain external peace, one, however, need not conquer the world. One need not be a super power possessing nuclear weapons to rule the earth. Those who can win the minds and hearts of the people living around them, become more powerful than super powers of modern days. Buddhism started in India but spread to the much of the then known world including China and Tibet in the north; Japan, Malaysia, and Indonesia in the east; Afghanistan in the west; and Srilanka in the south. Ashoka the Great (304–232 BC) demonstrated how one can become a real superpower by renouncing violence and all that has been won by force.

Jainism: Eternal peace is the credo of Jainism. The human soul can experience infinite bliss (*Ananda*) only when there is peace within (in the mind) and outside (individuals, family, society, nation, the world and the universe). All these are independent to each other yet inter-related. What is important is the welfare (*mangal*) of all living beings, from minute insects to human beings.

According to Jain thought, soul is the abode of Peace (*Shanti*) and peace the eternal quality of soul. Eternal peace can be achieved by conquering one self, i.e., ridding oneself free of all the vices (anger, jealousy, competition, attachment, and hatred, etc.). If one is at peace with oneself, his family becomes peaceful. Soon, peace spreads in the community, society; nation, the world and finally the whole universe. Jainism accepts differences of opinion (*Anekavad*) and hence respect views of others even if they are contrary. It considers non-violence (*Ahimsa*) as the foundation of peace and love the foundation of *Ahimsa*. There can be no peace so long as the welfare of all living creatures is assured.

Jainism, therefore, prescribes five vows or moral principles (*Panch Vratas*) to be observed by all. These are:

1. *Ahimsa* or non-violence,
2. *Satya* or truth,
3. *Astheya* or non-stealing,
4. *Brahmacharya* or chastity, and
5. *Aparigraha* or non-possession.

Since most people in the world share the above five principles at least in thought they do follow Jainism. But unless they put them into practice they are not true Jain. It goes against Jain principles if someone supports violence or remains expectator to the injustice been done to someone. Practice of non-violence should be limited to human beings; it should extend even to the lowest level of living species. That is why, vegetarianism is basic to Jainism. If the Jain code of conduct is mistakingly or otherwise violated, one should purify the body by fasting, purify the mind by doing *pratikraman* and then ask for universal forgiveness at least once in a year. That is why Jains observe a day every year as universal day of forgiveness.

Christianity: Christians see peace in six perspectives: Peace with God, peace within, peace with others, peace as non-violence, peace absence of conflict and peace as justice. Some Christians link peace with peace with all those around them. Many others claim that peace with others is not possible unless they are at peace with God. Some Christians understand peace as an inward reality derived from peace with God before it is an outward one. For others, inward peace is the prime means for working at peace in the world. But those who do not consider inner peace a prerequisite to outward peace contend that inner peace varies over time and within personal experience and hence can never be attained in all its fullness, at least in this life.

The perspective of peace with justice views peace and justice inextricably linked to one another. And so goes the saying: "There is no peace without justice." So even if there is no war, prevalence of violence and denial of basic human rights by the official and other institutions can negate peace. Poverty, oppression, racism, sexism, inequitable distribution of wealth are thus forms of violence and may give rise to reactive forms of violence, such as riots, armed resistance or terrorism. Thus, peace can be restored only when the injustices embedded within systems are redressed.

Islam: As in other religions, peace is a basic concept in Islam too. The root of term Islam in Arabic is *aslama*, which means "to surrender" or "resign oneself" to the will of God (*Khuda*). *Salam* in Arabic (green) is derived from the Hebrew *shalom* (in blue), which means "making peace." "As-Salaamu alaykum", the greeting that Muslims use literally means "Peace be upon you". So a good Muslim is one who submits to the will of Allah (Isalm) and who aspires to build peace. According to *Qur'an* the holy book of Muslims, one who carries out the will of God including the waging of the holy war (*jihad*), gets divine blessing of peace and eventually lives with God. Thus, in Islam total submission to the divine will lead to peace, both spiritual and temporal. Mohammad is reported to have said once, "Mankind are the dependents, or family of God, and the most beloved of them to God are those who are the most excellent to His dependents." "Not one of you believes until he loves for his brother what he loves for himself." Here, as per Ibn Hajar al-Asqalani and Sharafuddin al-Nawawi, brother refers to any person irrespective of his faith.

In His Last Sermon, the Prophet Muhammad told his believers:

1. "Hurt no one so that no one may hurt you";
2. "Woe to those…. who, when they have to receive by measure from men, exact full measure, but when they have to give by measure or weight to men, give less than due";
3. The *Qur'an* commends "those who show their affection to such as came to them for refuge and entertain no desire in their hearts for things given to the (latter), but give them preference over themselves";
4. "None [truly] believes until he wishes for his brother what he wishes for himself";

5. "Seek for mankind that of which you are desirous for yourself, that you may be a believer; treat well as a neighbour the one who lives near you, that you may be a Muslim (one who submits to God)";
6. "That which you want for yourself, seek for mankind"; and
7. "The most righteous of men is the one who is glad that men should have what is pleasing to him and who dislikes for them what is for him disagreeable."

In Islamic tradition many prophets were sent by God before Muhammad was sent. The difference lies in the area of their coverage. While earlier prophets were sent to convey their message to specific people or nation, Muhammad was sent to teach the whole world. So, for Muslims the whole world constitutes (*Ummatu Muhammad*) or nation of Muhammad. The establishment of *ummah* (the Islamic community) on earth based on the rules of *Shariah* is the ultimate goal of Islam.

According to Islam, Mahdi will ultimately come to save the world from chaos, injustice, and moral collapse. He would eradicate Godless ideologies and make Islam akin to what it was in the days of Prophet Muhammad. Further, he would ensure that the moral teachings of the *Qur'an's* were accepted by people throughout the world. The Muslims who consider it their duty to spread Islam all over the world, using *jihad*, if need be. They forget that all religions are open to all and hence are world religions. Further, *jihad* means fighting against the enemy within (lust, greed, violence, and untruthfulness, etc.); it does not mean doing injustice to all those who do not follow Islam.

Taoism: Ever since the beginning of Chinese history religion in China has never been monolithic. The indigenous Chinese religions being family-oriented, they do not demand total adherence. They are closer to 'cultural practices' or 'philosophies' rather than religious as commonly understood. Buddhism has been the most popular religion in China ever since the first century A.D. Along with Buddhism, the ethnic religion of the Hans encompasses Taoism and the worship of the Shens which include local ethnic deities, heroes, ancestors and figures from Chinese mythology such as Mazu (goddess of the seas and patron of Southern China), Huangdi (divine patriarch of all the Chinese), the Black Dragon (powerful monsters), and Caishen (god of prosperity and richness), etc.

Although Chinese statistics pertaining to religions is not very reliable, Shenism-Taoism and Buddhism have the largest number (around 30-40 per cent) of followers in China. However, the biggest part of the population, ranging between 60 per cent and 70 per cent, is classed as agnostic or atheistic. Why Mao's China even after embracing capitalism remained atheistic but the first Marxist state (USSR) remained theistic, is a question that deserves further exploration.

Taoism teaches:

1. "The past is just… the past… long gone and passed on by.
2. The future is not here yet…
3. That you are here now, firmly in the moment: dancing from moment to moment. By embracing the ride of now, a person quickly learns: to let go of false attachments to past pains, learns building a future is just a way of deceiving oneself away from now… In this process of embracing life now… a person can let go enough to actually have a chance to see himself truly by being present in his life."

Taoism, like other religions stands for peace and harmony. If people perform their duties as per the inherent rules, it would lead to a harmonious and orderly world where everyone is equal and kind to each other, so believe the Taoists. Taoism is always against wars because wars bring people nothing but disaster and suffering. Weapons are thought to be inauspicious. A peaceful is pro-nature; it protects nature instead of destroying it.

Taoism prescribes non-action and non-intention to purify the soul. The governments should so function that the society is not disturbed by their laws and actions. The Tao ideals have acquired new importance for the present society; a peaceful and harmonious society is sure to emerge if these principles are acted out.

Marxism: "The history of all hitherto existing society is the history of class struggles." says Karl Marx. Marxism considers class struggle as the main determinant of history and, therefore, war and peace too. It is economics that determines all social actions and institutions. Peace dawns when the working class seizes of power through the revolution and the dictatorship of the proletariat is established. A Marxist state will be a classless cooperative commonwealth; it will have control over production and distribution of wealth.

Once private ownership of property is abolished, the class distinctions would disappear and individuals will be free to contribute according to their abilities and take according to their needs. Karl Marx believed that human society has been marked by class struggle, i.e., struggle between the working class and the ruling class and it is this conflict that brings people to ruin. This status driven ways of society can be checked only through revolution. Once revolution takes place and the proletariats start ruling the country the society will become classless. Once the society is classless, peace will reign supreme.

This theory is self-contradictory and that is why it failed to gain ground in the world. How can a classless society have a dictator who has control over everything? No wonder then, that USSR had Stalin and China had Mao. They were responsible for maiming and killing of millions.

Swami Akhilananda (1894-1962) of Bangladesh has summed all that various religions have to say in following words:

> May He Who is the Father in Heaven of the
> Christians, Holy One of the Jews, Allah of
> The Muslims, Buddha of the Buddhists,
> Tao of the Chinese, Ahura Mazda of the
> Zoroastrians and Brahman of the Hindus
> Lead us from the unreal to the Real, from
> Darkness to light, from disease and death
> To immortality. May the all-Loving Being
> Manifest Himself unto us, and grant us abiding
> Understanding and all-consuming divine love.
> Peace. Peace. Peace be unto all.

BEYOND FAITH: CO-HABITANCE OF PEACE AND WAR

The religions of the world offer concrete guidelines for attaining both inner and outer peace but these guidelines are rarely followed. Guidelines for inner peace are ritualized and for outer peace camouflaged under the concept of Righteous War (*Dharma Yuddha*). Human beings all over the world are similar, if not the same, in their reaction to what goes around them in the family, community, society, country and the world. A friendly gesture is usually reciprocated with friendly gesture; a hostile gesture with a hostile one. Much, however, depends on the respective positions of the parties concerned.

Religions define what ought to be but the violation of the code of conduct prescribed by them is only to come to further emphasize here. It is often said that religious code of conduct is meant for a perfect world; in world of uncultured people, they do not work. That is why the concept of *dharma yuddha* has been evolved in each and every culture. Irrespective of the religion, its followers rarely adhere to its principles especially when they aspire to have more wealth, power and prestige or when they deal with their adversaries. It is unfortunate indeed that religion has now been confined to temples, mosques and churches. People pray God to condone their misdeeds of the past but they never stop committing such misdeeds in the future. And those who pray God to help them in their plan to rob, cheat or kill others are not rare.

Because the religious guidelines are known more for violation than adherence, does not mean that they are irrelevant. They are based on the individual as well as collective experience of the past and the path of human evolution traced by men and women of wisdom. Man cannot become a soulless robot nor can he go back to his animal stage. If human evolution is not over, then it is not his physiology that has to change; change has to come in his mental capability and emotional stability to get closer to *devas*.

The problem really lies in the evolutionary journey of man being marked with many twists and turns. Even if it has reached a stage where all concerned have mutually adjusted their desires, needs, expectations and interests to live in harmony never trampling on the inalienable rights of others, it does not last for too long. As time passes children become adults and their interests and perspectives change. The *status quo* that marks the social contract is not accepted by the new generation.

This leads to changes in the balance of power and the gap between what one has and what one expects widens. When the gap becomes too wide for good human relations to bridge, tensions develop and even minor issues rigger conflicts. As conflicts escalate, move to evolve new combinations and permutations to bring expectations and realities closer set in. Such to and fro social movements in due course of time lead to a balance which in turn leads to co-operation among the contending parties. Co-operation involves a harmony of expectations congruent with a balance of power achieved by conflict.

When the rules of the game are violated by one or the other party, the co-operative spirit gives way to antagonism and conflicts. New efforts are then made to readjust the interests and a new cooperative environment begins to take roots. Conflict and co-operation are thus interdependent and two sides of the same coin. They are alternative phases in a continuous social relationship. In a closed system, chances of co-operation and peace are evident. Contrariwise, more open a system greater the chances of conflicts. Both co-operation and conflict help people learn more about each other and thus move towards peace more confidently.

Peace is thus determined by a process of adjustment between what individuals, communities, groups, or nations want at a particular time and in a particular environmental setting, and what they can get given the traditions, customs, and laws on the one hand and individual and group aspirations on the other. The interaction between the two sets of forces that are dynamic both in content and timescale keep the social system stable. And so long as this stability remains intact individuals and groups live amicably sharing equitably whatever nature and human endeavours offer.

The most fundamental factor that makes peace and conflict dynamic is human mind. It is a factory of ideas, ideals, visions, hopes and aspirations. It can accept *status quo* only for a while and that too under very special circumstances. This dynamism of the human mind can lead humanity to heaven or hell depending on which direction it moves. If it moves in the direction of rights, privileges, hate, and violence it takes man to hell through conflicts and wars. But if it turns towards duties, equity, love and non-violence, the end result is peace and harmony. A single individual in power and position can cause World War as was the case with Hitler. At the same time, when the same individual acts otherwise, he leads to a peaceful world. Christ, Buddha, Mahavira, Muhammad and Gandhi turned the war torn world into a world of peace.

Peace being critical for continuing evolution of man into superconscious being, it is the responsibility of individual and nations to ensure that nothing comes in the way of peace. Moreover, even from a short-term perspective, who does not want to leave his next generation in a better and more secured world? As Gandhi had said "an eye for eye will leave everyone blind", conflicts will leave every one dead. True, man has at his disposal a negative alternative: to return to his animal past.

Modern science and technology have opened new avenues for man to advance forward or backward. He can use these new openings to move forward only when he is at peace mentally as well as physically. Otherwise, he would recede back as he often does may be only temporarily when his mind is enraged with anger, jealousy, hatred and killer instinct. Building a world on the foundation of competition rather co-operation, material prosperity without spiritual enrichment and self-aggrandizement at the cost of his fellow beings, takes man backward. Rarely do people realize that human beings a part and parcel of nature. If nature is a system and its various elements are interdependent and man cannot be out of it. Yet, it is he who destroys nature and invites global warming and climate change. We rarely realize that whatever progress man has made ever since, he came out of the animal existence and became *Homo sapiens* was more because of the co-operation between nature and man, and man and man. It is co-operation that led man to bind himself into families, communities, group and even nations. Some 5,000 years ago, the Vedics of India envisaged all that was living—plants and animals included—as integral parts of a single global family (*vasudhaiva kutumbakam*). How right were they? If we adhere to their principles, we would neither have conflicts nor the problem of global warming and climate change.

Peace is especially important because modern world is conflict ridden. As we look around us, we see internal as well external conflicts tormenting the individuals, communities, societies, and nations. Causes are many. There is hardly an individual who does not wear blinkers of self-interest on his eyes. For the developed countries, accumulation of money, material goods are the prime goals of life for they offer opportunities to acquire superiority complex, to torment the weak, and rule over the world. No wonder then that most of the developed countries have grown at the cost of their less fortunate brethren. Until very recently they were the masters of the world with huge colonial empires. Now, their old model empires are gone, but they continue to impose their will on smaller and weaker countries. Further, they are in search of new ways and means to maintain their supremacy. True, the developing countries are not less to be blamed. They want to follow the same path of development which developed countries used to colonize them.

It is perpetual restlessness that rules supreme over the people world over. None is happy, rich or poor, strong or weak, young or old, villager or citizen. Almost everybody is busy defending his existence rather than living a peaceful life. Pulling the legs of those who have managed to be ahead of them by fair or foul means has become the pre-occupation of most of the people. Jealousy, hatred and dishonesty mar relationship in and between families, communities, institutions, and nations. The end result is conflict: conflict within and conflict outside. It is because of this all-pervading environment of conflict that man has lost the synergy of his body, mind and soul. Even education has been so infected with the virus of conflict that highly educated men and women too commit heinous crimes. No wonder then that more people are dying of unnatural deaths than natural deaths.

The time has come to stop this drift. Gandhi showed the way but he was not allowed to live long enough to put peace as the agenda for thought and action. Man has advanced a lot in the fields of science and technology. In order that this knowledge is not utilized to destroy the natural and cultural heritage he has built so far and also to ensure that their benefits reach each and every individual no matter where he lives and what he does.

War has been denounced as inhuman no matter for what it was fought. "Thus, there never was a good war or a bad peace." (Benjamin Franklin, *Letter to Josiah Quincy* (September 11, 1773). Yet, there is hardly a culture which does not permit holy war (*dharma yuddha*). People have interpreted this concept of holy war to suit their own convenience and perspectives and goals. Even the World War I and II were justified as necessary means to secure justice and establish peace in the world. Even the most non-violent spiritual leaders like Buddha, Jesus Christ, Mohammad and Gandhi became victims of the ideology of *dharma yuddha*.

"There is no way to peace. Peace is the way." The preamble to the United Nations Charter sums up the existential dilemma of today: "Since wars begin in the minds of men, it is in the minds of men that defences of peace must be constructed". So to establish peace, we have to go beyond appreciating it as a concept. And we have to overcome our tendency to compete with others for power, prestige, wealth and status and fight violently. The time has come to devote more time and energy to build peace using means that go beyond long hours of prayers and meditations or indulging in wars to end wars. Life has originated from a common source, so proclaim the religions of the world. Man's mission of life is to pick up the threads from these religions and try to make this world a better place to live: a world without falsehood, hatred and jealousy and resulting tension, violence. For this to happen, peace must manifest in our lives.

All cultures have created their own models of paradise to guide humanity to create heaven on this earth. These models can be summed up under the following five principles:

1. Peace is our natural religion;
2. All that we do has implications for those around us;
3. Intellectual achievement unless circumscribed by spiritual values can lead to dangerous consequences;
4. Material well-being beyond the limits of needs and equity does not generate peace and harmony; and
5. To recharge our pure energies, we need to connect to the Supreme Source, call Him God, Truth, *Paramatma* or God particle.

By following the above principles, man will take himself and all those around him to a state of peace and thus will create heaven on earth.

Unfortunately, this paradigm of peace is neither followed nor promoted by the modern society. How else can we explain the wide acceptance of competition as the means to secure economic, political and other goals of life? Almost everyone appears to worship competition for wealth, power and prestige; rarely does anyone likes to share these with others. The only exception to this rule is the mother's attitude towards her newly born child. People know that competition generates jealousy, hatred, disharmony and conflict and makes their own life tense and sleepless. Yet, he remains a captive of competition and makes his and his associates' life conflict-ridden. The tragedy is that man has now eulogized trampling on the legitimate rights and interests of fellow human beings as the only path of progress and development. Even the religionists indulge in competition. Not infrequently, religion is misused to balkanize people, create suspicion and incite violence?

Peace is rarely a central theme of our social, economic and political agenda. The term development does not include inner development of man. Even human development is short of inner development. It is confined to only physical needs of man: food, clothing, housing, education and health. One wonders why our political leaders consider peace as a non-issue and opt for conflict to gain or regain power. Why do they not declare all out war against corruption in the same way as wage war to secure power? Why are there 'n' times more porn web sites than web sites dedicated to truth, honesty, human brotherhood, and peace on the internet? Why are the news channels full of detailed reports on the crimes committed but no mention of the sacrifices people make at the alter of truth, non-violence, honesty and human brotherhood? Why do they chant the word competition and refuse even to utter the word co-operation? Why is the term love downgraded to mean lust? Why we just watch our children going astray and consider their deviant behaviour as modernization? Interestingly the common man swayed by the propaganda and advertisement of the political and business leaders, inadvertently participates in conflicts.

BUILDING BLOCKS OF PEACE

Peace Education

The starting point of peace is the peaceful individual human being. And the first step in transforming conflict mongering humans into peaceniks is to reform our education system. Here education is seen in its broader meaning to include the training (*samskaras*) child gets from his parents, family, community and then the knowledge and skills he gets from various levels of formal educational institutions. But education does not stop here. Man learns from the natural, cultural, social and economic environment all through his life.

If peace is so essential for our well-being and yet so scarce, what role one can play to realize it? It is now clear that there can be no peace in the world so long as the very source of conflict is removed. And if this has not been possible so far, it cannot be realized in a day. It is related to the very nature of man—the man who has evolved from animal. To aim at absolute peace without any conflict amounts to being impractical. The best that can be achieved is to make the peace processes so strong that conflict gets subdued and in due course time becomes so weak that it is controlled before it gets out of control. To achieve that state work has to be done at several levels: from individual to the global society.

Family Education: Each individual begins his life in the womb of the mother. According to the Hindu philosophy, the character of the new born is influenced by what the mother eats, thinks and experiences during the nine months she harbours the foetus. Thus, a mother under stress would give birth to a child who would grow into an angry person. Once the child is born, its psychology and physiology will be influenced by what her parents, mother specially, think, talk and do. It would be a rare to children born of thieves not being thieves. As the child grows, he is influenced by the family, community and school environment. By the time the child is eight years old, he acquires all those traits or *samskara* that make him a man of peace or a man of war. Thereafter, he can add knowledge but not how to use the knowledge so acquired.

So, man should be so brought up from his early childhood that he becomes an instrument of peace rather an instrument of conflict. Bringing up involves not only the *samskaras* that parents especially the mother give to the child but also creating the cultural, social and economic environment conducive to peace and harmony. Unfortunately, our children are brought up in an environment of jealousy, hatred, greed and competition, each trying to leave others behind by hook or by crook.

Value based Education: As such much of our energy is spent in fighting wars both within and without. Each individual is engaged in the race for development and in doing so is trying to defeat others. He feels happy when he moves forward so fast that he leaves others behind. And development, progress and achievement are defined in terms of wealth, power and position. Since each one is a part of this rat race trying to surpass others, no one has rest or peace. Thus, man leads a life of tug and war. He does not have time to stop and talk even to his parents, leave aside the neighbours, friends, colleagues and acquaintances. He does, however, have time to wage mental, verbal and physical fights with whoever appears to come in the way of 'progress'. And he does not take rest unless the adversary is defeated and left behind. Since each one is a fighter and adversary at the same time, neither side lands himself in peace. The winner is so afraid of the losers that he tries to acquire more wealth and power to protect himself in the future and the losers either commit suicide or go berserk and use all the means available to defeat the adversary.

The efforts to maintain peace are limited to containing the conflicts. No one thinks of uprooting the root causes of conflicts. Each conflict is treated as a special case; efforts are made to resolve it as peacefully as possible and wait for the next conflict to show up. So, today we have organizations that try to stop conflicts from becoming deadly as wars. It is said that since conflict have but to arise in all societies, it is better to resolve them as peacefully as possible so that they do become too destructive. But, this is not the way to create a peaceful society. For a peaceful social order to come into being, we should have two pronged peace strategy: to build a society where conflicts are rare, if at all; and to find ways and means to resolve conflicts peacefully before they become violent. For both these strategies to succeed 'development' should be redefined as 'human development' and 'human development' as creation of an equitable society and all that promotes evolution of humans into 'super-conscious beings'.

Naturally, the development process has to be percolatory (upside down) and upwelling (bottom up) at the same time. We have to make peace a part and parcel of our life and living; we must pay far more attention in so bringing up our children that they become agents of peace in their adulthood. Education thus has a major role to play in creating a peaceful world order. Unfortunately, modern education trains our youth to compete with others and fight their ways to the top. They thus become agents of conflicts. If we scan through the curricula of various levels of modern education all the way from nursery to university, there is no place in it for character building; for creating a good human being. Much of the time is spent on teaching 3-Rs at the primary stage and on geography, history, literature, social sciences, sciences and engineering and technology at higher levels. We thus produce heartless and soulless youth.

They are trained to compete with others for wealth, power, prestige, and sexuality; not to be good human beings.

Today, there is no aspect of life which is not marred by lust for wealth and power. These two traits have become 'basic needs' of 'modern man'. Unless we reorient our educational system in creating humans with sharp minds, loving souls and skilful hands, we would neither have people "who love their neighbours" nor a world without conflicts and wars. And if this trend continues, humanity would reach a point of no return and would ensure its tragic end. The time has come for our education to sensitize and educate our children and youth to love, to be non-violent, to cooperate and move forward carrying their fellow beings with them.

Peace Education Programmes

For the last few centuries especially after European powers got control over the world, education has become a means to move forward economically, socially, politically and technologically. It is this education that helped Europe enslave the world and divide the world into two conglomerates of nation-states: developed and backward. Europe captured the whole world using the gun—the most powerful product of modern science and technology that dawned in Europe first.

Today, development has become co-terminus with westernization. It is the western thought and culture that rules the minds and hearts of the people. Further development of science and technology is the main focus of modern education; how the knowledge so gained would be used, is not its concern. It is only recently that peace became a talking point in educational and intellectual circles. And that too because the two World Wars of the twentieth century and freedom struggles of the so-called developing countries forced Europeans to rethink about what they did in the past *vis-à-vis* the other nations of Americas, Africa and Asia.

Concern for peace became more visible after the World War II. But peace continued to be seen as absence of war or at best, avoidance of war. The concept of peace as enunciated by different religions was by and large ignored; focus was conflict resolution and management as and that too when need arises. 'Peace education' programmes around the world, therefore, hover around conflict resolution and cover themes like international understanding, sustainable development, anti-nuclearization, human rights, tolerance of diversity and gender equality. True, a few have addressed inner harmony as a precondition for peace, but only as an appendage to the main theme.

A look at the peace education programmes of various universities and institution both in developed and developing countries points to overwhelming tilt towards training in Conflict Resolution. Instead of going to roots of why conflict, they take conflict as given and then try to find the ways and means of resolving them as and when they arise. The aspects covered are: symptoms and causes of inter-personal conflicts and the methods of resolving them using the techniques of negotiation and mediation. As stated by Van Slyck, Stern and Elbedour, the goal is "alter beliefs, attitudes, and behaviours…from negative to positive attitudes toward conflict as a basis for preventing violence". (Van Slyck, Stern and Elbedour, 1999, emphasis added). Managing anger, separating the facts from feelings and improving communication skills, constitute its main elements.

The programmes are run on the belief that in a truly democratic society, the peace processes would be so strong that conflicts would not be able to gain strength. This means that an educational programme that strengthens democracy will also strengthen peace. Unfortunately, education to improve democratic participation and balance in the forces that lead to conflicts and those that engender tolerance rarely succeed. The aim is to produce "responsible citizens" who will "assume the role of the citizen that chooses, makes decisions, takes positions, argues positions and respects the opinions of others": skills that a multi-party democracy are based upon. Assuming that democracy decreases the likelihood of violence and war, these skills are necessary for creating a culture of peace.

Some peace education programmes centre around human rights. If the human rights are ensured, there is greater likelihood of peace in the world. The students are trained to analyze the human rights situation and commit to work for a vision of structural peace that ensures the personal freedom of every member of the society institutionally and legally and violence, oppression and indignity would not be tolerated. Participants are familiarized with the Universal Declaration of Human Rights by the United Nations. How to detect the violation of these rights and how to stop these violations peacefully is the major focus of the programme.

All these programmes suffer from a serious drawback. They all aim at training in resolving conflicts rather than educating them to check conflict emerging. Helping people from their early childhood to grow into good humans with higher level of consciousness is yet to enter into peace education programmes boldly. They all work under the assumption that conflicts are natural to human beings as they are natural to animals and hence resolving them as and when they arise should be the main focus of peace education. They forget that conflict-promoting attitudes and behaviours take man to his animal past while the love-promoting attitudes and behaviours take him forward on his evolutionary journey. Both aspects are important and should form integral parts of peace education.

INTEGRATIVE THEORY OF PEACE

"Integrative Theory of Peace" calls for the integration of the psychosocial, political, moral and spiritual dimensions of peace education. According to Danesh, peace education should cover the following four aspects:

1. The nature of reality,
2. Human nature,
3. The purpose of existence, and
4. The principles governing appropriate human relationships.

Danesh has argued that the conflict-based worldviews are of two types correlated with phases of human development. These are:

1. Survival-Based Worldview, and
2. Identity-Based Worldview.

He feels that it is through the acquisition of a more integrative, Unity Based Worldview that alone can mitigate conflict, create unity in diversity and establish a sustainable culture of peace at home, school, work, or nation and the world. Those who are enrolled in our schools, colleges, and universities are not told that: "You are in the process of being indoctrinated. We have not yet evolved a system of education that is not a system of indoctrination. We are sorry, but it is the best we can do. What you are being taught here is an amalgam of current prejudice and the choices of this particular culture. The slightest look at history will show how impermanent these must be. You are being taught by people who have been able to accommodate themselves to a regime of thought laid down by their predecessors. It is a self-perpetuating system. Those of you who are more robust and individual than others will be encouraged to leave and find ways of educating yourself—educating your own judgements. Those that stay must remember, always, and all the time, that they are being moulded and patterned to fit into the narrow and particular needs of this particular society" (Doris Lessing).

In the words of Clarke-Habibi, "A general or integrated theory of peace is needed: one that can holistically account for the intrapersonal, inter-personal, inter-group and international dynamics of peace, as well as its main principles and prerequisites. An essential component of this integrated theory must also be the recognition that a culture of peace can only result from an authentic process of transformation, both individual and collective."

More and more people are now converging to the view that conflict is not an inborn human psyche and that peace education seen in its broader perspective to include both inner and outer peace can lead humanity to sustainable peace. (Clarke-Habibi)

GANDHI ON SUSTAINABLE PEACE

In the world of the twenty-first century where World War III rages inside, between individuals as among communities and nations, Gandhi, the apostle of peace is raising his head from Rajghat where his mortal remains were cremated on January 30, 1948, and telling loudly to the deaf world "Victory attained by violence is tantamount to a defeat, for it is momentary." "An eye for an eye makes the whole world blind." "What difference does it make to the dead, the orphans and the homeless, whether the mad destruction is wrought under the name of totalitarianism or the holy name of liberty or democracy? But the modern world has no time to listen him."

All those who dream about a world with peace and prosperity for all mankind, a world in which they live like brothers and sisters, differences in cultures, religions and ways of life notwithstanding, think of Gandhi and try to follow the path of truth and non-violence he laid for all. The Mahatma was a great soul residing in a visibly fragile body. What he achieved was miraculous—the mighty British Empire could not face his power of truth and non-violence. His life was a message—a message of peace and harmony.

Gandhi was a great teacher. He used all his sensory organs to convey his message of peace to all—children and adults, men and women, rich and poor, his countrymen and foreigners. His speeches and discourses kept the people spell-bound, his writings reached every nook and corner of the world to arouse what was best in each and every individual, and his three monkeys sitting close to him asked each one getting close to him: see not the evil, hear not the evil, and speak not the evil.

All those who have been interested in Gandhi's life and works tend to agree with Einstein that Gandhi was unique in his time that "Generations to come will scarcely believe that such a one as this walked on the earth in flesh and blood." It is now up to all of us to apply Gandhi's teachings in our daily life. Given below are the six lessons that capsule his thoughts and works.

"*Ahimsa* Paramodharmah"

The following three statements of Gandhi sum up his philosophy of life and living: One, "there are many causes that I am prepared to die for but no cause that I am prepared to kill for." Two, "An eye for an eye will only make the whole world blind." And three, Power is of two kinds. One is obtained by the fear of punishment and the other by acts of love. Power based on love is a thousand times more effective and permanent than the one derived from fear of punishment.

Buddha said over two millennia back as did the *Vedas* still earlier. When Christ prayed God to forgive his killers for they did not know what they were doing, he lived even after death to inspire his followers to follow the path of love. All through his life, Gandhi fought against the power of force and changed the minds of millions in South Africa and India to fight against injustice non-violently. He made the mightiest empire of the world to relent and leave India. His answer to the force of physical power was to bring the users of this force to his side by love. He demonstrated that we can make this world far more peaceful than it is today by seeking truth and pursuing non-violence.

Gandhi has proved that freedom and justice can be secured for one and all without inflicting pain on anyone, without making anyone homeless, without making a child an orphan and without taking away someone's legitimate rights. The world we live is full of all those anomalies which Gandhi wanted to remove from independent India. At least one-third of 1.2 billion people of India live below the poverty line; lakhs of children die of malnutrition and infectious diseases; at least a quarter of India's population is illiterate and the number of those who are ill-educated or uneducated is still larger. And yet we call ourselves a progressive and democratic nation "What difference does it make to the dead, the orphans, and the homeless, whether the mad destruction is wrought under the name of totalitarianism or the holy name of liberty and democracy?" said Gandhi.

The example of India given above does not mean that other nations are better off. There is conflict all around. Conflict within has made individuals seething with jealousy, hatred and ill-feeling towards others. Nations are poised against nations and within nations people following different religions and sects are fighting like mad dogs. Man is unable to live peacefully and harmoniously although everyone aspires to be at peace.

"Be the change you wish to see in the world"

One of the reasons for absence of peace in the world today that no one wants to apply the same standards of truth, non-violence, love, affection and fairness barring oneself. Gandhi gave first priority in transforming oneself and becoming an instrument of peace. He asked everyone to look inward and enrich your life with the standards of life and living that you expect from others. If we focus on changing ourselves to conform to the change we expect from others, we would be able to influence the world around us and solve the problems as and when they arise.

A good teacher is one who not only teaches but also practices what he teaches. This applies to all walks of life. If you want others to be honest to you, you must be honest to others first. If you want others to be brotherly with you, you have to be brotherly with others. Here it would not be out of place to repeat the story of a mother bringing her son to Gandhi. She told Gandhi that her son eats too much sugar (*gur*) and that he does not listen to her when she tries to stop him from this bad habit. She requested Gandhi to instruct him not to eat too much *gur*. Gandhi asked her to come after month or so. Gandhi too used to take more gur than necessary. So, he stopped his own intake of *gur* first. So, when the child was brought again to him, he asked him to follow his mother's instructions and eat less *gur*.

In other words, no one would listen to you if you don't follow what you want others to follow. First apply the principles that you want others to follow on yourself. If your life is message you want to give to the world, people would listen to you in the same way as they listened to Gandhi not too long ago.

"Live by the Dictates of Your *Atma*" (Inner Being)

While life is shaped by the values and passions we cherish but there hardly is a person who does not have an innate desire to live a peaceful life. Even Hitler wanted to have peace once he had control over the world. Now if we want peace, we cannot get it by violent means. Means and ends are not only the two sides of the same coin but also coterminous. Means turns into end and end into means as time and context changes. The greatest noble cause is to display our desire to bring about peace in this world by our own sacrifices and not that of those who oppose our views. The strength of cowardice is in using power to cause death and destruction for others. The strength of courage is in self-sacrifice for the benefit of all.

Mahatma Gandhi sacrificed his own lucrative law practice in Durban, South Africa to lead a simple life and to share the pain of the powerless and destitute. He won over the hearts of millions without ever reigning power over anyone—simply with the power of altruism. We too can bring peace to our world by showing our willingness to sacrifice our self-centred desires. Our utmost cause in life should be to win the hearts of others by showing our willingness to serve causes greater than ourselves.

Power is of two kinds. One is obtained by the fear of punishment and the other by acts of love. Power based on love is a thousand times more effective and permanent then the one derived from fear of punishment. – *Mahatma Gandhi*

Reduce, Reuse and Recycle (3-Rs) for Peace and Prosperity for All

"There is enough in the world for everyone's need, but not for everyone's greed", said Gandhi. His comments came in the context of the vast disparity in the world between rich and poor people and rich and poor nations. He saw luxury in which a few people lived in India in the midst of abject poverty of the masses; he also saw how the European countries were taking away the resources of the world to satisfy their comforts and luxuries whilst a great majority of people in the rest of the world were barely surviving.

This state of affairs has given rise to two great problems humanity is facing today. The first is the division of the world into rich and poor nations, rich and poor people and rich and poor individuals. It is the direct consequence of the disparities in styles of life and living unmindful of the interests of those who have been deprived of their right to lead an honourable life.

Globalization of business and technology is not enough for a new world order; peace and harmony too need to be globalized on a priority basis. This cannot be achieved unless need based life and living becomes a norm to be followed all over the world. Need based life and living is one in which everyone gets nutritious food; everyone has adequate clothing and shelter appropriate to the climate of the place, everyone gets health and education facilities to keep his body and mind in excellent state; and everyone should enjoy self respect so that he can respect others. It is unfortunate that millions of people in the world go hungry while

202 billion dollars are spent in the USA alone on alcoholic drinks and its aftereffects.

Second problem that has come up now boldly is global warming and climate change. The earth's temperature is likely to go up by 2 degree C by 2035 and 4 degree C by the turn of the century. If these predictions come true, much of life on the planet earth would be eliminated and even human beings would suffer from food shortage and series of incurable diseases. Unless the world finds a sustainable energy resource, the present style of life and living cannot be sustained for too long. The time has come when each one of us has to do our bit. And what is this bit: it is reduce, reuse and recycle (3-Rs).

Gandhi lived a very simple life. The very look of him invokes a feeling of respect for the man who started his career as an advocate and ended up with as a saint. He had very few worldly possessions and he preached simplicity and minimalism in all areas of life. He had only five material things to keep his body hail and healthy and in tune with the ethos of the poor of India. These were: 1. loin cloth (*dhoti*) to rap around the waist, 2. a pair of sandals (*chappals*), 3. a pair of spectacles, 4. a bamboo stick as walking aid, and 5. a watch to keep track of time.

When he visited England and met the King, he persisted with his simple Indian loin cloth. When asked if he was under dressed for a meeting with the King, Gandhi replied that the King had enough clothes on for both of them!

Start Today

In bridging "the difference between what we do, and what we are capable of doing, would solve most of the world's problems", says Gandhi. What it means is that it is the action that matters not the promises made. We all have our limitations. Further, we know that we cannot change the world single-handedly, but we can certainly make a difference to one or a few persons.

So, let us start in a small way. The opportunities are galore because the capabilities of those who want to change the world are different and problems to solve are also different. Even Mahatma Gandhi started in a small way. Let us take courage and begin today. Each one of us being different the skills we have are varied as are the problems to be resolved. So, each individual can contribute immensely to change the world for better. Let us not forget that each of us has a little Gandhi inside us. Let us arouse him to change the world.

If No One Walks with You, Walk Alone

A path breaking leader is instantly respected, but only gradually followed. To be a leader, therefore, one must lead a life that echoes his ideals and mission. Look at the life of Mahatma Gandhi, Swami Vivekananda, Subhas Chandra Bose, Nelson Mandela, Martin Luther King Jr, just to mention a few, they all led a very unique and simple life to live among the poverty stricken masses. They lived and died for the people. How different they were from the so-called modern leaders who promise heavens to the people but fill their own coffers. They cannot work for peace because they function as instruments of conflict. Their job is to divide the society on the basis of religion, caste and income, thus create vote banks, and get elected by all the unfair means at hand and rule as people's representatives. In fact the modern leader have put in their laptops which they have at the cost of the people, all the words that people wish to be translated in action: peace, harmony, *ahimsa*, truth, love, brotherhood, democracy, full employment, beautiful roads, clean water, subsidized food, houses, free education and health services, etc. They go to the people and deliver speeches prepared by their aides to mesmerize the people. Once the elections are over, they are not to be seen anywhere except in functions where they are honoured with garlands and mementoes (*smriti chihnas*) for the great public service they have been engaged in.

The great leaders like Mahatma Gandhi did not divide the people, they united the people under a single banner for "we are all children of God," our religion, colour of skin, caste, creed or any other differences notwithstanding. Look at what Gandhi wrote to Lord Irwin, the then Viceroy of India on March 2, 1930 when launched the famous Salt March. *"Dear Friend, I cannot intentionally hurt anything that lives, much less fellow human beings, even though they may do the greatest wrong to me and mine. Whilst, therefore, I hold the British rule to be a curse, I do not intend to harm to a single Englishman or to any legitimate interest he may have in India..."* Saying so, he marched on and saw to it that the British left India without any Englishman being hurt. Such were the qualities of justice and peace that made Mahatma Gandhi the world leader. His voice was heard outside India too; in the USA, South Africa, Poland, and now all over the world. As the world gets more enmeshed in conflict and war, Gandhi's popularity among the leaders and the iaity alike has soared up.

Albert Einstein was write when he said on Gandhi "Generations to come, it may be, will scarce believe that such one as this ever in flesh and blood walked upon this earth." Let us make a pledge to follow Gandhi and try to become a change that we would like to see in others.

Let the first act of every morning be to make the following resolved for the day:

1. I shall not fear anyone on Earth.
2. I shall fear only God.
3. I shall not bear ill-will toward anyone.
4. I shall not submit to injustice from anyone.
5. I shall conquer untruth by truth. And in resisting untruth, I shall put up with all suffering.

– *Mahatma Gandhi*

REFERENCES

Brabeck, K. (2001), "Justification for and Implementation of Peace Education. Peace and Conflict": *Journal of Peace Psychology*, Vol. 7, pp. 85-87.

Clarke-Habibi, Sara. (2005), "Transforming Worldviews: The Case of Education for Peace in Bosnia and Herzegovina", *Journal of Transformative Education*, Vol. 3, No. 1, pp. 33-56.

Danesh, H.B. (2006), "Towards an Integrative Theory of Peace Education", *Journal of Peace Education*, Vol. 3, No. 1, pp. 55-78.

Danesh, H B. (2007), "Education for Peace: The Pedagogy of Civilization" in Z. Beckerman and C. McGlynn (Eds.), *Addressing Ethnic Conflict through Peace Education: International Perspectives,* New York: Palgrave MacMillan.

Danesh, H.B. (2008), "Creating a Culture of Healing in Schools and Communities: An Integrative Approach to Prevention and Amelioration of Violence-induced Conditions", *Journal of Community Psychology,* Vol. 36, No. 6, pp. 814-32.

Danesh, H.B. (2008), "The Education for Peace Integrative Curriculum: Concepts, Contents, Efficacy", *Journal of Peace Education*, Vol. 5, No. 2, pp. 157-73.

Danesh, H.B. and R.P. Danesh (2002a). A Consultative Conflict Resolution Model: Beyond Alternative Dispute Resolution, *International Journal of Peace Studies*, Vol. 7, No. 2, pp. 17-33.

Danesh, H.B. and R.P. Danesh (2002b), Has Conflict Resolution Grown Up? Toward a New Model of Decision Making and Conflict Resolution. *International Journal of Peace Studies*, Vol. 7, No. 1, 59-76.

Danesh, H.B. and R.P. Danesh (2004), "Conflict-free Conflict Resolution (CFCR): Process and Methodology", *Peace and Conflict Studies,* Vol. 11, No. 2, pp. 55-84.

Danesh, H.B. and Clarke-Habibi, S. (2007), *Education for Peace Curriculum Manual: A Conceptual and Practical Guide*, EFP International Press.

Doris Lessing (1962), *The Golden Notebook,* London: Michael Joseph.

Deutsch, M. (1993), Educating for a Peaceful World, *American Psychologist,* Vol. 48, 510-17.

Galtung, Johan (1975), *Essays in Peace Research,* Volume 1. Copenhagen: Eljers, pp. 334-39.

Groff, L., and Smoker, P. (1996). "Creating Global-local Cultures of Peace", *Peace and Conflict Studies Journal,* Vol. 3, June Issue.

Hakvoort, I. and L. Oppenheimer (1993), Children and Adolescents' Conceptions of Peace, War, and Strategies to Attain Peace: A Dutch Case Study. *Journal of Peace Research*, Vol. 30, 65-77.

Halpérin, Daniel S., (editor), *To Live Together: Shaping New Attitudes to Peace through Education,* in series *Studies in Comparative Education,* Paris, UNESCO Bureau of Education, 1997.

Harris, I.M. (1999), Types of Peace Education, in A. Raviv, L. Oppenheimer, and D. Bar-Tal (Eds.), *How Children Understand War and Peace*, San Francisco: Jossey-Bass Publishers, pp. 299-317.

Harris, Ian and Synott, John. (2002) "Peace Education for a New Century", *Social Alternatives*, Vol. 21, No. 1, pp. 3-6.

International Conference on Education, 44th, Geneva, 1994.

Declaration and Integrated Framework of Action on Education for Peace, Human Rights and Democracy, 1995, p. 14.

International Conference on the Culture of Peace and Governance: Maputo: *Report,* 1997, p. 12.

International Forum on Education for Democracy, Tunis: 1992, *Report,* p. 136.

Jeffries, R., "Examining Barriers to Effective Peace Education Reform", *Contemporary Education*, Vol. 71, 19-22.

Johnson, M.L. (1998). Trends in Peace Education, *ERIC Digest* 151 (1994) http://www.ericdigests.org/1995-2/mandatory.htm.

Kevin Kester (2008), Developing Peace Education Programs: Beyond Ethnocentrism and Violence, *Peace Prints—A Bi-annual South Asian Journal of Peace Building*, Vol. 1, No.1, 37-64.

Meyer-Bisch, Patrice, *Culture of Democracy: A Challenge for Schools*, Paris: UNESCO, 1995, p. 143.

Manual for Human Rights Education: Primary and Secondary Levels; Preliminary Version. Savolainen, Kaisa. 1997, p. 128.

Page, James S. (2008) *Peace Education: Exploring Ethical and Philosophical Foundations,* Charlotte: Information Age Publishing.

Pitts, D. (2002), "Human Rights Education in Diverse Developing Nations: A Case in Point—South Africa", *Human Rights Education: Issues of Democracy*, Vol. 7, No. 1, March.

Reardon, Betty A., *Tolerance—The Threshold of Peace*, Paris, UNESCO, 1997, 3 V.

Reardon, Betty. (1997). "Human Rights as Education for Peace", in G.J. Andrepoulos and R.P. Claude (eds.) *Human Rights Education for the Twenty-First Century,* Philadelphia: University of Pennsylvania Press, pp. 255-61.

Roche, Douglas. (1993), *The Human Right to Peace,* Toronto: Novalis.

Salomon, G. (2002), "The Nature of Peace Education: Not All Programmes Are Created Equal" in Salomon G. and B. Nevo (eds.), *Peace Education: The Concept, Principles and Practices in the World.* Mahwah, NJ: Lawrence Erlbaum, pp. 1-14.

Swee-Hin Toh. 1997. "Education for Peace: Towards a Millennium of Well-Being", Paper for the Working Document of the International Conference on Culture of Peace and Governance (Maputo, Mozambique, 1-4 September, 1997).

UNESCO, Regional Conference on Human Rights Education in Europe: *Conference Report and European Implementation Strategy*, Turku: Abo Akademi University, 1997, p. 32.

UNESCO, Advisory Committee on Education for Peace, Human Rights and Democracy: Final report *Tolerance, the Threshold of Peace*, 4 July, 1995, p. 22.

UNESCO, Advisory Committee on Education for Peace, Human Rights and Democracy: *Final Report,* 23 May, 1996, p. 27.

UNESCO Advisory Committee on Education for Peace, Human Rights, Democracy, International Understanding and Tolerance: *Final Report*, 7 October, 1998, p. 17.

UNESCO (1998), Learning to Live Together in Peace and Harmony: Value Education for Peace, Human Rights, Democracy and Sustainable Development for the Asia-Pacific Region; a UNESCO-APNIEVE Source Book for Teacher Education and Tertiary Level Education, Bangkok: Principal Regional Office for Asia and the Pacific, p. 182.

United Nations General Assembly (1993) *Vienna Declaration and Programme of Action (World Conference on Human Rights),* New York: United Nations A/CONF. 157/23 on June 25, 1993, Part 2.

Van Slyck, M.R., Stern, M., and Elbedour, S. (1999), "Adolescents' Beliefs about their Conflict Behaviour", in A. Raviv, L. Oppenheimer, and D. Bar-Tal (Eds.), *How Children Understand War and Peace*, San Francisco: Jossey-Bass Publishers, pp. 208-230.

2

A Metaphor of Masks: Reflections on Peace Studies

R. Narayanan

"...perfect non-violence works perfectly..."

January is an ideal month for reflection. Like the Roman god Janus, we may look at the past before we look ahead into the future. We hark back not with the purpose of establishing a primacy for the origins of Peace Studies, rather to give ourselves the twin benefits—of hindsight and of perspective.

ORIGIN OF PEACE STUDIES

It is generally uncontested that Peace Studies emerged out of the violence of the twentieth century. That was perhaps the *raison d'ětre* of the Lentz Institute in St. Louis, Missouri founded in 1945 and the academic programme in Peace Studies in Manchester College, Indiana in 1948. Similar centres, programmes, and annual congresses dedicated to Peace Studies and Research sprung up over the last sixty years in North America.

As regards Europe, the founding of the Oslo Peace Research Institute in 1959 is acknowledged as being a cardinal moment. The Stockholm International Peace Research Institute (founded in 1966) and the Department of Peace and Conflict Research at Uppsala University in Sweden (founded in 1971) followed suit. The field acquired rigour with the publication of many academic journals, not the least of which is the *Journal of Peace Research*.

To name such like Bertrand Russell, Albert Einstein, and Cyrus Eaton must be added those of Kenneth and Elise Boulding and Johan Galtung. There are of course many more institutes like the International Peace

Research Association (IPRA) and the Consortium for Peace Research, Education and Development (COPRED) as well as individuals who ought to count to this list. The *Global Directory of Peace Studies* offers plenty more information and many more pointers. But, it is towards India that I invite your attention.

PEACE STUDIES IN INDIA

The fields of Peace Studies and Research as well as Conflict Resolution and Transformation found its way into Indian university departments, and 'independent' research centres. Apparently, while most, if not all, of these teaching and research programmes were intended to aid policy making, the research centres were or are led by people who were in government. It is not easy to list every university or college department in India that has attached importance to Peace Studies in their curricula. Nonetheless, Peace Studies programmes at Banaras Hindu University, at the University of Rajasthan, at the University of Calcutta, at Jadavpur University, at the University of Madras, and at Jamia Millia Islamia are some of these.

Added to university programmes are the endeavours of entities like the International Centre for Peace Studies and the Institute for Peace and Conflict Studies in Delhi. At the risk of generalizing, it appears that most of these programmes are affiliated to Political Science, International Studies, Strategic and Security Studies. This affiliation raises important issues regarding the nature and scope of Peace Studies. We shall deal with these in a while, but before we do so, it is pertinent to refer to Gandhian Studies.

There are well-established programmes in Gandhian Studies not only in the larger and smaller metropolises of India but also at Gujarat Vidyapith in Ahmedabad, Jain Vishva Bharati Institutes, Allahabad University and Mahatma Gandhi University in Kottayam. Innumerable other programmes are spread across the country. One can get an exhaustive and panoramic picture of Gandhian Studies at www.gandhiserve.org based in Berlin.

Although peace and non-violence are integral elements of Gandhian Studies, and although it is admissible that an important Peace Studies scholar like Johan Galtung was inspired by Gandhian thought and practice, the fields of Gandhian Studies and Peace Studies are different. They are different in conception and scope and, therefore, the two cannot be used interchangeably. Nonetheless, Gandhian thought and practice can vitally strengthen Peace Studies under certain conditions. What are these conditions? We shall explore some of these in due course. But, let us go back to the issue I raised a moment ago.

SCOPE OF PEACE STUDIES

The field of Peace Studies has been a Cinderella twin of Security Studies. The latter is principally concerned with national security issues of states. Traditionally, the security of a State is fortified not only by strengthening the police, the para military, and the armed forces but also through increased vigilance and draconian laws that deny or infringe upon civil liberties. Such measures vitiate human life and deny the very possibility of the right to peace. In brief, national security measures turn the state into an actor, and often the only actor, capable of maintaining peace for its own citizens and the neighbouring states. But, there are other peace constituencies besides the state, and Peace Studies should be intimately linked to them.

This is the central premise of the book edited by Ranabir Samaddar, 2004, *Peace Studies: Concept, Scope and Themes* published by Sage, Delhi. This book is the first in a four volume series, the last of which came out of the press in 2009. The work of Samaddar and other scholars who belong to, or are associated with, the Mahanirban Calcutta Research Group incorporates studies in International Relations, Nuclear Deterrence, Political Theory, problems of refugees, and conflicts in East and North-Eastern India, as well as other conflicts in South Asia. This book is a consequence of their labours during the preceding decade. It takes a sincere, thoughtful, and critical look at Peace Studies in the Euro-American West and the challenges confronted by Peace Studies in India and South Asia. As this is the most recent work in India on Peace Studies, I would like to engage with it briefly.

Samaddar and Samir Kumar Das of the Mahanirban Calcutta Research Group take off from the commonly agreed characterization of peace as the other of war, and of peace as going beyond conflict resolution. MCRG refuses to accept the dominant ideas of peace offered by national and international security establishments. This group believes that game theories and interest based approaches have obfuscated values of peace and justice in conflict situations. They have also falsified the myth that Western democracies are inherently peacemaking, for many of these have waged wars. They have characterised justice, human rights, and democracy as integral and defining elements of peace.

MCRG has made a case for our Peace Studies *versus* their Peace

Studies, without being fundamentalist in positing a binary opposition. Instead, the group has critically scrutinized the scope of every conceivable variant of the international modernist mega-projects, while warning against show casing indigenous micro-traditions of South Asia or attempting to romantically reinvoke them.

HOW ENDURING IS PEACE?

Perhaps, their questioning of the modernist mega projects is not invalid. The history of International Relations has sufficiently demonstrated that the peace secured between States in Westphalia, Versailles and Warsaw cannot be a just, enduring, and sustainable peace. The peace established by victors will and has always been a fragile peace. Immanuel Kant believed that perpetual peace could be ushering in through states that are democratic and republican. However, the recent history of the contemporary world has belied that trust. States that are apparently democratic and constitutionally republican cannot necessarily ensure peace. Or else, one could say that there is a democratic deficit in contemporary states despite the presence of electoral democracy. How else can we explain the invasion of Iraq?

Scientists, including those affiliated to international scientific bodies, doubted the claim of intelligence agencies that the Iraqi administration had the capacity to build weapons of mass destruction. The international civil society across the globe protested against the impending invasion of Iraq. But, elected leaders of democratic States paid little attention to such calls of reason. War ensued, civilians and soldiers died. They continue to die. If we have anything to learn from contemporary history, it is that peace cannot be entrusted to states, and states alone. Governments, bureaucrats, policy-makers, and those who belong to the military-industrial complex have far fewer stakes in peace than ordinary citizens and non-citizens like illegal migrants, refugees, poverty stricken women and children. This is why Machiavellian *realpolitik* refuses to go away.

ON THE CONCEPT OF JUST WAR

It is a fact that the politics of pragmatism resurfaces with surprising consistency. Barack Husein Obama is the most recent case in point. What was more astonishing that the award of the Nobel Peace Prize to Obama was his Nobel Lecture. There are at least three elements in his speech that may be disappointing to a student of Peace Studies.

1. Use of the term 'just war';
2. Reference to the definitive presence of 'evil'; and
3. Possibility that the non-violence of Gandhi and King may not always be feasible.

I quote below parts from the transcript of his speech of 10th December, 2009 delivered at Stockholm. *"And over time, as codes of law sought to control violence within groups, so did philosophers and clerics and statesmen seek to regulate the destructive power of war. The concept of a 'just war' emerged, suggesting that war is justified only when certain conditions were met: if it is waged as a last resort or in self-defense; if the force used is proportional; and if, whenever possible, civilians are spared from violence. ..."*

Is the concept of just war tenable at all? What is just about just war, except being a justification for war? Does 'just war' lead to a 'sustainable peace'? Or, will it lead to wounds that survive generations and centuries and take on new *avatars*? The Spanish theologian Francisco de Vitoria employed the concept of just war to justify the conquest of America during sixteenth century. In the succeeding centuries, Hispanic America witnessed innumerable instances of insurgent activity by the natives, many of which failed to make an impression on the pages of history until the Zapatista uprising of 1994 (Priti Singh, ed., 2009, *Indigenous identity and Activism*, Shipra, Delhi). This allowed a reconstruction of indigenous insurrections during the colonial and post-colonial periods. Hence, no war can ever be just, and an enduring peace cannot be procured through a just war.

In the twentieth century, the American scholar James Scott Brown idolised Vitoria as the father of international law. Thus, from theology through Political Thought and Theory to International Law, the concept of just war became a useful academic concept to be employed by political leaders. But again, if just war would lead to peace, it is difficult to explain how wars fought nearly a thousand years ago on the Eurasian landmass, in the name of God and religion, continue to rage as I talk. Not only Europe and Asia, but violence threatens America and Africa too. Not too long ago, the violence of the war in Somalia was dramatised in a Hollywood movie.

Black Hawk Down, directed by Ridley Scott and released in 2001, is based on a book with a similar title—*Black Hawk Down: A Story of Modern War*. The movie opens with a one-liner attributed to Plato: "Only the dead have seen the end of war." It is now learnt that the screenplay writers of this movie were far more inventive than Plato himself. The message nonetheless is clear. In war, there are no victors, only losers. At least, this was the message of Bhishma to his grand-nephew, as the latter lay dying on the battle field.

After the eithteen day long battle of Kurukshetra, which was fought between kinsmen, Krishna told the leader of the victors Yudhishthira to speak to Bhishma, the first commander of the opposing army, for calming the doubts that were troubling him. A part of that conversation between the grand uncle and the grand nephew is present in the '*Anushasana Parva*' of the *Mahabharata*.

Yudhishthira asks: "...O grandsire, what is flesn, of what substance it is, what are the merits of abstaining from it, and what the demerits of eating flesh."

Bhishma replies thus: "Abstention from cruelty is the highest religion. Abstention from cruelty is the highest self-control. Abstention from cruelty is the highest gift. Abstention from cruelty is the highest penance. Abstention from cruelty is the highest sacrifice. Abstention from cruelty is the highest power. Abstention from cruelty is the highest friend. Abstention from cruelty is the highest happiness. Abstention from cruelty is the highest truth. Abstention from cruelty is the highest *shruti*."

Shruti is the sound, or the voice, or the word that is passed down from one generation to another. The voice that said "abstention from cruelty is the highest religion", or *ahimsa paramo dharmah* in Sanskrit, resonated in Gandhi. This became the guiding principle of his thought and practice.

Place of Gandhi in Peace Studies

At this point, it is also important to warn ourselves against falling into the idolatry of Gandhism, or using the figure of Gandhi as a mannequin, as the one and only perfect antidote against violence. That Gandhi can be a creative inspiration is evident in the labours of the Mazdoor Kisan Shakti Sangathana. The people, especially women, associated with this organization in Rajasthan have shown how to nurture democracy, human rights and justice from below, and how to procure peace through non-violent methods. The moral of the story is that the University has much to learn from civil society.

Long before Peace Studies became an academic discipline, Confucius said that if the individual is at peace with herself, the family will be at peace, if the family is at peace, the community will be at peace, if the community is at peace, the country will be at peace, and if the country is at peace, the community, the family, and the individual will be at peace. The geometrical metaphor of peace, according to Confucius, is spiral, and all and every measure should be taken to guard against violence spiralling out of control.

REALPOLITIK UNDERLYING PEACE INITIATIVES

Let us now return to the second element in the Nobel lecture of Obama, which is another Machiavellian moment that justifies *realpolitik*.

> "…I make this statement mindful of what Martin Luther King Jr. said in this same ceremony years ago: "Violence never brings permanent peace. It solves no social problem: it merely creates new and more complicated ones." As someone who stands here as a direct consequence of Dr. King's life work, I am living testimony to the moral force of non-violence. I know there's nothing weak—nothing passive—nothing naïve—in the creed and lives of Gandhi and King. But as a head of state sworn to protect and defend my nation, I cannot be guided by their examples alone. I face the world as it is, and cannot stand idle in the face of threats to the American people. For make no mistake: Evil does exist in the world."

Evil might or might not exist. But what is dangerous is the belief that we are good, and they, the other, are evil. This distinction between "I and thou" is detrimental to what is common in all of us, our humanity. Gandhi accepted the obvious truth that the Indians and the British shared this common humanity. Therefore, he refused to employ the convenient political equation of "us *versus* them", or "good *versus* evil". Instead, while launching the Quit India Movement in 1942, he called the British his friends, but he described his fight as a struggle of right against might, not as one of good *versus* evil. This apparently insignificant emphasis on a different use of language is not a mere rhetorical tweet; instead, it reveals the soul of the man and what he stood for.

The young Gandhi, who had helped the British Empire during the Boer War at the turn of the twentieth century, refused to be as cooperative with the British government during the Second World War simply because Britain had dragged 400 million people in South Asia into violence, without caring to ask for their consent.

In the third and final quote that I have, Obama says: "… The non-violence practiced by men like Gandhi and King may not have been practical or possible in every circumstance."

What would Gandhi have done if he were present in Germany during the 1930s and 1940s? Would his politics of non-violence have worked? There are no easy answers to these questions. Human challenges, unlike mathematical problems, cannot be resolved with a working hypothesis. However, what we do know, and know for sure, is that Gandhi was unwavering in his commitment to non-violence, whatever may have been the idiosyncrasies of the man. To rule out, even in theory, or in a Nobel Peace Prize Lecture, that Gandhian politics may not be possible or practical in every circumstance is to shut the door on non-violent solutions to human challenges and open the floodgates of Machiavellian *realpolitik*.

While Obama won the Nobel Prize in 2009, Gandhi's efforts went unrecognized by the Nobel Committee till his death in 1948. That very same year the Nobel Committee declared that it did not find any living person worthy of the prize. Perhaps, the Committee decided to leave vacant a space, respectfully and silently, to that magnanimous non-violent soul, who died a violent death.

Nonetheless, had Gandhi been awarded the Nobel Peace Prize, the Nobel Committee would have only done a favour by ennobling itself. The point that deserves emphasis is not that Gandhi was denied a prize, however important that prize might be, but that the Gandhian politics of non-violence is being considered as not always practical by the Nobel winner of 2009, purely for reasons of state. This shows that for the logic of the modern state, Machiavelli and Hobbes are practical and useful, while Gandhi and King are dispensable. This utilitarian logic also pervades many aspects of Western modernity. Let us look at some of those.

EUROPEAN INFLUENCE ON PEACE STUDIES

European modernity shaped the rest of the world in her "image and likeness", to use the expression of Charles Trinkaus, a scholar of the Renaissance. Europe installed in her colonies the instruments of the modern nation-state, her legal systems and philosophies of jurisprudence. In doing so, it nearly destroyed other socio-political traditions and institutions of peoples in Africa, Asia, America and Australia. But above all else, European modernity instilled a new kind of epistemology.

The university system became the single most important institution for propagating this epistemology. This new knowledge system denied the possibility of other ways of thinking, especially for non-European peoples. With the advent of modernity, knowledge became more empirical than speculative. The research of Galileo of Galilee is a prime example of this kind of knowledge, and thus stands at the threshold of a new knowledge revolution, where truth became measurable.

Soon, this early Modernity paved way for the European Enlightenment, which may be understood as the use of reason in the public sphere. Such a use of reason also led to the growth and cultivation of social sciences in the nineteenth century. However, the goal of the social sciences was to search for truth in society, as the natural sciences sought truths of nature. But the search for truth separated itself from the quest for the good, the just and the beautiful. In other words, the sciences were separated from philosophy, the arts, and the humanities.

The Indian University system, which is a consequence both of the European modernity and the European Enlightenment, has before itself the task of retrieving, nurturing and bringing to the centre-stage of epistemological discussions, academic and otherwise, those South Asian knowledge systems that are holistic, but not anthropocentric, those that locate the human being as part of nature but not above or outside it, and those where the quest for truth, the good, the just and the beautiful are intertwined.

ROLE OF UNIVERSITIES IN PEACE STUDIES

What are the others tasks before us, as academics and as individuals in society? We could begin by questioning the received wisdom that life in the state nature is nasty, brutish and short. But a move away from this Hobbesian dictum to the belief that perfect non-violence will work perfectly, implies questioning the order of knowledge and the structure of the University that produces and propagates knowledge. In short, it is important to re-evaluate the epistemic foundation of the current state of knowledge in India.

How can we inculcate in young minds the importance and the necessity of Peace Studies? How can South Asian academics and scholars bring our own many and varied traditions into school and university curricula? What role does women and trans-gendered people have in these processes? What we are faced with is not merely this problem, rather its immediacy and its urgency. A resolution or transformation is possible only if academics have a social agenda that is not restricted to policy making for the State or turning into pedants in search of knowledge for its own sake. The University must also look to society, especially civil society, because the University is located in society not above it.

CONCLUDING REMARKS

We began with Janus, but Janus is also the god of endings. So, perhaps it is not inappropriate to close the circle by evoking him yet again. Janus Bifronte is a double faced god. While one face of Janus is melancholic, the other carries a smile. May we ask why Janus is melancholic?

Anyone who looks back at the greater part of the twentieth century, which was torn apart by war, is bound to feel melancholic. Anyone who looks back at the physical suffering and damages caused to human dignity during the centuries of colonialism in Africa, America, Asia, and Australia is bound to feel melancholic. Anyone who looks back at the way we have treated our only planet, her flora, her fauna, as well as her non-living elements during the last one hundred and fifty years, while mother Earth shrank and while the technological world expanded, is bound to feel melancholic. So, this metaphor of the melancholic mask of Janus ought to be taken seriously rather than literally.

But then again, Janus is not merely a god of beginnings and endings. He is also a god of change, and of transition. That transition is not of time alone, but also of vision and of perspective. I have attempted to outline the need to transcend some of the current modes of thought just as I have also endeavoured to suggest a possibility towards effecting that transition.

REFERENCES

Galtung, Johan, 1996, "Peace and Conflict Research in the Age of Cholera: Ten pointers to the future of Peace Studies", *The International Journal of Peace Studies*, Vol. 1, No. 1. http://www2.gmu.edu/programs/icar/ijps/vol1_1/Galtung.htm

Harris, Ian, Larry Fisk and Carol Rank, 1998, "A portrait of university peace studies in North America and Western Europe at the end of the millennium", *The International Journal of Peace Studies*, Vol. 3, No. 1. http://www2.gmu.edu/programs/icar/ijps/vol3_1/Harris.htm

Kant, Immanuel, 1795, *Perpetual Peace: A Philosophical Sketch* http://www.constitution.org/kant/perpeace.htm

Mazdoor Kisan Shakti Sangthan http://www.mkssindia.org/

Obama, Barack Hussein, 2009, "A just and lasting peace", Nobel Peace Prize Lecture, 10 December, 2009, Stockholm http://nobelprize.org/nobel_prizes/peace/laureates/2009/obama-lecture_en.html

Ovid, 2004, *Fastii*, translated by A.S. Kline http://www.poetry intranslation.com/PITBR/Latin/OvidFastiBkOne.htm

Trinkhaus, Charles, 1995, *In Our Image and Likeness: Humanity and Divinity in Italian Humanist Thought*, (2 volumes), University of Notre Dame Press, Indiana, USA.

Wallerstein, Immanuel, 1996, *Eurocentrism and its Avatars: The Dilemmas of Social Science*, Keynote address at the ISA East Asian Regional Colloquium, 22-23 November, 1996, Seoul http://www.iwallerstein.com/wp-content/uploads/docs/NLREURAV.PDF

3
On Conflicts and Conflict Resolution

R.P. Misra

The seeds of conflict have always been present in all human beings and the institutions created by them and the methods to resolve them have also been there since times immemorial. Love and conflict are quite common in the animal kingdom. Animals like dogs, cats, elephants, monkeys and chimpanzees and gorillas do love as well as fight each other. As human beings have evolved from animals, they have inherited the tendency to love and defense from them. Animals love their newly born siblings more intensely than human beings. They sacrifice their lives to save their youngsters. As the young mature to stand on their own feet, the old relationship fades away. They become part of the herd, not a part of the family.

Animals fight for self defence including protection of their habitat. Those who accept defeat are not harmed and those who are ready to fight are engaged in 'war' leading to the victory of one side or the other. Thereafter, the sides accept the reality, fight no more. As time goes the aggressive tendencies may develop again but not on the ground old animosities. The old is forgotten and conflicts emerge from new exigencies. Aggressive tendencies among groups are more common than within the group.

Human behaviour is not very dissimilar from animal behaviour especially when self-protection or the protection of livelihood is concerned. But it is far broader based. Humans have far great memory power and hence they are more guided by what happened in the past than the animals. Further, their interests are not limited to self-defence and to protect their livelihood sources. Their interests are far wider. They go beyond the self and extend their interests to family, community, group and national interests. As such the spheres of conflict as well as peace extend beyond the self defence and habitat.

While scope for conflict among humans and the institutions created by them is far more than the ones among the animals, the scope for peace too is wider because the human mind is tuned to two simultaneous tendencies enforced and re-enforced by human psychology and cultural traditions: to live and let live in peace and harmony or to rule over the world by hook or by crook. Often the differences among the warring camps are resolved through give-and-take. But in many cases the conflict ends in violence either because the weaker side has given in or both the sides have fought violently. In the past, people fought with sticks, now they fight with guns and atom bombs. When the population was small and density was low, the number of people killed or injured was also small. Now, with growing population and increasing use of modern technology to kill and destroy, the loss of life and property is far greater now than ever before.

Our ancestors were ever ready to face attacks from ferocious animals or neighbouring tribes often on move. When faced with such threats, they responded promptly and automatically. At the first sign of danger, amygdale (located deep within the emotional brain), triggered the release of epinephrine and/nor epinephrine from the adrenal glands raising the heart rate, elevating breathing, and diverting blood into large muscles. This prepares the body to fight or to flee, or to feign dead.

The responses are of three types: aggressive response engages the other side in an emotional or physical battle; the avoiding response engages the other side directly and tries to win indirectly; and the acquiescing response gives in to the other side either because of weakness or as a strategy and wait for the right opportunity to strike. Faced with a conflict, people employ one of these responses in pure or their variant forms, depending on the circumstances, timing, and mood. Which of these responses to adopt will depend on which one is likely to succeed in solving the problem at hand?

A person in a fighting mode sees only what he alone considers to be right. He is psychologically so convinced of his stand that he sees the other world black and his world white. This response is helpful when a legal or ethical issue is involved. Once the matter is settled, it does not leave behind a sour relationship for too long.

In the avoiding mode, one party refuges to be drawn in the conflict either because it considers fighting below its dignity or because it hopes the problem will get resolved in due course of time as circumstances change. The wait and see approach, gives time for both the parties to rethink and reassess their respective stands. Time heals some wounds, is the adage they believe.

The acquiescing mode, one party drops his demands and allows the opposite side to have what it wants. It does so because it considers "it is just not worth the fight" especially if the person aims at something big and he does not want to waste his time and energy in small things. He prefers to lose the battle in order to win the war.

Modern world is different but the ancient physical survival mechanisms continue more or less the same. True, the nature of threats has changed; it is as much psychological as physical. We face threat to our success, our self-esteem and our relationships. We dislike, hate, abuse and even attack physically but we are in such a great hurry to achieve what we consider success that we tend to be violent even at slightest provocations. Our face flushes, heart rate goes up, eyes become red, and palms get cold, voice quivers, and body trembles when anger overtakes us. We experience stress and strains and become prone to violence. The security mechanisms modern society has created to protect its members from what is not legal come in the way of going to extremes. We are forced to restrain ourselves and develop more peaceful styles of resolving conflict. But as pressures builds and ethical standards decline, the restrain is overcome and man crosses all moral and legal barriers.

TYPOLOGY OF CONFLICT

Conflict has multiple sources and hence can be classified in many ways. Daniel Katz a leading conflict theorist of 1960s has classified it into four: historical, economic, value and power centric. It must, however, be noted that most conflicts are not of pure type. The apparent source may be one of the above four, but as the problem escalates other sources get drawn into it. As such even simple problem can get so complicated that it becomes difficult to understand and resolve.

1. What happened in the past often haunts the present. Generations back, two individuals, families, communities or nations could have been engaged in some sort of conflict. Each side considered itself right and the other side wrong. This event becomes a part of the oral and written family history which makes it difficult for descendants to forget.
2. Economic conflicts involve competing motives to secure scarce resources. Each party tries to get the maximum it can and its behaviour and emotions are directed toward minimizing the benefits to the opposite party. It is clearly visible in the conflict

between trade union and management. The parties concerned have incompatible goals and try to slice up the 'economic pie'.

3. Value centric conflicts occur when there is incompatibility in the way of life and living, beliefs and ideologies. Religious conflicts at all levels – local to global, fall in this category. The so-called Islamic terrorism is not Islamic as such but it is practiced by some fundamentalist Muslims in the name of Islam. Not too long ago, the Cold War between the liberal West and Communist East had a strong ideological content. Each side asserted the superiority of its way of life, and politico-economic ideology. It ended only when the Communist world lost ideologically as well as economically.
4. When the parties concerned do not want to follow the "live and let live" rule, a power struggle ensues. Each tries to maximize its influence by overriding the other. A power struggle begins which ends in victory or defeat of one of the parties or in a 'stand-off' with a continuing tension. Power conflicts are most common today specially in Political and Economic spheres.

A survey of the current situation in the world points to conflicts being more common than peace? But let us not forget that peace is so imperceptible that it remains invisible. If conflict is more common and powerful than peace, human race would have not survived this long. Conflicts and wars would have swallowed our predecessors long back. Apparently, peace is the bed rock on which all life forms including human exist. It is the law of nature. Conflict on the other hand takes over peace when the negative forces governing human life supersedes the positive forces.

The question is: why negative forces? Negative forces are those that govern the animal life. Animal existence is based on the physical contexts of life and living. Animals do not have a philosophy of life. They just exist and anything that comes in the way of this existence has to be fought against. Survival of the fittest is the law that governs animal kingdom. Humans on the other hand are endowed with a mind far bigger than that of even an elephant. They have, therefore, been able to rise far above animal existence. They live and lead a life that is self-determined and this self-determination is based on the changing natural and social environment in which they live. Some of these are derived from the genes they inherit from their predecessors while many others are drawn from the environment they live in.

That is the reason why some human beings are ever peaceful; they are saintly and are not attached too intensely to the physical world in which they live. They are not only peaceful, but also carriers of peace. Like Mahatma Gandhi they are harbingers of peace: they have no enemies or adversaries. They have only those with whom they do not agree on one or more issues. They first try to get rid of their own weaknesses and then they try to win over the others. In doing so, they observe penance to cleanse themselves and all those who are around them –friends or enemies. We can say that they have reached a higher level of consciousness in their evolutionary journey.

Such men and women are present in this world all the time. They are sources of peace. But a great majority of people are still steeped in animal psyche. They are deeply attached to the physical world and are prepared to die and kill others to protect it by any means at their disposal. As mentioned earlier, this physical world consists of the natural resources nature has provided, the economic resources the society has created and the political power that society has created for better planning and management of the resources at the disposal of the human beings grouping themselves in families, communities and nations. These resources are the sources of conflict as each individual and the institution he creates tries to own or have control over not only its legitimate share but also the share of others.

Thus, peace and conflict co-exist in each individual, community, society or nation. They are interactive forces that give shape to all societies. Longer the duration and intensity of conflict, more is the pain, killing and destruction. Longer the duration and intensity of peace, happier is the people. Thus permanent peace can only be hoped and aspired; it has not occurred so far in this imperfect world. And hence, it deserves to be pursued more seriously than it has been so far.

Peace can be of two types: peace by choice and peace by force of circumstances. Let us take up the case of the status of women in Indian society. Women had a very respectful place in Indian society; they were even venerated as mothers/goddesses. In due course of time and in response to new challenges faced by Indian society, they needed protection and were confined to the four walls. Their male counterparts took the role of protectors of the so-called weaker sex. In course time, they became inferior to men and even ill-treated.

Now, the women have risen to protect their rights as human beings. They refuse to be treated as weaker sex and want to have equal access to education, income, power and privileges. When women protest, conflicts arise. Men want to stand by tradition, while the women want the traditions in this regard to be discarded. They want to be treated as human beings. Even though the two sexes play different roles in the society in some spheres, these roles are complementary and equally important.

The gender bias that exists in modern society has its roots in certain developments in the past demanding physical power for protection and safety. It might have been acceptable then but it cannot be accepted in today's context. The same applies to many other problems. Even competition for wealth and power is also a residue of the past. People have been fighting their way, defeating the weak, making compromises with the equals and giving in when confronted with stronger power. We cannot treat these traditions and practices as worthy of emulation and continuance.

So, we see that conflict and peace have co-existed ever since the *Homo sapiens* descended on this earth and they would go together in future too so long as man's evolutionary journey is incomplete or some catastrophe wipes the humanity out. Conflicts inflict pain that is difficult to forget; it changes the psyche of individuals and is ever remembered. Peace, once superseded by conflict does not last for too long in human mind, it is just a part of history. What makes conflict more apparent is the fact that it is a deviation from the norm set by persons like Mahatma Gandhi for civilized human beings.

Humans are still Closer to Animals

Conflict is inherent to animals as they lead an existential life. They consider all that they see around as theirs' and fight for it unmindful of the needs or rights of others. The moment they perceive or see a danger to their interests they set their defence mechanism on to protect their interests. True, all animals love their young offspring and are prepared to sacrifice their life to protect them. It is also true that all animals of the same species love to live in close proximity to each other and form herds. But the loving relationship between the mother and its young offspring's ends the moment the young is able to fend for itself. The herd mentality of the animals does not extend beyond the members of the same species and forever.

Animal needs are given and they cannot be tampered by others whether animals or humans. They don't have any feeling of duty even when they nurse and protect their babies. They love their babies, but their loving relationship is in-born. Like humans, animals too procreate to multiply themselves, but unlike humans, the animals do not have control over procreation. It is just a natural process and the time for sex is fixed. There is no family planning, nor is there an opportunity to hasten or postpone the time of sex. Animals eat whenever they feel hungry and whatever is available near them.

Human beings have evolved far beyond the animal stage of life. They are not only more sensitive but also more rational. Unlike the animals, the human do not snap their relations with their progenies once the baby becomes adult. They continue and give rise to families, communities, cultures and nations. While humans are conscious of the loving relationship with their progenies and further expand and transform it, animals remain self-centred. Competition with fellow animals is, therefore, a part of their existential life. When human traits of love and co-operation, is overtaken by the animal trait of self-centricity and competition, humans too behave like animals and their further evolution as super-conscious beings is stopped.

Great men and women of wisdom were born in all parts of the world and all cultures to bring man back to the human traits of love and harmony. They attained the status of super-conscious beings. But, their impact on their followers has not been too lasting. Once they passed away, their followers developed cults that often went against the very principles they lived and died for. Another way to putting man on the right path has been peace education both formal and non-formal that begins even before the child is born. Mahatma Gandhi has rightly said "If we are to teach real peace in this world, and if we are to carry on a real war against war, we shall have to begin with the children."

How far the human beings individually or collectively advance on their evolutionary journey depends on what their forefathers have left behind in terms of human values, the societal contexts in which they live and the knowledge and its application they have learnt from their parents, society and formal education processes. There are times when man moves forward rather rapidly towards higher level of consciousness; he becomes charitable; generous; truthful and non-violent. At times he turns back to his animal past; and makes his own life and that of others miserable. Some realize their folly and revert back to the path of sanity and some die in the filth of their own creation. Man has thus been moving forward and backward on the evolutionary path, but if we take a very long-term view, he has been inching forward to become more human. In Vedic terminology, he is moving slowly, but not steadily to become '*deva*'.

Conflict is thus an in-built trait of human beings. It is only through trial and error and conscious efforts on the part of man to advance on the road to super-consciousness that this trait can be subdued. And once he reaches a higher stage of consciousness, he enjoys peace both within and without. Each conflict teaches a lesson as if a warning to return to peace, but prolonged crises slow down or even interrupt the evolutionary journey. Millions of people die without ever having an opportunity to make their own contribution to human evolution. Many become victims of their own misdeeds. Natural hazards, wars, and avoidable diseases take millions of lives. Today more people die due to road accidents than any major disease. The chances of humanity being eliminated from the surface of the earth without stepping into the world of real humans, are now greater than ever before as the threats posed by atomic war and global warming, both unleashed by man become more eminent.

We are now passing through a period that is fraught with incalculable dangers and risks. The so-called modernization process has let loose a development process which is based on competition rather than co-operation. Children are brought up to compete with a view to defeat others not in the pursuit of honesty, charity and humility that makes man a better human being but in the mad race for money, power and privileges that further distance him from his ultimate goal of becoming a super conscious man. While the former subsumes and the latter arouses what is animal in him.

WHAT MAKES THE WORLD A BASTION OF CONFLICT?

Socio-Economic Inequities

Jean Jacques Rousseau, a French political philosopher (1712-1778) said in *The Social Contract* "man is born free but everywhere he is in chains". It is more so today than ever before. True, the world we live in is far more advanced than ever before materially but not spiritually. One finds poverty in the midst of plenty, and more unhappiness than happiness. There is so much available today that every individual can live comfortably. But the fact is that 25 per cent of the people are unable to meet their basic needs; 50 per cent live a normal life; and the remaining 25 per cent live in luxury. And they all are trying hard to deprive others of what they have.

There are different measures of poverty. In 1978, the Planning Commission of India fixed poverty line (PL) in terms of income/food requirements. Taking the food needs of a typical individual as 2400 calories in rural areas and 2100 calories in urban areas, the cost of

650 gm of grains that fulfilled this normative standard was set as PL. It amounted to Rs. 61.80 per person per month in rural areas and Rs. 71.30 in urban areas. In 2006, it amounted to Rs. 560 and Rs. 454 per head per month respectively. Those living below the PL were categorized as BPL.

During the Tenth Five-Year Plan (2002-07), the assessment of BPL was further refined. Thirteen parameters were used to measure the degree of deprivation in rural areas. Each parameter was given a score in the range of 0-4. Families with 15 marks or less out of a maximum 52 marks were classified as BPL. The parameters were: landholding, type of house, clothing, food security, sanitation, consumer durables, literacy status, labour force, means of livelihood, status of children, type of indebtedness, reasons for migration, etc. For urban areas the parameters used were: roof, floor, water, sanitation, education level, type of employment, and status of children. The results of this survey are yet to come.

Irrespective of the measuring rod, the number of BPL in the country falls in the range of 220-230 million although the net percentage of BPL population has come down from 36 per cent in 1993-94 to 22 per cent in 2004-05. Decrease in percentage has been offset by the increase in total population of the country. It means that the poverty alleviation programmes of the Central and State governments had only a limited impact [National Sample Survey (NSS) 2004-05].

The calculation of BPL is based on income per day suffers from conceptual weakness. It takes into account only the food requirements; it does not include shelter, education and health, leave aside other basic needs like self-esteem. That is why some people equate PL as SL (*starvation line)*. In a country like India where a mini-cup of tea costs Rs. 5, the Planning Commission has now fixed Rs. 26 per day in rural areas and Rs. 32 per day in urban areas as poverty lines. It amounts to Rs. 781 and Rs. 965 per capita per month for rural and urban areas respectively.

Abraham Maslow has classified human needs in two categories: Deficiency-needs (D-needs) and Being-needs (B-needs). Peace is possible only if both D and B needs are satisfactorily met. At the base of the pyramid of needs (Fig. 3.1) are the physical needs: air, water, food, clothing, shelter, and sex. Above the physical needs are safety needs: safety from natural disasters, famines, floods, wars, family violence, and childhood abuses, etc. Economic and social security form part of the safety needs. When economic crisis grips man's life, he suffers from stresses and trauma that make his behaviour abnormal and unpredictable.

Next to safety needs are the needs of belonging. The feeling of belonging is of particular importance for children. Deprived of these needs

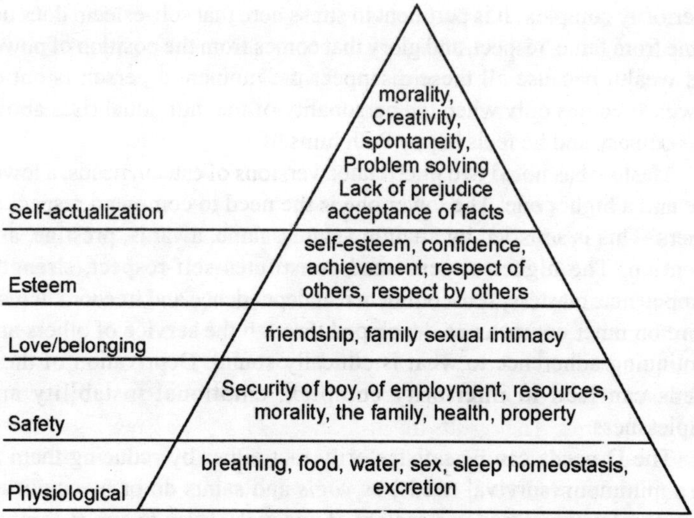

Fig. 3.1: An interpretation of Abraham Mallow's hierarchy of needs, represented as a pyramid with the more basic needs at the bottom. It is a theory in psychology, proposed by Mallow in his 1943 paper *A Theory of Human Motivation*. Mallow subsequently extended the idea to include his observations of humans' innate curiosity.

children fail to maintain loving relationships with other members of the family and community. For a satisfying life, all human beings want to have a feeling of belonging and acceptance by the family members, intimate partners, mentors, close colleagues, confidants and larger social groups like clubs, culture or religious groups, professional organizations, sports teams, etc. Everyone wants to love others close to him and be loved by them in return. In the absence of these loving relationships, people feel loneliness and become victims of anxiety and depression. This need for belonging can often overcome the physiological and security needs, depending on the strength of the peer pressure; an anorexic, for example, may ignore the need to eat and the security of health for a feeling of control and belonging.

Above the first three levels of D-needs are the needs for self-esteem and self-respect. No matter how rich and powerful an individual may be, he does not consider himself complete unless he commands respect from others in the society. These needs are satisfied when people so perform their duties that they get sense of achievement and also recognition of it from others. In the absence of self-esteem, people are gripped by inferiority complex. It is pertinent to stress here that self-esteem does not come from fame, respect, and glory that comes from the position of power and wealth because all these disappear the moment a person is out of power. It comes only when the personality of the individual rises above the ordinary and he feels happy with himself.

Maslow has noted two interrelated versions of esteem needs, a lower one and a higher one. The lower one is the need to command respect of others. This is satisfied by attaining status, fame, awards, prestige, and attention. The higher esteem need constitutes self-respect, strength, competence, mastery, self-confidence, independence and freedom. It rests more on inner competence developed through the service of others and continuing adherence to what is ethically sound. Deprivation of these needs can lead to inferiority complex, emotional instability and helplessness.

The D-needs can be satisfactorily met either by reducing them to bare minimum (survival needs) as *yogis* and saints do or by acquiring them to a level justified in a society of unequals. Even to aim at comfort level cannot be considered unjust in society of unequals like the one we find in the world today, but to try to raise it to luxurious and ostentatious levels is neither good for the individual or for the society. If the D-needs are satisfactorily met, man feels relaxed; he does not harbour any feeling of being sick and tense. He carries on his day-to-day business as a good member of his family, community, and nation. He is, however, neither a planner nor a visionary as he is not metamotivated, to use Maslow's term. For metamotivation, he has to get his B-needs also fulfilled.

Man is born with certain innate potentials for self-actualization. His parents, family and school further sharpen and strengthen these potentials and inspire him to become what he ought to be. One may desire to become a good artist, a good athlete, a good scientist, a spiritual *guru* or a servant of the people. To self-actualize, one must first have access to the D-needs discussed above. If the D-needs are not satisfactorily met it will be difficult to meet the B-needs. Viktor Frankl calls the B-needs as self-transcendence needs for they transcend the self-centric D-needs. Ingredients of the B-needs, according to Marlow are morality, creativity, spontaneity, problem solving, lack of prejudice (love), and acceptance of facts.

The D and B needs should not thus be considered as exclusive of each other. It is not that bottom layer of needs should be met first and rest of the needs should follow step by step. The categorization of needs and placing them in a hierarchic order are meant to help people understand their characteristics and relevance for peaceful life and living. In reality, they are intermixed and each individual makes his own concoction to achieve them. Further, each individual, culture, place and time has its own uniqueness. Hence, the hierarchy of needs given above should not be treated as rigid. Each individual would create his own hierarchy and work to get to the top, i.e., self-actualization.

Nearer one is to the meeting the D-needs, greater the chances of moving towards B-needs. When hate is replaced by love, people come together. Man forms families, friendship and professional groups, and larger entities like nations and United Nations only to bestow and share love. Millenniums ago the *Vedas* in India proclaimed *Vasudhaiva kutumbakam* (the whole world is a family) and the world they conceived included nature—animals, insects, and plants. Peace comes from the love man pours on his fellow human beings, on nature around him and on all that he creates and builds for himself and the generations to come.

While we plead for loving relations to ensure peace and harmony, we know that even such relations do not last long. Human society is ever changing. If it does not change, it would die. Many tribes and communities have disappeared because they did not change in response to the changing environment. Thus, *status quo* becomes dangerous even if there is no apparent conflict. Respect for the elders can make some elders misuse their privileges and come in the way of children growing into self-respecting human beings. Women get lowly status and hierarchic organization of society can make those who wield respect dictatorial. A stage comes when self-interest overrides love and rights supersede duties. Then the old order is challenged and love gives place to hate. Hatred leads to conflict. The challenge lies in individuals and collectivities being peace loving yet at the same time dynamic.

Religions have digressed from their Peace Mission

Religion came into being to promote peace and harmony. But more often than not it has been used as an instrument of death and destruction. William Blake, the English mystic, poet, and painter (1757-1827) had rightly said "this mystery never shall cease: the priest promotes war and the soldier peace." All through human history religions all over the world have been liberally used to secure political and economic ends. Religious education instead of giving deeper understanding of what the sages and saints have said and done, and what is enshrined in religious texts, produces fundamentalists who promote hate rather than love. The ritual of going to the temple, mosque or church is all that most religionists stand for. Religions stand for unity, equity, love, affection, and humility.

Unfortunately, the religious leaders are no less to be blamed for this. Most religions have become too ritualistic. Many so-called religious leaders aim at earning money by reciting passages from religious books. It is not easy to bring together two religious leaders on a common platform because they do not believe in equality of religions. People use and misuse religions the way they consider beneficial to them. The net result is hatred, violence, dishonesty and intolerance. Religions played a very important role in shaping the character of the people for they taught honesty, human brotherhood, sacrifice, ethical way of life and living. With the religions playing in the hands of those who wield power and prestige, their following has declined and they no longer inspire people to tread the moral path. Time has now come for the religious leaders to awake before it is too late and work for harmony and peace once again. They must rise above the ritualistic part of the religion and come down to the essence which is common to all religions.

Robert Green once said "Every man who expresses an honest thought is a soldier in the army of intellectual liberty." Religions are meant to produce such men and women. In some countries religions are shunned in the name of secularism, modernism, socialism, and even democracy; its widespread use to prepare vote banks notwithstanding. True, religion is a private affair of an individual, but to neglect the ideas and ideals that promote peace and harmony only because they are found in religious texts, amounts to being irrational.

The day the culture of accumulation and domination at any cost is superseded by the culture of share and care, peace would get the upper hand and conflict would not overtake the eternal inclination towards peace and harmony. Further, it would be easy to resolve conflicts as and when they arise.

Inadequate Efforts at Rebuilding Peace

Given the current state of affairs, we need peace builders all over the world. We need them in every village, community, city and nation. If building blocks of peace are the individuals, we need peace loving individuals: the people who are humble; the people who believe in justice for all; the people who respect others and respect themselves; the people who can sacrifice their own interests for the just interests of others; and the people who are ready to fight non-violently to restore peace and harmony.

But whence will these people come? They will come from amongst us. The institutions which once worked for peace are no longer active; many of them have gone astray. Our religions do not shape our way of life; our educational processes promote competition rather than co-operation; and the social institutions and organizations that promoted peace and kept the conflict at low key are now almost blunt. It is individualism that rules supreme; people tend to ignore their social responsibilities.

So, a new beginning has to be made. It has to be an initiative that uses modern science and technology together with ancient wisdom contained in our religious books and exemplified by the reincarnations, messengers, and sons of God. We have to look back to our past, live in the present, and create a new future.

APPROACHES TO CONFLICT RESOLUTION

Peace is possible only if conflicts are not nipped in the bud and not allowed to prolong. In this section of the chapter, we propose to discuss the often used approaches to conflict resolution. Which method should be used and when depends on the nature of the conflict and the intentions of parties concerned. Here the methods used are discussed below:

1. Aggressive

Styles of conflicts reflect the psychology and behaviour of the parties involved. One can see this more easily among animals like dogs. The moment an outsider enters into the area of influence of a dog, the two assess the physique and mood of each other make appropriate gestures. If the intruding dog is not strong enough to fight, it bends its tail downwards and tries to retreat. But in case, it feels it can give a fight and win, a physical fight ensues and one of them is ultimately defeated and runs away. Similar gestures mark the aggressive relations among other animals.

Human behaviour is not very different from that of animals. The principle of might is right is invoked, and priority is given to one's own rights and needs unmindful of the rights and needs of the other party. While asserting their views, they speak loudly and try to come in the way of the other side to put forth its point of view. Coercion is one of the usual methods used to browbeat the opponent.

People still in medieval times, mentally and culturally consider victory over the rival or supposed opponent as a great personal or group achievement. Hitler considered it his right to extend the sway of Germany in the name of Lebensraum. One often encounters this situation in traditional societies vertically divided into classes, races, religions, sects and castes.

The principles adopted in such confiicts are: "Might is Right"; "Eye for Eye"; and "Offence is the Best Defence". Where the followers of two religions or religious sects are involved in the conflict, each party considers its duty to wage a Holy War (*Dharma Yuddha*) to defend its religion that professes peace and harmony! Just wars are fought in defence of democracy, human rights, freedom from tyranny, etc. More often than not, the alibis are used to hide the real motives.

Realizing that the aggressive side is not interested in solving the problem except at its own terms and conditions, the other side too tries to pay in the same coin. And thus the level of threat increases and the possibility of any compromise further decreases. More often than not, the two sides resort to violence both in words and deeds leading to long-term enmity. One side wins and the other side loses.

The aggressive approach is highly destructive. The parties involved are more interested in hurting each other than settling the dispute. They are emotionally so apart that they feel happy if the other party is denied its share. In an interesting case of two brothers in the process of dividing the property left behind by their parents, failed to share a bullock cart. Neither side wanted the other side to get the cart. So, the cart was cut into two; the elder brother took one wheel and half of the body and the younger brother the other wheel and the rest of the body. The cart became a pack of wood but both sides were satisfied.

2. Transformative

Transformative style is just the opposite of aggressive style. Those using this style give more importance to establishment of cordial mutual relations than scoring over the other party by force, coercion or even third party mediation and arbitration. The style is well illustrated by a case of two brothers inheriting some agricultural land and jointly cultivating it. Once the parents were no more, the younger brother under the influence of his wife wanted the land to be divided in two equal parts. He approached his elder brother in an aggressive mood. The elder brother said: "Look, why should you be angry? Our parents are no more.

I am the eldest in the family. You being my younger brother, it is my duty to look after your interests. I am prepared to give all the ten acres to you if that satisfies you." Saying so, he sat down and started sobbing. The younger brother was so overwhelmed by this gesture that he fell on the feet of his elder brother and begged his forgiveness. Since then, they lived together and cultivated the land jointly. Here the elder brother was prepared to give up his rights to preserve brotherly relations. The gesture of the elder brother brought a sea change in the deteriorating family solidarity.

3. Accommodative

When both sides in the dispute try to accommodate each other's interests and needs, they find a mid way so, that neither side is a loser. In such cases, the relationship are maintained and even strengthened and both the parties are happy emotionally and otherwise. There are some people who by nature are outworldly in outlook. They are more likely to use accommodating style. Problems arise when they are confronted by people who are less social, more self-centred and short-tempered. At times, the generosity of one party works, but at many others it does not. This leads to painful experiences for both.

4. Collaborative

Collaborative style aims at a joint effort to pool individual needs and goals to find a solution that satisfied all the parties. It begins with mutual co-operation to reach a solution wherein neither side is a loser. This win-win outcome opens new avenues for future advances on the road to what is conceived as progress. It integrates the needs and aspirations of both the sides and offers new opportunities, energy, and ideas to solve not only the present, but also future disputes meaningfully. True, there is an element of risk in this style but it does produce an environment which is more conducive to healthy human relations.

Joint family system in rural India was a good example of collaborative style. As the family size increased, mutually agreeable and acceptable ways were found to allocate the assets to different members of the extended family. The authors have come across a case where the eldest member of a family used the available resources to build houses and made arrangements for livelihood for all on an equitable basis. Rarely did people go to the court of law for adjudication.

5. Compromising

In the case of compromising style, people involved in the conflict are flexible enough to settle the issue by give and take approach. Confrontation is avoided but neither side gets all that it claimed. And hence the outcome rarely satisfies either side as perception of need of various parties is too deeply engrained. So, the conflict appears resolved on the surface, but the lack of trust continues. Usually both sides feel cheated but since neither side is cent per cent right, the agreement arrived at is not violated.

At times, the contending parties are unable to arrive at compromise formula even if a mediator or arbitrator intervenes. This happens when emotional relations between them are highly disturbed because of breach of trust or family ties. In such cases, emotions overtake rationality and it becomes difficult to reach agreement and even if a compromise is arrived at, the relations remain sour.

6. Do Nothing

This style is marked by inaction from either side as they prefer to wait for a right moment to resolve the conflict. Because all conflicts are contextual, the circumstances at times so conspire that the bone of contention becomes irrelevant. This may happen if one or both sides pass through tragic experiences. In some cases the wait and see formula further widens the gulf and the problem becomes so complicated that it can neither be ignored nor resolved. Had it been handled differently, it could have been satisfactorily resolved.

SATYAGRAHA: THE GANDHIAN WAY OF CONFLICT RESOLUTION

Truth and non-violence were the twin end and means of Gandhi. To reach the truth means self-realization and the ultimate of human beings ought to be. Gandhi, however, considered humans so imperfect that they were "not capable of knowing absolute truth." The best that one can do is to seek relative truth. But in order that relative truth is closer to absolute truth rather than to untruth, one has to use non-violence as a means to while aiming at truth.

Since no individual can be sure of being absolutely right, no one is "competent to punish" others. This being the case, the first and the foremost requirement for peace to prevail effort should be made to accommodate the interests of the opponents and to bring them to a win-win solution without any coercion or force. Non-violence thus became the bed-rock of Gandhian approach to conflict resolution. Conversion of the opponent by non-violent means transforms him into a new man and leaves no rancour, resentment or revenge. Non-violence-in-action was *Satyagraha*, the most pragmatic and potent technique of conflict resolution.

The term *satyagraha* was derived from two Sanskrit words: *satya*=truth + *graha* = insistence, firmness. Alternative terms he used were: Truth-force and Soul-force. Gandhi considered Truth and Non-violence inter-related; truth being End and non-violence the Means. *Satyagraha* means "a relentless search for Truth". One who practices *satyagraha* is known as *satyagrahi.*

Satyagraha is often equated with passive resistance, a term Gandhi used while agitating for human rights of Indian indentured labour in South Africa. But Gandhi distinguished *satyagraha* (a weapon of the strong) from 'Passive Resistance' (a weapon of the weak). Unless one has the will power to resist any temptation to use violent means, he cannot be a *satyagrahi*. Thus, the basic unit of *satyagraha* is the individual. Even in mass scale *satyagraha*: "If a single *satyagrahi* holds out to the end, victory is certain."

Just a few months before his assassination, Gandhi once again reminded the world that non-violence alone would bring peace and harmony in the world. In his own words:

> "Perhaps never before has there been so much speculation about the future as there is today. Will our world always be one of violence? Will there always be poverty, starvation, misery? Will we have a firmer and wide belief in religion, or will the world be godless? If there is to be a great change in society, how will that change be wrought? By war, or revolution? Or will it come peacefully?
>
> Different men give different answers to these questions, each man drawing the plan of tomorrow's world as he hopes and wishes it to be. I answer not only out of belief, but out of conviction. The world of tomorrow will be, must be, a society based on non-violence. That is the first law; out of it all other blessings will flow. It may seem a distant goal, an impractical Utopia. But it is not in the least unobtainable, since it can be worked for here and now. An individual can adopt the way of

> life of the future—the non-violent way—without having to wait for others to do so. And if an individual can do it, cannot whole groups of individuals? Whole nations? Men often hesitate to make a beginning because they feel that the objective cannot be achieved in its entirety. This attitude of mind is precisely our greatest obstacle to progress—an obstacle that each man, if he only will it can clear a way."

INGREDIENTS OF *SATYAGRAHA*

"Non-violence, like charity, begins at home." "I learnt the lesson of non-violence from my wife, when I tried to bend her over to my will. Her determined resistance to my will, on the one hand, and her quiet submission to the suffering on the other, ultimately made me ashamed of myself and cured me of my stupidity. She became my teacher in non-violence," says Gandhi. *Satyagraha* can, however, be used to handle all conflicts: intra-personal, inter-personal, inter-group, national and international. Its starting point is the individual. For intra-personal conflicts, fasting is one of the very potent means.

A *satyagrahi* "grows from truth to truth", as moves forward on the path of duty for "The true source of right is duty." There is complete unison between what the *satyagrahi* "thinks, what he feels and what he says and what he does …". His "object is to convert, not to coerce, the wrongdoer." It aims at "a restructuring of the opposing elements to achieve a situation which is satisfactory to both the original opposing antagonists"; "it seeks to liquidate antagonisms but not the antagonists themselves." According to Bondurant, "In *satyagraha* dogma gives way to open exploration of context. The objective is not to assert propositions but to create possibilities. *Satyagrahi* involves himself in acts of 'ethical existence'."

One of the essential characteristics of *satyagraha* is humility: it never hurts. "It must not be the result of anger or malice. It is never fussy, never impatient, and never vociferous. It is the direct opposite of compulsion. It was conceived as a complete substitute for violence. The reformer must have consciousness of the truth of his cause. He will not be impatient with the opponent he will be impatient with himself."

The essential purpose of *satyagraha* is to arrive at a commonly agreed formula to solve a given problem. It is never to defeat or injure the opponent. The conduct of the *satyagrahi* must ever be transparent. In the event of committing a mistake, he must repent for it. In the ensuing dialogue, he must lay emphasis common interests of the disputants for "Three-fourths of the miseries and misunderstandings in the world disappear if we step into the shoes of our adversaries and understand their standpoint." The golden rule to follow is: "mutual toleration, seeing that we will never all think alike and we shall see truth in fragments and from different angles of vision. Conscience is not the same for all."

"A *satyagrahi* never misses, can never miss, a chance of compromise on honourable terms"—because I can never be sure that I am right." But, "essentials" or "eternal principles" should be defended at any cost. Gandhi asserted: "Human life is a series of compromises and it is not always easy to achieve in practice what one had found to be true in theory." And, "Compromise comes in every step, but one must realize that it is a compromise, and keep the final goal constantly in front of the mind's eye." Clarifying further, he said: "I could not have fought the Dutch and the English without love in my heart for them, and without a readiness for compromise. But my compromises will never be at the cost of the cause or the country."

One can understand why Gandhi at times called off his *satyagraha* midway. He never tried to exploit his opponent's weakness. Gandhi called off mass *satyagraha* launched by Indians in South Africa in 1914 because the European railway employees had gone on strike. The secretary of General Smuts appreciated this gesture and said to Gandhi: "I do not like your people. But what I am to do? You help us in our days of need. You will not injure even the enemy. You desire victory by self-suffering alone and never transgress your self-imposed limits of courtesy and chivalry. And that reduces us to sheer helplessness." *Satyagrahi* never humiliates cheats, or embarrasses the opponent; he addresses his heart directly by way of self-suffering, and if this fails, uses various strategies of non-co-operation and civil disobedience. But he would never resort to humiliation and violence.

Truth

Truth is an English term for Sanskrit term *sat*. *Sat* means God alone is; nothing else is. God is the all-pervading reality; He is the Absolute Truth that unites human beings with all that lives. "As long as I have not realized this Absolute Truth, so long must I hold to the relative truth as I have conceived it." As "the human mind works through innumerable media—what may be truth for one may be untruth for another." No one, therefore, "has the right to coerce others to act according to his own view of truth."

Differences in what constitutes truth have to be bridged peacefully through discipline, humility and self-suffering, i.e., *satyagraha*. A *satyagrahi* would publicly admit his mistakes. He would "magnify the mole-hills of (his) errors into mountains and minimize the mountains of others' errors into mole-hills." "A lover of Truth will never appear different from what he is. His thoughts, words and actions will be harmonious."

Non-violence (*Ahimsa*)

"*Ahimsa* is the means, Truth is the end. If we take care of the means we are bound to reach the end sooner or later." Violence begets violence. Hate the sin, not the sinner. In a conflict situation, violence hits the sinner not the sin. It is not possible to distinguish between justified and unjustified violence. In a conflict situation, violence hits the sinner rather than the sin. Gandhi asserted that "Individuals or nations, who practice non-violence, must be prepared to sacrifice their all except honour." As a corollary, "where there is only a choice between cowardice and violence, I would advise violence."

Since the legitimate goal of war is perfect peace, peace is always preferable to war. Since war involves "mutual violence" it is the breeding ground of hatred, revenge and bitterness—a poor foundation for greater peace. *Satyagraha* brings the issues out into the open and helps reach a settlement leaving behind no rancour or frustration.

Non-violence of Gandhi is "not merely a negative state of harmlessness but it is a positive state of love, of doing good even to the evil-doer. But it does not mean helping the evil-doer to continue the wrong or tolerating it by passive acquiescence. The active state of *ahimsa* requires you to resist the wrong-doer." "The very first step in non-violence is that we cultivate in our daily life, as between ourselves, truthfulness, humility, tolerance, loving kindness."

"Non-violence is never a method of coercion, it is one of conversion." The boycotts, strikes, or fasts do involve moral 'coercion', but if the cause and the means are right and love for the opponent is not diminished, the apparent moral coercion would also lead to peace and peace alone.

Self-suffering

Self-suffering is ever preferable to violence, "appeal of reason is more to the head but penetration of the heart comes from suffering. It opens up the inner understanding of man." It "does not mean meek submission to the will of the evil-doer it means the putting of one's whole soul against the will of the tyrant."

"Suffering injury in one's person—is the essence of non-violence and it is the chosen substitute of violence to others results in the long run the least loss of life." The *satyagrahi* as well as his opponent are transformed. If the opponent's conscience remains unchanged, he may yet be touched by the public opinion in favour of endured suffering. And, if self-suffering "is used in a cause that is unjust, only the person using it suffers. He does not make others suffer for his mistakes." And it keeps the resistance non-violent.

Faith in Human Goodness

A *satyagrahi* to be a true *satyagrahi* must have faith in human goodness. He must believe that the opponent is amenable to reason and has a conscience and hence he is likely "to respond to any noble and friendly action." Since "Everyone of us is a mixture of good and evil." The opponent must be as good or bad as the *satyagrahi*. "Even if the opponent plays false twenty times, the *satyagrahi* is ready to trust him for the twenty-first time, for an implicit trust in human nature is the very essence of his creed."

Unity of Means and Ends

"They say "Means are after all means." I would say, "means are after all everything." As the means so the end if one takes care of the means, the end will take care of itself." "I feel that our progress towards the goal will be in exact proportion to the purity of our means. The method may appear to be long, perhaps too long, but I am convinced that it is the shortest." No wonder then that Gandhi called off a major Civil Disobedience campaign in 1922 because it had gone violent.

Fearlessness

In *satyagraha* fearlessness "is a matter of heart" and not of physical strength. Possession of arms was not a sign of strength but a sign of fear and cowardice. Cowards can never be moral. "Non-violence and cowardice are contradictory terms." So, a violent person is better than a coward especially when violence "is offered in self-defence or for the defence of the defenceless." A violent person could become non-violent some day, but a coward can never become so. "If you feel humiliated, the use of force would be the natural consequence if you are not a coward. But if you have assimilated the non-violent spirit, there would be no feeling of humiliation in you."

Key to the success of *satyagraha* is the individual, "as we are so our environment becomes." "A small body of determined spirits fixed by an unquenchable faith in their mission can alter the course of history." Individual is like a part of the whole. They interact and influence each other. Gandhi did not subscribe to the sociological view that the social existence determines the individual's consciousness. Gandhi believed that moral development of the society is rooted in the individual. It is the individual's "duty to be disloyal" to the social institutions if they are not conducive to personal growth. Thus Gandhi's aimed at a morally enriched society constituting free and integrated individuals applying *satyagraha* to cleanse and further enrich it.

TIMING OF *SATYAGRAHA*

Right time launching *satyagraha* is the one when the role of the individual in a society is relegated to a secondary place, and power is concentrated in political and social structures. Gandhi looked upon "an increase in the power of the state with greatest fear because, although while doing good by minimizing exploitation, it does the greatest harm to mankind by destroying individuality which lies at the root of all progress." Digressing from the current biological and socio-psychological theories that humans, like animals, "are not gentle creatures who want to be loved. They are, on the contrary, creatures among whose instinctual endowment is to be reckoned a powerful share of aggressiveness." (Freud), Gandhi firmly believed in the basic goodness and non-violent nature of human beings. How else, they have continued to exist on the earth? If recorded human history is full of violence, it is because "History does not and cannot take note of this fact" of something that is expected.

In order that humans cultivate "truthfulness, tolerance, humility, loving kindness" and become soldiers of peace, they must be trained from their early childhood for the task ahead. If frustration triggers violence, then living in ways that cause less frustration to individuals and groups will promote non-violence. "Non-violence affords the fullest protection to one's self-respect and sense of honour."

Satyagraha has to be backed by an organization of devoted and trained *satyagrahis*. Gandhi was not a determinist who considered man to be a puppet of immutable laws. Gandhi believed that individuals could change themselves by force of will. In his model, the individual in a conflict situation is not innately aggressive and has the freedom of will to resolve conflicts in a non-violent way. The vows he prescribed helped in strengthening the will-power, "a vow really means unflinching determination without which progress is impossible."

Patience is a must to be a *satyagrahi*. Impatience implies inability to tolerate waiting and a belief that all desired change can be quickly brought about. The problem of mass impatience is even more serious. Patience is vitally connected with non-violence both in its techniques and in the wider objectives of the non-violent. A *satyagrahi* should, therefore, not crave for more active and unrestricted practice of a soldier or terrorist. And true patience means fortitude, endurance, and waiting; it is heroic, but rare.

It is these qualities that made Gandhi the greatest *satyagrahi* of our time. Decline in the values imparted by various religions has led to the search for fast track economic and technological remedies to solve emergent political, social and personal problems. These tendencies aggravate the difficulties in applying non-violent methods for solving present day human problems. Social discipline is a must for *satyagraha*. And for social discipline, some kind of socially useful Constructive Programme is a must. "Unaccompanied by the spirit of service, courting imprisonment, inviting beating and *lathi* charges, becomes a species of violence."

Apparently, Gandhi set a very high standard for himself. "I am an optimist because I expect many things from myself. I have not got them, I know, as I am not yet a perfect being." "All mankind in essence is alike. What is ... possible for me is possible for everybody." Louis Fischer had rightly pinpointed that Gandhi's greatness "lay in doing what everyone could do but doesn't."

SATYAGRAHA IN DIFFERENT CONFLICT SITUATIONS

Although the general principles of *satyagraha* are the same irrespective of the conflict situation, each category of conflict requires approaches specific to it.

Interpersonal Conflicts

Interpersonal conflicts can be resolved either by resorting to the court of law or non-violence. Courts can solve a given conflict but they cannot stop similar conflicts emerging again. In fact, they often create background for more conflicts because both the parties cannot be equally satisfied with court verdict. Unless the antagonists themselves become parties to the dialectic out of which Truth and justice emerge there can be no peace. In Gandhi's view: "Truly, men became more unmanly and cowardly when they resorted to the court of law. Surely, the decision of a third party is not always right. We, in our simplicity, imagine that a stranger, by taking our money, gives us justice."

The legal system offers institutional solution to conflict resolution among individuals or groups. The parties approach the court through their professional lawyers who plead the case to ensure victory of their respective clients. They use all the means at their command including untruth to prove their clients legally right. They do not want their clients to come together and resolve their problems without resorting to dubious means. Gandhi, himself was a lawyer, saw lawyers as mediators rather than mere conductors of legal proceedings. Talking of his first case which took him to South Africa and which he helped resolve out-of-court through an independent arbitrator and a time schedule for settling the agreed upon debts, he said: "I became disgusted with the profession. As lawyers, the counsels on both sides were bound to rake up points of law in support of their clients. The winning party never recovers all the costs. I felt it was my duty to befriend both parties and bring them together." He settled down into his legal practice in his singular way: "I realized that the true function of a lawyer was to unite parties riven asunder. The lesson was so indelibly burnt into me that a large part of my time during the twenty years of my practice as a lawyer was occupied in bringing about private compromises of hundreds of cases. I lost nothing thereby, certainly not my soul."

When interpersonal conflicts arise, ways of resolving them are either authoritarian leading to the imposition of their will on each other, or permissive wherein one party gives in. The former produces resentment and hostility in the loser and make the winner feel guilty; the latter fosters a feeling of guilt and helplessness in the loser and resentment and disrespect for the winner. The losers in either case cope by retaliation, dishonesty, submission, regression or rebelling. Where parties are balanced in power, stalemate is the normal result.

In such cases the ideal approach will be one in which the *satyagrahi* strives to "realize *ahimsa* in every walk of life and in a crisis act in a manner that is most natural to him." The *satyagrahi* should feel that neither of the two parties is unjust and evil. Then and then alone, both the parties would have faith in his impartiality. Each party is made to mind its own behaviour more than that of the opponent and try to arrive at a mutually acceptable understanding. Resolution of inter-personal conflicts using non-violent approach opens the door to further advances in the theory and practice of *satyagraha*: "For it will be by those small things that you will be judged."

Workplace Conflicts

Industrial disputes involving management and workers have several economic or social determinants, e.g., wages, management policies, employee-employer relations and feeling of powerlessness in employees. In order that disputes once settled do not arise again "labour should have the same status and dignity as capital." says Gandhi. Employees "should have the same access to the transaction of the mills as the shareholders." Gandhi wanted the workers to be organized: "When labour is intelligent enough to organize itself and learns to act as one man, it will have the same weight as money if not greater." Once this happens through *satyagraha*, the 'owners' will embrace the workers as partners. To bring about such a pleasant relationship both the management and workers should have patience, restraint, discipline, unity and faith in the organization. And neither side should dominate.

Satyagraha is not a one shot affair. It is a continuing process. *Satyagrahi* does not stop half-way for "in *Satyagraha* the minimum is also the maximum and as it is the irreducible minimum, there is no question of retreat, and the only movement possible is an advance." It, however, provides for reconciliation and a shifting of the position as new facts and experiences come to the fore and perception of Truth changes. Mediators do help the parties concerned to get a clearer realization of Truth.

In the event of everything else fails, the workers have the right to strike, "strikes are an inherent right of the working men but must be considered a crime immediately the capitalists accept the principle of arbitration." Gandhi warned: "Public has no means of judging the merits of a strike, unless it is backed by impartial persons enjoying public confidence." And the workers must follow the following six rules:

1. Workers and their leaders should not exaggerate demands and be ready for correction if convinced by the opponent.
2. Strikes should be resorted to as the last weapon if negotiation,

reconciliation and arbitration have failed. During strike, labour should remain ready for settlement or arbitration.

3. Labour must remain non-violent even under provocation and bear no ill-will towards employers.
4. Strikers should, out of self-respect, not rely on alms, public funds or union funds but find any available alternative work to maintain them.
5. Strikers, as *satyagrahis*, must not submit before force or hardship.
6. Strikers should be truthful, courageous, just, free from hatred or malice and ready for voluntary work with faith in God.

Conflict between People and the State

In the political field, *satyagraha* whether in the form of civil disobedience or civil resistance including fasting is resorted to oppose unjust laws and administrative practices. When such laws are broken, the *satyagrahi* (a) follows a higher law of conscience; (b) remains non-violent; and (c) is prepared to pay full penalty for violation. Gandhi emphasized that disobedience to be civil; it "must be sincere, respectful, restrained, never defiant, must be based on some well-understood principle, must not be capricious and above all must have no ill-will or hatred behind it."

Satyagraha should be the last resort and be used when everything else fails. The *satyagrahi* should try to negotiate. Then he should appeal to people, "educate public opinion, state his case calmly and coolly before everybody who wants to listen to him." And only then go for *satyagraha*. The moral pressure and public opinion paves the way for the possibility of conversion.

In a democratic set-up, the laws are passed by the elected representatives of the people. Gandhi, therefore, accepted the authority of the state in a democratic society. One must obey the state laws except those which are contrary to the conscience or have the potential to cause tangible harm to people's: "It is only when a person has thus obeyed the laws of society scrupulously that he is in a position to judge as to which particular rules are good and just and which are unjust and iniquitous." Further, "Civil Disobedience is not a state of lawlessness but presupposes a law-abiding spirit, combined with a self-restraint."

Thus in a democratic state, only 'defensive' civil disobedience — "involuntary or reluctant non-violent disobedience of such laws as are in themselves bad and obedience to which would be inconsistent with one's self-respect or human dignity"—may be resorted to. "Aggressive, assertive or offensive civil disobedience", i.e., "non-violent, wilful disobedience of laws of the state, whose breach does not involve moral turpitude and which is undertaken as a revolt against state", is resorted to where the state is corrupt, repressive or dominated by an imperialist power.

The state laws give two alternatives to the people: to obey the law itself ('primary' sanction) or to accept the ordained penalty ('secondary' sanction). Here disobedience is not 'criminal'; it is civil. That is why Gandhi said: "Civil Disobedience is the purest form of constitutional agitation." Obviously, 'criminal' disobedience has no place in *satyagraha*.

To sum up, progressive steps in a civil disobedience, *satyagraha* could be carried out in the following stages:

1. appeals,
2. negotiation,
3. mediation followed by arbitration,
4. agitation such as propaganda, marches, etc.,
5. ultimatum to the opponent if no agreement is reached,
6. economic boycott and strikes,
7. non-co-operation, non-payment of taxes, boycott of public institutions,
8. civil disobedience,
9. usurping the government's functions, and
10. parallel government.

International Conflicts

In international conflicts Gandhi tried to distinguish between aggressor and the defender even though both resorted to violence. In the context of World War II, he said: "While all violence is bad and must be condemned in the abstract, it is permissible for; it is even the duty of, a believer in *ahimsa* to distinguish between the aggressor and the defender. Side with the defender in a non-violent manner' because, "the [violent] defence has to resort to all the damnable things that the enemy does, and then with greater vigour if it has to succeed." The *satyagrahi* 'fights' a "war without weapons", aiming at the conversion of the opponent rather his destruction.

Modern War technology, particularly nuclear weapons, can only lead to mutual destruction. The concept of defence has almost become obsolete. *Satyagraha* tends to eliminate the very source of conflicts and thus eliminate the market for weapons. It brings us closer to peace through such constructive steps like conciliation, unilateral steps towards disarmament, a truth-seeking foreign policy and "civilian defence" if an invasion should nevertheless occur.

In the present political state, unilateral disarmament may not be practical, but a "graduated and reciprocated" initiative could give a productive start. Since armament and economy are interrelated Gandhi said: "real disarmament cannot come unless the nations of the world cease to exploit one another." Exploitation according to him begins when one claims as his own "more than the minimum that is really necessary for him...." Helping the neighbours in distress is not enough. We should invite our neighbours "to come and share our resources."

The state, according to Gandhi ".... can be administered on a non-violent basis if the vast majority of the people are non-violent." And if the non-violent people are attacked there are two options: "to yield possession, but not cooperate with the aggressor by the people who have been trained in the non-violent way. Or, offer themselves as fodder for the aggressor's cannon." The second option can be adopted only by a community of true and well trained *satyagrahi*s. "By laying down their arms they feel courageous and brave." "It was this unalloyed self-suffering which was the truest form of self-defence which knows no surrender." The aggressor is sure to realize "that it would not be paying to punish the other party and his will could not be imposed in that way."

Gandhi is often criticized for advising total surrender to the aggressor. He, however, defended by saying: "Everybody seems to start with the assumption that the non-violent method must be set down a failure unless he lives to enjoy the success thereof." while this is not said of war. "In *satyagraha* more than in armed warfare, it may be said that we find life by losing it."

Gandhi reminds that the essential nature in war is killing. It "demoralizes those who are trained for it. It brutalizes men of naturally gentle nature." Even if the non-violent people of a country are "hopeless minority" and cannot wean masses from war, they must still "live non-violence in all its completeness and refuse to participate in war." in two ways: First, to actively non-cooperate with the warring state, whether own or an outside aggressor: "Merely to refuse military service is not enough. Those who are not on the register of military service are equally participating in the crime if they support the state otherwise." Second, the hardcore *satyagrahis* should lead the masses so that "even common people would ultimately begin to subscribe inwardly to non-violence as a faith."

What India achieved through non-violence under the leadership of Gandhi remains unparallel to this day. India needs Gandhi today more than it needed in pre-independence days. It is not the foreign rule against which *satyagraha* has to be launched. It is against lack of *swaraj* and growing corruption in government and public life in general. As Horsburgh said, "the achievements of non-violence in India owe as much to Gandhi's moral greatness as to the techniques of *satyagraha*, the right method, if persisted in, can do much to produce the right man." As Gandhi said, training for violence could never do so.

Note: This section of the paper is based on Dr. Y.P. Anand, *Conflict Resolution: The Gandhian Approach*.

CONCLUDING REMARKS

It is now clear that conflicts arise because the parties involved whether individuals or nations perceive their interests differently. These differences result from factors like geography, race, religion, culture, ethnicity, caste, etc., which acts as perceptual filters. We are born and brought up in a given cultural and socio-political and economic setting. The values and beliefs that determine what wrong or right are shaped by what is taught to us from early childhood. As we grow we internalize these substantive, procedural and psychological inputs and rarely get rid of them even when confronted with different values and norms. When we are confronted with a conflict, we make up our mind on what is right and wrong through the filter of the values.

Gender too influences our perception of a situation. Men and women approach a conflict and its solution differently. Educational background of the individuals and knowledge about the issue at hand also influence a person's attitude towards the problem at hand and also his willingness to engage in efforts at conflict resolution. Age of the persons too plays a role. Older a person, more experience he is likely to have in handling conflicts. If the experience is negative, he is likely to be too careful and reluctant to take risks. It may also leave him confident and willing to take risk. In either case, the previous experience does play a role as a perceptual filter in handling conflicts.

Yet another factor that influences one's response to the overall situation is the character of the messenger. If he is known to be a wicked and scary person or is unknown, his impact on the parties concerned would be negative. People are more inclined to listen with respect to those who are credible and honest.

REFERENCES

Adam Roberts and Timothy Garton Ash, (eds.) (2009), *Civil Resistance and Power Politics: The Experience of Non-violent Action from Gandhi to the Present*, Oxford University Press.

Y.P. Anand, (1998), *Conflict Resolution: The Gandhian Approach* (*The Theory and Practice of Satyagraha*), New Delhi: National Gandhi Museum, 17 pages.

Augsburger, D. (1992), *Conflict Mediation Across Cultures,* Louisville, Kentucky: Westminster/John Knox Press.

Aureli, Filippo and Frans B.M. de Waal, (eds.) (2000), *Natural Conflict Resolution,* University of California Press, Berkeley, CA.

Bannon, I. and Paul Collier, (eds.) (2003). *Natural Resources and Violent Conflict: Options and Actions.* Washington, D.C: The World Bank.

Bar-Siman-Tov, Yaacov, (ed.) (2004), *From Conflict Resolution to Reconciliation,* Oxford University Press.

Bercovitch, Jacob and Richard Jackson (2009), *Conflict Resolution in the Twenty-first Century: Principles, Methods, and Approaches,* Ann Arbor: University of Michigan Press.

Blake, R.R.; Shepard, H.A.; and J.S. Mouton, (1964), *Managing Intergroup Conflict in Industry*, Houston, Texas: Gulf.

Bayazit, M. and E.A. Mannix, "Should I stay or should I go? Predicting team members intent to remain in the team", *Small Group Research,* 2003, *34*(3), 290-321.

Cormick, G; Dale, N.; Emond, P.; Sigurdson, S.G. and Stuart, B.D. (1996), *Building Consensus for a Sustainable Future: Putting Principles into Practice*, Ottawa: National Round Table on the Environment and the Economy.

Deutsch, M. (1973), *The Resolution of Social Conflict: Constructive and Destructive Processes*, New Haven, CT: Yale University Press.

Deutsch, M. and Coleman, P. (eds.) (2000), *The Handbook of Conflict Resolution: Theory and Practice*, San Francisco: Jossey-Bass.

de Waal, Frans B.M. (1989), "*Peacemaking among Primates*", Cambridge, MA. Harvard University Press.

Fisher, R.J. *The Social Psychology of Intergroup and International Conflict Resolution,* New York: Springer-Verlag, 1990.

Fisher, R.J. (1997), *Interactive Conflict Resolution,* Syracuse, NY: Syracuse University Press.

Fisher, R.J. "Third party consultation: A method for the study and resolution of conflict", *Journal of Conflict Resolution*, 1972, 16, 67-94.

Fink, C.F. "Some Conceptual Difficulties in the Theory of Social Conflict", *Journal of Conflict Resolution*, 1968, 12(4), 412-460.

Forsyth, D.R. (2009), *Group Dynamics* (5th ed.), Pacific Grove, CA: Brooks/Cole.

Goldfien, J.H., and Robbennolt, J.K., "What If the Lawyers Have Their Way? An Empirical Assessment of Conflict Strategies and Attitudes toward Mediation Styles", *Ohio State Journal on Dispute Resolution*, 22, 2007, 277-320.

Gray, B. *Collaborating: Finding Common Ground for Multiparty Problems*, San Francisco: Jossey-Bass, 1989.

Hicks, Donna (2011), *Dignity: The Essential Role: It Plays in Resolving Conflict,* Yale University Press.

Jarboe, S.C., and Witteman, H.R. (1996), "Intragroup conflict management in task-oriented groups: The influence of problem sources and problem analysis", *Small Group Research*, 27, 316-338.

Katz, D. "Nationalism and strategies of international conflict resolution", in H.C. Kelman (ed.), *International Behavior: A Social Psychological Analysis,* New York: Holt, Rinehart & Winston, 1965, pp. 356-390.

Kellett, Peter M. (2007), *Conflict Dialogue,* London: Sage Publications.

Kriesberg, L. (1998), *Constructive Conflict: From Escalation to Resolution,* Lanham, MD: Rowman & Littlefield.

Mack, R.W., and R.C. Snyder, "The Analysis of Social Conflict – Toward an Overview and Synthesis", *Journal of Conflict Resolution*, 1957, 1, 212-248.

Richard Arvid Johnson (1976), *Management, Systems, and Society: An Introduction,* Pacific Palisades, Calif.: Goodyear Pub. Co., pp. 148-142.

Sternberg, R.J., and D.M. Dobson, "Resolving inter-personal conflicts: An analysis of stylistic consistency" *Journal of Personality and Social Psychology,* 52, 1987, 794-812.

Tesler, Pauline and Thompson, Peggy (2006), *Collaborative Divorce: The Revolutionary New Way to Restructure Your Family, Resolve Legal Issues, and Move on with Your Life*, New York: Harper Collins.

Van de Vliert, E., and Euwema, M.C. "Agreeableness and activeness as components of conflict behaviours", *Journal of Personality and Social Psychology,* 66, 1994, 674-687.

Veenema, Hans *et al*. "Methodological improvements for the study of reconciliation" *Behavioural Processes,* 1994, 31:29-38.

Wilmot and Jouyce Hocker (2007), *Inter-personal Conflict,* New York, NY: McGraw-Hill Companies.

Winslade, John and Monk, Gerald (2000), *Narrative Mediation: A New Approach to Conflict Resolution,* San Francisco: Jossey-Bass Publishers.

4

Satyagraha: Gandhi's Approach to Conflict Resolution

Jai Narain Sharma

A path breaking method of conflict resolution was born more than a century ago, far away from India in South Africa. The father of the method was Mohandas Karamchand Gandhi, a lawyer by profession. Following Tolstoy, he called it passive resistance. But the action that followed was not passive, it was proactive. So, he renamed it *satyagraha*.

Satyagraha, as practiced by Gandhi, was a technique of action designed to set in motion a process to achieve lasting peace. It emerged from the realization that violence bred violence; war fought to end wars and bring peace brought greater and more devastating wars. *Satyagraha* replaced brute force by soul force, also known as love force through self-suffering with the sole objective of drowsing hatred in the opponent and arousing in him the inherent capacity, even if muted, to love the 'enemy'.

The doctrine of *satyagraha* was an extension of the rule of family life into the political arena. Gandhi held that family disputes and differences were generally settled according to the "Law of Love". The injured member had so much regard for the others that he suffered injury for the sake of his principles without retaliating and without anger against those who differed with him. As repressing of anger and self-suffering were difficult processes, he did not dignify trifles into principles, but in all non-essentials readily agreed with the rest of family and thus continued to gain the maximum of peace for himself without distributing that to others. Thus, his action whether he resisted or resigned was always calculated to promote the common welfare of his family.

The doctrine of *satyagraha* was meant to show how the man of conscience could engage in heroic action in the vindication of truth and freedom from all tyranny, in his appeal to justice against every social abuse sectional interest. Gandhi challenged the conventional notions of authority, law and obligation by appealing to his conception of natural law or *dharma* and self-suffering or *tapas*. *Satya* and *ahimsa* alone could secure an unending basis for social consensus and political loyalty.

In times such as ours when conflict is the order of the day and the potentials of technology offer more to fear than to hope, social and political theories face their gravest challenge. Theoretical and political systems have grown increasingly suspect and intellectual formulations tend less to challenge than to repel. But there is rapidly developing demand hitherto neglected by social and political theory: this is the demand for solutions to the problem of conflict not for theoretical systems of end-structure aimed at ultimately eliminating conflict, but for ways of confronting conflict when it arises: ways, which are constructive and not destructive. Such a demand must be met by a theory of process and of means and not of further concern for structure, for pattern and for ends; basic to such a theory is a philosophy of action.

In the arena of power politics, power experts meet power experts and the struggle continues to be cast in power-play maneuvers if not in terms of outright or subtle coercion. The framework of assumptions, which underlies the strategy of power conflicts, may make it impossible for rivals or antagonists to choose the mutually advantageous course because there is nothing in their experience, which allows them to make the assumption of similarity in regard to their relative positions. If they could do this, they might solve the dilemma to the benefit of both. Indulgence in *himsa* is the result of short-sightedness, lack of vision, arising out of the inability to put oneself in the position of the antagonist and to disarm or convert him so that he ceases to regard himself as an irreconcilable enemy.

Far from denying the existence or reality of conflicts of interest in human mind and society, Gandhi admitted their existence in every walk of life and sought to make *ahimsa* the basis of a method of action, which could cope with such conflicts by limiting, if not wholly removing, the *himsa* involved. It is part of liberal and democratic doctrine that the method of persuasion is morally and even practically superior to that of pressure; that free discussion and rational argument are better than coercion or brute force. We commonly distinguish between force, which usually means physical constraint; power, which implies the use of reason or of other skills, and authority, which presupposes the recognition by those who accept it of the moral and political legitimacy of its exercise by its holder.

T.H. Green's dictum "will, not force, is the basis of the State"; the earlier attempt to invoke the notion of a social contract; Locke's "tacit consent"; Hume's "appeal to political prudence and the artificial virtues"; and Rousseau's "general will", are all traditional examples of the present-day sociologists' concern with the social consensus, which provides the framework for peaceful conflict resolution under recognized rules of the game. The notion of non-coercion is essential to the respect that we accord to the human personality, and the concern with justifying minimum coercion as a necessary evil to secure a larger good is itself a recognition of the superiority of *ahimsa* over *himsa*. There was an anarchistic and utopian element in Gandhi's doctrine of *ahimsa* in that he proclaimed the ultimate need for the state and for all institutions totally to abjure all *himsa*. This was because he recognized that, in the broader meaning of *ahimsa*, even a liberal who abstained from physical force or shied away from slaughter could indulge in subtler forms of *himsa* or pressure. The main thing for Gandhi is that more and more people must be prepared to accept the absolute moral value of *ahimsa*, not as an elusive ideal or a pious hope, but as a widely relevant principle of social and political action. Force thrives on fear but if more and more individuals and groups become fearless, force increasingly fails to serve its intended purpose and its exercise may be effectively opposed and even consistently frustrated. Today, we are prepared to question the retributive theory of punishment and to condemn forms of *himsa* like capital punishment, duelling, slavery, torture, collective retaliation or revenge, acts of aggression by states, preventive wars, cruelty to animals, flogging and corporal punishment, which were all quite respectable at one time or the other. We are now stricter about the notion of minimal coercion or the use of force as a last resort and we also increasingly recognize that a progressive reduction of the content of minimal coercion is the mark of civilization, progress and enlightenment. But we still base our degrees of repugnance or condemnation of force upon our valuation of the rightness of the cause in which it is employed and upon our assessment of the amount of suffering caused in relation to existing suffering or the future suffering avoided.

Gandhi insisted that force did not change its immoral character according to the circumstances of its use, and denied that the use of force to prevent a greater evil could ever acquire any inherent moral or political legitimacy. His attitude towards *ahimsa* was never literalist, but it was nonetheless absolutist rather than utilitarian. He declared that a votary of *ahimsa* could not subscribe to the utilitarian formula. He would strive for the greatest good of all and die in an attempt to realize the ideal.

He was, therefore willing to die so that others might live. The absolutist's sphere of destruction will always be the narrowest possible. The utilitarian had no limit. Judged by the standard of non-violence, every war was wholly wrong. Judged by the utilitarian standard, each party was justified according to its idea of utility. Precisely on the same ground, the anarchist justified his assassinations. But none of these acts could possibly be justified on the principle of greatest-good-of-all.

Although Gandhi's conception of *ahimsa* was absolutist on the ethical plane, it was anything but an abstract moral attitude for he was convinced beyond doubt that individuals and groups and even the masses could be trained in "the white art of non-violence" just as they could be in "the black art of violence".[1] The individual votary of *ahimsa* must learn that he needed far greater physical and mental courage than the one needed for delivering of physical blows. He had to pass many a sleepless nights and go through many a mental torture before he could even be within measurable distance of the goal of utter humility and goodwill even towards his most bitter opponent. In any conflict between two parties, he was bound, when the occasion arose, to say, which side was just but he could not grade different species of violence according to whether it was defensive or offensive. Strength did not come from physical capacity but from indomitable will.

The votary of *ahimsa* must cultivate the habit of unremitting toil, sleepless vigilance, and ceaseless self-control. Such a man would not meekly submit to the will of an evil-doer but put his whole soul against the will of a tyrant. "Working under this law of our being, it is possible for a single individual to defy the whole might of an unjust empire." Gandhi recognized that it would be difficult to get large masses of men to be non-violent in this exalted sense, but he was convinced that if even a band of intelligent and honest men with an abiding faith in *ahimsa* could be formed and trained, it could ensure the non-violent atmosphere required for the working of civil disobedience in accord with *ahimsa*. It should be possible to train small communities in the difficult art of non-violence and use their influence for peaceful mass action and to get large number of people to learn to do without the protection of both the military and the police during communal troubles. Gandhi thought it was gross self-deception to believe that man could risk death only if they had learned and practiced the art of killing, but not otherwise. There was no *prima facie* reason why the masses, if trained in non-violent action, be incapable of showing the discipline displayed usually by a fighting force. The example of a few men and women if they fully imbibed the spirit of non-violence was bound to infect the whole mass in the end.

From *ahimsa* in politics flowed the individual freedom. Gandhi was against any kind of impositions even if it was imposed for the benefit of the person concerned. He upheld the dignity and authority of the individual throughout his life. In Champaran where he conducted his first *satyagraha* in India, he was served with a notice to leave the district. But he refused to comply with the directive. A summon was served on Gandhi to appear before the court. He pleaded guilty and read a brief statement before the court wherein he said, "I have disregarded the order served upon me, not for want for respect for lawful authority, but in obedience to the higher law of our being, the voice of conscience."[2]

Writing in 1939 in connection with the People's movement, he observed, "Civil liberty consistent with the observance of non-violence is the first step towards *swaraj*. It is breath of political and social life. It is foundation of freedom. There is no room there for dilution or compromise. It is the water of life. I have never heard of water being diluted."[3] With the outbreak of Second World War, India was made a party to the War. Rigorous curbs were put on civil liberties of the people. He strongly pleaded for freedom of speech as an inviolable fundamental right of the citizens even during the war. Explaining his mind at a greater length he observed, "But if they (the British) fight unto death for their freedom, and if they are at all reasonable, they must recognize our right.... It is our duty to fight for that right... This liberty is a concrete issue, which needs no defining. It is the foundation of freedom, especially when it has to be taken non-violently. To surrender it, is to surrender the only means for attaining freedom."[4] He asked, "If the individual ceases to count, what is left of society? Individual freedom alone can make a man voluntarily surrender himself completely to the service of society. If it is wrested from him, he becomes an automation and the society is ruined."[5] He regarded the individual as the centre of the power. He was categorical in his estimate of relation between individual and the state. He held that the state derived its existence and power from the individual.

The concept of the ultimate authority of the individual logically paved the way for the enunciation of the theory of non-violent non-co-operation with the state and the exploitative system that stood in the way of the all round evolution of the individual. The emphasis on the moral power of the individual was the keynote of his philosophy. His anguish and indignation expressed in the pages of '*Hind Swaraj*' against modern civilization was based on this fundamental belief.

Gandhi did, however, try to reconcile individual freedom with social obligation. He considered society like a family, and the relation between the individual and the society as interdependent. He rejected unrestricted individualism that ignored social obligations as well as the individual freedom as a mere cog in the social machine. He wrote, "I value individual freedom, but you must not forget that man is essentially a social being. He has risen to this present status by learning to adjust his individualism to requirements of social progress. Unrestricted individualism is the law of the beasts of the jungle. We have learnt to strike the mean between individual freedom and social restraint. Willing submission to social restraint for the sake of the well-being of the whole society enriches both the individual and the society of which one is a member."[6] But between the individual and society, the individual came first, though society was, by no means neglected. The individual was the unit and in any scheme of social progress the first step always began with him. Society must provide opportunities for the maximum growth of individual and individual in his turn must discharge his duties faithfully. In case, either of the two went wrong, the other must resist non-violently. Thus, non-violence reconciled individual freedom with social restraints. It implied that the mechanics of control, which maintained social cohesion, consisted of internal and non-coercive external sanctions. The individual used his opportunities to advance the greatest good of all while society gave to the individual maximum opportunity to be good.

Gandhi suggested a moral alternative to violence. The international community, so far, has adopted the method of violence, physical power, as the means for resolving conflicts, which accrue due to the clash of national interests as well as for other reasons. The achievements of science and technology have proved the futility of war, as in modern times, it means total annihilation of the world. This inadequacy of violence has raised the question of resolving conflicts without inviting disaster and use of physical power? We are in search of a functional alternative to violence.

Gandhi's contribution lies in the fact that he dispelled the common place notion that leads to a belief in the unavoidability of war. He applied his theory of unity and purity of means and ends in dealing with the problem of international relation also. War, as a method of struggle is the means and the object for which it is waged is the end. Even if the end of war is to get justice, it cannot be realized through the impure means of war. To get justice through war is unjust for if one cannot give life, how can one take it? Thus, he rejects even the concept of just war as a method of resolving conflict.

In modern age concept of "just war" is not tenable even if the peaceful methods prove ineffective. The destructive nature of war does not permit us to resort to war. The contention that war is in the interest of peace, is fallacious. For it overlooks the fact that the suppression of force can only prevent the expression of the evil in acts, but cannot remove the source of the evil itself. Gandhi held: "There is a law of Nature that a thing can be retained by the same means by which it has been acquired. A thing acquired by violence can be retained by violence alone while one acquired by truth can be retained only by truth".[7] Further, "It is an inevitable law that the weapon which is responsible for victory is the only one which can preserve the fruits of victory and win more."

Even the nuclear armament cannot prevent war. In his view, "The atomic weapons might have created a temporary revulsion against war, but the world would return to violence as soon as the feeling of revulsion was over." Thus, Gandhi rejects war as a method of conflict resolution and suggests a novel technique of *satyagraha* based on the principle of non-violence which may legitimately be regarded as moral alternative to war for the resolution of conflicts. He holds: "I do justify entire non-violence and consider it possible in relations between man and man and nation and nation, but it is not "a resignation from all real fighting against wickedness. On the contrary the non-violence of my conception is more active and real fighting against wickedness than retaliation whose very nature is to increase wickedness. I contemplate a mental and, therefore, a moral opposition to immoralities."[8] The Gandhian technique of inter-national conflict resolution consists in the principle of struggle without arms and, positively speaking, a fight with the help of truth, self-suffering, love, character and moral powers, which is known as the principle of non-violent resistance.

This technique of *satyagraha*, however, requires greater courage and training than is required for military personnel. "To seek to win in a clash of arms would be pure bravado. Not so if in defying the might of one who would deprive me of my independence, I refuse to obey his will and perish unarmed in the attempt." Further, "To kill and be killed in fighting an enemy is comparatively speaking an act of bravery but to stand the blows of your adversaries and not to retaliate is a greater form of bravery." The technique of non-violent resistance not only holds good for resolving the inter-personal conflicts but for the inter-national conflicts also. To Gandhi, "It is blasphemy to say that non-violence can only be practiced by individuals and never by nations which are composed of individuals."

Aggression by any nation on others takes place due to certain motive behind it. The motive may be certain natural greed or lebensraum. In the former case Gandhi suggests the proper study of the motives of the possible aggressor and removing that motive by providing suitable alternative. Speaking about the frequent tribal raids in the North-West Frontier Provinces Gandhi said in 1938 that the raider's motive was chiefly economic, i.e., the satisfaction of primary needs. He, therefore, suggested their training in handicrafts to remove their principal motive underlying their raiding habit.

If the possibility of invasion is due to certain differences, Gandhi forbids any resort to law courts. In his view, "We should use a variety of possible approaches dictated to us by our hearts and minds, including negotiation, conciliation, mediation, sharing of differences, co-responsibility and the co-creation of a valid and creative compromise, which is a recognition of the element of truth within the other out there."[9] He realized that "for two disagreeing parties to go to law court there could often be "another form of exhibition of brute force." "Having recourse to judiciary as a form of the Law of Aggression, rules out the chance for one to practice the Law of Love". If we resolve the differences with the help of judiciary, "it will amount to taking recourse to fear, constraint and force, which will never give us justice and the conflict finally will remain unsolved". Therefore, "A theory of non-violence must lay the greatest stress on negotiations as the chief peaceful means of inter-national disputes".

Gandhi prescribed another approach for a nation when it is faced with an armed attack. Here, the technique consists in fighting non-violently to the last consequences without any bitterness and hatred against the invader. In 1940, Gandhi wrote in the *Harijan* "if the Czechs, the Poles, the Norwegians, the French and the English had all said to Hitler, "You need not make your scientific preparation for destruction. We will meet your violence with non-violence. You will, therefore, be able to destroy our non-violent army without tanks, battleships and airships. The history of Europe would have been written differently," the same year in July, he appealed to every Briton "to accept the method of non-violence instead of that of war for the adjustment of relation between nations and other matters".[10] In this context his advice to Britain is also worth noting. He said, "I want you to fight Nazism without arms. I would like you to lay down the arms you have as being useless for saving you or humanity. You will invite Hitler and Signor Mussolini to take that they want of the countries, you call your possessions. Let them take possession of your beautiful island, with your many beautiful buildings; you will give all these, but neither your souls nor your minds. If these gentlemen choose to occupy your houses, you will vacate them, if they do not give free passage out, you will allow yourself, man, woman and child to be slaughtered, but you will refuse to owe allegiance to them."[11] The same type of advice is given to Abyssinia, Czechoslovakia, China and India during Italian, German and Japanese invasions. In 1935 he said: "If Abyssinia were non-violent, she would have no arms, would want none, she would make no appeal to the League of Nations or any other power for armed intervention. She would never give any cause for complaint. And Italy would find nothing to conquer. If Abyssinians would not offer armed resistance, nor would they give co-operation willing or forced. Italian occupation in that case would mean that of the land without its people. That, however, is not Italy's object. She seeks submission of the people of that beautiful land."[12] Against Japanese aggression to China, he advised. The Chinese would say to Japan, "bring all your machinery, we present half of our population to you. But the remaining two hundred millions won't bend their knee to you". If the Chinese did that Japan would become China's slave. He argued: "If it is brave, as it is, to die to a man fighting against odds, it is braver still to refuse to fight and yet to refuse to yield to the usurper. If death is a certainty, in either case, is it not nobler to die with the breast bared to the enemy without malice against him within."[13] During Second World War at the time of Japanese aggression, he advised people of India to opt for non-violent resistance. "The underlying belief in such non-violent resistance is that, the aggressor will, in time, be mentally, even physically, tired of killing non-violent resisters. He will begin to search what this new force is, which refuses co-operation without seeking to hurt, and will probably desist from further slaughter". But one can doubt its efficacy during aerial warfare and blast of atom bomb. Gandhi's reply was, "Behind the death dealing bomb there is the human hand that releases it, and behind that still is the human heart that gets the hand in motion." The remorse that gripped those who talked of atom bomb as also of those who dropped it on Hiroshima and Nagasaki is a sufficient proof of Gandhi's thesis.

Gandhi denounced not only the use of arms in war, but also the help of armed forces from other nations to one side or the other. He wrote in the *Harijan*, "It is clear that small nations must either come or be ready to come under the protection of the dictators or be a constant menace to the peace of Europe. In spite of all the goodwill in the world, England and France cannot save them. Their intervention can only mean bloodshed and destruction such as has never been seen before."[14] "If I were Czech, therefore, I would free these two nations from the obligation to defend my country. And yet I must live, I would not be a vassal to any nation or body. I must, have absolute independence or perish".[15] He always advised the nations small and big to fight with their soul-force, the force lying within, and not to take help from the outward circumstances.

In spite of the best of the efforts, if a nation loses its territory and becomes the slave of the aggressor, Gandhi prescribes a third type of behaviour called non-co-operation. A voluntary non-co-operation with the victor will make him realize his fault and arouse his moral consciousness. At least, it will not strengthen his evil designs and pride and will cause ultimate defeat to him. According to Gandhi "Non-co-operation is not merely an ideal but also a safe and quick way to freedom for India. I do suggest that the doctrine holds good also as between states and states". This is why, he suggested Abyssinia to non-cooperate with Italy. In 1942 during the anticipated Japanese attack on India, Gandhi wrote to Meera Behn: "Remember that our attitude is that of complete non-co-operation with the Japanese army. Therefore, we may not help them in any way, nor may we profit by any dealings with them. Therefore, we cannot sell anything to them.

The question of having any dealings with the Japanese does not and should not arise. They will handle nothing from Japanese hands".

To sum up, Gandhian technique of international conflict resolution consists in resolving differences with the help of violence and truth in the form of *satyagraha* and non-co-operation. In normal cases, it suggests the method of conciliation, negotiation, arbitration, and direct dialogue with the opponents for resolving conflicts.

According to the doctrine of *satyagraha*, social and political conflicts can best be resolved in an atmosphere in which the contestants respect each other's moral worth, distinguish between measures and persons, conduct their battles in a spirit of self-criticism, and abstain from the cruder forms of coercion. When the coercive clement is strong in conducting a conflict, it demoralizes the winner and humiliates the loser and leaves behind it a trail of continuing bitterness or suppressed resentment. Fear is always a bad counsellor, and solutions that rest on the appeal to fear are less lasting or satisfying than agreement achieved in the context of a consensus of goodwill. Further, when a conflict takes place between unequal parties, it is tempting for the stronger to regard itself as invulnerable, to identify it, interests with the general good or to think it can ignore with impunity the just claims of others. In such situations, the appeal to force is useless for the weaker party and merely increases the complacency of the stronger. The weaker can compel the attention of the materially stronger by showing their reserves of moral and spiritual strength and by casting doubt on the self-assurance and moral conceit of their opponents. Even if those who resort to *satyagraha* fail to secure their ends, they retain their self-respect and are morally enhanced, although they have some times to pay the price of political or physical martyrdom.

REFERENCES

1. D.G. Tendulkar, *Mahatma*, New Delhi, The Publications Division, Ministry of Information and Broadcasting, Government of India, 1952, pp. 209-10.
2. *The Collected Works of Mahatma Gandhi*, New Delhi, The Publications Division, Ministry of Information and Broadcasting, Government of India, 1965, Vol. XIII, p. 375.
3. *Ibid.*, Vol. LXIX, p. 356.
4. *Harijan*, 22-9-1940, p. 292.
5. *Ibid.*, 1-2-1942, p. 521.
6. *Ibid.*, 25-7-1939, p. 139.
7. M.K. Gandhi, *Satyagraha in South Africa*, Ahmedabad, Navajivan Publishing House, 1975, pp. 338-39.
8. *Harijan*, 12-11-1938, p. 328.
9. Guyde Mallac, *Seven Steps to Global Changes: Gandhi's Message for Today*, Santa Fe, New Mexico Ocean Tree Book, 1987, p. 33.
10. *Harijan*, 6-7-1940, p. 185.
11. *Ibid.*
12. *Ibid.*, 12-10-1935, p. 276.
13. *Ibid.*, 8-10-1938, p. 282.
14. *Ibid.*, 15-10-1938, pp. 290-91.
15. *Ibid.*

5

The Notion of Democratic Peace: The Kantian Roots

Sushila Ramaswamy

> A constitution where the subject is not a citizen, and which is therefore not republican, it is the simplest thing in the world to go to war…reason as the highest legislative moral power, absolutely condemns war as a test of rights – *Immanuel Kant*

The ideals of republicanism and democracy which were ushered in by the two major revolutions in the eighteenth century, i.e., America and France, and also saw the rise of a school of pacifism that rejected the medieval moral-legal doctrine of war, including that of just war. The pacifist writers like Desiderius Erasmus (1466/1469-1536), Thomas More (1478-1535), John Amos Comenius (1592-1670), Emeric Crucé (1590-1648), Francois Fenelon (1651-1715), William Penn (1644-1718), Abbé de St. Pierre's (1658-1743), Voltaire (1694-1778), Jean Jacques Rousseau (1712-78), Immanuel Kant (1724-1804) and Jeremy Bentham (1748-1832) derived their inspiration either from the Stoics or early Christian radical positions or the more recent European ideals of cosmopolitanism, humanitarianism and bourgeois internationalism. Common in their perceptions was their profound skepticism to war and the military profession and the great goal of life for European intellectuals was human happiness without any trace of the tragic.[1] There was considerable disagreement as to the means—whether through the application of scientific and technical reason or through man's return to nature and rediscovery of his original simplicity—but all alike were convinced that society was on the threshold of breaking away from the shackles of traditional authority and superstition, erase the historic curses of ignorance, disease and war and begin as articulated by Condorcet (1743-94) "upon the absolutely indefinite perfectibility of man, which knows no other limit than the duration of the globe upon which nature has placed us". There was complete cynicism about the doctrine of just war seen as smokescreen to hide the aggressive impulses of ambitious monarchs. However, none of them at the turn of the eighteenth century, including Kant, advocate world government, as they resisted the "very idea of concentrating power in the form of world government... The mood was one of suspicion of all political power and of faith in the beneficence of individual human reason and wisdom."[2]

Montesquieu (1689-1755) points out that reason would help human beings discover universally valid rules of reciprocity, which, if enforced by positive law, would maintain peace, security and a certain degree of fairness within civil society. Montesquieu counts on the transformation of human existence by the "spirit of commerce" guided by the new science of finance or economics. Commercialization helps human beings to get rid of their prejudices that veil their true needs. By recognizing the common need and aspirations, human beings discover their humanity thus transcending previous religious, ethnic and national sectarianism. Once captivated by the allure of peaceful trade, human beings look to military exploits and war with increasing disgust. Commerce brings in frugality, economy, moderation, work prudence, tranquillity, order and rule. Montesquieu's defence of manufactures, commerce, finance, riches and even luxury enables him to not only take his stand with the moderns and against the Greeks but influence Bentham and Kant to see trade and commerce as the basis of perpetual peace. Voltaire poked fun at the two kings each of whom had *Te Deums* sung in his own camp after the battle and defends a republican government as it allows people to constantly renew the sovereign power, a point that Kant makes central to his plan for perpetual peace. The general perception was that the transition from monarchical to republican institutions would eclipse wars and herald in an era of peace and moderation. The period was full of projects for abolishing war and establishing peace, namely that of Penn's *Essay Toward the Present and Future Peace of Europe* (1693), St. Pierre's *A Project for Making Peace Perpetual in Europe* (1713), Rousseau's *A Lasting Peace through the Federation of Europe* (1774), Kant's *Perpetual Peace* (1795) and Bentham's *Plan for a Universal and Perpetual Peace* (1789).

KANT'S PREDECESSORS

Among the various peace plans Penn is the pioneer to have envisioned disarmament as the most effective guarantee for international peace. He stresses the importance of peace in view of the suffering and destruction that war entails. War could be prevented within a framework of justice for both individuals and groups if conflicts could be resolved in a fair way. Justice could be ensured if governments enforced laws impartially. For maintaining peace in Europe, he proposes a Sovereign Parliament of European states to decide disputes collectively and enforce decisions though states could still maintain their sovereignty in internal matters, thus anticipating the European Union.

St. Pierre's peace plan tries to include all the nations of the world but then, for the purpose of making it feasible, he limits his confederation to Europe. After examining the various means to prevent wars, he suggests federation of states as the best solution. St. Pierre's plan is voluminous but Rousseau's project of a federation to establish lasting peace is a summary and a critique of Pierre. Rousseau points out that while private wars have been prevented with the institution of governments, larger wars could be prevented with the formation of a federation that would unite nations just as nations unite individuals under the authority of law. He observes that such an arrangement is not new as it existed, in an embryonic form, in the Germanic Body, the Helvetic League, and the States General of the Netherlands, and the ancients had the Greek Amphictyons, the Etruscan Lucumonies, Latin *feriae,* and the city leagues of the Gauls. For the success of the federation, Rousseau stipulates four necessary conditions: (1) every important power must be a member; (2) the laws they legislate must be binding; (3) a coercive force must be capable of compelling every state to obey the common resolves; and (4) no member may be allowed to withdraw.

Rousseau's plan proposes five articles. The first will setup a permanent alliance with a congress to settle and terminate by arbitration or judicial pronouncement of all conflicts. The second will decide which nations shall have a vote, how the presidency shall pass from one to another and how the contribution quotas shall be raised to provide for common expenses. The third declares the permanence of existing boundaries. The fourth specifies how violators shall be banned and forced to comply by the means of arms of all the confederates. The fifth recommends majority vote to begin with but three quarters after five years and unanimity to change the articles. Rousseau explains how his plan would remove the six motives that lead to war and these motives are: (1) to make conquests, (2) or to protect themselves from aggression, (3) or to weaken a too powerful neighbour, (4) or to maintain their rights against attack, (5) or to settle a difference which has defied friendly negotiation, and (6) to fulfil some treaty obligation. Rousseau is confident that with the exception of conquest the federation will be able to accomplish all the other purposes and even in conquest it will be able to deter by marshalling all the powers against the aggressors. Rousseau lists many of the evils and dangers that prevails in Europe of his time, such as injustice because of might, insecurity of nations, military expenses due to external attacks or their threats, no guarantee for international agreements, unsafe and expensive means of obtaining justice when wronged, risk and inconvenience of wars, loss of trade during crises and general impoverishment and lack of security. The benefits of arbitration are certainty of settling disputes peacefully, abolition of the causes of disputes, personal security for rulers, fulfilment of agreements between rulers, freedom of trade, smaller military expenses, increase in population, agriculture and public wealth and happiness. Rousseau also concludes that St. Pierre's plans were not adopted because the princes were short-sighted in their ambition and greed for power; were too proud to submit themselves to arbitration and too blinded by their self interest so as not to see wisdom of the general good. He points to revolution as the only means to establish the federation but sensing the violence it would unleash, he realizes that it would be dreaded as much as desired.

Bentham regards war as the chief cause of suffering and proposes two planks, that of reducing military forces in Europe and to emancipate colonies as a way of eliminating war. For the welfare of all civilized nations he suggests three goals—simplicity of government, national frugality and peace. He opposes international treatises and trade barriers and points out that trade is always advantageous to both parties but war is ruinous to all the participants in modern times. He desires the establishment of a common court of judicature to decide differences among states but does not want, unlike St. Pierre and Rousseau, the court to be armed with coercive powers. Establishing a judicial court is in the interest of all. Bentham recommends a Congress of deputies from each country whose proceedings would be made public. He distrusts secret diplomacy and is optimistic than Kant, about achieving lasting world peace and happiness if people are allowed personal contact with one another than through the abrasive relations between governments. Bentham's plan is quite sketchy and obviously not comprehensive. However, he demonstrates the usefulness of disarmament and warns about the dangers of colonialism and secrecy. Though he alludes to the power of public opinion in international affairs he was also conscious as to how it could be stifled. He also coins the word 'international'. "The basic Benthamite idea has persisted to this day that the ordinary citizen can have a vision of a more peaceful, just and happy world and has both the right and power to coerce his own government to policies consonant with this ideal."[3]

KANT'S PRESCRIPTIONS

Kant in the *Science of Right* (1790) discusses the rights of nations, international law and also the universal right of humankind. Inspired by Rousseau's emphasis on the dignity of the human being, Kant insists that ethically people ought to be treated as ends in themselves and that means a ruler has no right to treat his people as objects for his ambitions and wars. The people do not owe a duty to the sovereign. According to Kant it is sovereign who has a duty to the people.

Kant's insistence on human dignity leads him to emphasize on some important key concepts like individual rights, equality before law, the need for a correct legal procedure and an educational system that will enhance reason. Moral law and the autonomy of the individual will form the basis of freedom which is possible only under the rule of law. Hence laws are necessary and it is our duty to respect the law. But law can be administered only in a state which is a union of human beings and law has to be administered without prejudice to rank and privilege. Laws are the conditions by which the will of one particular individual is harmonized and united with the will of others within the framework of a general law whose basis is freedom. Only in a republican state all human beings are free, equal, independent and autonomous.

For Kant, morality and self-determination is the same thing and a person acts on the basis of categorical imperative which implies acceptance of general principles which one recognizes within oneself and is not self contradictory and is universally applicable. This framework allows Kant to make a synthesis between individual's own moral will and the universal law. Action follows a philosophy of right which allows the freedom of existence of an individual while allowing all others to exist equally on the basis of a universal law.

According to Kant, since human beings are endowed with reason by nature, the purpose of nature is to ensure the development of rationality for that constitutes the human essence. History is a process towards rationality and links progress with reference to the moral character of human beings. With his firm conviction in human rationality, Kant condemns servility and cherishes independence of mind. He regards paternalism as the worst form of despotism. Members of a civil society are united for the purpose of legislation and thereby constitute a state. Citizens endowed with three juridical attributes that inseparably belong to them by right. These attributes are constitutional freedom, civil equality and political independence. Kant does not dwell into the ways and means of achieving a republican constitution, but merely to indicate a set of absolutely valid principles to which to appeal in case of a conflict of interests. He is categorical that republican constitutions in individual states are the necessary stepping stones to achieve eternal peace among all nations. His faith in republican ideals of 1776 and 1789 did not waver despite the excesses in France during the reign of terror, ultimately helping in the rise of Napoleon. The overall optimism of the Enlightenment and the rise of republicanism and constitutional liberalism convinced Kant that perpetual peace can be envisioned within the plurality of nation states.

Moral practical reason within us pronounces the following irresistible veto: there shall be no war, either between individual human beings in the state of nature, or between separate states, which although internally law-governed, still lives in a lawless condition in their external relationships with one another. For war is not the way in which anyone should pursue his rights.... It can indeed be said that this task of establishing a universal and lasting peace is not just a part of the theory of right within the limits of pure reason, but its entire purpose.[4]

Kant believes that the history of human race is a progress towards a perfect political constitution and considers the republican constitution as the perfect one. He asserts that there is reason to believe that the natural process supports the ultimate goal of perpetual peace and explains this with reference to the idea of unsocial sociability of human beings, meaning that the personality of human beings is that of a split personality, they could not live with one another but also could not do without one another. In earlier times, human beings spread over the entire surface of the earth to escape others but the necessities of existence led them to develop trade and commerce and the latter too in turn brings people together. In the same process, he is convinced that nations would be brought together making the dream of perpetual peace a reality.. : "He applies the categorical imperative to the relations of states and rejects any action or policy that would make peace among nations impossible. Like individuals, he insists that nations must enter into a union of states, which is the only way to establish peace. This would make a permanent congress of nations a practical reality enabling nations to settle their differences in a civil process than by barbarous war. He bases the right to a universal peaceful union of all nations on the juridical principle of legal justice, namely that all people have a right to associate with one another as they originally share the entire soil of earth. He also insists that even though perpetual peace may not be a reality in the near future but must be worked for, as one's duty and states that "the universal and lasting establishment of peace constitutes not merely a part but the whole final purpose and end of the science of right as viewed within the limits of reason".[5] It is morality itself that vetoes war, as war treats human beings as mere means and persons as mere things. War is rejected by rational citizens out of legal motive of self love and conversely to wage war is to renounce reason.

Kant in his *Idea for a Universal History from a Cosmopolitan Point of View* (1790)[6] states that nature compels people to find a cosmopolitan solution making a league of nations the natural outcome of social evolution. Until that is realized human beings must suffer the cruelty of conflicts. The way out is a moral order which can be brought about only through education, as that would help in building character in accordance with moral principles. The justice and conscience within us, and not with help of governments, would enable us to realize our destiny, the sovereignty of God on Earth. Kant laments that rulers spend very little money on public because they spend it on paying for past and future wars and is convinced that the ever-growing war debt would eventually make war impractical economically. Reiterating Montesquieu, he highlights the value of inter-state commerce as paving the way eventually for an international government, as commercial activity and material prosperity are a panacea against war.

In 1795, Kant publishes his major work on peace entitled *Perpetual Peace: A Philosophical Sketch*[7] as a just treaty that could be signed by nations in the background of his indignation at the separate treaty of Basel in which Prussia ceded France territory west of the Rhine so that it could partition Poland along with Russia and Austria. Kant describes his proposed peace programme with reference to two steps: the preliminary articles and then three definitive articles to not merely attempt cessation of hostilities but to lay the foundations of peace. As far as the first is concerned he stipulates the following: (1) No Secret Treaty of Peace shall be held valid in which there is tacitly reserved matter for a future war; (2) No independent states, large or small, shall come under the dominion of another state by inheritance, exchange, purchase, or donation; (3) Standing Armies shall in time be totally abolished; (4) National debts shall not be contracted with a view to the external friction of states; (5) No state shall by force interfere with the constitution or government of another state; and (6) No state shall, during war, permit such acts of hostility which would make mutual confidence in the subsequent peace impossible: such are the employment of assassins, breach of capitulation, and incitement to treason in the opposing state. He adds that a state has no right to wage a punitive war because just punishment must come from a superior authority and not an equal. Like Bentham, Kant emphasizes that justice must be delivered publicly and open to scrutiny.

For enduring peace Kant suggests the need for three definitive articles: (1) the civil constitution of every state should be republican in which laws apply to everyone universally and fairly, a government by law and not by favoured persons. His hope lay on the mechanisms of checks and balances within a democratic set-up which is absent in authoritarianism. The public opinion would be the restraining element in a republic. His reasoning is that majority of the people would go to war only in self-defence and not otherwise. Therefore, if all nations are constitutional republics it would signal the end of war and aggression. For perpetual peace constitutional republics is only one of several necessary conditions. (2) The law of nations shall be founded on a Federation of Free States. If all wars have to be ended forever, then there must be a league of peace and if more republics associate with one another the more practical a federation becomes. (3) The law of world citizenship shall be limited to conditions of universal hospitality. He also concedes that realization of this ideal would be slow and long, but is confident that intensive education of all citizens in every country would make possible the ideal. Eventually, the conflict between the individual's obligation *qua* citizen to obey the law of the state and his obligation *qua* man to obey the cosmopolitan law will cease as the member states of the universal confederation cease to contravene the cosmopolitan law. As a result, the moral responsibilities of citizen and man will coincide and citizenship would become a universal status. Kant's argument for perpetual peace rests on the assumption that human beings have the singular potential for reasoning and moral development. But Kant does not advocate world government as centralized authority is detrimental to individual freedom.

KANT'S LEGACY

Kant's doctrine of perpetual peace is one of the most influential aspects of his political philosophy and has inspired many. H.G. Wells, writing in the early days of World War I, states that this War would be "the war to end all war" on the grounds that once popular government replaces Prussian militarism and autocracy there would be no war among European nations. In 1909, Norman Angell reiterating Kant points out, that war has become unprofitable due to modern commerce even for the technically victorious country and an interdependent European community based on economic self-interest then political wars would cease in the same way as religious wars have stopped in the West.[8] A rationalist, Angell believes that war could be eliminated through the growth and progressive application of human reason to international affairs. He points out that once human beings are convinced that war is meaningful except as a form of mutual suicide, disarmament and peace becomes possible. Angell fails to realize that most of the modern wars, including the First World War, are not necessarily due to economic reasons. Josef Schumpeter argues that modern states are inherently peaceful and oppose conquest due to capitalism's success in ensuring prosperity. Clarence Streit in *Union Now* (1938) proposes a federal union of democratic states modelled after the US constitution on the grounds that trade and peaceable ways of democracy would keep this Union perpetual. It included common citizenship, a defence force, a tariff-free market, and a common currency.[9]

Limits to the Notion of Democratic Peace

On the basis of this Kantian doctrine of perpetual peace, a thesis has emerged that democracies do not fight each other leading to the absence of wars between liberal states and the connotation, that peace dividend and commerce are much better alternatives than war and conflict is slowly becoming an integral part of universal consciousness. Ray (1998) points out that democracies rarely or never fight.[10] Small and Singer (1976) in their response agree with the aforesaid proposition but deny statistical significance to this pattern. They point out to the fact that the time span is too short to arrive at definite conclusions and thus initiate a widespread academic debate on the subject.[11] Doyle (1983, 1997) examines the debate at great length. Reiterating Kant, he argues that for past two centuries there has been a growing peaceful union of liberal states. He considers liberal democracy along with international organization and hospitality, as the three preconditions to ensure peace.[12]

> ...Kant and the other liberals were essentially correct about the benefits of democracy. Peace is more likely when societies have adopted non-violent means of conflict resolution, executive

> authority is constrained by a system of checks and balances, and intertwined commercial interests make conflict uneconomical.... There has been a dramatic increase in the number of democracies since second World War ....The pacific efforts of inter-dependence provide more reason than ever, therefore, to believe that Hobbesian anarchy is being reconstructed to reflect liberal values.[13]

An offshoot of this theory is the claim that democracies are generally more peaceful than authoritarian ones that may fight fewer and also smaller wars. But the facts do not substantiate this thesis, as democracies have fought as many wars as the authoritarian ones and these wars were also not smaller. The initiators of the largest number of wars for the last two hundred years was Great Britain which was a democracy for the entire period, followed by France, which was a democracy for substantial period of time and Russia, which was never a democracy. In fact, if one takes note of France's continued intervention in the Franco-phone countries from the 1950s to the late 1990s it would compare favourable with the erstwhile Soviet Union's use of force in the name of limited sovereignty. However, what is true is that while democracies do not fight with one another they do fight with authoritarian regimes. Furthermore, Mansfield and Snyder (2002, 2005)[14] point out that while mature democracies have abstained from wars democratizing ones are more warlike. Increase in the risk of war in democratizing countries happen only if many or most of the surrounding nations are undemocratic.[15]

As democracy is a recent development this theory's validity may just be a coincidence rather than based on experience of a long period of time. But even in propounding the doctrine of democratic peace, the theorists overlook important exceptions. The proposition that democracies have a larger consensual basis than authoritarian ones in taking crucial decisions like declaration of war is not vindicated by facts. The decision of the Truman administration to drop the atom bombs in Hiroshima and Nagasaki was taken by less than 10 persons. The theory of democratic peace fails to take into account the fact that democratic powers do perpetuate authoritarian rulers either overtly or covertly. For instance the overthrow of a democratically elected government of Allende in Chile in 1973 endorses this contention. In the 1971 India-Pakistan War, the US supported an authoritarian Pakistan rather than a democratic India. The biggest let down was the overthrow of the democratic government of Mohammed Mussadeq in Iran in 1953 through a coup led by democratic

US and Britain. The irony of it is that had Mussadeq been allowed to continue it could have led to the institutionalization of a liberal democratic regime in Iran with a spill over effect on its neighbours, just as India exerts a moral pressure on all the non-democratic regimes of South Asia. But this, the West did not allow in the Middle East when it was busy erecting a liberal democratic regime in West Germany, which was ruled by the Nazi dictatorships in the decade to the Second World War. For the rise of religious fundamentalist forces in the region, which happened due to the void following the throttling of liberal democracy, it is the Western powers that are be squarely blamed. In another context, the support that one democracy (US) gives to another (Israel) to quell some other democratic aspirations (Palestine) raises questions about the theory of democratic peace. What comes out of this survey is that the doctrine of democratic peace is restricted within the walls of advanced capitalist democracies and its universal legitimacy and sanctity is yet to be established. Furthermore, the Iraq fiasco has led to serious impediment in the present movement of democratic consolidation, as it may take a much longer period than anticipated earlier.

Another interesting evolution has taken place with the advent of the nuclear age which questions the main assumption of the doctrine of democratic peace. As articulated by Bernard Brodie (1910-87), the military strategist in 1946, that "thus far the chief purpose of our military establishment has been to win wars. From now on its chief purpose must be to avert them".[16] This is vindicated by the fact that the Cold War never became hot and though this period saw a number of small and limited wars in the Third World, the traditional theatre of war, Europe, remained remarkably peaceful because of the fear of nuclear holocaust and total annihilation and not because of what the theorists of democratic peace have claimed.

The hopes of the Enlightenment were also ill founded in the latter part of the eighteenth century. The French Revolution and the aftermath of Napoleon sparked off liberal nationalist ideologies resulting in intensification of warfare. The latter part of the nineteenth century saw spread of universal conscription in Europe, the mass production of new automatic weapons, armaments races, the creation of alliances, intense rivalry for colonies and commercial superiority among Great Powers. The twentieth century saw two world wars, atomic and nuclear eras and the cold war. The end of communism brought in its footsteps ethnic and religious wars. The Cold War ended but there is now a new threat in the form of international terrorism.

The march towards a peaceful and conflict free world within a reasonable period of time is taking place haltingly. For this to be achieved there is a need to apply the universal parameters of the rule of law, human rights, equity, justice and principles of international law under the auspices of the United Nations. Sakharov[17] rightly reminds us of the need to "have a universal responsibility to use a single standard in judging human misfortune and injustice wherever they may occur". Once achieved, then many disjunctions that globalization has placed on the actual sovereignty of the state, and the distrust between the North and the South may be tackled better leading to a more peaceful world. Lord Keynes points out the power and pivotal ideas play in human history. Kant's "kingdom of ends" where morality shapes politics by forbidding war, by insisting on eternal peace and rights of individuals is one such idea that is not for any one particular nation or a set of people but for entire humankind to make it a workable idea.

Kant put forward a form of ethics that enables people to be self-government and to know which actions are moral and are not. It can be devided into three formulations: the universalisation of actions; the treatment of people as ends; and that one should act as if in a kingdom of ends. The first formulation of Kant says man should "act only according to that maxim whereby you can at the same time will that it should become a universal law". This in practice means that we should never engage in acts that cannot be repeated if they are performed over and over again. The second formulation says that we should always treat humans solely as an ends, and never as a means to an end. Kant argued we should "act in a way that treats humanity, whether in your own person or in that of any other, never solely as a means but always an end". This in practice, means that a person cannot morally be used as an object.

And the third formulation is the formula of 'Kingdom of Ends'. This Kant argued, is where we should live by rules in a community where we all respect each other. Kingdom means the "union of different rational beings in a system by common laws". Here, people can be completely autonomous, regarding themselves as sovereign while making laws.

NOTES

1. Hazard, Paul. (1963): *European Thought in the Eighteenth Century*, trans. J. Lewis May, New York, World Publishing Company.
2. Heater, Derek (1990): *Citizenship*, England, Orient Longman.
3. Montesquieu, Charles de Secondat, baron de, *The Spirit of Laws*, trans. by Thomas Nugent and J.V. Prichard.

4. Kant, Immanuel. (1790): *Political Writings*, ed. H. Reiss, trans. H.B. Nisbet, Cambridge: Cambridge University Press.
5. Reiss, H. (ed.), *Kant's Political Writings*, trans.) H.B. Nisbet, Cambridge: Cambridge University Press.
6. Kant, Immanuel. (1790): *Idea for a Universal History from a Cosmopolitan Point of View,* in Reiss, H.S. Kant, History of Political Thought (2nd ed.). Cambridge: Cambridge University Press.
7. _______ (1795), *Perpetual Peace: A Philiosophical Sketch.* The book provides an outline of a treaty which does not leave any scope for future wars.
8. Angell, Norman. (1910): *The Great Illusion: A Study of the Relation of Military Power to National Advantage*, New York, G.P. Putnam's Sons.
9. Streit, Clarence K. (1938), *Union Now. Advocated North Atlantic Treaty Organization (NATO) to be converted into a Political Entity.*
10. Ray, James L. (1998): "Does Democracy Cause Peace?" *Annual Review of Political Science*, 1, pp. 27-46.
11. Small, Melvin & David J. Singer (1976): "The War Proneness of Democratic Regimes, 1816-1965", *Jerusalem Journal of International.*
12. Doyle, Michael W. (1983): "Kant: Liberal Legacies and Foreign Affairs", Part I & II; 12 (3 & 4) (Summer & Autumn), pp. 205-35; 323-53 see also his, *War and Peace.* New York: W.W. Norton, 1997.
13. Russett, Bruce (1993): *Grasping the Democratic Peace*, Princeton, Princeton University Press. See also his, The Democratic Peace: And Yet it Moves", *International Security.*
14. Mansfield, Edward D. & Jack Snyder (2002): "Democratic Transitions, Institutional Strengths and War", *International Organization,* 56(2), pp. 297-337. See also, their *Electing to Fight: Why Emerging Democracies Go to War*, Massachusetts, MIT Press, 2005; and 'War Proneness of Democratic Regimes' 1816-1965, Jerusalem Journal of International Reglations, No. 1, April 1976, pp. 839-43.
15. Ray, James L., *op. cit.*
16. Brodie, B. (ed.) (1946): *The Absolute Weapon,* New York, Harcourt, Brace.
17. Andrei Sakharov was father of the Soviet Hydrogen Bomb. He was awarded the Peace Prize in 1975 for his opposition to abuse of power and his advocacy for human rights.

6

Gandhi's Insights into Environmental Conservation and Sustainable Development

Shri Krishan

Mahatma Gandhi could foresee what has now become a major problem of humanity. Seeing the misuse of natural resources in the name of progress and development, he became a conservationist. In this respect, two inputs of Gandhi have to be emphasized. The first provides a parameter on how development choices be made; he insisted that whenever one is in doubt, one should recall the face of the poorest and the weakest man and think about how the steps one contemplates is going to be of any use to him? Will it bring back to him to control over his own life and destiny? In other words, the needs of the poorest should receive the highest precedence in development planning. His second assertion he made was that while aiming at meeting the basic needs of all people especially the poor, it should not lead to over-consumption and thus overuse of natural resources. Although the pressures on nature had not become so acute in Gandhi's lifetime and there was no problem of global warming and climate change, he had the prescience to see that our planet's capability to support consumption was not limitless. The Mahatma said: "The earth has enough for every man's need, but not for every man's greed."[1] This chapter would try to investigate these and other related issues.

It is now generally recognized that Gandhi provides the contemporary environmental movements with a vocabulary of protest as well as action.[2] He was not an environmentalist *per se*, but being an ideological critique of industrial modernity, he provides symbolic resources to contemporary activists in this field. Generally 'green-reading' of Gandhi is based on his mocking condemnation of Western civilization in *Hind Swaraj* (1909). Gandhi wrote there: "This land of ours was once, we are told, the abode of gods. It is not possible to conceive of gods inhabiting a land which is made hideous by the smoke and the din of mill-machinery and factories, and whose roadways are traversed by rushing engines, dragging numerous cars crowded by men who know not for the most part what they are after, who are often absent-minded, and whose tempers do not improve by being uncomfortably packed like sardines in boxes..."[3] This image of Gandhi remains stuck in popular mind as well as in scholarly discourses. It was this that moved Gandhi to his somewhat hyperbolic claim: "Machinery is the chief symbol of modern civilization; it represents a great sin".

However, by 1919 his views on machinery do begin to change right up to 1947 as he gradually comes to concede some of its positive contributions like time and labour saving, even as he warns against the negative ones of concentrating wealth and displacing workers. He was acutely sensitive to how machinery can dehumanize and technology alienate, and he extends his critique to the professions of medicine and law[4] (*HS*, Chapters 11, 12). The poor hardly benefit from these professional services, though they are often their victims. He backs up his criticism of these professions in *Hind Swaraj* with a later suggestion for their nationalisation.[5]

Gandhi envisioned the villages of India providing the ideal setting for maintaining traditional values and practices as well as defusing power. It was his local site for a just, equitable, stable community based on full employment and contentment, if not affluence of the scale which industrialism could furnish. Such an ideal economically insular village perhaps never existed in history; it existed in Gandhi's imagination only However, Gandhi's analysis and evaluation of the rural Indian society was far more complex than the agrarianism of Russian Narodniks.[6] Gandhi realized that absolute self-sufficiency was not possible to achieve in the modern world. He remarked that the humble cultivator had to depend for certain necessaries of life on middleman. In his own world, "Interdependence is and ought to be as much the ideal of man as self-sufficiency. Man is a social being. Without inter-relation with society he cannot realize his oneness with the universe or suppress his egotism."[7]

Speaking about the boycott of foreign goods, Gandhi once again emphasized interdependence in an article in *Navjivan*, "What Comprises Foreign Goods" in 1929. Gandhi wrote: "Boycott of all foreign goods is neither possible nor proper. The difference between *swadeshi* and foreign cannot be held for all times, cannot hold even now in regard to all things. Even the *swadeshi* character of *khadi* is due to circumstances...Today many things which we need for our sustenance and which are not imposed on us come from abroad. As for example, some of the foreign medicines, pens, needles, useful tools, etc. etc."[8] Ramchandra Guha, like many others, ascribes the Gandhi's village-centric notion of development and his decentralization zeal to the extent that villages assume the control of their own economic and political powers to his diagnosis of the ills of industrialism.[9] This is a simplistic reading of Gandhi because he addresses several strands of parasitism that need to be investigated in order to feel his "deep ecology". His metaphor of rural India as an ideal society is not meant to provide a determinant solution to the challenges of capitalistic or even socialistic modernization. The following words of Gandhi point to his broader concerns which can be guiding principles of a sustainable world culture:

> "Man is made to obey the machine. The wealthy and middle classes become helpless and parasitic upon the working classes. And the latter become so specialized that they too become helpless. The ordinary city-dweller cannot make his own clothing or produce and prepare his own food. The cities become parasitic upon the country and industrial nations upon the agricultural nations. Those who live in temperate climates are increasingly parasitic upon tropical peoples. Governments are increasingly parasitic upon the people they govern as armies are upon civilians. People even become parasitic and passive in regard to their recreation and amusements."[10]

Gandhi found modern technology applied to railways and hospitals as "necessary evil". He complains that modern transportation has turned pilgrimage sites into places of entertainment rather than places of devotion that they used to be once. To quote him:

> "What a contrast between Amarnath and lorries! There was a time when pilgrims travelled on foot from Kanyakumari to Kashmir and then, after suffering many hardships, ascended Amarnath.... Today, motor-lorries unload pilgrims at the foothills of Amarnath, just as they would unload goods and the pilgrims on their part regard it as a meritorious deed to travel in such comfort. The remaining distance has to be covered by foot or on horseback and this; the pilgrims somehow manage to do. They would readily accept if anyone was prepared to carry them right up to their destination or go in an aeroplane if it would take them straight to the top of Amarnath."[11] It is well known that

> Gandhi preferred walking to riding motorized vehicles. When his car accidentally crushed a man (named Padam Singh) to death in Almora in 1929, he felt deep anguish and remarked—"I have already felt the fact riding in cars makes men proud. The chauffeurs who drive them are vain and hot-tempered. But under the illusion that I will be able to serve better, I continue to use cars. I have reaped the fruit today. And yet I cannot promise to give up the use of cars, as I cannot give up the fond desire to serve the country."[12]

Gandhi knew, even if instinctively that the modern world had changed and the wheel of time could not be turned back. In a letter to Nehru, Gandhi agrees with him that simplicity he desired would not be possible and that "a number of things …will have to be organized on a large scale." He recognized that the elimination of "all machinery….requires a higher simplicity and renunciation than the people are today prepared for."[13] Gandhi noted, even much earlier than this, that he would "favour the use of the most elaborate machinery if thereby India's pauperism and resulting idleness be avoided".[14] Gandhi said that he was not opposed to industrialization as such but the manner in which it took place. In another context, Gandhi remarked: "I do visualize electricity, ship-building, ironworks, machine-making and the like existing side by side with village handicrafts. But the order of dependence would be reserved. Hitherto the industrialization has been so planned as to destroy the villages and village crafts. In the state of the future, it will subserve the villages and their crafts. I do not share the socialist belief that the centralization of necessities of life will be conducive to the common welfare when the centralized industries are planned and owned by the state".[15] Gandhi remarked that the physical geography of a country had a predominant role to play in determining its culture and form of economy. He believed that Europe could afford to urbanize as it had small countries and USA had no other options with its vastness and sparse population but a big country like India with teeming population could hardly imitate this model of development. How could India afford to replace human labour or "the solar power stored in 300 million Indians" with steam or such other power.[16]

Tracing the heritage of Gandhi, Guha (1997) emphasizes his lack of attraction for wilderness and turning his back on the city. As he puts it: "Nature lovers and those with a focus on the urban environment would, therefore, find little direct help from Mahatma Gandhi."[17] Here it has to be kept in mind that one of the major agitations organized by Gandhi was among the Ahmedabad urban industrial labour. Gandhi was just not only concerned with capital-labour relation in that city; he even bothered about its civic-planning and sanitation as can be seen from the following rather long passage:

> "If the wealthy and the educated wish, they can change the face of Ahmedabad. The biggest Jain firm is in Ahmedabad. It is said that the firm of Anandji Kalyanji is wealthier than any other firm in the world which can be described as a religious body. Ahmedabad is the capital of Gujarat and it is also the headquarters of the Jains. It claims a monopoly of compassion for all living beings. However, it has still to learn real compassion. Looking after cattle in some manner in crowded localities is a narrow form of such compassion and its least expression. The latter should be as wide as the ocean and, as the life-sustaining oxygen spreads its fragrance from the ocean all the hours of the day, so should the oxygen of compassion do and give happiness, peace and good health to human beings and all other living creatures….Nature has gifted Ahmedabad with such air and water that it could become a health resort. Its residents, however, pollute both these. The hospitals, temples, schools and orphanages of Ahmedabad should be removed to places outside the city. Its narrow lanes should be relieved of the congestion in them. There should be small open spaces in the city. We ought to have fragrance spreading all around instead of the stink that now pervades the city. This task is not beyond the capacity of Ahmedabad's citizens. It does not require crores of rupees to be spent. Moreover, it has been the experience of all cities in the world which have become prosperous that the amount spent is recovered twice over."[18]

Now let's turn our attention to 'Nature' and 'Nature Lovers'. William Cronon (1995) depicts natural world as changeable and entangled with human history, its meaning changing with the cultural context. The nature is not a stable, holistic, homeostatic community capable of preserving its natural balance more or less infinitely if only humans can avoid 'disturbing' it. 'Nature', in his words, is a human construction and the notion of the natural world as well as the human nature encompasses diverse and complex phenomenon. According to him, the metaphor of nature can be used as a moral imperative, as a moral vision of external reality, as a pristine beauty as for some modern Americans who worshipped 'wilderness', as the notion of Eden, the perfect, the benign and beautiful land of abundance or even as the demonic other, as the avenging angel or as the return of the repressed.[19] In another article in the same work, Cronon, further demonstrates that the 'wilderness' had negative meanings in the eighteenth century and the meanings associated with it were 'deserted', a place of 'savage', 'barren lands', etc. The imagery changed only in the nineteenth century when the ideology of 'the sublime' and 'the frontier' converged to remake wilderness in their own image, freighting it with moral values and cultural symbols that it carries even to this day. In this cultural context, wilderness became desirable and something to be preserved.[20] Gandhi's conception of the human nature and his social praxis based on this idea is the key to understanding his environmental ethic. Gandhi emphasized altruistic human motives as the supreme spiritual goal as they are essential to human survival. He wrote in 1907: "If we examine our desires, we shall see that we do not wish for what we have already. We always value more that which we do not have. But desires are of two kinds: one is the pursuit of mere self-interest. To attempt to fulfil this kind of desire is immoral. The other impels us constantly to improve ourselves and to do good to others."[21] Gandhi was as much opposed to the Fordist mass consumption as he was to Rockefellerian morality. He writes: "It is known the world over how Mr. Rockefeller, said to be the richest man in the world, violated many rules of morality in amassing his fortune. It is because such conditions prevail around them that many people in Europe and America have turned against religion."[22] He further felt that "there is no morality in my living a simple and unpretentious life if I have not the means to live otherwise. But plain, simple living would be moral if, though wealthy, I think of all the want and misery in the world about me—and feel that I ought to live a plain, simple life and not one of ease and luxury."[23] Gandhi was even keen to harness the scientific creed of Darwin for his altruistic conception of human naturc as evident from the following long account.

"Darwin was a great Englishman of the last century who made great scientific discoveries. His memory and his power of observation were amazing. He has written some books which deserve to be read and pondered. With a mass of evidence and arguments, he has shown how man came into being; how he has evolved from a particular kind of monkey. After a large number of experiments and much sifting of evidence, he realized that there was not much difference between the anatomy of man and that of the ape. Whether this conclusion is correct or not has not much to do with ethics.

Though Darwin did not write as a moral philosopher, he has shown how close the connection is between morality and environment. Those who think that morality is unimportant and that physical strength and mental capacity are the only things that matter should read Darwin. According to him, there is an instinct of self-preservation in men as in other creatures. He also says that those who survive the struggle for existence may be regarded as successful, that is, those who are unfit tend to extinction, but that the issue of the struggle does not depend on mere physical force. Comparing man with the bear or the buffalo, we find that, in physical strength, the bear and the buffalo are superior to him; in a tussle he will surely be worsted. Nonetheless he is their superior by virtue of his intelligence. .... The main distinction between man and other animals is that man is more selfless than the animals. He has sacrificed his life for others in proportion to his strength, that is, for his offspring, for his family, his community and his country. Darwin clearly shows that moral strength is supreme.[24]

Gandhi was obsessed with what Lorenz (1989) calls "the irreversible vicious-circularity of some aspects of technical and economic development".[25] Gandhi opposed the thought habits engendered by technology and the altruistic motives gave him a means by which he could challenge this "adversary of the soul." The technocratic religion that believed in technical viability of achieving anything that was technologically possible was a product of "the Great Promise of Unlimited progress, the promise of domination of nature, of material abundance, the Utilitarian greatest happiness of the greatest number, and of unlimited personal freedom had sustained the hopes and faith of generations".[26] Gandhi constructed the theory of '*Sarvodaya*' to counter this predominant mode of thinking of his times. Western capitalism breeds consumerism and accumulation of private capital. On the level of political thought, individual remains as the centre of political constructs. Gandhi turns into a worst critic of capitalism. He propounded a theory of social capital. He accepted the basic underlying principle of capitalism in the questions of human labour. Moreover, individual labour creates capital. But capital has a social utility. Society has a right over the individual capital. On the level of distribution, market should have a restricted role. Human consciousness has a role to play. Individual because of a higher level of consciousness allows the community to use one's own property. Human initiative should not be lost at any point. Gandhi reconstructed the concept of private property. One can have private property but not for one's own use. It should be utilized for societal needs. That is why individual needs need to be restricted to the minimum. This proposed restriction on human wants and needs makes Gandhi different from present day bio-economics dominated by a managerial ethos and notions of resource-engineering. This all was based on Gandhi's reading of John Ruskin. This is how Gandhi internalized and redefined Ruskin:

> "People some times believe, mistakenly, that by following certain precepts it is possible for everybody to become rich. But the true position can be compared to a water-wheel where one (bucket) empties out as another fills. The power of the rupee you possess depends on another going without it. If no one wants it, it will be useless to you. The power it possesses depends on your neighbour's lack of it. There can be wealth only where there is scarcity. This means that, in order to be rich, one must keep another poor. Political economy consists in the production, preservation and distribution, at the fittest time and place, of useful and pleasurable things....Careful reflection will show that what we really desire through acquisition of wealth is power over other men—[power] to acquire for our advantage the labour of a servant, a tradesman or an artisan. And the power we can thus acquire will be in direct proportion to the poverty of others.... So, that growing rich means contriving that as large a number of men as possible shall have less than we have. Economists generally assume that it is of advantage to the nation as a whole if the mass of people are thus kept in want. Equality among men is certainly not possible. But conditions of scarcity, unjustly created, injure the nation."[27]

The modern western industrial society which rested on private property, profit and a Machiavellian notion of power, did not appeal to Gandhi. To acquire, to have and to multiply wealth were considered sacred and unalienable right in the capitalist acquisitive society.[28] To oppose this Gandhi made use of the ancient Indian notion of '*Aparigraha*' or non-possession of unnecessary material goods.[29] Gandhi went to the extent of equating unlimited consumption and acquisition of wealth a kind to stealing. To again quote him:

> "If I take anything that I do not need for my immediate use, and

> keep it, I thieve it from somebody else. I venture to suggest that it is the fundamental law of nature, without exception, that Nature produces enough for our wants from day to day, an if only everybody took enough for himself and nothing more, there would be no pauperism in the world, there would be no starvation in the world. But so long as we have got this inequality, so long we are thieving…"[30]

Gandhi further contends that economic and natural resources ought to be better managed in the service of common good. The equity in the distribution of resources is central in his thinking. In his own words:

> "Wealth is like a river. A river always flows towards the sea, that is, down an incline. So, as a general rule must wealth go where it is needed. But the flow of wealth, like the course of a river, can be regulated. Most of the rivers run out their courses unregulated, their marshy banks poisoning the wind. If dams are built across these rivers to direct the water flow as required, they will irrigate the soil and keep the atmosphere pure. Similarly the uncontrolled use of wealth will multiply vices among men and cause starvation; in brief, such wealth will act like a poison. But the selfsame wealth, if its circulation is regulated and its use controlled, can, like a river whose stream has been properly harnessed, promote prosperity. The principle of regulating the circulation of wealth is ignored altogether by economists. Theirs is merely the science of getting rich. But there are many different ways of getting rich. There was a time in Europe when people sought to acquire wealth by poisoning owners of large estates and appropriating their possessions. Nowadays, merchants adulterate the food sold to the poor, for example, milk with borax, (wheat) flour with potato flour, coffee with chicory, butter with fat and so on. This is on the same level as getting rich by poisoning others. Can we call this either an art or a science of getting rich?"[31]

Gandhi discovered the profound and inherent connection between capitalism, colonialism, militarism and racialism and how they are about the exploitation of natural and human resources of the earth and advised like a first-rate teacher to develop an alternative value system. Let me quote the master again:

> "Economists do not take men's conduct into account but estimate prosperity from the amount of wealth accumulated and so, conclude that the happiness of nations depends upon their wealth alone. Hence, they advocate greater accumulation of wealth through more and more work in factories. In England and elsewhere factories have multiplied because of the spread of these ideas. Large numbers of men leave their farms and concentrate in cities. They give up the pure and fresh air of the countryside and feel happy breathing the foul air of factories...... Labour, in the real sense of the term, is that which produces useful articles. Useful articles are those which support human life. Supporting human life means provision of food, clothing, etc., so as to enable men to live a moral life and to do good while they live. For this purpose, large-scale industrial undertakings would appear to be useless. To seek to acquire wealth by establishing big factories is likely to lead to sin. Many people amass wealth but few make good use of it. If the making of money is likely to lead a nation to its destruction, that money is useless. On the contrary, present-day capitalists are responsible for widespread and unjust wars. Most of the wars of our times spring from greed for money......... Cultivators will find contentment in innocent labour and the nation will be happy. In the hands of bad men, it is used for the production, say, of gun-powder and bringing utter ruin on the people. Both those who manufacture gunpowder and those who fall victims to it suffer in consequence. We thus see that there is no wealth besides life. That nation is wealthy which is moral. This is not the time for self-indulgence. The western nations are impatient to fall upon one another, and are restrained only by the accumulation of armaments all round. When [the situation] flares up, we will witness a veritable hell let loose in Europe. All [white] nations look upon the black races as their legitimate prey. This is inevitable when money is the only thing that matters. Wherever, they find any territory, they swoop down on it like crows upon carrion. There are reasons to suggest that this is the outcome of their large industrial undertakings."[32]

Gandhi, it appears to me is not relying simply on the religious-ethical viewpoint in rejecting "modern way of life" or exemplifying the traditional reverence for nature and life-forms. He is not wedded to a romantic notion of nature and environment. There has been, of course, a great deal of stress lately on a kind of "eco-golden age", where preservation of sacred groves and other folk practices are viewed as "ecological practices".[33] This clearly is a case of "anachronistic projection of modern phenomenon onto the screen of tradition". Seen from such a perspective, all pre-industrial societies would exhibit a kind of harmony with nature. It has to be kept in mind that most of the times these societies and cultures were less harmful to the environment just due to demographic and technological factors, not because they wished to protect the whole canopy of the nature. Gandhi synthesized reinvented Indian traditions and the utopian and anarchist ideas drawn from Henry David Thoreau, John Ruskin, Morris, Tolstoy and Kropotkin to question the prevailing developmentalism which sought to maximize GNP at all costs, human and ecological. Thoreau romanticized nature and other living beings equally, believed in the extravagance and prodigality of nature in the midst of her simplicity of procedures, made contributions to the early ideas of forest conservation and warned against the "egotism of the race of humans"[34], Gandhi while having similar views on self-imposed limitations of wants in a simple rural life, free from corrupting influences of material luxuries, was more influenced by the humanistic traditions and privileged superiority of human reason. Some of the anarchist ideas of Prince Kropotkin[35] expressed in his *Fields, Factories and Workshops Tomorrow* (1899), especially peasant ownership, small business, a model of decentralized economy, and a critique of bureaucracies as wasteful and slothful, also resemble Gandhi's notions. "The civilization of the Megapolis and the Civilization of Latitudinal" both are equally resented by them. Gandhi himself candidly acknowledged the influence of Tolstoy's ideas on his thinking and behaviour. Foremost of these was the idea of "bread-labour". This was a mean to conquer the false distinction between manual and mental labour. Gandhi evaluated this concept in these words:

> "The cause of the inequalities we see in the world, of the contrasts of wealth and poverty, lies in the fact that we have forgotten the law of life. That law is the law of "bread labour". On the authority of Chapter III of the Gait, I call it yawn. The Gait says that he who eats without performing yawn is a thief and sinner. Tolstoy has said the same thing. We should not distort the meaning of "bread labour" and forget the real idea. Its simple meaning is that he has no right to eat who does not bend his body and work. If everyone of us did bodily labour to earn his food, we would

> not see the poverty which we find in the world. One idler is the cause of two persons starving, for his work has to be done by someone else."[36]

However, without romanticizing Gandhi, I would like to point out a few constraints of Gandhian ideas. First is his strong belief in individualism and second his equally fundamental faith in the sanctity of private property even to the extent of making the ruling people and the dominant social classes the guardians of public weal stemming from this private property. Two questions arise in my mind. One, will not the powerful and wealthy redistribute resources in their own favour, and two, has not the working of the harmonious, orderly nature, disrupted beyond individuals capacity to repair. The onus of saving the mother earth has to be collective.

REFERENCES

1. Quoted in Pyarelal, *Mahatma Gandhi: The Last Phase*, Vol. X, Part II, Navjivan Publishing House, Ahmedabad, 1958, p. 552.
2. It may be mistaken to speak of the Chipko Movement and the Narmada Bachao Andolan (Save the Narmada Movement) as 'Gandhian', since any such reading perforce ignores the traditions of peasant resistance, the force of customary practices, and the appeal of localized systems of knowledge, but the spirit of Gandhi has undoubtedly moved Indian environmentalists, contends Vinay Lal, see his writings "Too Deep for Deep Ecology: Gandhi and the Ecological Vision of Life", in *Hinduism and Ecology: The Intersection of Earth, Sky, and Water*, (eds.) Christopher Key Chapple and Mary Evelyn Tucker (Cambridge, Mass.: Harvard UP for Centre for the Study of World Religions, Harvard University, 2000), pp. 183-212; another version was published as "Gandhi and the Ecological Vision of Life: Thinking beyond Deep Ecology", *Environmental Ethics* 22, No. 2 (Summer 2000), pp. 149-68.
3. Quoted in Diane M. Jones, "The Greening of Gandhi: Gandhian Thought and the Environmental Movement in India" in Johnson Donald Hughes, ed., *The Face of Earth: Environment and World History*, M.E. Sharpe, New York, 2000, p. 171.
4. Parel, Anthony J. (ed.) (1997): *Gandhi: Hind Swaraj and Other Writings,* New Delhi: Foundation Books, pp.164-170.
5. Gandhi, Mahatma, *Collected Works*, Vol. 68, p. 97.
6. Once the serfs of Russia got emancipated in 1861, the Narodniks arose under Tsar Alexander II), and argued that the change was not deep enough. Bourgeoisie had replaced landowners freed and the former serfs were being used as labourers. Narodniks did not like the uprooting of peasants

from the traditional communes (obshchina). Narodniks used the growing conflict between the peasantry and more prosperous farmers (*kulaks*) to organize the peasants to usher in socialism.

In the spring of 1874 the Narodnik intelligentsia left the cities and went to the villages where peasants lived and taught the people there their moral imperative to revolt. They could not impress the peasants as they came from the middle and upper middle classes. On arriving into some villages Narodniks were viewed with suspicion by Russian peasants who were completely removed from the urban culture. They decided to learn peasant customs.

7. "Our Helplessness", *Navjivan,* February 24, 1929, Gandhi, *Collected Works*, Publications Division, p. 23.
8. "What Comprises Foreign Goods", *Navjivan,* May 12, 1929, in *Collected Works*, Publications Division, Vol. 41, p. 374.
9. Ramchandra Guha, "Mahatma Gandhi and the Environmental Movement" in Ramchandra Guha and J. Martinez-Alier, (ed.) *Varieties of Environmentalism: Essays North and South*, Earthscan Publications Ltd., London, 1997, pp. 156-57.
10. 'Notes', *Young India*, April 15, 1926.
11. "Blind Faith" *Navjivan,* 16-9-1928 in Gandhi, *Collected Works*, Vol. 43, pp. 26-27.
12. "Speech at Almora", *Aaj,* 4-07-1929, Mahatma Gandhi, *Collected Works*, Vol. 41, The Publications Division, Government of India, p. 70.
13. Letter to Jawaharlal Nehru, October 5, 1945, in *Collected Works*, Vol.81, Publications Division, pp. 319-20, quoted in Ronald Terchek, *Gandhi: Struggling for Autonomy*, Rowman and Littlefield, 1998, p. 124.
14. *Young India*, November 3, 1921.
15. *Harijan*, January 27, 1939.
16. 'Urban *vs* Rural', *Young India*, July 25, 1929, Gandhi, *Collected Works*, Vol. 41, pp. 220-21.
17. Guha (1997), "*Mahatma Gandhi and the Environmental Movement*", pp. 167-68.
18. "Ahmedabad and its Deaf and Dumb", (From Gujarati), *Navjivan,* 16-9-1928, Mahatma Gandhi, *Collected Works*, Vol. 43, pp. 22-23.
19. See William Cronon's Introduction to his edited work, *Uncommon Ground: Rethinking the Human Place in Nature*, W.W. Norton & Company, London, 1995, pp. 24-51.
20. William Cronon, "The Trouble with Wilderness, or, Getting Back to Wrong Nature" in his work *Uncommon Ground: Rethinking the Human Place in Nature*, pp. 69-90.
21. Gandhi summarized, into Gujarati, *Ethical Religion* by William MacIntyre Salter, the founder of the Society for Ethical Culture, Chicago.
22. The book, one of a series issued by the Rationalist Press Association, was published in America in March, 1889 and later in England in 1905 and

above lines are from Gandhi's paraphrase. See Gandhi, *Collected Works*, Vol. VI, p. 222.

23. Gandhi, *Collected Works*, Vol. VI, p. 212.
24. *Ibid.*, p. 247.
25. *Indian Opinion*, 19/2/1907, Gandhi, *Collected Works*, Vol. VI, pp. 267-269.
26. Konrad Lorenz, *The Waning of the Humaneness*, Unwin Paperbacks, London and Sydney, 1989, p. 6.
27. See the Introduction of Eric Fromm to his celebrated work *To Have or To Be*, Bantam Books, Toronto, New York, 1981, p. xxiii.
28. Indian Opinion, 13/06/1908, Gandhi, *Collected Works*, Vol. VIII, pp. 368-69.
29. R.H. Tawney, *The Acquisitive Society*, Harcourt Brace, New York, 1920: The term *aparigraha* is just the opposite of *parigraha* which means 'to amass', 'to accumulate', 'to compile', 'to seize', 'to hold', and 'to receive or accept gifts'. It is defined as that which entangles one from all sides. (*Parigahanam Parigraha*) *Parigraha* has two implications according to Jainas (i) *Bahya* (outer) meaning worldly possessions, (ii) *Abhyantara* (inner) meaning attachment. Both these implications together refer to an attitude of mind towards material objects. These are not two kinds of *parigraha* but are actually two components of *parigraha*. *Parigraha* thus means not only possessions but also possessiveness.
30. Speech on 'Ashram Vows' at YMCA, Madras, *The Indian Review*, February, 1916. Quoted in Thomas Weber, *Gandhi as Disciple and Mentor*, Cambridge University Press, Cambridge and New York, 2004, p. 210.
31. *Sarvodaya*, VIII, *Indian Opinion*, 4/7/1908, Gandhi, *Collected Works*, Vol. VIII, pp. 419-21.
32. *Sarvodaya*, IX, *Indian Opinion*, 18/7/1908, Gandhi, *Collected Works*, Vol. VIII, pp. 455-459
33. Emma Tomalin, *Bio-Divinity and Bio-Diversity: The Limits to Religious Environmentalism*, Ashgate Publishing Ltd., 2009, p. 87.
34. For a description of Thoreau's ideas and contribution to ecological ideas see Donald Worster's work, *Nature's Economy: A History of Ecological Ideas*, Cambridge University Press, Cambridge, 1985, pp. 60-110.
35. See Anna Bramwell, *Ecology in the 20th Century: A History*, Yale University Press, New Haven and London, 1989, pp. 6, 70.
36. Speech on Birth Centenary of Tolstoy, September 10, 1928, in Gandhi, *Collected Works*, Vol. 43, pp. 8-9.

7

Water as a Security Concern: Conflict or Cooperation in South Asia

Yogesh Nair

In the modern security discourse, the definition of security is being expanded to include a host of non-traditional issues such as environmental degradation, resource depletion and number of new tenets previously considered beyond the realms of traditional security paradigm.[1] With burgeoning populations, growing poverty, and little hope of commensurating expansion in agricultural sector, the sustainability of food supplies is acknowledged as a serious security concern in many Asian nations. Similarly, in some quarters lack of adequate quantity and quality of potable water is increasingly being characterized as a security issue.

One could argue that perhaps water security really is not a security concern in itself, or that it should fall under the larger rubric of "environmental security" or "resource depletion".[2] Nevertheless, regardless of how it is defined, it is well established that freshwater scarcity poses a very serious, complex and potentially wide-ranging threat to regional stability. This threat could manifest itself in a number of different ways, such as directly in the form of violent conflicts over freshwater resources, or indirectly, by causing large-scale migration and food shortages. Further, water scarcity, accelerated by climate change, affects water availability which in turn may threaten peace and security of the region. In fact, the challenges associated with water scarcity and management has pushed "environmental security" into the broader security lexicon and established the notion that environmental scarcity and competition may induce migration and conflict.[3] Thus, water security is gradually becoming an epicentre of interstate relations and water scarcity is rapidly becoming the miseries of the people.[4] This chapter attempts to explore the dynamics of water security with regard to conflict and co-operation scenarios in South Asia in general, and India and its neighbours, in particular.

WATER SCARCITY AND ITS IMPLICATIONS FOR SECURITY

The world's freshwater supply is finite. Most of the world's water, about 97.5 per cent exists as salt water in the Oceans and Seas. Of the world's 2.5 per cent of freshwater, roughly 99 per cent is either trapped in glaciers and ice caps, held as soil moisture or located in watertables too deep to access. Thus, only about one per cent of the world's total freshwater supply is readily available for consumption by humans, animals and for irrigation.[5] Moreover, the world's population is growing by about 80 million people a year, implying increased freshwater demand of about 64 billion cubic metres a year.[6] Water stress occurs when a country's annual water supplies drop below 1,700 cubic metres per person. When these levels reach between 1,700 and 1,000 cubic metres per person, occasional water shortages are likely to occur.[7] Today, many South Asian countries are beginning to experience moderate to severe water shortages, brought on by the simultaneous effects of agricultural growth, industrialization, and urbanization. As the region's population growth continues to surge, the demand for water is increasing substantially, without a concomitant increase in water resources,[8] is causing the water scarcity.

In order to understand the contours of relationship between water and security dynamics it is essential to analyze varied facet associated with water security that can impact socio-political, economic and ecological development of a region. To fully appreciate the complexity of the water security issues, it is analyzed into various dimensions as under:

Human Security

Freshwater can become a security issue when it is linked to "human security," encompassing variety of issues that have an impact on human health and well-being. From this perspective, water is a clear security problem if one considers the large number of human deaths that occur as a result of unsafe or inadequate water. Approximately 25,000 people die every day from water related diseases. In Bangladesh, it is estimated that three-quarters of all diseases are linked to unsafe water and inadequate sanitation facilities. Experts estimate that about 60 per cent of all infant mortality throughout the world is tied to infectious and parasitic diseases, most of them related to water.[9] Diarrhoeal diseases are more prevalent in many South Asian countries with inadequate sewage treatment. An estimated 4 billion people per year contract diarrhoeal disease and among that number approximately 3-4 million die annually. Unsanitary water is clearly a major health threat for millions in the developing world.

Internal Security

The specific impact of freshwater on intra-State security is far more complex and difficult to ascertain. Water insecurity constrains economic development and contributes to a host of corrosive social behaviours that can, in turn, produce violence within societies.[10] Freshwater scarcity, often causally related with other factors, such as poverty, population growth, infrastructure problems, environmental degradation, can escalate the "human security" problem into a national security issue. Water security can be catalyst for large-scale migration and ethnic conflicts, which ultimately, in more dire situations, can result governance menace, potentially leading to a "failed state".[11]

International Security

Water security issues can have a destabilizing effect on regional and international security. Consequently, when one or more countries share water resources, the potential for disputes and conflicts is always present. Spawned by globalization, the increasing economic and political interdependence of nations ultimately means greater potential for spillover of problems. Ethnic unrest, mass migration, and declining economic conditions, fanned by freshwater scarcity, are not likely to be confined within a country's borders. This can have an adverse affect on country's relationship; inter-State business avenues, international agreements; having wider security, economic and environmental ramification, which may in turn erode country's ability to interact at international level. Consequently, when one or more countries share water resources, the potential for disputes/conflicts is always present. Although no nation has yet gone to war over water, this potential scenario could unfold given the right conditions. According to one study, factors such as demographic change, rising water demands due to improved living standards and predominance of upstream over downstream by way of control of flow of rivers are likely to stoke smouldering conflicts.[12]

WATER AS A CAUSE OF CONFLICT

Fierce competition for fresh water may well become a source of conflict and wars in the future.[13] Poor quality and mismanagement has further aggravated the problem. Increasing scarcity of clean fresh water impedes development, undercuts human health, and plays a crucial role in the conflict continuum between and within states.[14] Today, population growth, surging demands for food and biofuels, global rise in living standards, and changing weather patterns are some of the factor contributing to water scarcity. These, along with inadequate regional and global management issues have fuelled tensions both within and between nations. United Nations carried out study of 300 potential conflicts over water that exists around the world.[15] It highlighted that water-related violence often occurs at local level rather than international extent, and the intensity of conflict is generally inversely related to geographic scale.[16] However, while conflicts often remain local, they can also impact stability at the national and regional levels. Even if international disputes over water-related issues do not typically cause violent conflict, they have led to inter-State tensions and significantly hampered development[17], such as Mekong, Indus, and Ganges rivers. The likelihood of conflict rises as the rate of change within the basin exceeds the institutional capacity to absorb that change. Water security and conflict dynamics at different level are analyzed in the succeeding paragraph.

Intra-State Conflicts

Within States, water scarcity can assume an increasingly contentious and violent character when water-dependent sectors such as agriculture can no longer sustain farming livelihoods, leading to destabilizing migration flows.[18] At the local level, competition over water use, its availability and allocation can lead to low-scale violence, which can escalate into instability within States and across sub-regions. Tensions between citizens and authorities over water issues may initially manifest themselves in the form of civil disobedience. They may, however, also escalate into acts of sabotage and violent protest if adequate political initiatives are not taken.[19] As pressure on fresh water supplies rises due to population growth, economic development and pollution, access to water, and its allocation and use, are becoming increasingly critical concerns that may have profound consequences on societal stability. Intra-State conflicts may be of the following kinds:

1. Conflict over access to adequate water supplies;
2. Water, livelihood loss, and civil conflict; and
3. Water management and conflict.

Conflict is most likely to occur over water when disputes involve access to water of adequate quantity and quality. Even when water supplies are not severely limited, allocation of water among different users and uses, viz., agriculture and urban residents can be highly contested.[20] Degraded water quality, which can pose serious threats to health, is also a source of potentially violent disputes. Finally, when water supplies for broadly irrigated regions decline either in terms of quantity or quality, those declines can spur migrations that could politically destabilize the receiving cities and/or neighbouring countries.[21]

Water's importance in sustaining human livelihoods can indirectly link it to conflict. Water is a basic resource for agriculture, which is traditionally the largest source of livelihoods. If this livelihood is no longer available, people are often forced to search for job opportunities in the cities or turn to other, often illicit, ways to make a living. Migration, induced by lack of water, sudden droughts and floods, infrastructure construction, pollution disasters, or livelihood loss can produce tensions between local and incoming communities, especially when it increases pressure on already scarce resources.[22] And poverty due to livelihood loss has been identified as a common denominator of the causes of conflict in most of the violent conflict that emerged in South Asia region during the last decade.[23]

Another reason of water related conflicts are due to the inadequate ways the resource is governed and managed. There are many reasons why water management fails, including lack of adequate water institutions, inadequate administrative capacity, lack of transparency, ambiguous jurisdictions, overlapping functions, fragmented institutional structures, and lack of necessary infrastructure. Disaggregated decision-making often produces divergent management approaches that serve contradictory objectives and lead to competing claims from different sectors. And such claims are even more likely to contribute to disputes in countries where there is no formal system of water-use permits, or where enforcement and monitoring are inadequate. Controversy also often arises when management decisions are formulated without sufficient participation by local communities and water users, thus failing to take into account local rights and practices.[24] Direct violent conflicts over water are most likely on a local level, for example, over privatisation of drinking water or access to a water point.

Inter-State Conflicts

The world is rife with conflicts over waters, especially over use and management of trans-boundary waters. Rivers with trans-boundary nature, Brahmaputra, Mekong, Barak, etc., are becoming subjects of controversy over the right to manage the waters. Given that water flow ignores political and community boundaries, decisions in one place affect water use elsewhere. In the case of shared river basins, water use upstream can affect downstream quality and quantity, thus creating the potential for conflicts of interest. Stronger countries use both, technical capacity and infrastructure to exploit water resources. Complex physical, political, and human interactions can make the management of shared water systems especially difficult.[25] The UN's "World Water Development Report", presented ahead of the fifth "World Water Forum" warns of increased regional rivalry over water-related issues which will threaten fragile states by mounting security challenges.

Climate Change and Water Security in South Asia

Climate Change is one issue which is likely to affect the entire world. Global temperatures are anticipated to rise by 2 to 5 degrees Celsius over the next half century. This will result in melting of glaciers. As these glaciers melt, the rivers they source will experience massive flooding in the short-term and recede in the longer-term. As regards South Asia, the impacts of climate change in the form of higher temperatures, more variable precipitation, and extreme weather events is likely to threaten the water supply to millions of people living near numerous river basins. The Ganges river basin alone is home to some 500 million people. The massive concentration of people around river basins, compounded by high and persistent poverty rates illustrates the vulnerability of the region to current hydrological shocks and longer-term climate change. The region remains highly vulnerable to droughts and floods that not only devastate lives and livelihoods, but also undermine progress on economic growth and poverty alleviation. Every year, some part of the region is usually in the grip of a devastating drought or in the fury of a flood. Climate change might exacerbate the damage caused by such events. With its heavy reliance on the monsoons and snow-fed rivers, water availability in the region is highly sensitive to climate change. If this continues unabated, rivers like the Brahmaputra could become seasonal rivers. At the same time, the rainfall patterns changing will compound the effect of climate change on the rivers. Any minor change in the monsoon pattern has an immediate and discernible effect on rivers. Further, fewer days of rain will lead to inadequate amounts of water percolating down to the ground watertables, further jeopardizing the precarious water situation. Increased temperatures will also increase the rate of evapo-transpiration, the simultaneous movement of water from the soil and vegetation into atmosphere through evaporation and transpiration. This will reduce the actual amount of water that is available for human use. Given the inextricability of water with the already tense politics over its control and supply throughout the subcontinent, climate change is no longer viewed as only environmental problem but a matter of concern for security as well. With China in control of Glaciers, feeding major rivers of South Asia, climate change strengthens China's hand over South Asian waters and adds a great dimension to the Asian power dynamics.

WATER AND COOPERATION

Water is a fundamental resource, indispensable to all forms of life on earth. Reliable freshwater resources are crucial to human and environmental health, as well as economic development. Furthermore, as water flows ignoring state boundaries, water resources are often shared at the local, national and international levels, requires efficient and integrated water management to balance competing interests. Without a mutual solution, water users can find themselves in dispute and even violent conflict.[26] Although there has been history of water-related violence at a sub-national level, but for nation-states, the potential for violent conflict over water is actually relatively low.[27] A total of 1,831 water related events that occurred between states in the years 1948-1999 were investigated, of which two-thirds resulted in co-operation; 37 incidents reached an acute conflict level and the vast majority of the remaining, only escalated to political tensions and violent rhetorics.[28] Indus water treaty between India and Pakistan stood through several wars is the testimony of the strength water sharing treaty has, withholding larger social cause. The fact that cooperative action overwhelms conflictive incidents and that co-operative water management institutions prove resilient even in conflict environments, has led researchers to focus on the potentials that water could hold for peace-building. Water and the environment in general can be related to peace in three main, partly overlapping ways[29] as under:

Sustainable Water Management

The most basic relation between water and sustainable peace exists in the important role water plays for human health, food security, securing basic incomes, and thus ensuring human security. Sustainable water management in social, environmental and economic contexts can thus help prevent potentially related conflicts and is a prerequisite for establishing the socio-economic foundations for peace.

Preventing Water-related Conflicts

Where water-related issues represent structural causes contributing to conflict, a sustainable and just solution to these issues will play a part in conflict transformation and peace accordingly. Conflict-sensitive approaches to balancing competing interests and inequalities related to water can help prevent conflicts arising in the future. Co-operative water management mechanisms, such as river basin organizations or water user committees, offer the most advanced approach. They can anticipate and mediate water-related conflict, provided that all stakeholders are included in decision-making processes and given the means (information, trained staff and financial support) to act as equal partners.[30]

Co-operation on Environmental Issues as an Instrument for Building Peace

Sharing an ecosystem, such as river basins or other water resources, creates complex interdependencies between parties. Based on these interdependencies, environmental problems can provide incentives for co-operation and collective action across political boundaries and ethnic divides. In many instances, parties whose relations are otherwise characterized by distrust and hostility have found that environmental issues, such as shared water resources, are one of the few areas in which they can sustain ongoing dialogue.[31] There are several pathways along which environmental co-operation could contribute to peace. Working together on solving common problems can help replace distrust, uncertainty and suspicion with shared knowledge and a tradition of co-operation. The interdependencies created by shared water resources can further reveal mutual benefits of co-operation. In another ideal scenario, co-operation over environmental issues could lead to the creation of regional identity and regional interests over safeguarding ecosystems.[32] Some of the specific characteristics of environmental issues further support the argument that environmental co-operation could translate into broader forms of long-term co-operation and solutions. The ramifications of environmental co-operation can, therefore, encourage local and non-governmental participation and constitute "high" and "low" politics.[33] Since water management, in particular, requires horizontal coordination between different economical sectors, as well as vertical coordination efforts from local to international levels of society, water co-operation offers particular opportunities for spillover of positive impacts. Still, it cannot be expected that environmental co-operation *per se* will contribute to peace. The way in which cooperative processes are designed and implemented remains critical for the peace and conflict impacts. In this regard, aspects of ownership, transparency, participation and power relationships become utmost importance.

Environmental co-operation could be introduced at different levels of society with the aim of contributing to peace. Social interest groups can take advantage of ecological interdependence across territorial borders to facilitate co-operation between academia and/or civil society actors. This can bring changes in the attitudes, values or perceptions of individuals. At the governmental level, regional water co-operation can range from sharing data and conducting joint research, to infrastructure projects to institutionalized co-operation mechanisms such as joint water commissions or river basin organizations to manage water resource co-operatively. Regional mechanisms for water co-operation between states have the potential to contribute to further regional integration.[34] While the effectiveness depends on the conditions prevailing in the region, the main challenge is to transform environmental co-operation into broader forms of political co-operation and to initiate a social and political dialogue that moves beyond environmental aspects.

INDIA AND ITS NEIGHBOURS

Asia is home to two fastest growing economies of the world. Dispute over sharing of river waters will have a direct impact on the economies of the region. Many treaties have been put in place so that there is no undue utilization of river water by one country which affects the other, however, dwindling water resources and added fear of unilateral action or expression by some country has brought the water issues into league of confrontation and conflict. India has entered into a number of treaties with its neighbours; some of these focus on sharing of water while some pertains to irrigation power and flood control.

Pakistan

Indus Waters Treaty was signed by India and Pakistan at Karachi on 19 September, 1960, by the then Prime Ministers, Jawaharlal Nehru and Mohammad Ayub Khan along with W.A.B. Illif of the World Bank. As per the treaty the waters of the Eastern Rivers were allocated to India and those of Western Rivers were largely allocated to Pakistan. Since then water has been shared amicably, however, as India controls the headwaters there are ill founded fears in the minds of the Pakistani establishment that they are being denied their rightful quantity of water as per the Indus Water Treaty including numerous analysis of "water war" between India and Pakistan by analysts in media time to time. Some Pakistani analysts have even equated it to be another core issue and the trigger for a Nuclear War. However, despite strained relation and several wars the Indus Water Treaty has stood the test of time and is a good example of co-operation between two countries.

Bangladesh

Appropriate allocation of the Ganges' Water was a long standing issue between India and Bangladesh. A new chapter in the Indo-Bangladesh relation opened up in December 1996 with signing of a long term Treaty on the sharing of the River Ganges water. The Treaty shall remain in force for a period of thirty years to be renewed thereafter by mutual consent. A Joint Committee has been set up for monitoring the implementation of the Treaty. Discussions have also been continuing with Bangladesh for sharing of waters of the Teesta River, and likely to be finalized soon. Besides, agreement on transmission of flood forecasting data on major rivers like Ganga, Teesta, Brahmaputra and Barak during the monsoon seasons from India to Bangladesh has continued without any problem; enabling the Civil and Military authorities in Bangladesh, to shift the population of flood affected areas to safer places.

Nepal

There are no major problem areas regarding sharing of river waters between both the countries and mechanisms are in place for joint exploitation of the water resource. Management of the Koshi, Gandaki and Karnali river systems and communication of their conditions to India is vital for the prosperity of both the countries. India and Nepal have entered into large number of agreement for setting up multi-purpose projects on the rivers emanating in Nepal for joint utilization. Some of the co-operation includes treaty on integrated development of Mahakali River for power, irrigation and incidental flood control benefits for both the countries; a plan scheme called, "Flood Forecasting and Warning System on rivers common to India and Nepal", operational since 1989; a Standing Committee on Inundation Problems, functioning since 1986; Nepal-India Joint Committee on Water Resources headed by Water Resources Secretaries of both the countries, functioning with the mandate to act as an Umbrella Committee of all committees and groups.

Bhutan

India and Bhutan have a cordial relation with regard to sharing of water resources. A scheme titled "Comprehensive Scheme for Establishment of Hydro-Meteorological and Flood Forecasting Network on rivers common to India and Bhutan" is in operation. The network consists of 33 hydro-meteorological stations has been set up in Bhutan with funding from India. The data received from these stations is utilized in India by Central Water Commission for formulating the flood forecasts. A Joint Group of Experts on Flood Management has been constituted between India and Bhutan to assess the probable causes and effects of the recurring floods and erosion in the Southern foothills of Bhutan and adjoining plains in India and some mutually acceptable remedial measures are likely to be instituted soon.

China

China and its control of flow of water emanating from Tibet by constructing dam over River Brahmaputra is emerging as an area of contention between the two countries. China has the 'potential' power to disrupt water flow into India by diverting or damming the receding waters either to increase supply to their water thirsty Northern provinces, to generate more electricity or to use it as a punitive measure against South Asia. Large scale diversion of water would adversely affect production of foodgrains, fisheries, in land waterways, hydropower, etc., and thus the economy of the India's North-Eastern States. For Bangladesh, the consequence will be even bigger as it will render Bangladesh incapable of meaningful agriculture production, leading to a major food crisis; which will push Bangladeshis to migrate, having security implication to India. Further, since the region falls in the regular Seismic Zone, destruction of dam due to earthquake can cause devastating consequence downstream. Hence, there is an urgent need to get into dialogue with China to arrive at a mutually acceptable solution. It is important that any solution / agreement to the water issue between India and China will have to be regional and cutting across different countries of the region. In that direction, greater significance needs to be given to basin wide co-operation on water management. Protection of water sources, improving and maintaining water quality, issue of drainage, flood controls, water harvesting and watershed management are some potential areas where co-operation can be envisaged between the countries. Given the scale of the emerging challenges, a treaty with China along the lines of the Indus Water Treaty will be needed to pre-emptively address any sharing, diversion or communication issues.

CONCLUSION

Water is increasingly viewed as a strategic resource, one that has to be protected and valued.[35] Water, like religion and ideology, has the power to move millions of people. Since the very birth of human civilization, people have moved to settle close to it. The great civilizations of the world have evolved around water and South Asia is no exception. In South Asia, water encompasses the cultural, social, economic and political fabric in the lives of some 1.5 billion people. Water resources is key to agriculture, hydropower, and to sustain the aquatic environment. The region is endowed with great rivers that are the lifelines of the regional economy. Water is giving life, not only to organisms, but also to economies. The region's economy and predominantly rural livelihoods heavily depend on the timely arrival and performance of the monsoons. Because water is of critical importance for human survival, the well-being of nations often depends on its access to water.

Water scarcity, deteriorating water quality, increasing water demands and no visible prospects of workable solution has led to increase in competition for control of water resources including political stresses. Given these conceptual and practical limitations, the link between water and conflict is at best contextual. However, water has an important role to play as a nexus of co-operation between states. As such the cooperative approach is overwhelmingly the most frequent response to water challenges between states. In fact, co-operation is the dominant response to a shared water resource. Additionally, co-operation on the water issue could act as a nucleus for further co-operative arrangements in other spheres, triggering linkages between states at a multiplicity of levels and opening communication channels normally severed by conflict. And while water acting as a social and political panacea in the 'developing' world is unlikely, the potential for co-operation needs continued and sustained exploration. Water needs to be utilized as a tool of co-operation, which may potentially lead to synergistic benefits in meeting wider social justice challenges.

REFERENCES

1. Stucki, P. (2005). "Water wars or water peace: Rethinking the nexus between water scarcity and armed conflict". *Programme for Strategic and International Security Studies*. PSIS Occasional Paper 1, Number 3, p. 11. Available at<http://www.psis.org/ pdf/ PSIS-OccPap-2_2004-Stucki.pdf.
2. Alexander Cariou (2003). '*Water, Conflict and Cooperation*', Institute of Peace and Conflict, Canada, p. 54.
3. *Consortium of Non-Traditional Security Studies in Asia*. (2008, September). 'Water Security: Issues and Challenges in SEA', A Fortnightly Bulletin of Current NTS Issues Confronting Asia, Centre for NTS Studies, S. Rajaratnam School of International Studies, NTU, Singapore, p. 2.
4. World Water Assessment Programme (2009). The United Nations World Water Development Report 3: Water in a Changing World, Paris: UNESCO, and London: Earthscan, p. 29.
5. Paul J. Smith & Lt. Col. Charles H. Gross. (1999, September 17). "Water and Conflict in Asia?" A Seminar Report, Asia-Pacific Centre for Security Studies (APCSS), Honolulu, Hawaii, 1999, p. 1 available at http://www.apcss.org/Publications/Report_Water & Conflict _99.html.
6. *Ibid*.
7. Mukand S. Babel and Shahriar M. Wahid. (2009). '*Freshwater Under Threat: South Asia*', jointly published by United Nations Environmental Programme (UNEP) and Asian Institute of Technology, Kenya: Nairobi, 2009, p. 22, available at http://www.roap.Unep. org/pub/southasia_report.pdf.
8. Thomas F. Homer-Dixon. (1999). *Environment, Scarcity and Violence*, Princeton University Press, p. 69.
9. *Consortium of Non-Traditional Security Studies in Asia*. (2008,

September). "Water Security: Issues and Challenges in SEA", A Fortnightly Bulletin of Current NTS Issues Confronting Asia, Centre for NTS Studies, S. Rajaratnam School of International Studies, NTU, Singapore, p. 2.

10. France Bequette. (1998, June). "Water: Will there be Enough? Fresh or Drinking Water," *UNESCO,* p. 42.
11. Quoted in Wolf Aaron T., *et al.* "Water, Conflict and Cooperation", p. 1, available at http://wilsoncenter.org/news/docs/Carius_Dabelko_Wolf.pdf.
12. *Ibid.*
13. "The Big Question: Will Global Conflict Flow from the Quest for Water Security?" Published in *World Policy Journal,* Vol. 26, No. 4, Winter 2009/10, World Policy Institute, 2009, p. 5.
14. Wolf Aaron, T. (Junc, 1999). *Water and Human Security* (*AVISO 3*), Victoria, Canada: The Global Environmental Change and Human Security Project.
15. Wolf, Aaron T., *et al.* "Water, Conflict and Cooperation", p. 1, available at http://wilsoncenter .org/news/docs/Carius_Dabelko_Wolf.pdf.
16. *Ibid.*
17. OECD-DAC. (2005). *Water and Violent Conflict* (drafting of report led by the United States Agency for International Development); Issue Brief; p. 2.
18. Wolf Aaron T., *et al.* "Water, Conflict and Cooperation," p. 1, available at http://wilsoncenter.org/news/docs/Carius_Dabelko_Wolf.pdf.
19. *Ibid.*
20. *Ibid.*
21. Ohlsson. Leif. (2000), *Livelihood Conflicts: Linking Poverty and Environment as Causes of Conflict*, Stockholm: Swedish International Development Agency, Department of Natural Resources and the Environment.
22. *Op. cit.*, p. 2.
23. OECD-DAC. (2005). *Water and Violent Conflict* (drafting of report led by the United States Agency for International Development); Issue Brief; p. 2.
24. A.T. Wolf *et al.* (2005). "Managing water conflict and co-operation" in The Worldwatch Institute (Ed.). *State of the World 2005: Redefining Global Security*. New York & London: WW Norton & Company.
25. A.T. Wolf (1999). *Water and Human Security*, AVISO, No. 3. Victoria, Canada: The Global Environmental Change and Human Security Project.
26. S. Postel and A.T. Wolf (2001), 'Dehydrating Conflict', *Foreign Policy*, September/October. See http://www.globalwaterpolicy.org/pubs/FP_Conflict.pdf.
27. K. Conca, *et al.* (2005). "Building peace through environmental co-operation" in The Worldwatch Institute (ed.). *Op. cit.*
28. A. Kramer (2004). *Water and Conflict – Briefing Paper for USAID*. Berlin, Bogor and Washington, DC: Adelphi Research, Centre for International

Forestry Research and Woodrow Wilson International Centre for Scholars. Available at http://rmportal.net/tools/water-and-fresh-water-resource-management-tools/toolkit-water-and-conflict-04-04-02. pdf/view.

29. K. Conca, *et al.* (2005). *Op. cit.*
30. A. Carius (2003). "Naturschutz als Beitrag zur Friedensentwicklung" in *Naturschutz (Aus-)Löser von Konflikten?*. Documentation of a conference by the Bundesamtes für Naturschutz and the Heinrich Böll Foundation, 25th-27th November, 2002 in Berlin. Bonn, Germany. p. 26. Available at http://www.bfn.de/fileadmin/MDB/documents/script 98.pdf.
31. G.D. Dabelko (2006). *Analyzing Environmental Pathways to Peace*. Paper presented at the annual meeting of the International Studies Association, Town and Country Resort and Convention Centre, San Diego, California, US, 22nd March, 2006. Available at http://www. allacademic.com/meta/p99621_index.html.
32. D. Phillips *et al.* (2006). *Transboundary Water Co-operation as a Tool for Conflict Prevention and Broader Benefit-sharing*. Global Development Studies, No. 4. Stockholm: Swedish Ministry for Foreign Affairs.
33. Paul J. Smith & Lt. Col. Charles H. Gross. (1999, September 17). "Water and Conflict in Asia?" A Seminar Report, Asia-Pacific Centre for Security Studies (APCSS), Honolulu, Hawaii, p. 4 available at http://www.apcss.org/Publications/Report_ Water&Conflict _ 99.html.
34. "The Big Question: Will Global Conflict Flow from the Quest for Water Security?" Published in *World Policy Journal,* Vol. 26, No. 4, Winter 2009/10, World Policy Institute, 2009, p. 5.
35. Stucki, P. (2005). "Water Wars or Water Peace: Rethinking the Nexus Between Water Scarcity and Armed Conflict".

8

India's Energy Security in the Context of Global Warming and Climate Change

A. Subramanyam Raju

Energy security has become an important concern to most of the countries including India. Energy availability is one of the foremost requirements for India's economic growth. Economic reforms, population growth, urbanization, demographic transition and growing transport sector in India are resulting in a rapid demand for more and more energy. The demand for energy consumption is likely to increase in future. India is largely dependent on coal[1] to meet its energy needs, which produce more CO_2. India is the fourth largest emitter of green house gases[2] (GHG) in the world. However, its emissions are less than five per cent of that of the world. Carbon-dioxide emission reduction imposes costs in terms of lower GDP and higher poverty. For instance, a thirty per cent CO_2 reduction over a period of thirty years using annual emissions reduction targets leads to a fall in GDP of four per cent and raises the number of poor by 17.5 per cent.[3]

On one hand India has to provide sufficient commercial energy for growth and on the other hand it has to minimize the inequality between urban and rural people's consumption levels of energy.[4] Many people (500 million people) in India still lack access to electricity for their basic needs. Thus energy security is linked up with both growth and poverty. India realized the need for coherent and enduring foreign energy security policy to secure energy imports at reasonable price and without any disturbance. However, it is essential for India, on one hand, to improve the efficiency of coal and electricity use and on the other hand to reduce its dependence on coal that could reduce emissions.

Total global energy consumption will expand by seventy one per cent between 2003 and 2030.[5] Increase in energy demand will occur in developing countries that depend upon the combustion of hydrocarbons such as coal to produce the electricity to meet their energy needs. Carbon dioxide emissions from developing countries are projected to exceed those of the industrialized nations soon after 2010. Oil and gas are not as abundantly available as coal. Projections indicate that under current policies and trends fossil fuels will remain the dominant source of energy in the future. The International Energy Agency (IEA) forecasts that between 2004 and 2030, fossil fuels will account for eighty three per cent of the overall increase in global energy demand. There is a need to find alternative sources of energy that can supply the burgeoning energy needs of the world. Further development and deployment of sustainable energy technologies on an unprecedented scale is needed.

Climate change is more likely to act as a threat multiplier than as a primary source of insecurity. Climate change cannot be addressed without discussing the issue of energy. This chapter analyzes the existing energy situation in India and how climate change would prevent/challenge India's growth and eradication of poverty. Further, it focuses on how India would reorient its energy strategy to reduce its carbon emissions.

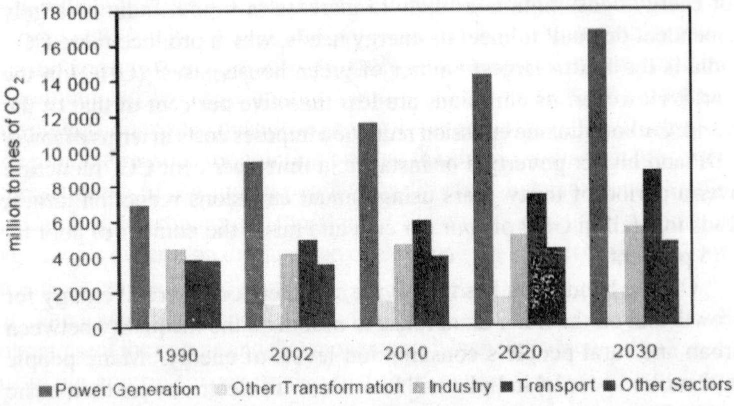

Fig. 8.1: Evolution of CO_2 Emissions

Source: International Energy Agency, *World Energy Outlook*, Paris, 2006.

The Figure 8.1 reveals that source of CO_2 emissions are largely from power generation, transformation, industry, transport and other sectors. During 1990- 2030, it is estimated that power sector is largely contributing to emission of CO_2. developing countries, like India, are more depending on coal for power production. The power sector is responsible for the highest direct CO_2 emissions in India (42%), followed by iron and steel, road, railways and air transport and coal. Improving the efficiency of coal and electricity use could significantly reduce emissions from these sectors.

Table 8.1: Fossil Fuel Emission Levels (Pounds per Billion BTU of Energy Input)

Pollutant	*Natural Gas*	*Oil*	*Coal*
CO_2	117000	164000	208000
Carbon Monoxide	40	33	208
Nitrogen Oxides	92	448	457
Sulfur Dioxide	1	1,122	2,591
Particulates	7	84	2,744
Mercury	0.000	0.007	0.016

Source: EIA – Natural Gas Issues & Trends 1998 http://www.naturalgas.org/environment/naturalgas.asp

From the Table 8.1, it is clear that CO_2 emission from coal is more than from natural gas and oil. Compared to other GHGs, it is CO_2, which contributes emission levels more from oil, gas and coal. Since, CO_2 is playing a significant role in contributing more towards GHGs, it becomes difficult task for many developing countries to reduce their emission levels. Emission growth rates in developing countries increased until the 1990s, but are showing signs of deceleration in major countries such as India and China due to reduced population growth as well as reduction in energy intensity of GDP (due to substitution of coal with oil and gas). The energy intensity is more by the developed countries. On average, each American emits more than four times as much carbon dioxide from energy use as a Chinese, and as much as twenty Indians. India and other developing countries feel strongly that they are not responsible for the threat of climate. Unsustainable consumption patterns of the rich industrialized nations in the world are responsible for it. Yet, India and other developing countries' economies may be highly vulnerable to climate change.

INDIA'S ENERGY SECURITY SCENARIO

To meet the future demand, the Indian government had set up a group on *India's Hydrocarbon Vision 2025* in February 1999. The recommendations put forth by the group are: 100 per cent exploration coverage of Indian sedimentary basins by 2025; exploration in frontier and deep water areas;

offering of attractive fiscal terms; abroad investment in exploration of oil and gas resources; Self-sufficiency in Petroleum refining; and Storage of oil in various locations.

India's economy is growing since the economic reforms were undertaken. If it has to grow at the rate of eight per cent as per projection, there should be uninterruptible supply of oil, gas and power.

Table 8.2: India's Position in Global Energy Production and Trade, 2004

	Crude Oil (Mt)	*Coal (Mt)*	*Natural Gas (BCM)*	*Petroleum Products (Mt)*
Global Production	3923	5878	28721	3719
Indian Production*	34 (0.87)	430 (7.32)	32 (0.11)	108 (2.9)
Indian Consumption*	130 (3.31)	454 (7.72)	32 (0.11)	107 (2.9)
Global Trade*	2235 (56.97)	778 (13.24)	838 (29.18)	825 (22.18)
Indian Imports**	96 (4.30)	37 (4.76)	6.9	9.75 (1.18)
Indian Imports Dependence	73.85	8.15	—	—

* Figures in parentheses are percentage of global production.
** Figures in parentheses are percentage of global trade.
Source: EIA, *International Energy Outlook* 2006, Washington DC: US Energy Information Administration, 2006, cited in Nitya Nanda, "Trading in the World Energy", in Logia Noronha and Anant Sudarshan (ed.), *India's Energy Security* (London: Routledge, 2009), p. 52.

India's energy production and its trade are given in the Table 8.2. Table reveals that India is depending more on importing oil than on other sources. It is the sixth largest importer with a share of 4.3 per cent. Though India produces a large amount of coal but it has become the sixth largest importer of coal. India's trade in natural gas is not a significant because of infrastructure constraints and liquefied natural gas imports started only in 2004. India's most important source for energy is coal. More than half of India's energy needs are met by coal and seventy per cent of its electricity generation. With more than 90,000 million metric tonnes of proven coal reserves (about ten per cent of the world's total), the country could be self-sufficient for more than a century. India's coal consumption increased from 360 million tonnes in 2000 to 460 million tonnes in 2005

(5.5 per cent year over this period). Sixty eight per cent of India's CO_2 emissions are from coal.

In most of the industrialized countries, there is relatively little disparity in energy consumption between the urban or rural areas or between different parts of the country. However, it is not the case in the developing countries, particularly in India. The rural people in India still use cycles or animals for transportation, and consume only a small amount of electricity due to its high cost or no access. Table 8.3 shows the distribution of direct and indirect consumption of coal, oil and electricity by different rural and urban income groups in India and their contribution to carbon emissions. It is to be noted that fifty per cent of rural people emitted in 1990 only fifty four kilograms of carbon per person per year. The richest ten per cent of urban people emitted twelve times as much as 656 kg carbon per person per year. India needs to address to minimize the disparity in energy consumption. It cannot eradicate poverty unless takes initiatives to provide access to electricity to every rural Indian. Also savings in GHG emission by the poor should not be expected at the expense of development. It is time for the Indian government that disparity between the rural and urban must be addressed, because seventy per cent of people live in rural areas. It is to be noted that the poor people, who live in the proximity of the plants such as Singrauli and Dabhol plants, do not have access to power and laying grids and pipelines for urban areas. The government must focus on developing infrastructure including power in the rural areas; otherwise rural people may migrate to cities, which would cause disaster in future.

Table 8.3: Per Capita Annual Energy Use (Direct and Indirect), 1989-90

Income Group	*Coal (Kg)*	*Oil (Kg)*	*Elec (Kwh)*	*Carbon (t)*
Rural				
Bottom (50%)	74	22.5	95	054
Middle (40%)	127	39.7	152	093
Top (10%)	262	89.8	284	204
Urban				
Bottom (50%)	130	45.6	164	101
Middle (40%)	302	118.6	366	246
Top (10%)	765	332.3	858	656
EDR@ Extreme Disparity Ratio – Urban top / rural bottom	10.3	14.8	9.0	12.0

Source: Jyoti K. Parikh and Kirit Parikh, *Climate Change: India's Perceptions, Positions, Policies and Possibilities* (Paris: OECD, 2002), p. 10.

INDIA'S ENERGY CO-OPERATION WITH ITS NEIGHBOUR COUNTRIES

In order to reduce its dependence on coal based energy production, India is exploring ways and means to meet its energy demands through agreements with other countries. Following are some of the bilateral and multilateral initiatives taken by India.

India and Bangladesh

Bangladesh contains natural gas reserves of around 16.3 trillion cubic feet (tcf). Further, it is estimated an additional 32.1 tcf in undiscovered reserves. If these figures are proved to be correct, then Bangladesh could certainly become a major gas producer. Many people in Bangladesh want gas resources to be used for domestic purposes and oppose exporting gas to other countries particularly to India. Bangladesh will benefit if it exports gas to India. An analyst rightly pointed out "Dhaka's inclusive, and perhaps increasingly irrelevant debate on gas exports reflects the tragic sub-continental tradition of wallowing in isolation and poverty rather than creating shared wealth."[6]

India and Pakistan

India's relationship with Pakistan is very important because any gas pipeline to India from the Middle East/Central Asia would require Pakistan's involvement and partnership. Abdullah Yusuf, Secretary for Petroleum and Natural Resources of Pakistan, stated "Pakistan may start buying up to 5 million tonnes of diesel from India instead of Kuwait because it makes "better economic sense", that is, would prove cheaper."[7] Yaswant Sinha, India's External Affairs Minister, addressing the SAARC Chambers of Commerce and Industry in Islamabad on 2 January, 2004, expressed that "If Pakistan can find within itself the strength and wisdom to change its current approach towards India, there are immense benefits that it can derive as a transit route for the movement of energy, goods and people."[8] If this comes into reality then both countries can mutually be benefited. Thus economic interdependence will make it easier for the two countries to resolve their political problems.

Pakistan has a 500 KV primary transmission system extending from Jumshoro in the south to Tarbela and Peshawar in the north. All the lines are close to India's borders and may not require very complex transmission extensions. Pakistan's Power Minister stated, "There is a complete network on our side of course, on their (India) side as well. What we need are the connections, which would take a couple of weeks."[9] If Pakistan exports its surplus of 200 MW, it will get $1.2 billion a year over a period of twenty years.[10] Also it can help the power plants to use their power at eighty per cent capacity than the present sixty per cent. If the plants run at eighty per cent capacity utilization, the tariff would decrease to Rs. 3.5 (4 cents). However, Pakistan is demanding Rs. 3.00 (7 cents) per unit, whereas India is willing to pay for Rs. 1.26 (3 cents) per unit. It wants to sell power in cents and not in rupees. This will require setting up of foreign exchange reserves. India gets for Rs. 1.30-1.50 per unit from National Thermal Power Corporation (NTPC), whereas Pakistan government is paying Rs.3.60 per unit to the Independent Power producers (IPPs). It has to balance the both internal and external prices. India cannot buy power if it goes beyond Rs.1.50 per unit. There has been an asymmetry in the power tariff between these two countries. They have to sort out their differences and as a result both will benefit from power deal.

India and Bhutan

India and Bhutan had an agreement related to hydroelectric power supply. Under this agreement Bhutan is supplying power to India from Chukha Hydro Electric Project (336 MW). There is another project –Tala Hydro-Electric Project (1020 MW), which is under construction and the surplus power from this project will be supplied to India. Bunakha (180 MW) and Wang Chu (900 MW) projects are planned and Sankosh project (4060 MW) is under process. Bhutan is exporting eighty per cent of its energy generation to India, which accounts for thirty per cent of its GDP. According to Indian sources, about sixty per cent of Bhutan's GDP accrues from exporting of surplus power from three hydro-power station (Kurichu, Chukha and Tala) and the generation will increase once work on four more stations (Punatsangchu, Wangchu, Bunakha and Sankosh) is completed.[11] Through Chukha Project, Bhutan earned Nu 1,454 million as profit in 1998-1999 from its power export to India. As a result it is in a position to increase revenues through the supply of energy to India and tc its own industries in the country. India provided technical and financial aid to this project. Its share was Rs. 2.45 billion with sixty per cent grant and forty per cent loan. Bhutan was able to redeem the entire cost of the project in five years. India is able to supply power to West Bengal, Orissa and North-Eastern parts of India. However, India has to upgrade its transmission lines to increase its access to Bhutanese power. The energy co-operation between India and Bhutan proved to other neighbours in South Asia that a smaller country can benefit more from a larger country (India).

India and Nepal

Nepal is possessing largest hydropower potential (83,290 MW) in South Asia. However, due to various reasons, Nepal is not able to tap its hydro resources. It is able to install only 283 MW capacities. There are proposals between India and Nepal for hydro-electric co-operation. Projects like Pancheswar Project, which has the capacity of about 6,000 MW, needs special institutional and financial assistance. The other project—West Sati (750 MW) is also proposed to develop to export power to India. Due to factors such as technical, production and supply constraints and political differences, co-operation between the two countries could not be reached.

India and Other Countries in South-East Asia

Economic relations with the ASEAN will certainly help India's quest for energy security. Presently India imports crude oil from Malaysia and Brunei and it is about 5.4 per cent of its total imports from the world. It also imports 3.5 per cent LPG from Malaysia. Since the ASEAN countries—Indonesia, Malaysia and Vietnam have about one per cent of world's proven oil reserves and three per cent of the world's proven gas reserves[12], India can work towards enhancing its energy trade with them.[13]

India-Pakistan-Iran Gas Pipeline

India and Pakistan had signed a memorandum of Understanding in July 1993 regarding exploring the prospects of a natural gas pipeline from Iran to India *via* Pakistan. In 1995, Pakistan and Iran had signed an agreement to construct a pipeline from South Pars gas field in Iran to Karachi in Pakistan and with an extension to India. However, due to various factors it has not been materialized. Pakistan insists for onshore gas pipeline, whereas India prefers to offshore pipeline project.

It was estimated that a 2,700 km overland gas pipeline through Pakistan would cost about $3.1 billion. Out of this amount, India has to bear about $1 billion and the rest by Pakistan and Iran. Later the BHP Billiton revised the cost to about $7 billion. If it is materialized then

Pakistan will get $700 million as transit charges from India every year.[14] India has reservations about the onshore pipeline project on the following grounds: (a) India is keen on full-fledged economic relations with Pakistan. It would be possible only if Pakistan gives MFN to India. India has already granted MFN to Pakistan in 1995; (b) India has doubts about the safety and security of the gas line in the light of ongoing tensions between the two countries; (c) India has to live at the mercy of Pakistan; and (d) there may be threats from the fundamentalists and terrorists of Pakistan to the pipeline.

In spite of these reservations on the part of India, the proposed project can still be pursued on the ground, as it is mutually beneficial for both. For instance, the Indus Water Treaty between the two countries was successful. Even the fundamentalists and disruptive elements obstruct the proposed line, the governments can take steps to prevent those activities. It is to be noted that the project is not a trilateral Government-to-Government project but it would be owned by an international consortium made up of the national companies of three countries concerned together with other international partners (may be companies from China, Russia and Australia).[15] Hence, it would not be possible for Pakistan to disrupt the supply of gas to India. It is to be noted that Pakistan own gas lines from the Sui gas field were being blown up by insurgents (in Baluchistan) and Indian own crude oil pipelines are being blown up in Assam regularly, but the respective governments are able to manage the situation.[16] Hence, India should not bother about the threat from militancy. Meanwhile, India has signed an LNG deal with Iran and some of the companies such as Tatas and Essar who are interested in investing in the latter. However, this deal was yet to be materialized because it was to be approved by Iran's Supreme Economic Council. This may be because India cast its vote against Iran in the IAEA on the nuclear issue and also gas prices had gone up.

Turkmenistan-Afghanistan-Pakistan-India (TAPI)

The Turkmenistan-Afghanistan-Pakistan-India (TAPI) line will run from the Dauletabad gas field to Afghanistan. From there it will be constructed from Heart to Kandahar and then through Quetta and Multan in Pakistan. The final destination of the pipeline will be the Indian town of Fazilka, near the border with Pakistan. The 1,680 km pipeline from Turkmenistan will transport 100 million standard cubic metres per day (mscmd) of gas from the Dauletabad gas field and India will have share of 60 mscmd.[17]

The pipeline will be 1,420 mm in diameter with a capacity of 3.3 billion cubic metres (bcm) of natural gas annually. The cost of the project is estimated at $3.5 billion in 2005. However, the cost was now estimated about $7 billion.

Myanmar-Bangladesh-India Pipeline

Myanmar possesses significant energy reserves: gas in Yadana field and another deposit in the Bay of Bengal. Two Indian energy firms, OVL and GAIL own twenty and ten per cent stake respectively in the Burmese field, A-1 and in the adjacent A-3 Block. The 290 km pipeline passes through Arakan State in Myanmar and the Indian States of Mizoram and Tripura crossing through Bangladesh and Kolkata. GAIL conducted feasibility studies for a 550 to 600 kms. long offshore pipeline to connect India through Bangladesh. In case of Bangladesh's continued refusal to permit gas be supplied to India, an alternative route of the pipeline will have to go under the sea in the Bay of Bengal, where pipes may have to be laid as deep as 6,560 ft. under water. This would also be highly expensive. The pipeline cost may be more than $2 bn even if an economical route is followed.

Before signing an agreement with India, Myanmar signed a MoU with Chinese company Petro China in early 2006 to supply gas to China from the A-1 field over a thirty years period. China gave soft loan of $84 million to Myanmar for laying a 2380-km pipeline connecting the gas site at Kyaukphyu (Myanmar) to Ruili (Yunnan province of China). China also agreed to pay $150 million annually for thirty years as a transit fee for the 990 km stretch through Myanmar. However, in the case of supplying gas to India, Bangladesh wants pipe line to be laid along its existing roads and highways and the project to be managed jointly by both; all the problems to be discussed in a package deal; allow Bangladesh a free trade corridor to Nepal; India to remove the existing trade barriers between the two countries. It is very unfortunate that Dhaka refuses to allow supply of gas through its soil when it will also benefit through the pipeline in the form of $100 million per annum as transit fee.

India's Shift in Energy Production

India has been relying on hydro-power for years to reduce its dependency on fossil fuels. One-fourth of the country's electricity comes from hydro-power plants and new dams will go online in the coming years, especially along the Brahmaputra River.[18] Himalayan glaciers that feed India's major rivers are essential for a steady supply of hydro-power. With climate change and shrinking glaciers, the most important source for India's rivers, the country risks of experiencing even more blackouts during dry seasons are increasing. India has renewable capacity to over 11,000 MW, in which 7,000 MW is based on wind power. Nuclear generation[19] is attracting countries to increase the diversity of their energy supplies, improve energy security and provide a low-carbon alternative to fossil fuels. For instance, China, the US and India, which are the world's three largest coalconsuming nations, are projected to expand their nuclear capacity significantly over the next twenty five years.

India is presently able to produce about three per cent (4,000 MW) nuclear energy. In 2002, the installed electricity capacity was about 139 giga watts. During 2002-2003 electricity production was about 639 terrawatt hours (twh), where sixty seven per cent from coal-based stations, twenty per cent from oil and gas, ten per cent from hydro and three per cent from nuclear. India's requirements of energy by 2052 indicate that the total installed capacity will have to be about 1,350 giga watts and the total generation about 8,000 twh. Of this, the coal and hydrocarbon (oil and gas) contributions would have gone down to forty seven and sixteen per cent and hydro to eight per cent. The nuclear component is required to go up to twenty six per cent.[20]

Realizing its energy needs, India has recently signed an agreement with the US on peaceful nuclear energy co-operation. Through this agreement India is expected to produce about 20,000 MW by 2020 and double this by 2030. The Nuclear Supplier Group (NSG), which treated India in the past three decades as a pariah, has agreed to trade nuclear commerce with the latter after the agreement with the US. India's main focus on nuclear energy is not only to meet the demands but also to reduce its green house emission. The global estimated oil reserves were estimated to be 1,188 billion barrels (one barrel is equal to 160 litres) and proven gas reserves were estimated to be 6,400 tcf (one tcf is equal to 100 million barrels of liquid fuel) as per the 2004 figures.[21] It is expected that oil will be available for about forty to sixty years, whereas gas for 100 years. If this is going to be the reality, then India, which is depending heavily on imports, should explore alternatives to secure its energy needs.

High prices for fossil fuels allow nuclear power to become economically competitive with generation from coal, natural gas, and liquids despite the relatively high capital and maintenance costs associated with nuclear power plants.

CONCLUSION

India is making significant progress in limiting GHG emissions through initiatives such as those aiming to improve energy and economic efficiency of the energy and industrial production capacity, as well as energy development, both conventional and renewable, which improve environmental quality and limit human health hazards from air pollution. India has to join with other countries in a collaborative effort to bring about a strategic shift, across the globe, from production and consumption patterns based on carbon-based fossil fuels to those based on renewable energy and non-carbon fuels, because it is question of life and death for every human being in the world. India must prioritize areas such as: energy efficiency in lighting, transport, power generation and reduce the energy-intensity of industrial production. For instance, India is about 4½ times more inefficient than the US in production and even more so than some European countries (China is almost twice as inefficient as India). For every unit of consumption, India generates about two to three times more CO_2 emissions than do the industrial countries. The US per capita consumption of energy is forty nine times that of India and of transport 146 times that of India.

Climate change poses different challenges for India. It does not want any constraints on its development prospects and it seeks to be seen as an emerging global power. On the other hand, it has become compulsory to concentrate to mitigate its emission of CO_2. India's energy security is linked up with its growth and poverty. The demand for energy consumption is likely to increase. It is largely dependent on coal to meet its energy needs, which produce more CO_2. Economic growth is the major cause of rising emissions. There would be a major reorientation of its energy strategy, if India has to reduce its carbon emissions, i.e., a shift from their current coal-based to other based energy system.

India maintains that it does not want to be a part of the problem but want to be a part of the solution and "India with per capita carbon emission of a little more than one tonne cannot create a problem for the survival of the world."[22] India is ready to reduce twenty to twenty five per cent in energy intensity in 2020 compared to 2005. It is to be noted that India can reduce its contribution to climate change, if it concentrate more on non-fossil sources. Further, India has to concentrate more on energy efficiency, clean energy, prevention of air pollution, afforestation and wasteland development and population reduction. Besides, India needs to focus on bilateral as well as multilateral agreements with other countries to import gas/oil/hydro power to meet some of its demands and thereby it would be able to reduce CO_2 emissions.

REFERENCES

1. Coal provides energy at a cost between $1 and $2 per MMBtu compared to $6 to $12 per MMBtu for oil and gas and coal prices are relatively stable. However, it is highly polluting and more carbon-intensive than other energy alternatives.
2. The six green house gases (GHGs) are: CO_2, methane, nitrous oxide, hydro fluorocarbons, perfluorocarbons and sulfur hexafluoride.
3. Jyoti K. Parikh and Kirit Parikh, *Climate Change: India's Perceptions, Positions, Policies and Possibilities* (Paris: OECD, 2002).
4. For details see Anant Sudarshan and Logia Noronha, "Contextualizing India's Energy Security", in Logia Noronha and Anant Sudarshan (ed.), *India's Energy Security* (London: Routledge, 2009), p. 3.
5. *World Energy Outlook* (Paris: International Energy Agency), 2006.
6. *The Hindu*, 12 November, 2002.
7. Prem Shankar Jha, "Big Gulps of the Peace Pipe", *Outlook*, Vol. 44, No. 3, 26 January, 2004, p. 10.
8. *The Hindu*, 3 January, 2004.
9. *The Hindustan Times*, 16 January, 1999.
10. Mahendra P. Lama, "Economic Reforms and the Energy Sector in South Asia: Scope for Cross-Border Power Trade", *South Asian Survey,* Vol.7, No.1, January-June, 2000, p. 18.
11. See *The Hindu*, 22 December, 2009, p. 10.
12. Partha Pratim Pal & Mitali Dasgupta, "Does A Free Trade Agreement with ASEAN Make Sense?", *Economic & Political Weekly*, Vol. 43, No. 46, 15 November, 2008, p. 11.
13. For more details see A. Subramanyam Raju, "India-Southeast Asia Energy Cooperation", in T. Nirmala Devi & A. Subramanyam Raju (ed.), *India and Southeast Asia: Strategic Convergence in the Twenty-first Century.*
14. G. Parthasarathy, "The Quest for Energy Security", see http://www.rediff.com/news/2001/jul/106gp.htm.
15. Talmiz Ahmad, "Geopolitics of West Asian and Central Asian Oil and Gas", in Noronha and Sudarshan (ed.), n. 4, p. 74.
16. Ravi Kumar Batra, "Natural Gas Pipelines: Geopolitics, Affordability, Security Dimensions", in Noronha and Sudarshan (ed.), n. 4, pp. 88-90.
17. See *The Hindu,* 23 April, 2008.
18. There was a debate in the Lok Sabha on 8 August, 1974. P.V.G. Raju, a Congress member of the Lok Sabha emphasized the importance of nuclear technology for producing energy. He quoted Professor Swamy Gnanand, Professor of Nuclear Physics in Andhra University, who told him when China attacked India: "It is very important that we hold the area (north

Assam) because it is very important for us to develop nuclear energy, electric energy in the area". According to Swamy "... the Brahmaputra reaches India in that area... and then it flows into the valley on the right hand side and the left had side of the valley... about 5,000 to 7,000 metres high, and the Brahmaputra flow in between.

Swamiji told that it is possible to produce electricity by blasting tunnels in those mountains and allowing water to flow into these tunnels. We can have first class hydro electric machinery there. We could produce electricity in that area as much as what the whole of Europe is producing today". Cited in *Lok Sabha Debates*, Vol. 12, No. 14, 8 August, 1974, col. 226-227.

19. Despite the nuclear accidents like US 3 Miles and the Chernobyl disaster, countries are in favour of exploring energy from nuclear reactors. An accident was occurred at Kalpakkam Atomic Plant and some workers received high doses of radiation in January 2003. The Bhabha Atomic Research Centre took six months to acknowledge the incident. This incident raised doubts about the safety of nuclear power plants. See T.S. Subramanian, "The Kalpakkam 'Incident'", *Frontline*, Vol. 20, No. 17, 16-29 August, 2003, http://www.frontlineonnet.com/fl2017/stories/2003082404400.htm
20. M.R. Srinivasan , "New Opportunities for Nuclear Energy", *The Hindu*, 2 August, 2005, p. 10.
21. *The Hindu*, 19 February, 2008.
22. M.R. Srinivasan, "One Month after Copenhagen", *The Hindu*, 30 January, 2010, p. 8.

9

Indian Commitment to 'No First Use' of Nuclear Weapons: The First Step towards Global Nuclear Disarmament

P.M. Kamath

After Indian declaration of its newly acquired nuclear status, as the sixth Nuclear Weapons State (NWS) in May 1998, the then Prime Minister, Atal Behari Vajpayee and others in the foreign policy establishment stated that Minimum Nuclear Deterrence (MIND)[1] is not negotiable. But India had to determine when, under what circumstances and how it is going to use its nuclear weapons. Thus, the Prime Minister in the Parliament in May 1998 had stated rudiments of its impending doctrine of MIND. Vajpayee had also declared India's adherence to No First Use (NFU) of Nuclear weapons. Hence, NFU became the main Principle of the Indian doctrine of nuclear deterrence. NFU of nuclear weapons establishes that India is not trigger happy and will not be the first to take recourse to the use of nuclear weapons. India put NFU into nuclear discussion in the country, as well as in the world,[2] which was also to become a firm formulation within Indian nuclear doctrine.

The draft of Indian nuclear doctrine—MIND as prepared by the National Security Advisory Board (NSAB) was released by Brajesh Mishra, the then National Security Adviser to Prime Minister, Vajpayee on 17 August, 1999.[3] However, draft was officially adopted by the National Democratic Alliance (NDA) government at the meeting of Cabinet Committee on Security on 4 January, 2003 with minor changes.[4] The annual report of the Ministry of External Affairs 2002-2003, however, dropped the term 'minimum'. Later in September 2004 as P.S. Chari points out, India's the then Defence Minister, Pranab Mukherjee reportedly said that India needs a 'credible' nuclear deterrence, dropping the term—minimum.[5]

There were doubts as to whether Indian doctrine of nuclear deterrence will continue in force if the government's political complexion changes after periodical elections. I had opined then that there is a national consensus on nuclear weapons programme as such there will be no change in the policy even if the BJP goes out of power.[6] This was proved correct after May 2004 General Elections, which saw the Congress, led coalition government of the United Progressive Alliance (UPA) at the centre assuming power. Prime Minister, Manmohan Singh more than once reiterated that the doctrine of nuclear deterrence would continue to be the Government policy. In an interview to the CNN in Washington, DC on 20 July, 2005 Prime Minister stated that his government is very much committed to no first use of nuclear weapons.[7]

NO FIRST USE OF NUCLEAR WEAPONS

If the credible[8] nuclear deterrence is the mind controlling the Indian national security policy, its heart is NFU—an Indian commitment not to be the first one to use nuclear weapons. This clearly establishes that Indian nuclear weapons are for defence and not for offence. India has already offered to sign a treaty with Pakistan on NFU. The offer is also applicable to China since it has also made commitment to a similar doctrine since 1964.

The doctrine of NFU has been in the Indian strategic thinking since its first nuclear test in May 1974. Vajpayee, as the Minister for External Affairs, in the first non-Congress government led by Morarji Desai in 1977 is said to have used the concept of NFU first time while attending the UN General Assembly session in 1977. If UPA dropped minimum in favour of credible, heart of the Nuclear Doctrine has remained intact even after the UPA coming to power.

Though NFU came prominently into Indian strategic thought after May 1998 nuclear tests, Indian commitment to NFU was very much in Indian political thinking much before the NDA's adoption of it. V.P. Singh's government in 1990 spoke of commitment not to use nuclear capability as an instrument of first strike. In his cabinet Arun Singh was committed to it, as the then Army Chief General Sundarji was also an advocate of the concept. During his visit to Washington DC in May 1994 Narasihma Rao also offered to reassure Pakistan by pledging no first use of nuclear capability. Earlier in January 1994 the then Foreign Secretary, J.N. Dixit had also made a similar offer to Pakistan.[9] But once India declared herself as the sixth NWS had to come out with the nuclear doctrine wherein it made NFU as the soul of the doctrine. This makes it clear that NFU has evolved over the time particularly since the 1970s, and was not developed after the nuclear tests in May 1998 as a tactic to defuse international adverse reactions to Indian tests.

Early Origin of the NFU

However, NFU has had a global appeal. America has unique distinction of having invented Atom Bomb and also of experimenting with its use and consequent realization of catastrophic destruction it could bring about. Hence, Americans were also first in proposing an NFU principle in its application. Republican Senator from Vermont, Ralph Flanders, made earliest suggestion of NFU of nuclear weapons in 1949. He introduced on 27 June, 1949 a resolution in the US Senate stating "the Atom Bomb like biological warfare, wholesale poisoning, is not properly a military device directed against the armed forces of the enemy, but rather is a means for the mass murder of civilians." Hence, he called upon the Truman administration in US to adopt NFU policy.[10]

Around the same time George Kennan, then Head of the Policy Planning Staff in the State Department made a similar proposal within the Truman administration on 20 January, 1950. In a memorandum to the Secretary of State, Dean Rusk, he wrote that the US faced a fundamental choice on the nuclear weapons. Without naming the options as one of First Use (FU) and second as NFU of nuclear weapons, he asked, "Are we to rely upon weapons of mass destruction as an integral and vitally important component" of US "military strength...." Or, "to retain such weapon" in the US "national arsenal *only as a possible means of retaliation*...." In the first case, "something which we have resolved, in the face of all the moral and other actors concerned, to employ forthwith and unhesitatingly at the outset of any, great military conflict."[11] He elaborated in the case of NFU, nuclear weapons as "something superfluous to our basic military posture—as something that we are compelled to hold against the possibility that they might be used by our opponents."[12]

Kennan considered, this memorandum as "one of the most important, if not the most important, of all the documents," he "ever wrote in government."[13] Kennan, of course, favoured the second alternative of not using the nuclear weapons, but bemoaned that the US paid lip service to the idea of abolition of atomic weapons. He wanted the US to take a public position that "We deplore the existence of all weapons of indiscriminate mass destruction. We regret that we were even obliged to make use of one."

The Chinese, so to say, borrowed the American intellectual property. It is clear that Chinese even before they went nuclear had a firm commitment to NFU of nuclear weapons. At least one year before their first test, China reaffirmed its faith in NFU. Second, it declares that "China will never at any time or under any circumstances be the first to use nuclear weapons." It has also during the later years added its commitment not to use or threaten to use nuclear weapons against any non-nuclear weapons states.[14]

Main Principles

Then, what are the main principles of Indian policy of NFU? First, India will not be the first one to use nuclear weapons in any war with a nation that is known to possess nuclear weapons. Second, India has pledged not to use nuclear weapons "against states which do not possess nuclear weapons, or are not aligned" with other nuclear weapon states.[15] However, if a non-nuclear power uses biological or chemical weapons (BCW), India will keep the option of using nuclear weapons open against such a state. It is fair proposition as India is a signatory to the Chemical and Biological weapons treaty and as such has destroyed all its holdings of BCW.

Third, in the event India becoming a victim of first strike with nuclear weapons by an adversary, India will use nuclear weapons as weapons of second strike to retaliate and "to inflict damage unacceptable to the aggressor." Clearly Indian intentions were to prevent any adversary from using tactical nuclear weapons to gain battlefield advantages. In case that fails, India will respond with a massive second strike. In fact amongst the members of strategic community, credibility of the deterrence depends upon the effectiveness of the second strike capability. Of course, if India becomes a victim of first strike by an aggressor, it is a failure of deterrence and NFU cannot be a doctrine to communicate a sense of vulnerability to an adversary.

Hence, fourth, the credibility of such deterrence would depend upon not only sufficiency but also survivability of nuclear weapons. Of course, there is no clarity as to what constitutes a sufficient level of nuclear weapons; it all depends on the situation at a given time and thinking of policy makers. Minimum of nuclear weapons and delivery system needed in case of one adversary would vary from another. There is no need for Indian government to ever define what it stands for. Hence, it was strange for the Clinton administration to pressurize India to declare what constitutes its minimum! It is next to impossible mathematically to state an accurate figure at any given time or to determine exactly the number of nuclear weapons required to make deterrence effective. This shows the dynamic nature of nuclear deterrence. Even if one makes an intelligent guess today, it might become outdated after some time.

Fifth, the survivability of nuclear weapons, keeping with the doctrine of NFU, depends on dispersal of those weapons. Triad consisting of air force based bombers, army controlled missiles and navy held submarines should help. India is obligated to make its nuclear weapons invulnerable to a surprise first attack by an adversary. Triad assures dispersal of nuclear weapons assuring flexibility of use, makes defence complex deterrence stable. Chinese have given maximum attention to make their defensive nuclear weapons safe by placing them "in caves and deep canyons" well hiding them from adversaries.[16] Indian nuclear doctrine proposes to develop a triad of land, sea and air based assets. It is necessary to disperse nuclear weapons to avoid those becoming easy sitting duck targets in a first strike.

The land based nuclear assets are very easy targets in a nuclear strike against India. To make its commitment of NFU credible enough to any would be adversary, it is necessary to develop air-based nuclear weapons. India has developed a missile programme of series of Agni missiles. While medium range nuclear-capable Agni II missiles with a range of 2500 km are developed and test-fired, what is crucial is Agni III missile with a range of 3500 km which can retaliate against any attack from China.

Submarine Launched Ballistic Missiles (SLBMs) play a very important role in the successful implementation of NFU. Land based bombers and even if we develop ICBMs, they have increasingly become vulnerable. On the other hand, Super Powers have so far not been able to find a means to locate a Submerged Ballistic Missile Submarines on patrol. This has meant that submarine based nuclear weapons have become more important in nuclear deterrence. Submarines have also become quieter with the technology development, which makes them more difficult to detect.[17]

Hence real test, utility and credibility and efficacy of triad under the commitment of NFU, in the ultimate analysis, depend upon the acquisition of sea-based missile capability to carry nuclear weapons. Sea based assets really can provide a capability in stealth operations. Sea based missiles can also ensure greater invulnerability of the second strike capability against the enemy attack and hence their higher survivability that enhances credibility of the doctrine.

Sixth, the NFU is a declaratory policy; hence what are the verifiable means that distinguish it from the FU? There are at least three ways in which the NFU policy distinguishes itself from the FU policy. First, the nuclear weapons are not physically deployed. Second, nuclear warheads are maintained in dealerted or deactivated way. Removing warheads from the delivery system is the easiest way of dealerting nuclear weapons.[18] Third, the nuclear weapons are maintained by the Atomic Energy Commission and not by the Armed Forces. Though as an exception, the SLBM based nuclear weapons have to be in the submarine, but dealerting would be achieved by technical means such as "pinning open the motor ignition switches of missiles, making it impossible to fire them until the pins have been manually removed."[19]

Advantages

Indian Policy of NFU is not without its own rationale. Indian philosophy and foreign policy mind is accustomed to negative thought process. *Brihadaranyaka Upanishad* (chapter II, section iii) teaches *Neti, Neti* (nothing). After watching the destruction brought about by Atom Bomb, Robert Oppenheimer is said to have uttered *Neti, Neti*. India began its foreign policy with a negative approach of non-alignment. Indian independence was an outcome of Gandhian non-violence. As a reluctant nuclear weapon state, a commitment to NFU is logically and philosophically, indicative of policy of restraint in the use of WMD.

The doctrine of NFU is more democratic in contrast to the FU. In first use the nuclear weapons, per force have to be placed with the armed forces for instant use. But in NFU since nuclear weapons are used only for a second strike, the weapons could be held by a different agency other than the armed forces. Indian democracy as a nascent experiment did not bestow much confidence in the nation's armed services, at least in the early period. After sixty two years of independence the distrust in the armed services has by now been considerably reduced. As a matter of fact, there is a small beginning in co-operation between armed service and nuclear scientists with the initiation of co-operation for involvement of three service men in the BARC in weapons' manufacturing.[20]

Beyond that, there are political—global and national, economic, moral and even practical advantages of the policy. Globally as a late entrant to the nuclear weapons club, who is yet to be admitted even as a full member,[21] it is in India's interest to maintain a low profile on use of nuclear weapons. Since international society has not yet grown beyond self-help stage in protecting once own security, others accepted seriousness of Indian security threat perceptions only when India went nuclear.

India faced national security threat from two fronts—from Pakistan on north-western and China from north-eastern. Since India's potential security threat emerged from China, India would not have been able to enter into an arms race with that country. China is also committed to NFU policy; even then Chinese nuclear weapons in terms of quantity and quality are superior to those of India. China has also in relation to India well developed means of delivery system of nuclear weapons. A policy of minimum/credible nuclear deterrence with no first use only enhances India's sense of security. It shows that India is not in competition with China in developing nuclear weapons. These weapons of mass destruction, if used at all, are used as weapons of self-defence make sense globally.

In domestic politics, though a majority was in favour of India going nuclear, there are sizeable politically left leaning—supporters of Communist Parties but more so China-inspired and independently left leaning forces which were opposed to Indian nuclear tests. It was not uncommon to see communists demonstrating in India against the US bomb (India was no where in the picture in 1980s talking about bomb). For them NFU is like a soothing balm for pain relieving and expected to make it more acceptable. NFU as a politico-military doctrine should help to increase communist loyalty to India!

It is also economically sensible, since Indian main concern has been economic development to uplift millions of people above the poverty line. As a policy, India had always limited resource allocation to armed forces at an absolute minimum level. P.V. Narasimha Rao had reduced the defence budget. When the Kargil Committee asked him as to why the defence was cut during his time he had replied, "That was because the nuclear deterrent was under development and that had priority."[22] This shows budgetary crunch experienced by the government and compulsions of limiting at one end to meet the needs at the other.

Alternative to the NFU is the First Use (FU); it would have meant India as an aggressive nation willing to strike fear of destruction by threatening the use of nuclear weapons. Such a position would inevitably mean keeping nuclear weapons in hair-trigger alertness inevitably in ready to fire position. That could mean also an invitation for pre-emptive attack by any adversary. It would have been an invitation in a developing democracy to armed forces to play a major role. NFU in association with minimum/credible deterrence really limits the role of nuclear weapons as weapons of retaliation. Hence, their role in military planning and budget should get limited. This would really help India to strengthen civilian control over the armed forces that it has been so fortunate to maintain since independence.

The NFU also, in a practical sense has certain benefits in policy formulation. India might say that its policy to go nuclear was compelled by the potential security threat from China. But having identified the source of threat and gone for a few nuclear weapons—is only a part of the solution. But India needs to develop a delivery system for the nuclear weapons, which are going to be used only in a second strike, but in a massive way. India is yet to achieve the triad capability. It takes time, and the NFU provides that time for the policy makers.

A commitment to the doctrine NFU prevents or at least minimises the possibilities of accidental start of nuclear wars; it lowers the risk of nuclear war by miscalculation. There have been several incidents of false alarms raised by failures in computers in western nuclear weapons states, creating a false alarm over the incoming of enemy nuclear capable missiles. In the US, there have been many such incidents. In June 1980 there was an alarm over the Soviet Union launching an SLBM attack, which was a computer malfunctioning.[23] At least in case of countries committed to NFU, they would not insist on taking any pre-emptive strike, as it would amount to First Use of nuclear weapons!

NUCLEAR DISARMAMENT

Despite these advantages, there are a few who would like India to denuclearize and move towards nuclear disarmament. Former Chairman of Atomic Energy Commission, P.K. Iyengar, for instance, stressed the need "to evolve a national consensus on the country's short-term and long-term policies on nuclear deterrence and disarmament."[24] George Perkovich, an American scholar who worked on Indian Bomb from American perspective, says: "India lost much of the moral credibility it had as a champion of disarmament in the eyes of other states."[25] But certain questions arise: Can India pursue unilateral nuclear disarmament, particularly, when you are threatened by two nuclear neighbours? Did moral credibility help India to enhance her security, in any way? Does morality govern the nuclear policy? Isn't that in world politics, morality also depends on power?

On the other hand, I think, H.V. Kamath, former member of the Constituent Assembly was right when he described, in the aftermath of first Chinese nuclear test in October 1964, Indian pronouncements that "we can make the bomb, but we would not do it" as pig-headed.[26] Similarly, it is appropriate here also to recall the words of another member of the Constituent Assembly, Prof. Shibban Lal Saksena, who had said: "If we have not got the knowledge and the ability to use this power [of atom], there is no virtue in our saying that we shall not use it for destructive purposes and that other people should not use it...."[27]

Critics of Indian nuclear weapons ought to note the fact that the US decided to seek China as a partner in geopolitical balancing of the then Soviet Union in 1971 only because 7 years earlier it had become a NWS. The US also could agree to detarget their nuclear weapons against China only when China acquired modern nuclear weapons and capability to deliver them against the American territory. It shows the states respect power, and only those who have power are listened to on international issues of significance. Hence, Indian NWS status should help her to pursue seriously idea of nuclear disarmament.

Thus, the Indian nuclear doctrine states, "global, verifiable and non-discriminatory nuclear disarmament is a national security objective." Advocacy of nuclear disarmament has been an important principle of Indian foreign policy since independence. India had played a significant and positive role in promoting nuclear disarmament through Partial Test Ban Treaty 1963. It is undeniably true that India has consistently taken an anti-nuclear stance in its foreign policy. In 1978, India proposed an international convention prohibiting use or threat of use of nuclear weapons. During Rajiv Gandhi's tenure as Prime Minister India took a global step in promoting Four Continent Peace Initiative in 1988.[28] Hence, Indian military strategy, even after acquisition of nuclear weapons is not based on the use of these weapons of mass destruction.

However, nuclear disarmament has to include all those who possess nuclear weapons and all those on the threshold of it. India now sees that she can speak on nuclear disarmament more authoritatively. But in pursuit of global disarmament, we need to change our approach: instead of pushing for total nuclear disarmament, in the beginning, we need to move step by step towards that goal.

HYPER SUPER POWER: MOVER OR MOWER?

In the ultimate analysis, the goal of nuclear disarmament could be met only when the major nuclear powers like the five nuclear weapons states—the US, Russia, Britain, France and China—who are also five permanent members of the UN Security Council, take lead in reducing drastically nuclear weapons held by them with the aim of achieving time-bound nuclear disarmament. Of these, the US needs to play an active role in giving up nuclear hegemony and its NATO allies need to exercise their influence towards that goal.

Towards that goal, the doctrine of NFU can be strengthened and made more relevant to the goal of nuclear disarmament globally if the Hyper Super Power of the day—the US is made to take the NFU doctrine seriously and lend its moral and political support to it. But it is not being able to do it, despite enjoying unchallenged power, and to rise gradually above its narrowly interpreted national interest. It has to ponder over the fact that if every nation pursues its national interest in a narrow perspective as done by it, there will only be proliferation of number of NWS. Since the PTBT of 1963 left underground tests as legal—only because of the US and USSR's national interest—India conducted its first nuclear test in 1974 and declared itself as a NWS. Pakistan followed it. Instead, if the comprehensive test ban treaty had materialized in 1963 itself in place of PTBT, probably India would have limited itself to computer simulated tests in a later period![29]

If the US adopts a NFU policy, it will be a major step towards nuclear disarmament. Such a pledge on the part of the US can be unilateral, bilateral or multilateral since NFU is a declaratory policy to begin with. It is not that the US is totally unaccustomed to the NFU. An element of it, of not using nuclear weapons against a non-nuclear weapons state was briefly practiced for four years by the Carter administration. There is no need for any international mechanism for its enforcement. For the US such a policy even if it is unilateral, it would be less subjected to bureaucratic infighting between State, Defence and the White House in policy making. Once there is the greater domestic consensus, NFU could also be considered for inclusion as an element of War Powers Act 1973. A policy of NFU restrains President's use or threat of use of nuclear weapons to an extent of making other nations' willingness to break such a pledge. President has always power to use the nuclear weapons for retaliation in the unlikely event of a first strike.

The US might argue that NFU could always create uncertainties as nations could break their pledge making NFU very fragile. This fear is similar to the one it had on reliability of verification before it went ahead with the then Soviet Union on Partial Test Ban Treaty in 1963. But it has worked fairly well in protecting the global environment much before nations became conscious of global warming or the role-played by clean 'environment' in human welfare. But if the US wants to add teeth to NFU it can enter into a treaty on a bilateral or multilateral basis.

The US was hyper-critical of Indian nuclear tests.[30] Biggest anomaly in the US response to Indian nuclear doctrine is its failure to explain why does it need 12,000 nuclear warheads, when it has proposed to detarget them against Russia and China? According to former CIA Director, Stansfield Turner, the US needs only 200 warheads for an effective deterrence against a threat from Russia and China.[31] The US now justifies nuclear weapons on the ground of challenge from rogue states and terrorist groups. For even to deter rogue states and friends turned adversaries, so many nuclear warheads are unnecessary and waste of resources. In reality, is there any need to exceed the mass destruction 6 to 10 times more than Hiroshima?

MOVE TOWARDS INTERNATIONAL TREATY ON NUCLEAR DISARMAMENT

In conclusion, Indian nuclear tests of 11 and 13 May, 1998 have given a new direction to International relations. It has given an impetus to the emergence of a multipolar world with India as one pole with others like the US, Russia, China, UK and France. Even though, India would not like another nuclear armed nation on its north-west with Iran pushing its nuclear ambitions forward, India or to that matter even the US would not be able to prevent emergence of new nuclear weapons states as long as they feel threatened. If China becomes politically more aggressive in East Asia, it may give birth to Japan to come out from its virtual NWS status. In the event Iran going nuclear, it is obvious no force on the earth could prevent Israel from overtly becoming nuclear.

NFU of the Indian strategic doctrine could be considered, therefore, as a first step towards ultimate emergence of No Use of nuclear weapons. Hence, India will continue to advocate—from a position of strength—global nuclear disarmament. In other words, with nuclear power, a nation is believed more than a non-NWS, when it advocates nuclear disarmament. India is weaker than five other NWS, yet, India has now acquired nuclear know-how, power and capability. It is time for India to lead other NWS with their destructive power of nuclear weapons to unite them to achieve global disarmament.

The step has to be taken for a global treaty amongst the known nuclear powers and threshold states on no-first use of nuclear weapons.[32] The 1995 Noble Peace Laureate, Sir Joseph Rotblat had called for a treaty among nuclear weapon states that commits them never to be the first to use nuclear weapons. No first use Rotblat rightly thought "would open the way to the gradual, mutual reductions of nuclear arsenals, down to zero."[33] Only obstacle today in achieving that goal is the US and Pakistan which have based their doctrines of nuclear deterrence on the basis of a first use. That was it; nothing more was heard later on about it.

A multilateral agreement under the UN Conference on Disarmament could bind the nations to a greater extent to follow the spirit of treaty. The definition of the use of nuclear weapons under the treaty should be so constructed as to include use of those weapons to blackmail non-nuclear nations as well. Indian plea for a treaty on NFU of Nuclear Weapons as a first step towards nuclear disarmament cannot be dismissed as mere idealism in an anarchical international society, emerging from its comparative weakness of power.[34] When President Woodrow Wilson sought to promote collective security through the League of Nations, he was not pleading for world body acting on collective security on the basis only of weakness.

Movement even on this new treaty on NFU has necessarily to be slow. Since China is the first one to internationally commit on NFU and continue it as the state policy and successfully maintain the policy during the post Cold War period, it should not have any problem in joining hands with India which has also declared NFU as its stated policy on the use of nuclear weapons. However, as there is lot of historic baggage of mistrust between the two as a result of the Chinese aggression of October 1962, and their unresolved border conflict, two coming together may take some time.

In this regard, Russia has a history of ambiguous commitment to NFU doctrine. But since the end of the Cold War, Russia had often spoken of a strategic triangle between Russia, China and India. An analysis of the background of its reference to the strategic triangle shows that its frustration with the US policies in international relations affecting its friends or former allies has made it to speak of forming a strategic alliance.[35]

But with the end of the bipolar world of the Cold War period, major powers today, other than the US, which obviously wants to retain its status as number one power unchallenged, clamour for emergence of a multipolar world. Russia, European Union, India and China among others have all preferred a multipolar world. In a multipolar world there could be issue-based alliances but there cannot be any strategic alliance as proposed by Russia.

However, Russia could take initiative in promoting an understanding between India and China on the issue of NFU by joining them in making it a first stage of nuclear disarmament. Russia's predecessor state, the Soviet Union and China had announced during the Cold War their commitment to NFU of nuclear weapons. But after the end of the Cold War, Russia and China have been ambiguous on the issue. Hence, a successful conclusion of No First Use treaty will greatly reduce the threat of nuclear war.

But even here, gradual movement towards the goal could be envisaged. Since the US, globally and Pakistan regionally see the need for retaining their nuclear weapons, India can pursue more vigorously, such a treaty on NFU of nuclear weapons with China. Since Russian Prime Minister, Primakov had in December 1998 proposed a strategic triangle between itself, China and India, India could persuade Russia to take lead in bringing India and China together on the issue of signing a NFU treaty. Later others could be persuaded to join.

With Russia joining in the efforts by the NWS to pledge themselves on NFU of nuclear weapons, India and China could firm up their efforts on the promotion of the treaty on NFU. There is absolutely no perception of a security threat in the UK and France. These two together with Germany constitute troika in the European Union. European Union has developed in the background of long experience of war and destruction a better appreciation of human rights.

The treaty on NFU of nuclear weapons is a measure to ensure human rights and human life are promoted on a global plane. If the EU also joins in the promotion of a treaty on NFU of nuclear weapons, who is left out? Only two countries—US and Pakistan, which have nothing in common, except their love for first use of nuclear weapons. If global democracies come together to promote denuclearization, the US could join other democracies in committing itself to NFU doctrine.

While rejecting NFU offered by India, Pakistan in its pursuit of one upmanship, in politics of unknown in nuclear arena, had offered in May 2003 nuclear disarmament if India does the same, knowing full well that Indian nuclear programme is not –Pakistan-specific.[36] Yet there are saner voices in between in Pakistan. It is worth noting that then Pakistani Foreign Minister, Sartaz Aziz stated in November 1998 that Pakistan would not deploy nuclear weapons if India agrees to a similar restraint. This was a good offer, which should be taken up at the diplomatic level for further negotiations and formal agreement. These steps suggested could be unilaterally implemented.

Once the US joins the movement for treaty on NFU, Pakistan can be brought around to fall in line. However, Pakistan is likely to ask for its pound of flesh. The trends in India-Pakistan bilateral strategic relations seem to indicate that a claim for strategic equality is going to be future emphasis in Pakistan's policy. Having considered nuclear weapons, as equalizer of strike force, it is bound to maintain it that way in all aspects of nuclear weapons and related agreements. It might agree for NFU if there is a parity of nuclear weapons. If the parity is the only condition, global community could agree for it, on the condition that its economy is not pumped with oxygen by way of foreign aid by the global community. Destination of nuclear disarmament through NFU is not easy to reach, but it is better to move in that direction than embrace nuclear annihilation by insisting on use of nuclear weapons.

REFERENCES

1. Americans are fond of creating very attractive and meaningful acronyms. Under their influence, Mind is an acronym to indicate Indian doctrine of nuclear deterrence.
2. Former German Foreign Minister Fischer made a suggestion in mid-November, 1998 that in the absence of a threat, NATO adopt the proposal of no first use of nuclear weapons. In another instance, at a meeting held in Maryland in March 2006 a listener asked President George W. Bush, whether he will ponder over a proposition "to consider a 'no first use' policy to help the prospect of nuclear [non] proliferation in the long run." See P.M. Kamath, *India's Policy of No First Use of Nuclear Weapons: Relevance to Peace and Security in South Asia* (New Delhi: Anamika Publications, 2009), pp. 213, 218.
3. For the complete text of the draft of Indian Nuclear Doctrine, see *Observer of Business and Politics* (Mumbai), 20 August, 1999.
4. There are two changes. One while the draft had promised "assured retaliation" final document speaks of "massive response". Second, draft uses the term "unacceptable damage" while the final document speaks of "unacceptable punishment."
5. IPCS's Special Report 13, "India's Credible Minimum Deterrence: A Report, February, 2006, http://www.ipcs.org/IPCS-Special-Report-13.pdf However, for the convenience, in this article, I propose to use MIND as the acronym throughout the discussion, irrespective of whether it meant a reference to it during the NDA term or the UPA since May, 2004.
6. See P.M. Kamath, "Indian Nuclear Strategy: A Perspective for 2020," *Strategic Analysis*, Vol. 22, No. 12 (March, 1999), pp. 1941-42.
7. See transcripts of Wolf Blitzer's interview, *Strategic Digest,* Vol. 35, No. 9 (2005), p. 1151.

8. Minimum can be credible if every component of the nuclear deterrence, particularly triad, is in place.
9. In an interview with K. Subrahmanyam in New Delhi in November, 2004.
10. Quoted by Morton H. Halperin, *Nuclear* Fallacy: *Dispelling the Myth of Nuclear Strategy* (Cambridge, MA: Ballinger Publishing Co.), p. 8
11. See "Memorandum by the counsellor (Kennan)", *Foreign Relations of the United States*, 1950, Vol. 1, p. 29 (Emphasis added).
12. *Ibid.*
13. George F. Kennan, *Memoirs,* 1925-1950 (Boston: Atlantic Monthly Press, 1967), p. 472.
14. For details see P.M. Kamath, "No First Use of Nuclear Weapons: Sino-Indian Doctrine of Peace," *India Quarterly: A Journal of International Affairs*, Vol. 63, No. 2 (April-June, 2007).
15. For the text of the doctrine see *The Observer of Business and Politics* (Mumbai & New Delhi), August 20, 1999.
16. Lewis and Litai, *China Builds the Bomb*, p. 215.
17. Laurence Martin, *The Changing Face of Nuclear Warfare*, pp. 120-22.
18. For details of de-alerting and various ways, techniques, and benefits see Arjun Makhijani, "De-Alerting: A First Step," http://www.ieer.org/latest/de-alert.html
19. *Ibid.* (Author's footnote ignored).
20. Army Chief of Staff, General J.J. Singh lauded Army and BARC co-operation in having three officers trained in BARC, *Times of India* (Mumbai), 26 August, 2005.
21. US-India Civil Nuclear Deal of 2005, is a *de facto* recognition of India as a NWS.
22. K. Subrahmanyam, "Narasihma Rao and the Bomb," *Strategic Analysis*, Vol. 28, No. 4, 2004, p. 593.
23. Ann E. Weiss, *The Nuclear Arms Race: Can We Survive It?* (Boston: Houghton Mifflin Co., 1983), pp. 50-51.
24. P.K. Iyengar, "Imperatives before India", *Frontline*, Vol. 17, No. 15, (July 24-August 4, 2000).
25. George Perkovich, *India's Nuclear Bomb*, p. 439.
26. Quoted in George Perkovich, *India's Nuclear Bomb: The Impact on Global Proliferation* (Berkeley, CA: University of California Press, 1999), pp. 118-19.
27. Quoted in George Perkovich, *India's Nuclear Bomb*, p. 19.
28. See http://parliamentofindia.nic.in/ls//lsdeb/ls12/ses2/0527059801.htm
29. Perkovich raises a hypothetical question: "…whether if a comprehensive ban had been agreed to in 1963 India would have gone forward with its nuclear weapon option." *India's Nuclear Bomb*, p. 58.
30. For details see P.M. Kamath, "Indian Nuclear Strategy: A Perspective for 2020," *Strategic Analysis,* Vol. 22, No. 12, (March, 1999), pp. 1934-46.
31. Stansfield Turner, *Caging the Nuclear Genie: An American Challenge for Global Security* (Colorado: Westview, 1998).

32. See P.M. Kamath, "Post-Pokhran Permutations," The *Tribune* (Chandigarh), June 17, 1998.
33. As quoted by David Krieger and Carah Ong, "No First Use", April, 2002, http://www.wagingpeace.org/articles/2002/04/00_krieger_no-first-use_print.htm
34. I had first put forward this idea of a treaty on NFU of nuclear weapons in an article, "Indian National Security Policy: Minimal Nuclear Deterrence," published in *Strategic Analysis*, Vol. 23, No. 8 (November, 1999).
35. P.M. Kamath, "Is Primakov triangle theory workable?" *Free Press Journal* (Mumbai), 14 January, 1999.
36. Owen Bennett-Jones, "Have nuclear weapons made South Asia safer?" http:/newsvote.bbc.co.uk/mpapps/pagetools/print/news.bbc.co.uk/1hi/world/south_asia/3015…

10
Traditional to Ideology-based Terrorism: Case for Alternative Policies

P. Lazarus Samraj

The Maoist violence-estimated to cause 600 to 700 deaths annually and the displacement of 100,000 civilians has spread to 182 of India's 602 districts and has been declared by the then Prime Minister of India Dr. Manmohan Singh as the country's single biggest internal security challenge. The Maoists have stepped up violence across eastern and central India. They have attacked schools and police stations, and used landmines and Improvised Explosive Devices (IEDs) to disrupt infrastructure development projects. They also target the informers as counter revolutionaries. The main objective of the Maoists is to prevent the development of infrastructure in remote areas, which so far has remained their exclusive domain. Thousands have been killed by Maoists in the recent past. The Maoists claim that they are fighting for the rights of poor farmers and landless labourers, but they are denying all the government initiatives to help the people of tribal areas to the fast losing credibility as they continue attacking schools, hospitals and infrastructure projects. The outlawed Communist Party of India, Maoist, CPI (Maoist), named a terror outfit by the central government last month, has issued a threat to the then Prime Minister Manmohan Singh, Congress President Sonia Gandhi and dared Home Minister P. Chidambaram to visit Jharkhand. "Home Minister P. Chidambaram says the government will end Maoism in the country. His statement will remain a dream. It is not possible to end the Maoist movement… If Chidambaram has the courage, he should come to Jharkhand," the CPI (Maoist) said in a press release issued here late Monday. It also threatened Manmohan Singh and United Progressive Alliance (UPA) Chairperson Sonia Gandhi. "Both the PM and Sonia Gandhi will meet a fate like former Prime Minister,

Late Rajiv Gandhi," said the release issued by Anup-ji, a member of the Jharkhand State Central Committee of the CPI (Maoist). The CPI-Maoist, in the statement, has also threatened Congress leaders in Jharkhand, asking them to quit the party or face dire consequences.[1]

To address the serious domestic menace the Central and the State governments are competing with each other in implementing problems as solutions. At one side Prime Minister says that the Central government will not use military forces against its own people and another side Home Minister is for using all means to eradicate the menace. At the same time Maoists are answering the government initiatives with series of bandhs, propaganda, threats and violent attacks. Against this background this chapter makes an attempt to suggest the problem solving other non-traditional ways and means to address the menace of Domestic terrorism.

SHARING THE CAKE OF DEVELOPMENTS

One of the important causes for the growth of ideological based domestic terrorism in and around the red corridors of India is the successive government's failure to share the cake of development with the tribal people of the jungles and the continuous exploitation of their resources and depriving them with other basic facilities. The sixty plus years of electoral democracy has failed to address their genuine demands and pushed them towards accepting the ideology which believes in violence and instant action and result. The socially and economically deprived people who are ideologically indoctrinated cannot be tamed or reformed or forced to join the main path through the negative means adopted by the State and Central government agencies. Instead they have to go for a new paradigm. Without meeting their genuine demands of basic needs of livelihood it is impossible to win them back into the main stream. When Indian economy was liberalized there was mixed reaction from the Indian intelligentsia and some of them even criticized the government policy as Americanization and helped the rich by sacrificing the concept of welfare states. The fifteen years of liberalization experience undoubtedly depicts the negative picture of India mainly because of widening the income gap between the rich and the poor. At one side, the rural people are losing their livelihood and the poor people are moving towards the urban areas for their survival to avoid hunger death or suicide. At another side both the Central and the State governments are continuously neglecting the tribal and rural India. For instance the situation in the red corridor States like Jharkhand, Bihar, Orissa, Chattisgarh and part of Andhra Pradesh there are thousands of villagers living without any primary school, water tank, health facility, electricity and road facilities. Who is responsible in spite of the pitiable condition for the sixty plus years of Independence?

The time has come to address the need of the hitherto neglected people of India. We cannot deny the cake of development and expect them as silent spectators ready to suffer silently. They have their own valid justification of violence. To overcome their violent agenda the State and the Central governments should formulate strategies to implement developmental programmes in war footings. Firstly all the tribals in rural areas should be connected through proper roads in all the direction with the urban India. This will help the people to move freely to the town. Secondly cheap public transport facilities should be given to all the neglected areas and the people should be allowed to carry their agricultural products to the urban markets and *vice versa* through government transport facilities. Thirdly, all the dark parts should be lighted with electric connections. In Tamil Nadu the then Chief Minister M.G. Ramachandran provided one free electric light to all the huts of rural and urban Tamil Nadu. These schemes can be implemented in the States where Naxalites are active. This may be followed by other freebies as discussed elsewhere. Fourthly, all the villages should be provided Primary or Middle school or High school facilities according to the population. These schools should be provided with necessary infrastructure facilities so that the teachers can stay and work and even conduct adult education programmes in all the villages. This educational revolution will definitely bring a lot of positive changes. Instead of investing the resources on recruiting new Para Military forces, arming and aiding the government sponsored counter terrorist forces like Salwa Judum, the government can invest its resources on developmental activities. There are so many negative reports on the activities of Salwa Judum, a tribal army armed, supported and aided by Chattisgarh government. Challenging the State government's decision to arm the private groups with latest weapons two cases were filed in the Supreme Court and the Chief Justice K.G. Balakrishnan and Justice Aftab Alam gave a historic judgment on 31 March, 2008. The judges said: "It is a question of law and order; you cannot give arms to somebody (a civilian) and allow him to kill. You will be an abettor of the offence under Section 302 of the Indian Penal Code (murder)[2]. Instead of adopting these kinds of hasty and negative means, the government should meet the challenges with positive agenda of development programmes. In Costa Rica one of the Central American states they dissolved the army in 1949 and invested in education. Increased schooling rated a more stable society, less prone to the conflicts that have raged elsewhere in Central America.

Education also boosted the economy enabling the country to become a major exporter of computer chips and improving English language skills so as to attract American eco-tourists. In Costa Rica, rising education levels fostered impressive gender equality also so that it ranks higher than the United States in the World Economic Forums gender gap index. This allows Costa Rica to use its female population more productively than any other country of the world. Likewise, education nurtured improvements in healthcare, with life expectancy now about the same as in the United States. Rising education levels also led the country to preserve its lush environment as an economic asset. Costa Rica is an ecological pioneer, introducing a carbon tax in 1997. The Environmental Performance Index, a collaboration of Yale and Colombia University, ranks Costa Rica at No. 5 in the world, the best outside Europe. Indeed, Costa Rica is one of the few countries that are seeing migration from United States. Costa Rica's national decision to invest in education rather than arms has paid rich dividends.[3]

If the government is really serious to find a time frame solution for the Maoist problems, it should invest heavily on education. If there is any paucity of funding facilities for infrastructure, the Centre should direct all the Multinationals and Indian Big business houses to divert all the funds for Social responsibility to the tribal and rural areas for another ten years. If the MNCs and other Indian business houses are encouraged to adopt one or more villages it will make a greater impact on rural and tribal India. The government should take utmost care to provide health facilities to the tribal and rural India. Even today thousands are suffering from malaria and other communicable as well as serious diseases without any medical facilities. The Government should encourage the doctors to serve for the needy by providing hospital facilities. As discussed elsewhere, medical missionaries from all the religions may be encouraged to work in the remote parts of India with necessary incentives. Unless the government is ready to address the basic needs of the people and to share the cake of development with the underdeveloped it is impossible to win them back in the peaceful path of non-violence.

DEEPENING PARTICIPATORY DEMOCRACY

Based on the vision of our founding father it is necessary to systematically decentralize the powers by politically and financially empowering the people of the remote and neglected regions of India. The colonial and feudalistic mind set of the opinionated bureaucracy should be convinced that without sharing the power with the local people it is impossible to win them back into the main stream. Of course experimenting democracy among the inexperienced and uneducated people is a Himalayan task. Here, it is necessary for drafting a separate Pantheist law suitable to their conditions. For instance, the proposed law can accommodate more non-elected members as advisors without voting rights. Keeping these things in mind, a teacher or the Head Master of the nearest school, a Doctor from the nearest health centre and one or two faculty from the nearest college may be given special representation for the proposed Pantheist. If possible they can accommodate one or two NGO representatives who are working among the villagers. These members may continue to guide the newly elected representatives with adequate inputs on good governance and also train them on policy formulation and implementation. This new set-up will help the local administration to act without much interference from the corrupt bureaucracy and traditional power centres like the feudal lords, religious heads and other tribal chieftains who are continuously exploiting the people. The local higher educational institutions can periodically evaluate the performance of the local administration and give them valuable inputs for future policies and programmes. If government has succeeded in forming a new coalition of well trained local leaders, committed NGOs, dedicated teaching community along with the active support of the bureaucrats the local problem will be definitely addressed in the long run. The untrained, inexperienced and directionless local leaders can bring more harm than help to the local people by fuelling on the fire of frustration. Because they have no other alternative but to form an unholy alliance with the Police, corrupt bureaucrats, landlords, arrack traders and other anti-social elements to loot the government fund and to exploit the poor people and claim legitimacy in the name of popular election which are strongly opposed by the Maoists. To overcome the problem the only solution is to provide good governance to the neglected people by winning their support by implementing welfare measures and by involving them in developmental activities.

INVOLVING NGOs AND EDUCATIONALISTS IN POLICY MAKING AND IMPLEMENTATION

One of the legacies of British colonial administrative set-up in India is the neglect of Higher Educational Institutions in policy making and implementation. Though we proudly claim that we have gained independence from the colonial yoke, our people are not free from the colonial Bureaucratic bondages. The red tapism, formalities, secrecies, etc., are not allowing the administration to tune according to the changing environments and developments. However, the economic liberalization initiated by Narasimha Rao government and other administrative reforms in one way created a lot of positive impact in the Indian economy. But, unlike the other developed democracies, the Indian policy makers are not ready to accommodate and listen to the voices of the intelligentsia of higher educational institutions. This negative trend is prevailing from central administrative set-up to local administrative set-up. We are at the early stages of twenty-first century which is well known for accountability, transparency, right to information, all forms of justice, judicial activism, participatory democracy and respecting the sentiments of the local people mainly because of the electoral democracy. In this context, it is must to go for a paradigm shift in Indian administration from top to bottom. First we should allow all the higher educational institutions to take part in policy formulations, implementation and periodical evaluation. To do these exercises in a fruitful manner, the government should finance these institutions to enable them to undertake problem solving and socially relevant research projects to help the policy makers to introduce necessary amendments in their future programmes. As discussed elsewhere, each local administration should be represented with one or two ex-officio members from the local higher educational institutions, one doctor from the Primary Health Department wherever they are available, and one or two senior staff from NGOs who are working for the betterment of the local people of the region. The newly added educated representatives will definitely help the inexperienced and uneducated local leaders to run the administration and to initiate and implement people oriented programmes in a successful way. Moreover, it will help a corrupt free and bureaucratic free administration at the local level. Good local administration is the best cure for the ills of ideological based local violence.

INTRODUCING POPULAR SCHEMES TO ADDRESS THEIR IMMEDIATE NEEDS AND TO PROVIDE THEM ADEQUATE TRAINING ON OPPORTUNITIES

Welfare State concept emphasizes the importance of taking care of the basic needs of all sections of the people. The universal adult franchise and the multiparty elections directly and indirectly influence the political agenda of almost all the political parties of India. Most of the ruling parties and parties in waiting are generously giving promises to the people living below the poverty line. One of the causes for violent revolution is the denial of the basic needs and poverty in spite of plenty. One cannot prevent the hungry stomach from indulging in violent actions. Understanding the reality, the ideological based parties are justifying their agenda on violent revolution among the frustrated youths. To address the threat the government can take multidimensional approach. One way is to provide them the basic needs of life as the Tamil Nadu State government is doing. Tamil Nadu government under Karunanidhi is successfully implementing some welfare schemes like one kg rice for one rupee and free colour TV to all the people, free dress during festival times apart from implementing Central government programme of hundred days working hours under the MGNREGA. These programmes are supplemented by women self-help groups. If the State and Central governments join together in introducing more welfare schemes aimed at meeting the basic needs of the tribals of India, they will slowly ignore the ideology based violent groups. Further, the information technology can be effectively used to convey to the marginalized people in life building opportunities.

Here, it is pertinent to point out that Tamil Nadu is free from ideology based violent groups for the past two and half decades. The major reason being the implementation of a number of welfare schemes directed to improve the living conditions of the poor. Though there are political parties, media and think tanks who often criticize the exercises of the ruling parties for the overdosing with freebies, directly and indirectly these freebies are helping the poor to shed violent means to achieve their livelihood. Further, these free benefits are helping them to stand on their own instead of looking at the hands of the local affluent for alms. Trusting and expecting some good things from the government at least for a short run make the people violent free. Tamil Nadu experiments can be successfully implemented among the tribal areas where the poor people are struggling for their survival and continuously exploited by the landlords and middle men for decades together.

Further, through media and other NGOs government can help the poor people with the windows of opportunities available for them, for unawareness of the development facilities and benefits is one of the causes for the underdevelopment as well as frustration which may lead to violence. Further, the government and the Panchayati Raj with the help of NGOs who are really interested and committed can start training centres for the educated youths and women to prepare them to enjoy the benefits available to them. One of the important causes for frustration among the youths is that they are not adequately prepared to enter the door of development to enjoy the fruits of development. Therefore, preparing them to enter the door of opportunities should be given utmost importance. These initiatives will definitely give a lot of dividends in the long run.

OPENING THE GATES OF OPPORTUNITIES TO OTHER PARTS OF INDIA

At present the Constitution of India guarantees reservations for Scheduled Tribes along with the Scheduled Castes and Other Backward Classes. However, the past experiences reveal that the fruits of reservations are enjoyed repeatedly by the microscopic affluent minorities of each community leaving the majority to continue to suffer. Most of the silently suffering majority will not be aware of the benefits available to them unless somebody shows them the windows of opportunities available and their benefits. Moreover, most of the entrance and recruitment examinations are conducted only in urban centres which are far away from most of the tribal areas. Therefore, most of the allotted vacancies are not filled up by most of the Central and State sponsored institutions. Another area of concern is that most of the ST vacancies are enjoyed by the North-Eastern people because of their higher educational standard and standard of living. Moreover they are well connected with all the information technology and other networking. Consequently, the youths of the red corridor States are deprived of the benefits given to them. For instance, for the year 2008, 66 seats of the 720 total numbers available for SC & ST candidates at the six new IITs are lying vacant. Of these 66 seats, 47 are for ST candidates. According to their information, it has been difficult to find ST students for IITs said Prof. Dhande.[4] In this context, it is necessary to formulate strategies to address the problems of the people. First, there should special training centres to conduct preparatory course in the Tribal areas or the government should establish special hostel facilities in the urban areas with cent per cent subsidiary. Secondly, there should be separate reservation for first generation candidates within the ST community for another twenty five years in admissions in schools and institutions of higher education apart from in job openings. Thirdly, with the consensus the government can allocate certain percentage of seats exclusively for the red corridor areas just as it is done for the candidates of Kashmir origin (including migrants from Kashmir).[5] Similarly, special recruitment training centres should be established in the tribal areas for identifying suitable candidates for various jobs in different parts of India. Opening the windows of opportunities and guaranteeing suitable jobs for the youths of the sensitive areas will create a lot of positive impact in the long run. Further, government can initiate many women Self-Help Groups and Self-Employment Opportunities based on the availability of natural resources.

ADOPTING FLEXIBLE JUDICIAL INSTRUMENT AND GUARANTEE OF DECENT LIFE AFTER SURRENDER

Forgiving the mistakes of others and accepting and accommodating them with genuine generosity may change the heart of the offender than cruel punishment. Almost all the religions preach the need of forgiving the mistakes of others. One of the important causes for the continuous involvement of the youths in violence without surrendering is that they don't have any guarantee for forgiveness but to face the brutal cruelty of the Police force or death. Therefore, the ideologically addicted youths are not ready to surrender and determine to fight till their death instead of undergoing the torture of the Police and the judicial procedures. Here, the Indian administration should learn from the Italian experience. During 60s Italy was beset with Leftist, Rightist as well as Mafia oriented violent groups which disturbed peace at all levels. Moreover, the lack of political stability and change of governments every week led to the breakdown of the administrative machinery. In this context the Italians have undergone series of terrorist threats and subsequently, the government initiated so many harsh laws against the violent groups. However, they found it counter productive and destructive for the harsh pursuit policy generated series of violence of different nature. It was reported that from 1969 to 1986 both the leftist and the rightists carried out 14,569 attacks and 415 people lost their lives and 1,181 seriously wounded.[6] Consequently, after a lot of indepth discussion and rational thinking the Parliament of Italy introduced two farsighted laws. The first law entitled Legge Cossiga No. 625 was passed in December 15, 1979 assuring the individuals and groups indulged in violence with many concessions and benefits if they are ready to cooperate with Judiciary and Police. It also assured that there will not be any harassment by the Police against the surrendered people. The second Act was passed in 29 May, 1982 named Legge Sui Pentiti No. 304, which encouraged the youths to disassociate from the terrorist groups and also guaranteed them peace and security.[7] Consequently, some youths started disassociating themselves from the terrorist groups. Because of the sincerity of the government officials who were in charge of the projects so many Italian youths volunteered to surrender or disassociate from the terrorist groups.

The successful Italian model for addressing the terrorist menace was successfully experimented in Jammu & Kashmir in 2004 through the joint initiatives of the State and Central governments. Consequently, the terrorists who were operating in the hill regions of Magur and Uthambur districts for more than seven years under the banner of Hizbul Mujaheedin and Jaish-e-Mohammed surrendered before the senior army officials. The government showed their generosity to the surrendered youths with one and half lakh fixed deposits and monthly livelihood allowance of Rs. 2,000 per month.[8] This positive offence may be initiated by the State and Central governments with the help of the educational institutions, NGOs and even missionary movements for the local groups pursuing violence are not ready to trust the government machineries. The people involving in negative means will never trust the government machinery which believes in violence. For instance, accepting the invitation of the great social worker Jayaprakash Narayan the Sambal valley dacoits surrendered by laying arms and similarly the famous Jungle robber Jembulingam of Donavur area surrendered under the feet of famous Christian missionary mother Kar Michael. History shows that even the worst criminal is ready to surrender under the feet of selfless god loving people with service mentality.

PROVIDING SPECIAL LEADERSHIP TRAINING TO THE BUREAUCRATS AND THE PEOPLE'S REPRESENTATIVES

> "I am afraid of an army of ten thousand goats led by a lion than an army of ten thousand lions led by a goat".
>
> – *A Russian General*

Leadership makes a lot of difference in all walks of life. A good leader is one who thinks ahead of times and shows the way, walks the way and leads the way to his followers by setting the best example based on his vision. A leader without vision is like a mission without purpose. Now we live in a period of visionless and directionless leaders. Obviously, the greatest crisis of the twenty-first century is the leadership crisis at all levels. Opinionated, parochial, short-sighted, self centred, corrupt and visionless leaders can do more harm than help to any system. Understandably, it is high time for the educational institutions and other leadership training centres to take special initiatives to offer short term and long term leadership training courses to the local people representatives as well the bureaucrats who are working in the sensitive areas on development works. The course curriculum should include time management, goal setting, integrity, leadership qualities, decision making, consultation, accepting criticism, accommodating dissent voices of different people groups, development opportunities, sharing the cake of developments and information, involving talented people in policy making and implementation, fund raising techniques, project preparation, planning the work and working the plan, family building with integrity, handling the sensitivity of the different people groups, women empowerment, child care, youth empowerment, preserving and promoting their culture, moral and ethical living, saving techniques, investment opportunities, scientific tools and techniques available for farming, e-governance, initiating collaborative and cooperative works with other people groups, NGOs, other non-profit agencies, conducting meetings, keeping the records, reaching the unreached, etc. This kind of comprehensive and higher level training should be imparted with the collaboration of educational institutions, leadership training institutes, NGOs and other non-profit agencies committed for the welfare of the rural and tribal India. If these people are dedicated to work with real commitment with a visionary plan without doubt we can change the tribal belt by liberating them from the clutches of the violent ideological menace.

REFORMING THE BUREAUCRACY WITH ADEQUATE TRAINING WITH LATEST TECHNIQUES

Untamed, arm chaired and corrupt bureaucracy is the liability for any system of governance for it will spoil the spirit of team work, transparency, adjustability, adoptability, change and instead counter productive with its traditional and negative mentality. One of the reasons for the collapse of the vast Soviet Empire was over bureaucratization of administration at all levels which resulted in corruption at all levels. The bureaucrats had an unholy alliance with the Communist Party leaders and indulged in all forms of negative activities resulting in the breakdown of the communist system of governance with one part dictatorship. Even in India there are series of criticism on the functioning of the bureaucracy since the dawn of India's independence. However, taming the dragon of India so far has been next to impossibility. The dissent voices raised by the opposition leaders and the intellectuals have become a cry in the wilderness. But allowing the bureaucracy without proper focus on the reality may create more harm than help. Therefore, it is necessary to train them with the latest means of administration like e-governance, accountability, transparency, promptness, people friendly, interpersonal relationship, periodical consultations, evaluation, etc. The ivory tower bureaucracy should be changed into a people centred and problem solving agency for development.

INITIATING PROPAGANDA ON THE NEGATIVE IMPACT OF POSITIVE APPROACH

Propaganda is an effective instrument often used for positive as well as negative purposes by government and non-governmental agencies. The purpose of propaganda is to convince the people about the organization's policies and programmes, to win the support of the majority for active involvement and to present the positive aspects of the organization as well as the negative mentality of the oppositions. It also intends to convince the people on the government's harsh decisions justifying that there is no other alternative. Throughout history almost all forms of governments used propaganda machinery of different kinds to win the support of the people. The advent of multiparty electoral democracy and the participatory democracy further increase the importance of propaganda machinery. The Naxalites and Maoists believing in violent revolution had a systematic propaganda machinery to indoctrinate the frustrated youths about the atrocities of the upper class, feudal lords, judiciary, government machinery, multinationals, private institutions and the ruling class against the tribes, poor farmers, and other deprived people of the society. Through their ideological education they successfully convinced the frustrated youths about the need for taking arms against the oppressors of the rights of the poor and they justify that there is no other path except carrying bloodshed revolution. Convinced by the teaching the ideologically committed are even ready to give their precious life for the so called noble cause of total revolution.

Unfortunately, the Central and State government agencies and other NGOs working among the tribal areas failed to counter the propaganda of the Maoists with empirical evidences and the opportunities available. They have failed to convince the tribal youths about the other better alternatives offered by the Central and State governments and also the ways and means to develop themselves through hard work. Most of the youths are not aware of the special privileges given by the States and Central Government of India. They have also failed to encourage the tribal youths to look outward for the opportunities available for them. They should teach them the failure of violent movements in Nepal, the positive sides of globalization, the Chinese model of State controlled capitalism, the Vietnamese changing attitudes on developments after the bloody war against the Americans, importance of multiparty democracy, transparency in administration, accountability, universal adult franchise, participatory democracy through local self-government, failure of communist model of growth in Russia, China, Vietnam and other former socialist countries and above all the need for forming a peaceful coalition of various people's movements, civil rights movements, tribal rights movements, labour movements, and other workers against the negative forces of globalization. The best way to counter the negative features of globalization is not through violence but through international and national people movement because democratic election is the ultimate weapon available to the ordinary people of the world. The need of the hour is organizing workshops and special seminars and orientation programmes for the deprived and oppressed people on the importance of silent and knowledge based revolutions to fight the negative forces of globalization through Gandhian means not violent means. If the people of the Peace movements and other peace loving people are ready to form an alliance with the active support of the governmental machinery there is a possibility for the misguided tribal youths to adopt the peaceful and constructive path in future.

EMPOWERING WOMEN WITH SPECIAL SCHOOLS AND TECHNICAL INSTITUTIONS

Terrorism or counter terrorism, the immediate victims are the women and the children in all areas of violence. Women are the victims of male dominated society in rural and the tribal areas. The ignorant and uneducated women are not in a position either to build their homes or children with value and life based education. If the women are educated and liberated from ignorance and from the social bondages, they can build not only their homes but also their children by showing the right direction. In most of the rural and tribal areas education and other developmental opportunities are continuously denied by the male dominated tribal or rural male leaders. This guardian knot should be broken with the help of government agencies, NGOs, educational institutions and other missionary movements by starting special schools for girls and also creating self-help groups for women of rural and tribal India with adequate training. If the women are liberated and adequately equipped with education and financial facilities they will help their children and the youths showing the right path of life. The women can initiate a great silent revolution without much noise if they are properly empowered. It is the failure of the successive Central and State governments for the sixty long years of our democratic experiments not to address the genuine needs of the tribal and rural women considering them as non-entities and vote banks. It is the time for initiating new measures to address their genuine needs to change the social, economic and political milieu of rural and tribal India. This silent revolution will change the mind-set of the youths who have belief in violent revolution in the long or short run.

RECRUITING THEM FOR ARMY AND BORDER SECURITY FORCES

The Maoists or the Naxalites who are pro active in tribal areas succeed in recruiting the unemployed or underemployed or unemployable youths by indoctrinating them on ideological grounds convincing them that it is impossible to get anything from the so called feudalistic electoral democracy of Indian model and justify that bloodshed and total revolution is the only way to get rid of all their sixty years of suffering and train them with all the available weapon system. The ideologically addicted youths with necessary weapon training are willing to sacrifice everything for their cause for they don't have any other hope but to fight for their so called noble cause of total revolution for they are very much committed and devoted. It is appropriate to recall the Maoist's experience in Nepal who waged a long armed revolution against the autocratic monarchial rule with the purpose of establishing a one party communist government. Having realized that proletarian dictatorship rule in the era of globalization and multi-party democracy is next to impossibility, they started accepting the multi-party democracy and the electoral democracy although they demanded the government to accommodate their cadets into the regular army. Accommodating the ideologically oriented Maoist communist volunteers along with the main line army created a lot of heated debates in Nepal for the same cadets fought a bitter war with the national army for more than a decade. However, Indian Maoists are different from the Nepal Maoists in many respects. Firstly, Maoists in India didn't fight with the Indian army in any area of their operation. Their fighting was with the Police forces of their region of operation and the State government agencies. Therefore, if any opportunity is given to them with proper governmental backing there is a possibility for sizable cadets to join in the mainstream considering their future. However, this initiative should go along with other initiatives as discussed elsewhere. Offering a job in the Indian military without adequate home work and preparation will be counter productive. Indian government has already initiated this programme in some parts of India recruiting the youths for Central Police Force when Shivraj Patil was the Home Minister.[9]

TAKE THEM AWAY FROM THEIR SO CALLED COMFORT ZONES TO BETTER COMFORT ZONES

Most of the great men of history took their career changing decisions when they were away from their so called comfort zone. The Central government of India has already directed all the Central educational institutions to reserve specific number of seats for the Kashmiri youths to provide them opportunities to pursue higher education in rest of India. Now, the Kashmiri youths have started entering different higher institutions of India which help them to understand and appreciate India's pluralistic culture and civilization and to, re-enter their homes with a lot of positive and fresh experiments. The same methodology can be adopted in the tribal areas also. At one hand, most of the tribal youths are not aware of the developmental opportunities offered to them by the Central and State governments of India and on the other hand, they are not prepared to enter the gates of development opportunities. In this context it is necessary to take special initiatives by taking the youths from tribal areas to different parts of India to provide them necessary training on empowerment and self-employment. These people should be trained and educated by the specially trained teachers so that they can inject the positive seeds of patriotism, positive humanism, pluralism, tolerance, perseverance and the art of adjustment apart from informing them the opportunities available for them for development. To achieve this mission the Central government should allocate special funding facilities with additional package to address the needs of national importance. Instead of modernizing the Police and Para military forces, empowering the youths by giving them proper direction will help a lot. Taking them away from their discomfort zone to comfort zone to give them insight about the opportunities that can transform their lives and thus to help them to opt for a paradigm shift in their life. Moreover, they will educate their fellow villagers based on their training and experiences.[10] Further, organizing periodical tours for the rural and tribal Indian students in and around the parts of developed India will help them to understand the plurality of India and other opportunities available in other parts of India to avail. They should be given the feeling that India belongs to everybody and there is sufficient space for all people group to develop without any disparity. The J&K government and the Central government often arrange tours for the youths of the State taking them to Delhi and other parts of India to educate them how people of different religions are living together peacefully. These trips change the negative mentality of the Kashmiri youths on the secular credential of Indian Republic. (Referred by Farook Abdullah, the former Chief Minister of Jammu & Kashmir).

INVOLVING THE RELIGIOUS MISSIONARIES OF ALL RELIGIONS AND OTHER COMMITTED NGOs WITH ADEQUATE DEVELOPMENT ASSISTANCE

Working among the poor and illiterate people of remote tribal areas braving the environmental challenges and lack of basic facilities is a Himalayan task. The urban educated, career and money oriented youths rarely accept the mission to serve the people of tribal and rural India who are doomed and dying without hope and basic facilities. The Union Health Ministry under Dr. Anbumony Ramadhas took some initiatives to provide the basic health facilities to the tribal and rural India by directing the Medical students to serve at least one year for the unprivileged people of India to get the M.B.B.S. degree. However, with the backing of the affluent and political power houses the medicos launched series of protests against the order of the Health Ministry. This is a test case to study the seriousness on the service mentality of the new generation who are willing to get the benefits from the society without giving anything back. Similarly, in Tamil Nadu there are so many negative reports of the non-serious nature of the doctors who have been appointed to serve the rural people of India as well the teachers who work in the Primary and Middle schools of rural Tamil Nadu. The doctors and the teachers are complaining that without providing the basic facilities it is very difficult for the family people to work among the rural as well as tribal people of India. Of course, it is difficult for the government to connect these remote areas with adequate road facilities, drinking water, electricity and infrastructure facilities within a short span of time. However, it is not an excuse for the government servants with service mentality to serve the needy and deserving people. But the reality is different. Half hearted service is considered as disservice which is worst than no service. Because these so called civil servants are doing more harm to the people by sinning than winning them with their noble service.[11]

In this context, the government should go for better available alternatives. To serve the deprived people with a lot of sincerity and dedication the government can engage the service of the Missionaries of different religion, Multinational Organizations like the World Bank, The IMF, The UNDP, the Global Fund to fight AIDS, Tuberculosis and Malaria, Non-profit organizations like the Gates Foundation, CARE, Ford Foundation, Carter Foundation, Clinton Foundation, Oxfam International, and other networks of NGOs like the Interaction as well as other smaller groups like ACCION and Transparency International agency who are ready to work in rural and tribal India.[12] The government can help them to start educational institutions, health centres, Creech facilities, women empowerment measures and other developmental activities. This will avoid the corruption at the bureaucratic and other levels and help the people to get the genuine and required services. For instance Dr. Ida Scudder a medical missionary from the United States of America was well known for her noble service in and around Vellore, once one of remote regions of Tamil Nadu. Similarly, Sree Narayana Guru and his disciples in Kerala and Ramakrishna Mission in different parts of India have been doing a lot of social and educational services to the poor people in India. Another great social worker started forty five schools in Pakistan and ten in Afghanistan. He achieved great things by initiating a famous "Pennies for Pakistan" programme in the United States.[13] There may be some healthy competitions among the clashing religious groups or the NGOs or social groups in different areas but government agencies can serve as trouble shooters and catalysts with the vision of providing the basic needs of the people of rural and tribal India by allocating different areas to different groups to avoid unwanted clashes and to create healthy competitions.

CONCLUSION

The roots of Maoist menace lie on the continuous negligence of the tribal areas by the State and Central governments for the past sixty plus years of our Independence. According to their perspective the electoral democracy failed to address their even genuine and basic demands. Instead all the successful administrations in collaboration with the landlords, bureaucracy, politicians and the Private companies including the multinationals continue to exploit their resources and other benefits. Their justification for taking arms against the, informers, oppressors to destroy their infrastructure and other networks and even denying the peanut benefits in the name of developmental programmes should be understood in rational and objective ways. At present India is facing two types of terrorism, one is from across border aided by extra territorial players and the other is Maoists menace organized at the domestic levels. In this context, the hard hitting techniques adopted against the cross border terrorist groups should not be a total success in dealing with domestic terrorism which needs an entirely different approach. According to Kautilya, a great strategist of ancient India, a frustrated and scattered army is more dangerous than an organized army. At present Maoists are not working in interior jungles alone. They are spreading their network throughout India and their cadets are from the tribal, oppressed people of the rural India, frustrated youths of urban India, ideologically trained educated youths of India apart from the white collar employees of both private and public organizations. Defeating this movement by adopting bureaucratic arm chaired policies and the military oriented hard hitting approach alone will not get the desired result. Instead it will compel the armed youths to target all the possible urban and sensitive places of better parts of India like that of the Italian terrorists practiced during 60s and 70s. Therefore, the policy makers should concentrate more on comprehensive and multifaceted development plans to address the socio-economic needs of the deprived people of India than to pursue with more and more offensive agenda to win the war against them in the long run. The need of the hour is a policy with more and more carrot and soup and lesser and lesser big stick approach.

The Village Panchayat receives funds allocated to carry out for the implementation of certain works allocated through Indira Awas Yojana, Sampoorna Grameen Rozgar Yojana (SGRY), Swarnajayanti Gram Swarozgar Yojana (SGSY), Member of Parliament Local Area Development Scheme (MPLADS), Pradhan Mantri Gram Sadhak Yojana (PMGSY), Anaithu Grama Anna Marumalarchi Thittam (AGAMT), Member of Legislative Assembly Constituency Development Scheme (MLACDS), Panchayat Union School Renovation Programme, Nammakku Naame Thittam, Rural Roads under NABARD, Rural

Infrastructure Development Fund (RIDF), Pradhan Mantri Gramodhaya Yojana, Central Rural Sanitation Programme, State Finance Commission Grant, Biogas and Central Finance Commission Grant.

NOTES AND REFERENCES

1. Rajiv Gandhi was assassinated by a *Liberation Tigers of Tamil Eealam (LTTE)* woman suicide bomber at an election rally in Sriperumbudur near Chennai in May, 1991.
2. *The Hindu* 25th November, 2009, Chidambaram committed more paramilitary battalions to fight Maoist rebels after the forces were relieved of prolonged deployment and patrolling in the worst-hit eastern Jharkhand during the nearly month-long State polls held between November 25 and December 18, 2009 and also for Chhattisgarh.
3. *The Kashmir Times, (Jammu)* June 21, 2008, p. 11.
4. Nicholas D. Kristof, "Happiest people on Earth live in Costa Rica" *Deccan Chronicles*, 9 January, 2010, p. 8.
5. *The Hindu,* 18 August, 2008.
6. Department of Higher Education*, Government of India* Notification dated 06/05/2000, D.O. No.F. 10-1/96-Desk (U).
7. Franco Ferracuti, "Ideology and repentance: Terrorism in Italy" in Walter Reich (ed.,) *Origin of Terrorism* (Washington D.C. Woodrow Wilson Center Press, 1996, p. 58.
8. *The Hindu,* 1 April, 2004.
9. *The Tribune,* June 1, 2004, p. 20.
10. According to the Home Ministry report in the year 2004 alone, 29,000 youths have been selected for Central Police Force from Naxalite areas *Deccan Chronicle*, 23 May, 2006, p. 10.
11. Hillary Rotham Clinton, the US Secretary of States emphasized the need for the net working of various groups and organisations working with deep commitment to humanitarian mission. *Deccan Chronicle,* 8 January, 2010, p. 11.
12. *The Christian Medical College in Vellore is the living example of the great service of the American medical missionary.*
13. For details see Khalid Hassan, "Three cups of tea" *Kashmir Times*, (Jammu) June 21, 2008, p. 8.

11
Principles of 'Natural Frontiers' and 'Settled Population': Solutions for the Sino-Indian Border

L. Premashekhara

It is an irony of history that the frontier separating Asia's two giants – China and India—was transformed from the one guarded by a few hundred club-wielding policemen into world's highly militarized one in a surprisingly short period in the latter half of 1950s. The frontier erupted almost suddenly, led to acrimonious charged and counter-charges eventually culminating into the border war of October-November 1962 that wounded India's pride. Although several attempts were initiated by both governments in the form of bilateral talks and confidence building measures in the 1980s that led to several agreements initiating an era of mutual economic and scientific co-operation, the border issue remains unresolved and raises its ugly head like a hydra time and again. This chapter attempts to analyse the actual nature of the problem and raises certain questions about the very genuineness of the problem itself. In other words, the aim of the chapter is to probe with the help of the "Three Frontiers Theory" (see next page for details) whether there is really a border problem between the two countries *now*. At the same time, this chapter suggests that the "Principles of Natural Frontier and Settled Population" are the remedy of formally ending the Sino-Indian border problem.

I

All that happened in the realm of Sino-Indian relations during 1949-62 has become an inseparable and unforgettable chapter in the history of modern India. The plethora of material painstakingly researched and compiled by numerous scholars[1] conclusively establishes that there were two broad sets of reasons for the war of 1962. The Indian insistence on the legitimacy of one of the several lines that put the whole of Aksai Chin under its control and New Delhi's undue haste in getting it accepted by Beijing either through negotiations or through low-key military operations during 1959-62 described as "Forward Policy" belong to the first set of reasons. On the other hand, frequent changes and shifts in China's claims and stances form the second set of reasons.

Before proceeding further it is relevant at this point to introduce the basic principles of the "Three Frontiers Theory" in order to properly equip the reader to understand and appreciate the contents and conclusions this chapter tries to present.

The Three Frontiers Theory classifies the frontiers between the states of the world into three categories:

(i) Single-edged frontiers,
(ii) Double-edged frontiers, and
(iii) Dull frontiers.

Single-edged frontier is the one that gives strategic advantage to one of the two states say State A. Double-edged frontier provides strategic advantage to both State A and State B. The Dull frontier does not give any strategic advantage to either.

The frontier that existed between and the boundary line that separated Germany and France during 1871 to 1919 was a very good example of single-edged frontiers. It provided considerable amount of strategic advantage to the newly unified Germany *vis-à-vis* France thereby acting as a single-edged frontier in Germany's favour. There are innumerable examples for double-edged frontiers and perhaps the most striking one is the Radcliffe Line that separates India and Pakistan. This Line provides strategic advantage to both countries thereby forcing the two to maintain constant vigil on each other's motives and moves. The present line of control or the *de facto* frontier between India and China is the best example of dull frontiers. It doesn't provide any kind of strategic advantage to either and has eliminated the usefulness of an armed conflict between the two neighbours ever since it was created as a result of the border war of 1962.

For the sake of convenience the state that enjoys strategic advantage in case of a single-edged frontier is referred to as **Ridge State**, and the one that is deprived of that advantage as **Valley State.** This nomenclature has been coined on the basis of the general assumption that one who positions himself on a ridge tends to possess advantage *vis-à-vis* the one in the valley below. In the case of a double-edged frontier, the two states on its either side can be called **Plain States** since both of them are on equal footing just like two contenders standing on an even surface enjoy relatively equal amount of advantage among themselves. Similarly, in the case of dull frontiers, the states that lie on either side of that can be called as **Canyon States** since a canyon hardly allows the two adversaries on its either side to gain any advantage against one another. (Premashekhara, 2008: 13-14)

The Sino-Indian frontier saw military activities in a major scale in its eastern flank during the beginning of the second decade of the previous century. It was India that initiated those military activities and China did the same in the western flank forty years later. These military moves, first by India and followed by China later, together are, according to the "Three Frontiers Theory", attempts on the part of New Delhi and Beijing to convert "Single-edged Frontiers" against themselves into "Dull Frontiers."

II

There existed no linear boundary[2] between India and China before an attempt for creating one for the first time in history was initiated by India during 1911-14. In fact, no linear boundary existed between empires/kingdoms of Asia in the historical past. What separated one from the other was a broad stretch of land of varying width usually being a geographical landmark like a mountain, or a desert and the like. Interestingly, rivers which are closer to linear boundaries in nature hardly acted as lines that separated one empire from the other. Usually, these frontiers (between two empires) were uninhabitable areas or areas with sparse tribal or nomadic population which was numerically a minority and militarily insignificant and consequently played no role in the regional politics of the time thus posed no threat to or undermined the interests of the empires which they separated. The reason for Asiatic states not attempting to establish linear boundaries was probably the frequent changes in the location of frontiers. The constant warfare between the states never allowed a particular stretch of land to remain as a frontier for a time span adequately enough for it to secure acceptance and legitimacy. Thus, absence of permanent frontiers was the reason for absence of linear frontiers or at least attempts at establishing them.[3] It was so in the case of India and China too. Of course, the mighty

Himalayas were regarded as the traditional frontiers between the two civilizations. But the fact is that it was not quiet most of the time. Military activities involving the armies of Tibet, Nepal, Punjab (the Sikhs), Kangra, Jammu, Kashmir, Ladakh, Hunza, Baltistan and, occasionally, imperial China were common during the historical period causing constant shifts in frontiers. As a result, when "the Republic of India and the People's Republic of China, after they came into existence had faced an unfinished task: How to convert their frontiers into legal boundaries (Swamy, 2001: 39).

Before 1911, Tibetan suzerainty extended to areas south of the Himalayas in the eastern sector.[4] In other words the present north-eastern State of Arunachal Pradesh was not under the political and military control of British India. The traditional frontier between Tibetan territories and British India ran roughly along the northern edges of the Brahmaputra plains far below the mighty Himalayas which were traditionally believed to be an impassable wall providing absolute protection to India from any invading army from the north.[5] The British Indian troops in the Assam would have been put under tremendous stress if Tibet became expansionist or it came under stricter Chinese control once again as was the case before the decline of the Beijing-based imperial authority.[6] In this way this line acted as a Single-edged Frontier in favour of Tibet of which China was the suzerain and thus India found itself in the unenviable position of a Valley State.

In order to eliminate any future threat from either Tibet or China or Russia a section of the British Indian authorities conceived a plan of pushing the Indo-Tibetan frontier to the higher reaches of the Himalayas and also delineate it. Colonel Francis Younghusband led an expedition in 1911 into the Tibetan territories south of the Himalayas and successfully established Indian authority there. These territories which British India established *de facto* control were christened "North Eastern Frontier Agency (NEFA)."[7] An unsuccessful attempt to formalise Indian sovereignty over these newly acquired territories was made by the British Indian authorities during 1913-14. When the tripartite negotiations involving India, China and Tibet held in Shimla in 1913 failed to produce the desired result, Sir Henry McMahon, the then Foreign Secretary of the Indian government arranged bilateral talks with Tibet in New Delhi in March 1914. The boundary line he proposed and got accepted by the Tibetan representative in this meeting bore his name and ran almost right along the crest of the Himalayan Mountains thus establishing a natural boundary between India and Tibet. The Tibetan authorities in Lhasa, however, soon repudiated their representative's action of accepting the McMahon Line. As a bigger blow to the Indian official's plan the Chinese government too declared that any agreement between Tibet and India would be "illegitimate and null" (*Ibid*., 42).

Sir Henry McMahon had a vision about the necessity of linear boundary for the security of India which, unfortunately, was not understood and shared by his superiors in New Delhi and London at that time. His efforts which were aimed at converting the Single-edged Frontier against India in the eastern sector into a Dull Frontier were met with opposition not only from Chinese side but by the very government he represented. The then Viceroy, in his report to London, disowned McMahon's dealings with the Tibetan representative. The British government too expressed its disapproval of McMahon's moves by transferring him from India to Egypt (*ibid*.). Even the Survey of India did not include NEFA in India in its maps. Thus Sir Henry McMahon became a tragic hero in the saga of India's quest for converting Single-edged Frontier into Dull Frontier in the eastern sector.

The British authorities finally accepted the relevance of McMahon Line in the 1930s and maintained that it was India's legal boundary with Tibet and the Survey of India too followed suit by publishing maps that showed NEFA as Indian territory for the first time in 1938. After some initial hesitation the government of independent India too echoed this view when Prime Minister Jawaharlal Nehru asserted in the Parliament: "Our maps show McMahon Line is our boundary and that is our boundary—map or no map. The fact remains that we stand by that boundary, and we will not allow anybody to come across that boundary." (Maxwell, 1997: 75). This assertion by Nehru is a clear indication that the government of independent India accepted the perception of the erstwhile British colonial regimes regarding the necessity of McMahon Line for India's security. It demonstrated its resolve to continue the policy of converting Single-edged Frontiers against India into Dull Frontiers when it annexed in February 1952. Tawang which the British had left with the Tibetans despite it being located south of the Himalayas as well as the McMahon Line. China which had established politico-military control over Tibet a year ago did not react to the Indian move at all. "This puzzling silence can be construed as China's acquiescence in India's filling out in the McMahon Line" (Maxwell, 1997: 73). In the Sino-Indian War of October-November 1962, the Chinese People's Liberation Army (PLA) violated the McMahon Line, crossed the Himalayan Mountains occupied Tawang and made significant gains further south.[8] The Chinese government, however, declared unilateral cease-fire after a month long campaign, vacated all the occupied areas including Tawang and withdrew its army to its own territory north of the McMahon Line. Though this action of Beijing has all elements of a typical Chinese riddle, it is not difficult to decipher it. Had the PLA remained in the areas south of the Himalayan Mountains for some more times it would have been cut off from China once the mountain passes got closed due to heavy snowing during winter which was about to set in. In such an eventuality the Chinese soldiers would have become sitting ducks for Indian army and the impressive victory achieved by the PLA would have turned into a great fiasco for Beijing (Premashekhara, 2008: 17). The Chinese realized the fact that it would be difficult or even impossible for them to keep NEFA (present Arunachal Pradesh) under their control during winter since the Indians enjoyed easy access to that territory throughout the year including winter months. The peculiarity or uniqueness of this region is that a Chinese controlled Arunachal Pradesh would act as Single-edged Frontier in India's favour during winter and in China's favour during the rest of the year! It would, in a way, act as a Double-edged Frontier. It means this frontier would never be quiet. In order to avoid such a situation Chinese authorities realized the fact that it would be wise to regard the McMahon Line as boundary line since it was a Dull Frontier and did not provide strategic advantage to either of the powers, did nothing to disturb it except issuing statements staking their claim on the territories south of the McMahon Line. Thus the Sino-Indian frontier in the eastern sector was first converted by the British into a Dull Frontier during 1911-14 and was accepted by the Chinese as such later 1962.[9]

III

The Sino-Indian frontier in the western sector is more complex in nature than its eastern counterpart. Here, it was China that converted a Single-edged Frontier in India's favour into a Dull Frontier. There existed no clearly delineated boundary between Ladakh region of Jammu & Kashmir and Uyghur Xinjiang (formerly Sinkiang) and the British exhibited least interest in having one ever since they came to possess Kashmir following their victory over Maharaja Ranjit Singh in the Fourth Sikh War in 1839. The governments in both London and Kolkata,[10] however, were alarmed when an Imperial Russian army led by Çapt. Grombechevsky reached Hunza in northern Kashmir in 1888 after his successful campaigns in Central Asia. The Russians, if allowed, were capable of threatening the densely populated Punjab which also had the distinction of being the bread basket of British India.

A careful study of British India's frontier policy in the north shows that London and Kolkata always wanted "friendly buffers" lying between densely populated regions of northern India on one hand and imperial Russia and China on the other. Their attitudes towards and dealings with Afghanistan, Swat and Tibet were all demonstrative of this policy. Capt. Grombechevsky's entry into northern Kashmir evidently disturbed British India's "friendly buffers" policy, exposed densely populated northern India to potential dangers unless London did something drastic against the Russians. The British apprehension and their threat perception *vis-à-vis* the Russians were demonstrated by Capt. Algermon Durand, the well known frontier expert when he said "the game had begun" (Woodman, 1969: 72). Northern Kashmir suddenly assumed strategic importance and led to the British efforts at defining Kashmir's boundaries with Afghanistan in the north-west and China in the north-east. They did conclude an agreement with Kabul formally delineating Afghanistan's border with India in 1893. The Russian threat in the north-west was considerably reduced when the British signed a treaty with Moscow on 11 March, 1995 according to which a narrow corridor called 'Wakhan' was created between the Russian controlled Tazhik territories on the one hand and Swat Valley of the newly created North-West Frontier Province (NWFP) and Gilgit region of the princely state of Jammu & Kashmir of the British Indian Empire on the other, and the same was placed under the control of Kabul (Premashekhara, 2008: 22).

With regard to the issue of delineating Kashmir's boundary with China in the Aksai Chin region,[11] the British contemplated three lines Ardagh-Johnson Line, Macartney-MacDonald Line, and Trelawney Saunders Line.[12] While the Ardagh-Johnson Line,[13] running along the Kuen Lun Range in the north and northeast, placed the whole of Aksai Chin within the territory of Kashmir, the Macartney-MacDonald Line,[14] on the other hand, put much of Aksai Chin in Sinkiang. The earlier Trelawney Saunders Line[15] ran along the Karakoram Range and thus placed the whole of Aksai Chin in Sinkiang (Lamb, 1964: 86).

The British, however, did nothing serious to get anyone of these lines accepted by Beijing as there appeared to be no consensus among various officials and bodies dealing with Indian affairs in London and Kolkata. Initially John Ardagh's views of placing the entire Aksai Chin in India gained acceptance in London when he argued that China's weakness made it useless as a buffer between northern frontiers of British Indian Empire and the Russian Empire. Highlighting the eagerness with which Russia annexed the whole of Central Asia in less than forty years and advanced its borders towards India, Ardagh predicted that Moscow would eventually annex western part of Sinkiang and pose serious threat to India's security in the Kashmir region and argued for extending Indian sovereignty right up to the Kuen Lun Range with the whole of Aksai Chin within Indian territory (Maxwell, 1997: 32). Although he conceded that in general sense the Karakoram mountains formed a natural boundary, "easy to define, difficult to pass and fairly dividing the people on either side", he rejected this mountain range as proper border as its very "physical condition" would deny Indian army of proper information regarding the movement of the enemy on the other side (*ibid.*). The officials in India, however, rejected Ardagh's views as "impractical theorising of an armchair general" (*ibid.*). The Viceroy Lord Elgin "warned" London that any attempt to implement the Ardagh-Johnson Line and bring Aksai Chin under Indian control would "entail a real risk of strained relations with China and furthermore might precipitate the very Russian advance which Ardagh wished to forestall".[16] London accepted the Indian officials' point of view and approved the Macartney-MacDonald Line and the same was proposed to the Chinese on 14 March, 1899 (*ibid.* 33). Thus, this Macartney-MacDonald Line was the only border line British India officially ever proposed to China. The Chinese, however, never replied to this proposal.

The British lost their interest in the issue once the Russian threat disappeared following the Anglo-Russian Convention of 1907 and China ceased to be a source of threat as it plunged into political instability following the revolution of 1911. These developments, and several other similar ones which the history of the British Empire, in Asia in particular and the world in general, is replete with, amply demonstrate that London's attitude towards India's borders with its neighbours was determined not by India's interests and it was the empire's interests *vis-à-vis* other empires that guided the British in this regard. It was the two variables of Russia and China that shaped London's policy towards India's borders. In the words of Stephen A. Hoffmann:

> They [the British] had to be concerned with the political and strategic implications for the empire of any boundary agreement concluded with other powers bordering India. Such powers included Russia and China, and relations with them were seen from London as set by such matters as Anglo-Russian dealings in Europe and the Middle East and British interests on the

> mainland of China. Thus, London tended toward avoidance of forward claims and lines. (1990: 14).

Thus, the "British approach towards the border was that of an imperial power and not one of defending Indian nation-state." (Swamy, 2001: 42). Despite these historical ambiguities and absence of any formal treaties the government of independent India unilaterally accepted a slightly modified Ardagh-Johnson Line as the international boundary between India and China insisting on New Delhi's sovereignty over the whole of Aksai Chin. This stand was not effectively challenged as long as civil war raged on in China and Chinese frontier remained receded far away from India as Tibet enjoyed independence and Sinkiang experienced Russian influence. Once China achieved political stability under the communists following their victory in the civil war in 1949. Tibet lost its independence to the new central government in Beijing, Sinkiang was once again reverted to Chinese rule and consequently China's frontier once again came closer to that of India. History repeated itself then and Aksai Chin once again became a *disputed* territory.

The British maps had shown no marked boundary at all in the Sino-Indian frontiers from Nepal to Afghanistan. The Survey of India continued to reproduce the same maps for several years after independence. It, however, published maps in 1954 marking a definitive boundary between India and China in the western sector which placed the whole of Aksai Chin in India. India did insist time and again that Aksai Chin belonged to it but did nothing to establish its authority there. New Delhi became aware of Chinese presence in that region only when the Chinese media announced in 1957 that their frontier guards and about three thousand civilian builders had completed the construction of a road there. Although the Indian ambassador in Peking reported this matter to New Delhi in September 1957, the latter took ten full months to send a patrol team in Aksai Chin to find out whether the Chinese claim on road construction was true.[17]

Then onwards began a series of allegations, accusations, counter-accusations and failed negotiations with China firmly holding on to its claim. Beijing on its part changed its claims lines frequently pushing the same westward every time thus arousing Indian anxiety greatly (Woodman, 1969: 245-78). All these finally led to the border war of October-November 1962 which resulted in the Chinese occupation of all the areas right up to the Karakoram Mountains. Beijing's attitude here was markedly different from its policy in the eastern sector. Here, the PLA didn't withdraw from the region as it did in the east; instead, maintained that the Karakoram Mountains were the traditional frontier between Kashmir and Sinkiang and the same must be accepted as international boundary between the two countries. Beijing was reasonable in thinking that the extension of Indian sway over areas beyond the Karakoram Mountains would make Aksai Chin a Single-edged Frontier in India's favour throughout the year except the winter months and seriously undermine Chinese security in and control over Tibet. Hence, they wanted to limit Indian control up to the Karakoram Mountains only thus creating a natural and Dull Frontier between the two countries.[18]

Neither any government in London nor any British Administrator in India had ever attempted to extend India's control beyond the Karakoram Mountains although such an idea was contemplated whenever Russian, and Chinese to a lesser extent, threat came closer to India's northern frontiers. At the same time they never accepted any hostile element being present on this side of the Mountains. In other words, they wanted mighty mountains ranges to form India's northern frontiers in both eastern and western sectors. They extended Indian authority up to the Himalayas in the east during 1911-14 and maintained that Macartney-MacDonald Line which ran almost along the eastern slopes of the Karakoram Range was India's limit in the western sector. They were well aware of the danger the empire was to face should it crossed the Karakoram as the areas beyond that mountain range were indefensible from Indian side. The government of independent India, however, lacked such wisdom and followed an ill-conceived and audacious policy and challenged Beijing's authority over Aksai Chin when China emerged, with a fiercely nationalist government under the communists, stronger out of decades of chaos and re-united all the regions under strong central authority. The British had avoided such a daring policy during their heydays as global power and when China was incapable of offering effective military resistance. The policy India followed towards China with regard to the border issue was geographically unscientific, strategically illogical, politically irresponsible and militarily suicidal. It was doomed to end in disaster and humiliation, and that is what happened finally.

IV

The above analysis shows that the Sino-Indian frontier which was single edged in India's favour in the western sector and in China's favour in the east was converted into a Dull Frontier during the period between 1911 and 1962. Although Beijing and New Delhi have not officially accepted the change, they have not done anything significant to disturb the *status quo* and alter the so-called "Line of Actual Control" (LAC) since the end of the war of 1962 giving the indications they feel that the mutual border today runs along the natural frontiers and consequently there exists no border dispute between India and China. Of course, there have been minor incursions into each other's territories, the Somdorong Chu incident of June 1986 and the Kongka Pass incident of July-August 2009 being the major ones. Such incidents are bound to occur when borders are not defined in written agreements and delineated on land. Both countries handled these incidents in positive manner and never allowed the situation on ground to deteriorate. The Indian government's handling of the situation in the present case is particularly remarkable. It has not given into media outrage and remained calm maintaining that there were inbuilt mechanisms to handle these kinds of situations effectively. This is markedly different from New Delhi's attitudes during similar situations before the war of 1962. Reality being so, it is unlikely that India and China will go to war over the boundary issue again. Such a war will alter the Dull Frontier created over a period of half a century of military moves and push India and China to situations similar to the one existed before 1962 which is not going to serve the interest of either country.

In fact, New Delhi and Beijing have concluded, apart from the significant "Agreement on the Maintenance of Peace and Tranquillity along the Line of Actual Control in the India-China Border" signed during the official visit of Prime Minister P.V. Narasihma Rao to the Chinese capital in September 1993,[19] several agreements to maintain peace along this LAC. Therefore, it can be safely assumed that both New Delhi and Beijing have realized the fact that the present LAC is the scientific boundary between the two countries. Their hesitation to officially convert the LAC into official international border is understandable. Such a move will, especially in India, create strong public resentment. Such resentment is actually the result of lack of understanding of history on the part of the Indian people. A careful analysis of the historical documents and proper understanding of events in the past 120 years demonstrate clearly enough that India has been the gainer in its border row with China. India now possesses Arunachal Pradesh, which was in fact not a part of its territory before 1911. On the other hand, Aksai Chin now under Chinese control was part of Indian territory only in maps as a result of British India's ambiguous policies and independent India's cartographic expansion in 1954. In reality India never controlled that region.[20] If the Indian public is properly educated on historical facts they may not oppose any move by their government to convert the Line of Actual Control into international boundary.

In fact, the Chinese offered to convert the Line of Actual Control with minor modifications into international border between the two countries in the fifth round of border talks held during 1983-84. This meant China was ready to recognize Indian sovereignty over Arunachal Pradesh provided India accepted Chinese sovereignty over Aksai Chin. The Indian government, however, rejected it (Sali, 1998: 113, Ganguly, 2009: 14). The Chinese offer was wise in more than one respect and Indian acceptance of the same would have solved the vexed border row, freed Indian armed forces from the tremendous burden it has been shouldering and radically overhauled Sino-Indian relations. It is difficult to gauge whether China still favours such a solution to the border problem. However, it is in the interest of the Indian people and government to probe the matter and work for legitimizing the Line of Actual Control as international border and formally establish "Dull Frontiers" which will remove the threat of any armed conflict between the two Asian giants. A Dull Frontier with China is very much in India's interest. It will free India from the tremendous tension along its northern borders and help New Delhi to deal with challenges and threats emanating from other sources and directions more effectively and decisively.

On China's part, the "Principle of Settled Population" agreed upon by Prime Ministers Manmohan Singh and Wen Jiabao during the latter's official visit to New Delhi in April, 2006 should be accepted by Beijing and used as means for final solution to formally end this boundary dispute and officially establish Dull Frontiers between the two countries (*Times of India*, 2006). The Chinese, however, changed their position a year later when their Foreign Minister told his Indian counterpart in June 2007 that the "mere presence" of settled population did not affect China's claims across the border (Shourie, 2008). This stand of China was categorically rejected by Dorji Khandu, the Chief Minister of Arunachal Pradesh when he declared on 12 October, 2009 that "the people of Arunachal Pradesh are *Tibetans of India*" (*Times of India*, 2009, Emphasis added). Even the general public in Arunachal Pradesh, especially in Tawang are totally averse to the idea of any change in their present nationality. Some even expressed their readiness to fight the Chinese along with Indian Army if China resorted to use force to settle the border issue in its favour (*Indian Express,* 2009). Reality being so, it will be wise for Beijing to accept the present arrangement in which the Sino-Indian border is aligned along the natural frontiers and both New Delhi and Beijing should settle the vexed border row and convert the present '*de facto*' frontiers into '*de jure*' frontiers.

NOTES AND REFERENCES

1. Some of them are: Hoffmann, Steven (1990), *India and the China Crisis*, Oxford University Press, Delhi; Lamb, Alastair (1964), *The China-India Border: The Origin of the Disputed Boundaries*, Oxford University Press, London; .... (1966), *The McMahon Line*, 2 Vols. Routledge and Kegan Paul, London; .... (1975), *The Sino-Indian Border in Ladakh*, University of South Carolina Press, Columbia; Maxwell, Neville (1970), *India-China War*, London; Swamy, Subramanian (2001), *India-China Perspective*, Konark Publishers Pvt. Ltd., New Delhi; Woodman, Dorothy (1969), *Himalayan Frontier*, Barrie and Rockliff; London.
2. A Boundary is a geographic line agreed to in diplomatic negotiations (delineation), jointly marked out on the ground (demarcation), thereafter visualized on a map (cartography), and accurately formalized between two sovereign governments (treaty), in which each thus recognized the limits of its own and that of its neighbour's territory. See: Swamy, Subramanian, (2001), *India's-China Perspective*, Konark Publishers Pvt. Ltd., New Delhi, p. 39.
3. Perhaps the first ever linear boundaries in continental Asia were established by the Russians to separate their newly conquered Central and North-East Asian territories from Sinkiang and Manchuria of Imperial China in the second half of the nineteenth century. British and French colonizers followed suit in South-East Asia at the end of that century.
4. The areas lying south of the Himalayas and north of the Assam plains were not parts of Tibet in strict sense. Arunachal Pradesh, as that region is known today was fragmented and was under the control of several tribal chieftains. These chieftains in turn owed their allegiance to the Tibetan rulers in Lhasa.
5. In other words the boundary line that now separates India's two north-eastern States of Assam and Arunachal Pradesh was roughly the boundary between British India and Tibetan territories.
6. The threat the British rulers were apprehensive of at that time was in fact not coming from either the Chinese or the Tibetans. The Imperial Russian advance into Central Asia had begun in the middle of the nineteenth Century. The Russian campaign was swift and decisive and by late 1880s the Russians annexed what are now called Central Asian Republics and their armies were knocking at the doors of Kashmir and Chinese Turkestan. A Russian arrry led by Captain Grombechevsky actually landed in Hunza in Northern Kashmir in 1888. At the same time Peking's authority over the remote western province of Sinkiang was gradually weakening because

of various politico-social, ethnic and religious reasons. There was a danger of Russians extending their sway over that region and then entering into the adjoining Tibet. Had they succeeded in that adventure then they would have posed serious threat to both Northern and North-Eastern regions of India.

7. NEFA was a part of the state of Assam for some time. In 1972 it was accorded the status of a Union Territory with a new name of Arunachal Pradesh. Full statehood followed suit fifteen years later in 1987.
8. The Chinese army came right up to Bomdila, just 80 kilometres north of Tezpur and 40 kilometres away from oil fields at Dig Boi and thus threatening to enter the Assam plains.
9. Though the Chinese have not given up their official claim over Arunachal Pradesh yet, the fact remains that they have not done anything significant to disturb the McMahon Line since 1962 despite their overwhelming superiority against the Indians as far as military strength is concerned. Though the Somdorong Chu incident of 1986 created some resentment in New Delhi it was amicably settled by the end of the year and was soon forgotten.
10. Kolkata, or Calcutta as it was known till recently, was the capital of the British Indian Empire during the nineteenth century and it enjoyed that position until the capital was shifted to the newly built city of New Delhi in 1911.
11. Aksai Chin is a triangular elevated tableland lying between the Karakoram Mountains in the west, Tibetan Plateau in the east, and Kuen Lun mountain range and low lying Uyghur Xinjiang (Sinkiang) beyond in the north. Geographically, it is an extension of the great Tibetan plateau. It is easily accessible from the Chinese side whereas the high-rise Karakoram Mountains deny India similar easy access.
12. These names were coined by Alastair Lamb in his book: *The China-India Border: The Origin of the Disputed Boundaries*, Oxford University Press, London, 1964.
13. This line is called 'Ardagh-Johnson Line' as it was prepared way back in 1863 by Survey of India explorer W.H. Johnson and later proposed to the Government of India in 1897 by the Chief of British Military intelligence in London, Major General Sir John Ardagh. See: Woodman, Dorothy (1969), *Himalayan Frontier*, Barrie and Rockliff; London, pp. 360-65.
14. This line was suggested to the Viceroy Lord Elgin by George Macartney, the British representative in Kashgar and proposed to the Chinese, on behalf of the Viceroy, by Claude MacDonald, the British Minister in Peking.
15. This line was drawn by the India Office cartographer Trelawney Saunders for the Foreign Office in 1963.
16. The full text of Viceroy Elgin's official communication to London can be found in Dorothy Woodman, (1969), *Himalayan Frontier*, Barrie and Rockliff, London, pp. 364-65.

17. One of the two patrols that went towards the southern section of Aksai Chin reported in October that the Chinese had indeed built a road there. The other patrol that went to the north disappeared. It was later learnt that they had been detained and later 'deported back' to Indian territory by the Chinese. The unfortunate patrol team was lucky to be discovered and rescued after being dumped by the Chinese at the Karakoram Pass far away from any nearby Indian post.
18. Karakoram Mountains are the second highest mountain ranges in the world next only to the Himalayas.
19. For the full text of this Agreement, see Sali, M.L., (1998). *India-China Border Dispute—A Case Study of the Eastern Sector*, A.P.H. Publishing Corporation, New Delhi, pp. 288-92.
20. It is interesting to note that Indians learned Chinese presence in Aksai Chin only when Beijing officially announced in mid-50s that it had completed the construction of a road in that region.

OTHER CONSULTED REFERENCES

Ganguly, Swagato, "Grouchy Tiger, Misread Dragon" in *Times of India*, (Chennai), 8 October, 2009.

Hoffmann, Steven (1990), *India and the China Crisis*, Oxford University Press, New Delhi.

Lamb, Alastair (1964), *The China-India Border: The Origin of the Disputed Boundaries*, Oxford University Press, London.

—— (1966), *The McMahon Line*, 2 Vols., Routledge and Kegan Paul, London.

—— (1975), *The Sino Indian Border in Ladakh*, University of South Carolina Press, Columbia.

New Indian Express (Chennai), 4 October, 2009.

Maxwell, Neville, (1997), *India's-China War*, Natraj Publishers, Dehra Dun.

Premashekhara, L., (2008), "Three Frontiers Theory: An Explanation to India-Pakistan Animosity" in *International Journal of South Asian Studies* (Pondicherry), Vol. I, No. 1, January-June, 2008, pp. 13-32.

Sali, M.L., (1998). *India-China Border Dispute—A Case Study of the Eastern Sector*, A.P.H. Publishing Corporation, New Delhi.

Shorie, Arun (2008), Are We Deceiving Ourselves Again? ASA, Rupa & Co., New Delhi.

Swamy, Subramanian (2001), *India's-China Perspective*, Konark Publishers Pvt. Ltd., New Delhi.

Times of India (Chennai), 13 April, 2006 and 12 October, 2009.

Woodman, Dorothy (1969), *Himalayan Frontier*, Barrie and Rockliff, London.

12
The Democratic Experience of India

Rohit Wangcho

The rise and triumph of liberal capitalism after the collapse of socialism early two decades ago has led to a substantial revaluation of the history of economies and polities during the twentieth century. The short twentieth century that Eric Hobsbawm wrote about looks a lot different to those who do not share his Marxist perspective.[1] The study of the Indian economy and society has also been influenced by this change.[2] There is definitely a need to look at the Indian experience in a comparative perspective although the focus of this chpater is on India.

The left in India has for long believed that the history of India had to be examined in terms of its failure to produce a viable socialist movement.[3] Many regarded the transfer of power by the British to the Indian nationalist elite as a form of "passive revolution" in the sense somewhat of Antonio Gramsci.[4] India's performance has for long been compared unfavourably with that of China and the socialist bloc in general. For over two decades now the rise of liberal and neoliberal ideology has led to the revaluation of the past in terms of the failure to produce a vibrant capitalism. The turning points and missed opportunities in these two narratives of India's past can hardly be expected to have much in common.[5] It is quite clear that the country could not have moved in the direction of capitalism and socialism at the same time. Therefore, the counterfactuals of historical interpretation have to be subjected to some kind of reality check.[6]

There is a need to look at the record of post-independence India in terms of specific conditions that shaped its evolution. India emerged as an independent country after a long and largely non-violent struggle against a colonial power that ultimately handed over power to the leaders of the national movement without an armed struggle. The members of the Constituent Assembly adopted a democratic system of government with adult franchise in a country where the levels of literacy were very low. The national movement had roused the masses considerably and people had high expectations about significant economic and social transformation of the country. India's mixed economy had to evolve in a poor country with immense linguistic and cultural diversity. The manner in which independence was achieved also determined independence period. Any comparison between countries has to be based on the given historical conditions under which they had to develop.

THE NATIONAL MOVEMENT AND ITS LEGACY

The Indian struggle for independence was a long drawn one, which under the control of the Indian National Congress remained largely non-violent. There were those on the left who argued that the Gandhian leadership imposed a rigid ideology based on non-violence and class accommodation that prevented the fullest development of the anti-imperialist mass movement. Some Marxists believe that the Gandhian leadership blunted the edge of the popular movements that emerged against both colonial rulers and the Indian landlords and moneylenders.[7] Subaltern historians have argued that there was an inverse relationship between the strength of the Congress as an organization and the development of popular struggles. The anti-imperialist struggle was broader than the national movement led by the Congress. Many tribal, peasant, and popular movements flourished outside the control and influence of the Congress.[8] The political reasons for pointing out that the Congress was not the 'true' representative of the Indian people are different, but the accusation of the Cambridge scholars and the Marxist-Subalterns is similar. Where the two schools differ is on the question of assessing the impact of colonialism on India's economy and society.

The Cambridge School pointed out years ago that the Congress did not represent the people and that movements it launched frequently slipped out of its control.[9] They argued that the Congress movements against British rule led to a forging of an alliance between the rich peasants and the Congress. The effectiveness of the Congress in thwarting the efforts of the British Government to raise the land revenue was responsible for its popularity among the peasants.[10] The demands of the tenants against landlords, of debtors against moneylenders and of the agricultural labourers and sharecroppers were not taken up by the Congress. Therefore, the Congress did not genuinely represent the poor and the underprivileged.

The Subalterns have argued over many years that the nationalists have tried to incorporate the history of subaltern sections of the population within elitist and nationalist narratives. A few scholars argue that the role of the peasants in India's freedom struggle has been misunderstood; they were forced to make greater sacrifices for securing class collaboration but their participation influenced political outcomes after India won freedom. Given the immense differences in the impact of colonialism on India and China peasant based revolution was not an option in India.[11] A National Liberation Movement in Vietnam succeeded because the option of a non-violent middle class based movement was unavailable. In some countries like Indonesia and Malaysia communist uprisings were suppressed. Therefore, the evolution of India and Indian democracy was decisively shaped by the success of a non-violent mass movement that produced a certain consensus about the future of India's economy and society. The crucial importance of the middle class in shaping policies in India, as opposed to the basic social classes, has been articulated in various ways. Even the concept of an "intermediate regime." has been used to explain Indian economic development in diverse ways.[12]

BROAD CONSENSUS ON THE PATH OF DEVELOPMENT

In the realm of economic policy the national movement did throw up the ideal of an independent path of economic development with a strong emphasis on self-reliance, industrialization and state intervention to achieve desirable social objectives. The growth of state intervention worldwide as a result of the Second World War and the post-war emphasis on full employment and Keynesian ideas in Britain, made socialist ideas broadly acceptable.[13] The growth of a socialist orientation within the Congress from the time of the Karachi Congress in 1931 made the path of economic development in India more socialist or less capitalist than it might otherwise have been. Nehru was a product of the national movement and he helped to carry forward that legacy when he became Prime Minister.[14] Even prominent capitalists accepted the need for some state intervention in the economy and the need to accept some socialist ideology.[15]

The ideology of socialism was not dominant but the concern for the common man was shared by orthodox socialists and those with a Gandhian bent of mind as well. The communists were not happy with the mixed economy that evolved subsequently during the 1950s but nor were the supporters of free enterprise. The post-independence path of development represented the consensus of the period and articulated the aspirations that had emerged during India's freedom struggle. The broad consensus was on state-backed economic development with emphasis on social justice.[16] Whenever we think of counterfactual alternatives we have to keep the legacy of the national movement and the broad national consensus in mind. There were alternative paths of development but they were not equally popular or politically feasible. The Communist party and the *Swatantra* party were not in a position to mount a serious political challenge to the Congress during the 1950s.[17] The significance of the consensus eroded steadily as the Congress party failed to deliver on its promises and those groups and ideologies that had been pushed to the margins began to assert themselves by the 1960s.

PAKISTAN AND INCLUSIVE NATIONALISM

The two nation theory and the birth of Pakistan constituted a major blow to the ideology of composite nationalism that the Congress party had tried to articulate during the national movement. Many radicals argued that Muslim League was a party that represented the feudal and elitist sections of the Muslim community in India. These elites used communal ideology to mobilize the common man in support of Pakistan. At an abstract level some Marxists argued that uneven development of capitalism led to the emergence of nationalities and their ambition to acquire control over national markets led to demands for independent nation-states. The Communist party in India supported the demand for Pakistan as a product of nationalism.[18]

The work of recent scholars has tended to blame the Congress leadership and Hindu majoritarianism for compelling the Muslim community to demand Pakistan. Other scholars have argued that Pakistan became a popular demand during the 1940s and the League became a representative of Muslim nationalism. The rise of multiculturalism in the west and communitarian perspectives has led to substantial rethinking about the religious and cultural diversity of India.[19] Nevertheless, it is best to conclude that Indian nationalism was neither derivative nor unitary. As Sudipto Kaviraj observes Indian nationalism was "a second-order identity, but not something insubstantial, fraudulent or artificial."[20] The political management of the immense diversity of the country has been difficult at certain points of time but pragmatism and political flexibility have eventually prevailed.

The national movement espoused the ideals of inclusive nationalism—or composite nationalism—in the vocabulary used at the time of the freedom struggle. This has been contested by the subaltern and communitarian scholars and by the articulate and radical spokesmen of various communities in the country today.[21] The national movement cannot be held accountable for the denial of the claims of communities that had not emerged politically before independence. That it did not meet the expectations of the most radical sections of the marginalized groups of that period is another matter. In many ways the right of the Indian national elites to 'represent' the people was more credible than that of many European national movements of the late nineteenth and early tweentieth centuries. The failure of the Indian national movement was primarily in terms of the inability to reach out to the Muslim community not so much other communities or nationalities. The *Dalits* and the Backward Castes were not mobilized sufficiently at the time of independence.

Building on the traditions of the national movement the Congress party was able to carry forward after partition a broadly secular and inclusive nation building ideology. It was this tradition that sustained the Indian political system's ability to manage or accommodate the claims of various politically mobilized groups over time.[22] An Indian political scientist has argued that whenever democracy is introduced in a developing country it "nearly always exacerbates political conflicts over the short to medium term." If the elites are accommodating then the problem of ethnic group mobilization can be handled reasonably well. Flexible policies enabled the Indian state to eventually pacify and win over ethnically mobilized groups in Tamil Nadu and Punjab.[23] This was facilitated not only by well managed institutions in a liberal democratic polity but also the conception of nationalism that the political elites have.

The Indian state could cope effectively with identity politics because there was the possibility of democratic opposition. Even more there was no single ethnic group that controlled the Indian state and determined its identity. Although the politicians of the Hindi belt dominated, they could neither disproportionately corner the rewards of controlling state power nor were they in control of the business and cultural resources of the country. Even if the North Indian pro-Hindi bias restricted the proper articulation of inclusive nationalism this was often despite the official proclamations and initiatives by the State.[24] Unlike in Pakistan where one State and ethnic group became predominant in India there has been a balance between regions and communities. The survival of India as a plural society owes as much to this demographic and economic reality as it does to the legacy of the national movement and the wisdom of the men who wielded power during the 1950s.

It must be acknowledged even by the spokesmen of groups that felt neglected or marginalized that the state did respond to the needs of different groups in terms of political recognition and economic concessions. Undoubtedly the grievances of *Dalits*, Muslims and the Backward Castes have been more forcefully articulated in recent years. What has to be kept in mind is that popular as well as elite conceptions of inclusive nationalism are always restricted by the standards of democratic and group rights prevailing at any point of time. Although the conceptions of inclusive nationalism have become more expansive in recent times there has also been the rise of illiberal tendencies in Indian society. Sharper religious and caste identities in India today may be regarded as part of a global trend of illiberalism that a perceptive observer has written about.[25]

DEMOCRACY AND ECONOMIC GROWTH

There is a need to look at the connection between the maintenance of a plural society and the path of economic development based on democracy in India. There is an argument that the slow rate of economic growth in the country after independence is closely linked to the need to keep the diverse communities of India in good humour and to ensure the harmonization of interests within a democratic framework. There is no denying the fact that rational dictators can achieve fairly good results if they manage their economy well.[26] The Chinese economic surge since the 1980s has been greatly facilitated by the control over labour, rural-urban migration, political opposition groups and the media. In a democracy like India strikes, bandhs, ethnic and religious and caste based protest movements have the capacity to disrupt public life and slow down growth. Democracy may be desirable for its own sake but enlightened dictators at least in China have made great strides in terms of economic growth with a fair measure of concern for the ordinary man.

In the case of India, a country with far greater linguistic and cultural diversity than China, the working of democracy might arguably be necessary to preserve the political unity of the country. In order to maintain regional balance and manage diversity democracy might be more desirable in India than in China. The rate of growth in India might be somewhat circumscribed not only because of the working of Indian parliamentary democracy but the political management of unity within diversity. However, the rates of growth depend on many variables and democracy and diversity are just two of them. A larger population in the working age group is a factor that helps countries grow and experts have argued that this worked for East Asia between 1965 and 1990 and is likely to work in South Asia's favour in the years ahead.[27] Also dictatorships find it difficult to survive loss of legitimacy and economic decline. This happened in the Soviet Union during the 1980s. Finally, we do not know how societies and economies will evolve in the long run. Enlightened dictatorships historically have done well for short periods of time, but they could also evolve into democracies later. This has happened in the case of the Soviet Union and Eastern Europe.

DEMOCRACY, EDUCATION AND GROWTH

The existence of democracy in any society does create certain constraints affecting the rate of growth and savings, the sacrifices that can be imposed on the present generation for the benefit of the next one, the ability to acquire control over resources like land, mineral wealth and water resources and the ability to maintain law and order necessary for rapid growth. The USA for instance could not ignore the public protests against the loss of human lives in Vietnam.[28] By contrast the USSR could allocate huge sums to defence without a public outcry. Casualties in Afghanistan during the 1980s took a long time to erode the credibility of the government. The USSR could ask a whole generation during the 1930s to endure hardships that any elected government would have found impossible to impose on its people. It has now been acknowledged that the high budgetary allocations for the capital goods sector in the Soviet economy helped the USSR to industrialize rapidly during the 1930s.[29]

Nevertheless there are choices available to capitalist democracies in the form of foreign investments to boost economic growth. It was the substantial investment of foreign capital in export oriented economies like South Korea and Taiwan that enabled them to grow substantially during the 1960s and 1970s.[30] The imperatives of the cold war that led the west to prop up countries under threat of subversion by communists from within and without is only part of the reason for the inflow of capital. The substantial improvement brought about by land reforms and investment in human capital enabled these countries to develop as export oriented economies.[31] Therefore, authoritarian capitalism, without communist totalitarian regimes, has also made considerable progress in the post-World War II period. The countries in which such rapid growth did take place were those which had few nationality issues to grapple with and also did not make any special provisions for the minority groups that existed.[32]

The critics of democracy argue that it promotes redistributive policies and higher taxes and also discourages savings and capital accumulation. An empirical study has shown that the negative implications of democracy can be outweighed by the rise in education and investment that are also a consequence of democracy. Although education contributes to growth "differences in education levels" do not explain the differences in the growth rates among Asian countries.[33] Recent empirical studies of a large number of countries have shown that the implications of democracy for growth are difficult to measure. One scholar has concluded that there was a negative relation between democracy and growth during the 1960s and a positive one during the 1980s. For three of the four decades between the 1960s and 1990s "both the pro-democracy and anti-democracy argument can be completely rejected."[34] Also the implications of democracy for growth depend on the time period of study and the statistical significance depends on the choice of specifications. The issue of comparison is greatly complicated by the fact that notions of democracy and the levels and quality of education are difficult to capture in large studies.

When considering the case of India we find that the country after independence had very little chance of adopting the harsh methods of totalitarian communist countries like China or even those of the more humane totalitarian regimes like Cuba. Yet the rate of development would have been higher if the country had made greater investment in human capital.[35] It is clear that universal primary education could not have been achieved in the country without outlays that were considerably higher than were made. Addressing people at Chatham House in England Mahatma Gandhi had said that if we want the costly conventional kind of education it would take almost a century to provide compulsory primary education.[36] Therefore, he supported the idea of basic education. Also the size of the country meant that what could have had a catalytic affect on a small country or economy would not have the same impact on a large country like India. Nevertheless literacy and the quality of life and democratic culture are intimately linked and the benefits of higher levels of literacy would have been substantial.[37]

Literacy could have made the propaganda about family planning more effective and the general public more careful about whom it voted into power. In China the one-child norm worked not only because of higher levels of literacy but also because of the incentives and disincentives put in place by the one party state. In India the acceptance of family planning has been constrained because of lack of literacy and awareness. The southern states with higher levels of literacy have a better record than the northern states where literacy is lower. The fears of adverse popular reactions, particularly after the backlash against policies introduced during the period of Emergency in 1975-1977, have also reduced the enthusiasm for family planning programmes. A rise in literacy also increases political awareness. It partly accounts for the decline of caste as a factor in politics in the villages of North India during the 1990s.[38] Yet the politics of caste- based reservation erupted violently in Rajasthan with the Gujjar community engaged in a fierce struggle for their rights not long after the optimistic findings cited above were published.

There is no reason why a capitalist democracy controlled by enlightened elite should not be able to achieve a substantial rate of growth. Yet certain negative consequences of electoral democracy have to be kept in mind. One of the problems is that politicians seeking election are reluctant to take hard decisions or to stick to them faced with a popular backlash. Even in a more advanced society with far greater literacy like that of Britain the Conservative Margaret Thatcher fought against the spendthrift policies of the Labour party that accepted the role of State intervention in the economy, high levels of public spending and welfare policies. Keynesian policies were challenged by Smithian liberalism and monetarism. So, it is arguable that the benefits in terms of electoral maturity and wise economic decision making that flow from universal literacy can be exaggerated. After all either the Keynesians or the neo-conservative ideologues had messed up the economy, depending on individual political preferences. Nevertheless for developing countries the impact of literacy is definitely positive in terms of well-being and political awareness whatever the implications for growth might be.

The need to gain a majority of the votes in a political system does take its toll even with a literate electorate. The quality of the politicians does improve, as does the life of the ordinary citizen, but wise economic decisions are still hard to arrive at. Economic competitiveness of nations is connected to both education levels and wage levels.[39] The levels of education in the United States rose substantially after Second World War but US economic competitiveness declined by the late twentieth century.[40] Arguably the rewards from literacy could add to personal well-being in more developed countries but lead to loss of jobs owing to imports from low wage countries.

DIVERSITY, DEMOCRACY AND GROWTH

The problem of pluralism in India is far more complex than that of most countries. In the USSR the problem of plurality, based on language and ethnicity, was handled in a more rigid manner. All those who were deemed bourgeois nationalists were declared enemies of the state and socialism. They were arrested, deported to Siberia or exterminated. The right to national culture and identity was recognized within the framework of socialism and the dictatorship of the proletariat. The Soviet citizen had two passports—one of the republic to which he belonged and one of the Soviet Union.[41] While this policy made the Kazakhs in the post-Soviet period relatively mild nationalists the Armenians developed essentialist nationalism.[42] The absence of democracy meant that regular feedback from the national minorities was not required. In India there is only one citizenship and only one passport despite the fact that the linguistic and cultural rights of the individual in the states of the Indian union are taken far more seriously and there is no attempt to impose a straitjacket ideology or culture.

Indian national ideology has been sufficiently loosely defined to make pragmatic adjustments to changes in group demands over time. The survival of India as a single nation despite its evident diversity is because the notion of Indianness is sufficiently inclusive to keep the various groups within the country content to remain within the Indian nation. There have also been moments of extreme stress when those who were dissatisfied with their lot had to be retained by coercion within the Indian Union as in the North East and Kashmir. The alienation of the Indian Muslims from time to time and in some parts of the country is also a reminder that Indianness is often not sufficiently inclusive.[43]

There is no reason to argue that democracies cannot take the right decisions or adopt a consistent policy but there are certain constraints. The problems increase in a plural society.[44] The need to win votes leads political parties to use caste and religious identities to win electoral support. The Congress party too since the time of independence has tried to keep the caste and religious profiles of candidates in mind when fielding candidates in different constituencies. Parties appealing primarily to religious identities and regional or linguistic identities also exist in India and their numbers and influence have grown with the decline in the dominance of the Congress party.[45] The under representation of the "lower castes" in North India[46] became a first class political controversy after the V.P. Singh government endorsed the Mandal Report in 1990. The rise of leaders like Mayawati and the Bahujan Samaj Party are a part of this process. Mandal II and the Sachar Committee Report have highlighted the problems of the Other Backward Classes and the Muslims recently. These efforts have led to short-lived periods of political agitations and backlash but the terms of public discourse and political alignments within the country have been altered as a consequence.[47] These movements have built on differences between groups that are divisive from a liberal standpoint but the need for widening opportunities cannot be denied. The political and social costs are difficult to estimate because such an evaluation is influenced by the different outcomes for the parties involved.

The economic and political costs of movements for the affirmation of linguistic rights as in Andhra during the 1950s and of communitarian or religious identity as in the Punjab during the 1980s have been the cause of much anxiety in India. The problems of alienation in the North-East and in Kashmir have imposed a heavy financial and military burden on the country. The use of religion for mobilization by the *Ramjanmabhoomi* movement led to a vast change in the politics of the country. The communal polarization contributed to the defeat of the Congress in 1989 and culminated in the collapse of the Babri Masjid in 1992. Therefore there is a feeling among some experts that the need to secure electoral support leads politicians to fan religious and linguistic sentiments to come to power.[48] As political awareness spread the unequal rewards of development produced the basis for ethnic and religious mobilization. The electoral system allows politicians to exploit differences and perceived injustice but there has to be some basis for this mobilization.[49] Wise States in a democratic system can handle these problems by initiating appropriate policy changes.[50]

Some of these movements may be regarded as those which try to empower the disadvantaged groups like the *Dalits* and the OBCs. As a consequence of various factors the notions of caste hierarchy have become very weak even if caste identities are still important.[51] Some movements are actually a kind of nationality demand. Therefore, the costs that these movements impose on society may partly have to be offset by the fact that they provide some opening for disadvantaged groups. The costs imposed by bandhs, political stalemates and agitations are high but are the consequence of real as well as perceived neglect of some group or groups. The democratic political system allows groups to assert themselves, often in ways that are far from liberal, because the liberals have ignored the needs of specific groups. If the liberal tradition takes care of their needs then the problems will not become so intractable. The negotiation of the relationship between ethnic and linguistic groups in a democracy should be possible in a more durable manner if the elites are sufficiently wise.[52] Of course, wars can also be a great catalyst for change. The socialist tendencies in Europe were greatly weakened by World War I which strengthened nationalist sentiments in Europe.[53] Two World Wars led eventually to the rise of democracy and social democracy in Western Europe by the 1960s.

In a dictatorship since such identities are suppressed they do not obstruct development or impose costs on the country till the regime loses its power or legitimacy. When a regime loses its legitimacy, as was the case of the Soviet Union, various ethnic political groups go their own way. The various Soviet republics became independent countries when the USSR broke up after 1991. When the power of the regime weakens there are revolts against it as in the case of the Austro-Hungarian and Ottoman empires. Of course in these two cases the First World War played an important role in dismembering them as did the diplomatic maneuvers of the victorious powers at Versailles.[54] The growth of ethnic political conflicts and fascism in interwar Europe was based on movements that used scapegoats and built mass support on the basis of resentments that were produced by economic distress. The possibility of the subversion of democracy by such authoritarian and fascist movements has been the subject of many studies.[55] Dictatorships and authoritarian regimes are more successful in reducing the economic and political costs of competition among religious and linguistic groups while they are in control but face the risks of breakdowns and disintegration when they lose their grip on the state and society.

In India the use of caste identities has been reinforced by electoral mobilization and the system of constitutional and administrative arrangements. To some extent the recognition of such differences has allowed the Indian political system to cope with Indian diversity.[56] On the other hand the use of strategies to gain a majority of votes by mobilizing on the basis of ethnic and caste or religious identities has a tendency to produce more and more polarization that is disruptive and retards development. The use of money and muscle power also distorts the democratic process and makes the authoritarian regime seem a preferable alternative to such ineffective democratic regimes. Some regimes are so overwhelmed by their opponents and militant groups that they are declared failed states instead of just soft states.[57] Therefore, the democratic countries are better placed to deal with ethnic differences if they can handle the issue pragmatically. Where they fail to do so the regimes become repressive and where their repressive capacity proves inadequate there are civil wars, widespread secessionist movements and long and costly wars of attrition. The examples of Rwanda, Sri Lanka and Northern Ireland come to mind. Democracies in principle can handle diversity better but very often they function badly and produce terrible consequences.

The broad conclusion is that the differences between regimes that are more or less democratic and those that are authoritarian or totalitarian do not adequately explain their economic performance or the handling of diversity. If the Indian government had invested in human capital development after independence it might have been able to slow down population growth, increase democratic participation and economic growth. Higher levels of literacy are no guarantee of democracy and harmony. Although the levels of literacy were much higher than in India, the mishandling of Tamil grievances during the 1980s, led to bloody civil war. This setback the Sri Lankan economy and society by a few decades. Appropriate investment in human capital has beneficial effects regardless of the system in which it is introduced but cannot compensate for the absence of other favourable factors. Public investment that sustained the green revolution enabled Punjab and Haryana with much lower levels of literacy to enjoy a higher per capita income than Kerala. Literacy, however, enabled Malayali labour migration to the Gulf region and other parts of India which compensated for a less diversified regional economy. Greater ethnic and linguistic diversity has a certain negative impact on a polity and economy because balanced regional development and affirmative action policies become necessary. The need to manage the consequences of diversity may be less in non-democratic regimes, but they are definitely there.

In the case of India the diversity is greater than that of most other countries and the need to cope with this diversity definitely imposes limitations on the policies that can be followed. If there were vast inequalities between regions and politically sensitive communities the political stability of India would be adversely affected. Prolonged neglect could even lead to secessionist movements and a break-up of the nation-state. In a more homogeneous society these problems are less complex and impose fewer constraints. Even if India were controlled by a dictatorship it could not afford to ignore the needs of various ethnic, linguistic and religious groups in the country. The rate of economic growth and the path of development in India can be partly explained in terms of the management of the needs and aspirations of diverse communities in

India if the electoral system gets distorted it imposes greater burdens on society than in a well ordered democratic system.

HOW INCLUSIVE IS INDIAN DEMOCRACY?

There is a question mark against India's democratic credentials at the beginning of the twenty-first century although the idea of democracy is no longer confined to the middle classes and the upper castes.[58] The country was ruled by the monolithic Congress party after independence based on the support of a cross section of society but of the Scheduled Castes and Tribes, Muslims and upper castes in particular. The rise of the intermediate castes and of peasant based parties challenged this dominance during the 1960s. The rise of the Backward Castes as a political force and the growth of regional parties challenged this hegemony of the Congress during the 1990s. In fact Mandal produced such anxieties that those opposed to it almost regarded it as anti-national.

The process of democratic mobilization is a legitimate activity, but excessive demands and expectations by both advantaged and disadvantaged groups can cause serious economic and political difficulties. The demand of various farmer interests for subsidized electricity and fertilizers can impose a serious burden on the exchequer.[59] The state as a great dispenser of largesse tends to distort the proper functioning of the economy because of the presence of distributional coalitions.[60] Identity politics grows as a result of the need felt by disadvantaged groups to create the basis for a greater share in the allocation of funds and subsidies by the State. Identity politics and the politics of distribution are intimately connected. In fact a recent study claims that *Hindutva* is a cover behind which "the classes of the former intermediate regime" gather to cope with the strains of national development and globalization. The intermediate classes which benefited from shortages and stagnation in the past have adopted castist and neo-Swadeshi agenda.[61]

The ability of the state to provide subsidies is limited by its tax revenues and excessive demands can create financial problems. On the other hand the subsidies themselves do not help the farmers as much as the fertilizer companies; cheap power supply worsens the financial viability of the state controlled power supply companies and the farm support policies are of far greater benefit to the rich farmers rather than the poor and middle peasants. The need to win the support of the peasants drives the political leaders to promise subsidies and the waiver of farm loans and electricity bills.[62]

The political system tends to distort the economic system. The milking of public sector companies by political leaders for various reasons also affects the viability of the sector. The overstaffing to appease local interests also distorts the functioning of the public sector units. Therefore, the political system produces economic affects that tend to distort the proper functioning of public sector units. The interest groups that fund political parties seek favours from government and try and derive benefit from the state. While some of these problems are inescapable when the scale becomes very substantial it definitely makes the working of democracy seems a rather costly affair. The cost seems particularly high because it tends to put the less organized groups at a definite disadvantage in dealing with this politics of patronage and distribution of benefits.

Those who are outside the framework of this politics of distribution, which is closely linked to the politics of identity, are the ones who are least persuaded that India is a democratic society. However, what has been called the "second democratic upsurge" has led many members of the disadvantaged groups to feel that the logic of electoral competition and majority rule will eventually bring benefits. Inclusive nationalism and inclusive democracy are intimately linked to each other. So, the OBC groups have reason to be optimistic but many in the tribal hinterland, because they do not have similar expectations, come under the spell of various groups, some times loosely called Maoists in various parts of tribal India. Some scholars believe that the number and influence of such Maoists has been greatly exaggerated,[63] but they definitely do not have as much faith in the politics of identity and electoral democracy as other disadvantaged groups.

THE COSTS AND BENEFITS OF DEMOCRACY

One needs to sum up the argument about the political and economic costs and benefits of democracy. Any assessment must take into account different parameters. There is no doubt that at certain points in time the economic progress of democracies is likely to be slower than that of enlightened dictatorships, whether communist or capitalist. The performance of the Indian economy has improved over the last two decades, although there are signs of rising disparities. The growth rate has accelerated partly because of the enormous achievements of the pre-liberalization period in creating the infrastructure for growth. What is most relevant is that economic growth has accelerated within a democratic system.[64] Where there is a lack of economic incentive for the work force, a slowing down of innovation and excessive allocation for defence, as in the Soviet Union, there is a slowing down of growth. Capitalist democracies fared better than the Soviet Union during the 1970s and 1980s. Where the rate of growth has to be given less importance than income inequalities and minimum standards for the bottom half of the population then capitalist democracies may not be ahead of the Soviet Union during the same period in terms of certain indices.

If the emphasis is on democratic rights like civil liberties and a free press then the capitalist democracies are way ahead. Once the minimum requirements of large sections of the population have been taken care of then the value that people place on such democratic rights becomes higher than when they are underfed and without basic necessities of life. The value of democracy becomes greater for the bottom half of the population in any part of the world when their minimum expectations have been fulfilled. So, the people who had achieved minimum standards of living under actually existing socialism were open to the appeals of consumerism and capitalism. Many in the Third World, where standards of living are still precarious, continue to be inspired by socialist ideals. Even actually existing socialism of the 1980s seemed a step forward to many victims of slow growth in certain parts of the world.

In India the benefits of growth and democratic rights are tangible benefits for at least a quarter of the population. The rest of the population could in fact set fewer stores by the virtue of capitalism and democracy. Nevertheless the workings of democracy have so entered the culture and consciousness of the majority of the Indian population that they have sufficient faith in it to work the system.[65] Besides, caste and communal politics has grown so much over the last quarter of a century that old style class based mass mobilization also seems a rather uphill task. After studying more than a hundred countries between 1970 and 1996 two scholars have concluded that some features of globalization—trade openness and portfolio investment—adversely influence democracy, but foreign direct investment has a positive influence. Only the dissemination of democratic ideas strengthens democracy over a long period of time.[66] Therefore, the rise of democratic ideas in India, despite numerous inadequacies of the Indian political system, bode well for the future of Indian democracy.

Democracy has struck deeper roots in India than in many countries with a similar level of economic development and literacy. The growth of a large number of identities, spawned as much by unequal development as well as by the logic of electoral competition and the politics of distribution, also makes it unlikely that democracy can function effectively or ensure the most conducive climate for rapid growth. The situation in India seems to be one in which growth will have to be maximized in a context in which identity based politics and distortion of choices as a result of electoral compulsions will remain factors to reckon with. The question that has to be asked is: Do the elite think the rate of growth needs to be accelerated even if it means the denial of democratic rights and the claims of various disadvantaged groups to preferential treatment? The answer is that whatever they might prefer the system cannot be wholly transformed to resemble that of China or even South Korea and Singapore.

As far as considerable sections of Indian society are concerned the prospects of using democratic rights and institutions to promote their interests seem bright; newly mobilized groups appear fairly optimistic about their future.[67] Identity politics can be used to secure some form of distributive justice and democratically elected governments can be counted on to further their agendas. Those who are unable to see a brighter future for themselves are the ones who might prefer a dictatorship that favours their interests as opposed to that of the rich and privileged. So, there are those who would favour a non-democratic solution to India's problems from the standpoint of the privileged and those who would do so from the standpoint of the underprivileged. At the moment the possibility of either one or the other succeeding is highly unlikely.

The broad consensus that sustained Indian democracy and the mixed economy with a socialist bias during the first-two to three decades of the post-independence period has vanished. A new consensus has not been fully worked out but it seems to favour a liberalization of the economy with a commitment to social justice in terms of the needs of disadvantaged groups like the OBC's and the Muslims.[68] This has emerged out of the logic of electoral politics and competition rather than economic ideology but it represents a point on which the major political parties seem to agree. This is a kind of consensus too, though not born out of a long period of ideological and political struggles. As the costs and benefits of democracy will be viewed differently by the elites, the newly mobilized groups and the marginalized the question cannot be addressed without keeping these social class and political differences in mind. When we consider the costs and benefits of British imperialism the question of social class differences have to be kept in mind. The consequences of democracy for India have to be judged by the same yardstick.

CONCLUSION

When we look at the problem of change in societies that have evolved from merchant capitalism to industrial capitalism and to others that have evolved from Maoist communism to a market friendly economy under a communist party dictatorship we are confronted with the problem of deciding whether to see continuity or change, a gradual change or a sharp break. In the case of the British economy the gentlemanly capitalist argument about relatively gradual transition is still around.[69] In the Chinese case the policies of Deng and his ideological heirs marked a sharp departure from those of the past but there were continuities in terms of the structure of power in China. The Chinese communists control the Chinese polity although the market is dominant in the economic sphere.

In India we find elements of both continuity and change. Indian pluralism and diversity are still factors that the liberal elite cannot ignore. In a sense the breakdown of the traditional vote banks and the assertion of the disadvantaged has influenced the political perception of caste and religion. The supporters of a hard secular ideology within the Congress have declined over the last decade or so because the party is not sure if that will help it win elections. After all, if the Yadav-Muslim alliance in Uttar Pradesh will not be dented then there is no point in antagonizing the Hindu voters. Those who broadly support secular values vote for many parties like the Samajwadi party, the Congress and regional parties. There is also evidence of fragmentation of vote banks which worked till not so long ago. Muslims and *Dalits* may vote for different parties and so communitarian appeals may be insufficient to attract them to any single political party. Therefore, the hard secular stand may not yield electoral dividends because there is no monolithic Muslim community that will turn *en masse* towards the rejuvenated secular Congress. Since the supporters of *Hindutva* too cannot mobilize enough support, the Indian political system will probably remain one in which two broad but unstable coalitions struggle for dominance. National parties purportedly representing secularism and Hindu majoritarianism or Hindu cultural nationalism have been unable to secure a dominant position on their own within the framework of Indian parliamentary democracy for quite some time.

While the state can be pushed out of the sphere of production by the votaries of the free market the logic of electoral competition compels them to deal with problems of identity politics. The state can divest itself of responsibilities in one sphere but has to accept the need to provide for those groups which are excluded from the mainstream. Those whom development had offered little in the pre-liberalization phase and those no better off after liberalization—sections of the peasantry and large swathes of the tribal population—have to be provided a measure of support by the democratically elected governments today to make India an inclusive democracy and a just society. There is a sense of deprivation and marginalization that drives men and women into organizations of the extreme left and right today. By whatever name we wish to call the groups the marginalized turn to or they choose themselves the issues have to be tackled. Indian democracy has to tackle the consequences of uneven development and neo-liberal economic policies.

The Indian economy can grow at a satisfactory rate even while protecting democratic rights in a plural society. Authoritarian governments have certain advantages, but we do not know how long they can last. Once the system opens up and democratic institutions are introduced they may face far more acute problems than India does today. In the case of China the situation appears better than that of the Soviet Union in the 1980s. When the Soviet Union introduced glasnost and perestroika their economy was sluggish and inefficient; by contrast the Chinese economy is growing by leaps and bounds. There are clear signs of growing income and regional inequalities in contemporary China.[70] The problem of ethnic and religious minorities is less likely to become explosive while the Chinese continue to grow at the pace they have maintained so far. The rapid growth that took place in China after 1980 led to the neglect of the welfare needs of working people as the proportion of contract workers employed by the state as well as private employers rose substantially.[71] The Chinese have managed to achieve higher growth within an authoritarian system but their economic reforms have created problems as well.

The Indian economy could grow faster if economic or community based grievances and agitations did not frequently act as a dampening influences. The Indian record of handling diversity within a democratic framework, though not without its flaws and failures, is reasonably satisfactory. Therefore, it serves as a model of an economy that can grow reasonably fast while trying to handle problems of distributive justice in communitarian terms in a democratic polity. The Indian national movement is considered a remarkable example of a primarily non-violent struggle that secured independence from British rule. There were votaries of violence but their influence never matched that of the mainstream national movement. The Indian state working within the framework of democracy has to ensure that the groups that are marginalized are incorporated in society even using methods that involve a burden on the exchequer. Violence does not have to be met with violence in all cases; it can be made less attractive to the groups that are engaged in violence. State and non-governmental organizations can play a role even in the context of neo-liberal policies and globalization.[72]

The achievement of Indian industrialization after independence until liberalization has been based primarily on domestic resources and within a democratic framework which has few parallels. The opening of the economy after 1991 has created both problems and opportunities. The success of the political elites and the much more numerous middle class would lie in accelerating growth within a socially inclusive and democratic framework. Inclusive nationalism espoused by the Indian National Congress helped to unite the diverse linguistic and cultural groups before independence but could not avert the vivisection of the country. The conceptions of inclusive nationalism and inclusive democracy espoused by the Indian elite today, political as well as economic, have to be sufficiently broad minded if the country has to move forward surely and confidently.

REFERENCES

1. Eric J. Hobsbawm, *Age of Extremes: The Short Twentieth Century,* 1914-1991, Delhi: Viking, 1995.
2. Compare the economic history of India written by Irfan Habib and Tirthankar Roy. I. Habib (ed.), *Essays in Indian History: Towards a Marxist Perspective*, Delhi: 2002 and T. Roy, *The Economic History of India, 1857-1947*, Delhi: OUP, 2000.
3. The aim of the subaltern studies school was to write a history from below but it implicitly compared India with the movement in China under Mao Tse-Tung. See Introduction, in Ranajit Guha, (ed.), *Subaltern Studies*, Volume I, Delhi: OUP, 1982.
4. Partha Chatterjee, *The Nation and its Fragments: Colonial and Postcolonial Histories*, Delhi: OUP, 1994. D.L. Sheth regards the changes at the time of independence as a form of counter-revolution from a Gandhian point of view.
5. See I.G. Patel in Dwijendra Tripathi, ed., *State and Business in India: A Historical Perspective*, Delhi: Manohar, 1987.
6. For the incorporation of counterfactual perspectives in mainstream works see Roderick Floud and Paul Johnson, eds. *The Cambridge Economic History of Modern Britain*, Vol. I, *Industrialization*, 1700-1860, Cambridge: Cambridge University Press, 2004 and Vol. II, *Economic Maturity*, 1860-1939, Cambridge: CUP, 2004.

7. M.N. Roy, *India in Transition,* Geneva: 1922 and R.P. Dutt, *India Today*, Bombay: 1949; Muzaffar Ahmad, *Communists Challenge Imperialism from the Dock: The Meerut Conspiracy Case, 1929-33,* Calcutta: 1967.
8. Sumit Sarkar, *Popular' Movements and 'Middle Class' Leadership: Perspectives and Problems of a 'History from Below.'* Calcutta: 1983.
9. Anil Seal, *The Emergence of Indian Nationalism: Competition and Collaboration in the Late Nineteenth Century*, Cambridge: CUP., 1968); D.A. Low, ed. Congress and the Raj, Delhi: 1978.
10. David Hardiman, *Peasant Nationalists of Gujarat: Kheda District, 1917-1934,* New Delhi: OUP, 1981.
11. See Bipan Chandra., ed., *The Indian Left: Critical Appraisals*, Delhi: Vikas, 1983. Also see Mridula Mukherjee, *Peasants in India's Non-Violent Revolution,* New Delhi: Sage, 2004. See especially, chapter 8.
12. M. Kalecki, *Essays on the Economic Growth of the Socialist and the Mixed Economy,* London: 1972; and K.N. Raj, The Politics and Economics of Intermediate Regimes, *The Economic and Political Weekly,* 7th July, 1973.
13. Robert Skidelsky, *John Maynard Keynes*, Penguin, 2005. Also see A. Booth, The Keynesian Revolution in Economic Policy Making, *Economic History Review*, Vol. XXXVI, 1983.
14. S. Gopal, *Jawaharlal Nehru,* Delhi: OUP, 1978.
15. Stanley Kochanek, *Business and Politics in India*, California: California University Press, 1974 and Claude Markovits, *Indian Business and Nationalist Politics 1931-39*, Cambridge: CUP. 1985.
16. T. Byres (Ed.), *The State and Development Planning in India*, New Delhi: OUP, 1993.
17. Howard Erdman, *The Swatantra Party and Indian Conservatism*, Cambridge: CUP, 1967.
18. K.N. Panikkar (Ed.), *Nationalist and Left-wing Movements in India,* Delhi: 1980.
19. See Peter van der Veer, *Religious Nationalism: Hindus and Muslims in India,* California: 1994; and Dipesh Chakrabarty, *Habitations of Modernity*, Delhi: Permanent Black, 2002.
20. Sudipto Kaviraj, Modernity and Politics in India, *Daedalus,* Vol. 129, No. 1; Multiple Modernities, Winter, 2000, pp. 137-162, Quote p. 154.
21. Ayesha Jalal, *Self and Sovereignty: Individual and Community in South Asian Islam since 1850,* New Delhi: OUP, 2001. Also see Kancha Illiah, Dalitism *vs* Brahmanism: The Epistemological Conflict in History, in Ghanshyam Shah (ed.), *Dalit Identity and Politics,* New Delhi: Sage, 2001.
22. Narendra Subramanian, Bringing Society Back in Ethnicity, Populism and Pluralism in South Asia in Zoya Hasan (Ed.), *Parties and Party Politics in India*, Delhi: OUP. 2002.
23. Atul Kohli, Can Democracies Accommodate Ethnic Nationalism? Rise

and Decline of Self-Determination Movements in India, *The Journal of Asian Studies*, Vol. 56, No. 2, May, 1997, pp. 325-344.

24. Mushirul Hasan, *The Legacy of a Divided Nation: India's Muslims since Independence*, Westview press, 1997; Bipan Chandra, Mridula Mukherjee and Aditya Mukherjee, *India after Independence*, Delhi: Sage, 1999.
25. Fareed Zakaria, The Rise of Illiberal Democracy, *Foreign Affairs*, Vol. 76, No. 6, November-December 1997, pp. 22-43.
26. A critic of the Soviet Union still regards Stalin as a rational dictator who twice reduced investment in order to provide consumer goods to workers to boost output. See Paul Gregory, *The Political Economy of Stalinism: Evidence from the Soviet Archives,* New York: Cambridge University Press, 2004.
27. David Bloom and Jeffrey G. Williamson, Demographic Transitions and Economic Miracles in Emerging Asia, *The World Bank Economic Review*, Vol. 12, No. 3, September 1998, pp. 419-455. This demographic dividend can fail to deliver positive results if education and skill levels do not rise. If the rate of increase in the working age population is primarily going to be in India's less developed North Indian States it is likely that labour migration to neighbouring States could fuel ethnic and linguistic conflicts.
28. For a comparison between the USA and the USSR see Samuel Huntington and Zbigniew Brzezinski, *USA/USSR: Political Power*, New York: Viking, 1968.
29. For the older views see Maurice Dobb, *Soviet Economic Development since 1917,* New York: 1948 and Abram Bergson, *The Real National Income of Soviet Russia since 1928,* Cambridge: Harvard University Press, 1961. For more recent views see Robert C. Allen, *Farm to Factory: A Reinterpretation of the Soviet Industrial Revolution*, Princeton: Princeton University Press, 2003 especially chapter 5, pp. 91-110 and chapter 8, pp. 153-171.
30. For an early Indian Marxist assessment of East Asian growth see Sukhamoy Chakravarty, Marxist Economics and Contemporary Developing Economies, *Cambridge Journal of Economics*, Volume 11, No. 1, March, 1987, pp. 3-22.
31. See John R. Hanson II, Human Capital and Direct Investment in Poor Countries, *Explorations in Economic History*, Vol. 33, 1996, pp. 86-106.
32. Outcomes in countries varied according to the nature of state and society linkages. See Peter Houtzager and Marcus Kurtz, The Institutional Roots of Popular Mobilization: State Transformation and Rural Politics in Brazil and Chile, 1960-1995, *Comparative Studies in Society and History*, Vol. 42, No. 2, April, 2000, pp. 394-424.
33. John Helliwell, Empirical Linkages between Democracy and Economic Growth, *British Journal of Political Science*, Vol. 24, No. 2, April, 1994, pp. 225-248.
34. Jonathan Krieckhaus, The Regime Debate Revisited: A Sensitivity Analysis

of Democracy's Economic Effect, *British Journal of Political Science*, Vol. 34, No. 4, October, 2004, pp. 635-655. Quote p. 653.

35. For the emphasis on literacy for empowerment see the emphasis on the Kerala model in development literature. For a broad perspective see Amartya Sen, *Development as Freedom*, Delhi: OUP, 1999.
36. M.K. Gandhi, The Future of India, *International Affairs*, Royal Institute of International Affairs, Vol. 10, No. 6, November, 1931, pp. 721-739. Mahatma Gandhi said, "I defy anybody to fulfil a programme of compulsory primary education of these masses inside of a century," p. 728.
37. According to Peter Lindert, in India "the voter turnout rate…correlates with the relative development of primary education and average incomes." See Peter Lindert, Voice and Growth: Was Churchill Right? *The Journal of Economic History*, Vol. 63, No. 2, June, 2003, pp. 315-350. See especially pp. 333-339. Observes Lindert, "As the importance of human skills and individual decision-making discretion grows, autocracy may obsolesce, just as the gains from slavery obsolesced." p. 345.
38. Anirudh Krishna, What is Happening to Caste? A View from Some North Indian Villages, *The Journal of Asian Studies*, Vol. 62, No. 4, November, 2003, pp. 1171-1193.
39. For the argument about labour market imperfections, see a review by Patrick K. O'Brien, Britain's Economy Between The Wars: A Survey of a Counter-Revolution in Economic History, *Past & Present*, Number 115, pp. 107-130. Also see Barry Eichengreen and T.J. Hatton, (ed.), *Interwar Unemployment in International Perspective*, Dordrecht/Boston/London: Kluwer Academic Publishers, 1988.
40. Michael Porter, *The Competitive Advantage of Nations*, New York: The Free Press, 1990.
41. Yuri Slezkine, The USSR as a Communal Apartment: or How a Socialist State Promoted Ethnic Particularism, *Slavic Review*, 53, No. 2, Summer 1994, pp. 414-52. Also see David Shearer, Elements Near and Alien: Passportization, Policing, and Identity in the Stalinist State, 1932-1952, *Journal of Modern History*, December, 2004, pp. 835-881.
42. Ronald Grigor Suny, Constructing Primordialism: Old Histories for New Nations, *The Journal of Modern History*, Vol. 73, No. 4, December, 2001, pp. 862-896.
43. Gyanendra Pandey, Can a Muslim Be an Indian? Comparative Studies in *Society and History*, Vol. 41, 1999, pp. 630-59.
44. Paul Brass, *The Politics of India since Independence*, Cambridge: CUP, 1990.
45. Christophe Jaffrelot, *The Hindu Nationalist Movement*, Delhi: 1996.
46. Christophe Jaffrelot, *India's Silent Revolution: The Rise of the Low Castes in North Indian Politics*, Delhi: Permanent Black, 2003.
47. See Zoya Hasan, *The Politics of Inclusion: Castes, Minorities and Affirmative Action*, New Delhi: OUP, 2009.

48. There is an argument that the Congress tried to appease Muslim and Hindu Communal Groups by turn during the 1980s. Sumit Sarkar, *Beyond Nationalist Frames: Relocating Postmodernism, Hindutva, History*, Delhi: Permanent Black, 2002.
49. In Bihar after a certain point in time the nature of backward class politics was itself transformed. See Sanjay Kumar, New Phase in Backward Caste Politics in Bihar, 1990-2000, in Ghanshyam Shah, (ed.), *Caste and Democratic Politics in India*, Delhi: Permanent Black, 2002.
50. A. Beteille, *Antinomies of Society: Essays on Ideologies and Institutions*, New Delhi: OUP, 2000, pp. 83-107. Beteille believes that it is necessary to accept the co-existence of secular as well as religious ideas and institutions, *ibid.*, p. 91. Social harmony can be achieved only by "limiting and subordinating the totalizing claims of every kind of ideology, whether religious or secular." *Ibid.,* Quote p. 104.
51. M.N. Srinivas, The Future of Indian Caste, *Economic and Political Weekly*, Vol. 14, Nos. 7/8, February, 1979.
52. Baruah has argued how the immensely popular music of Bhupen Hazarika and his entire career "are texts that underscore the compatibility and dialogical relationship between Assamese subnationalism and pan-Indianism." Chapter 4, pp. 86-90. Sanjib Baruah, *India Against Itself*, Delhi: 1999.
53. Eric Hobsbawm, *Nations and Nationalism since 1780: Programme, Myth, Reality*, Cambridge: CUP, 1990.
54. E.H. Carr, *The Twenty Years Crisis, 1919-1939: An Introduction to the Study of International Relations*, London: 1939.
55. Ernest Nolte, *Three Faces of Fascism: Action Francaise, Italian Fascism, National Socialism*, London: 1965; Alan Bullock, *Hitler and Stalin: Parallel Lives*, Vintage: 1993 and Ian Kershaw and Moshe Lewin, eds., *Stalinism and Nazism: Dictatorships in Comparison*, Cambridge: 1997.
56. Yogendra Yadav, Understanding the Second Democratic Upsurge: Trends of Bahujan Participation in Electoral Politics in the 1990s, in Francine Frankel, Zoya Hasan, Rajeev Bhargava and Balveer Arora, (ed.), *Transforming India: Social and Political Dynamics of Democracy,* Delhi: OUP, 2000, pp. 120-145.
57. Gunnar Myrdal, *Asian Drama: An Inquiry into the Poverty of Nations,* New York: Pantheon, 1968; and idem, *The Challenge of World Poverty*, New York: Pantheon, 1970.
58. Ashutosh Varshney, Is India Becoming More Democratic?, The *Journal of Asian Studies*, 59, No. 1, February 2000, pp. 3-25.
59. Pranab Bardhan, The Political Economy of Reform in India, in Neerja Gopal, (ed.), *Democracy in India*, Delhi: OUP. 2001, pp. 397-414.
60. See Mancur Olson, *The Rise and Decline of Nations: Economic Growth, Stagflation and Social Rigidities,* New Haven: Yale University Press, 1982; Michael Lipton, Agriculture, Rural People, the State and the Surplus in Some Asian Countries: Thoughts on Some Implications of Three Recent

Approaches in Social Science, *World Development*, Vol. 17, No. 10, October 1989 and Jan Breman and Sudipto Mundle, eds., *Rural Transformation in Asia*, Delhi: OUP, 1991.

61. Matthew McCartney and Barbara Harriss-White, 'The Intermediate Regime' and 'Intermediate Classes' Revisited: A Critical Political Economy of Indian Economic Development from 1980 to *Hindutva*, *Queen Elizabeth House Working Paper Series, QEHWPS,* 34, February, 2000, p. 49.
62. The burden of these subsidies, direct and indirect, reached 15 per cent of GDP by 1987 according to an estimate by Mundle and Rao in 1991. Cited in Matthew McCartney and Barbara Harriss-White, 'The Intermediate Regime' and 'Intermediate Classes' Revisited, *QEHWPS*, 34, February, 2000, p. 28. The authors argue that *Hindutva* as an ideology was a cover for the former intermediate classes trying to resist national development and globalization, p. 49.
63. Dipankar Gupta is convinced that there are very few Maoists in Jharkhand: statement made in a seminar at Nehru Memorial Museum and Library, New Delhi, November, 2009.
64. Siva Sivasubramonian, *Twentieth Century Economic Performance of India*, in Angus Maddison, D.S. Prasada Rao and William Shepherd, eds., *The Asian Economies in the Twentieth Century,* Edward Elgar: Aldershot, 2002.
65. John Harriss, Anthropology of the Modern Indian State, in John Harriss, *Power Matters: Essays on Institutions, Politics, and Society in India,* Delhi: OUP, 2006, pp. 193-211.
66. Quan Li and Rafael Reuveny, Economic Globalization and Democracy: An Empirical Analysis, *British Journal of Political Science*, Vol. 33, No. 1, January, 2003, pp. 29-54.
67. See S. Mitra and V.B. Singh, *Democracy and Social Change in India*, Delhi: Sage, 1999.
68. While the rights of the OBCs are constitutionally protected, the extension of quota for the Muslims is still a matter of discussion. The Ranganath Misra Commission has recommended that *Dalit* Muslims and Christians should also get the benefit of reservations. The five per cent quota for the Muslims of Andhra Pradesh introduced by the Government in 2004 was struck down by the High Court in September 2004 and in November 2005. The Supreme Court on 25th March, 2010 upheld a four per cent quota in jobs and educational institutions introduced by the Andhra Pradesh government for 'backward' groups among Muslims and struck down by the High Court in February 2010. Poor Muslims benefit by quotas in four States: Kerala, Karnataka, Bihar and Tamil Nadu. It also decided to refer the matter to a five judge constitutional bench. *The Times of India*, Delhi, 26 March, 2010. This was reported on the front page and page 13.
69. P.J. Cain and A.G. Hopkins, *British Imperialism: Innovation and Expansion*, 1688-1914, Vol. I and idem, *British Imperialism: Crisis and Deconstruction*, 1914-1990, Vol. II, London: 1993.

70. De-Qiang Liu, Income Disparity and Social Instability in China, in Ryoshin Minami, Kwan Kim and Malcolm Falkus, eds., *Growth, Distribution and Political Change: Asia and the Wider World*, MacMillan: 1998.
71. Sheying Chen, Economic Reform and Social Change in China: Past, Present, and Future of the Economic State, *International Journal of Politics, Culture and Society*, Vol. 15, No. 4, summer 2002, pp. 569-589. Chen argues that the Chinese economic state that emerged after the 'transfer' in 1978 needs to address the 'tensions' that have surfaced "between its economic and socio-political functions," p. 570. The share of contract workers rose from 0.6 per cent in 1983 to 50.7 per cent of the workforce in 1996 which reduced their welfare, pp. 573-577. He advocates a second 'transfer' in China to facilitate "socialist welfare pluralism with Chinese characteristics."
72. For a discussion of the new situation and its possibilities see Arjun Appadurai, Deep Democracy: Urban Governmentality and the Horizon of Politics, *Public Culture*, 14, 1, 2002. Also see James Ferguson and Akhil Gupta, Spatializing States: Toward an Ethnography of Neo-Liberal Governmentality, *American Ethnologist*, Vol. 29, No. 4, November 2002, pp. 981-1002.

NOTES

A Note on the progress and activities of the Arya Samaj based on the materials provided by Pandit Rahas Behari Tewari, Secretary of the Arya Pratinidhi Sabha, United Provinces, Census of India, 1931, pp. 505-508.

A.C. Pradhan, *The Emergence of the Depressed Classes*, Bookland International, Bhubaneswar, 1986, pp. 115-116, 204.

A.C. Pradhan, *The Emergence of the Depressed Classes*, Bookland International, Bhubeneswar, 1986, p. 204.

B.R. Ambedkar, *What Congress and Gandhi Have Done to the Untouchables*, 1945, (Reprint) 1991, p. 156.

Badri Narayan, Inventing Caste History: *Dalit* Mobilisation and Nationalist Past, in Dipankar Gupta (ed.), *Caste in Question: Identity or Hierarchy?*, Sage Publications, Delhi, 2004, pp. 195-98.

Census of India, 1931, pp. 626-628.

Census of India, 1931, pp. 631-638.

Census of India, 1931, *United Provinces of Agra and Oudh*, Vol. XVIII, Part-I, Report, Allahabad, 1933, p. 533.

Census of India, OUP, 1931, p. 630.

Census of India, Report, 1921, cited in Census of India, 1931, *United Provinces of Agra and Oudh*, Vol. XVIII, Part-I, Report, A.C. Turner, Allahabad, 1933, pp. 528-529.

Chandrika Prasad Jigyansu, Swami Achhutanand, Lucknow, Bahujan Kalyan

Prakashak, 1960, p. 100, cited in Christophe Jaffrelot, *India's Silent Revolution: The Rise of the Low Castes in North Indian Politics*, Permanent Black, New Delhi, 2003, p. 201.

Christophe Jaffrelot, *India's Silent Revolution: The Rise of the Low Castes in North Indian Politics*, Permanent Black, New Delhi, 2003, pp. 199-200.

Christophe Jaffrelot, India's Silent Revolution: The Rise of the Low Castes in North Indian Politics, pp. 202-3.

Correspondence Regarding Council Reforms, Vol. I, Part-I, Calcutta, 1908.

E.A.H. Blunt, *The Caste System of Northern India* (April, 1931), Reprint, New Delhi, 1968, p. 208.

File No. 163/III/30-R, Reforms Office, NAI.

File No. 199/32-R, Reforms Office, NAI.

Government of India, Reforms Office, File No. 111/32-R, NAI, New Delhi.

Government of India, Reforms Office, File No. 199/19032, NAI, New Delhi.

Ibid., p. 205.

Ibid., p. 84.

Ibid., pp. 177, 182.

Ibid., pp. 74-75.

In the Indian caste system people belonging to the lowest social order were referred by various names such as 'Untouchables', 'Depressed Classes', '*Harijans*', 'Scheduled Castes', etc. The reference to the term '*Dalit*' describing the lower castes is found in the 1920s. Although Sudha Pai writes that 'The word *Dalit* has been used in Uttar Pradesh only since the late 1980s', we find the references of '*Shraddhanand Dalit Uddhar Sabha*' in Delhi in 1920s, '*Dalit Jat Sudharak Sabha*' in United Provinces in 1920s and also a weekly '*Dalit Bandhu*' started in 1928 by P.N. Rajbhoj. (Sudha Pai, *Dalit* Consciousness and Movements in the United Provinces: Colonial Legacies, in R. Basu and S. Dasgupta (eds.), Narratives of the Excluded: Caste Issues in Colonial India, Kolkata, 2008, pp. 45-46). AICC Paper, File-AP-9,10,16,17/1928, NMML, New Delhi, Indian Franchise Committee, Vol. II, Government of India, Calcutta, 1932, p. 415, R.K. Kshirsagar, *Dalit* Movement in India and its Leaders, M.D. Publications, New Delhi, 1994, p. 135). But the usage of the term *Dalit* got momentum in the early 1970s following the *Dalit* Panther movement in Maharashtra. (S.M. Michael, Introduction, in S.M. Michael (ed.), *Dalits in Modern India, Vision and Values*, second edition, Sage Publications, New Delhi, 2007, p. 16). In this paper I have used the word '*Dalit*' in place of words like 'Untouchables', 'Depressed Classes' to refer the lower castes in caste hierarchy.]

Indian Franchise Committee, Vol. II, Government of India, Calcutta, 1932, pp. 412-420, 429, 1932.

Indian Franchise Committee, Vol. IV, Government of India, 1932, pp. 823-24.

Indian Statutory Commission, Oral Evidence-United Provinces, Vol. II.

Indian Statutory Commission, Vol. III, Reports of Provincial Committees, Calcutta, 1930, pp. 241-43.

Indian Statutory Commission, Vol. XVI, Selections from Memoranda and Oral Evidence, Calcutta, 1930, pp. 347-363.

Indian Statutory Commission, Written Evidence, United Provinces, Vol. I, Calcutta, 1930.

Indian Statutory Commission, Written Evidences, Vol. I.

Kapil Kumar, *Peasants in Revolt: Tenants, Landlords, Congress and the Raj in Oudh*, Manohar, New Delhi, 1994, pp. 47, 66, 224-225.

Kapil Kumar, Rural Women in Oudh 1917-47 in Kumkum Sangari and Sudesh Vaid (eds.), *Recasting Women: Essays in Indian Colonial History*, Rutgers University Press, New Jersey, 1990, pp. 362-63.

Kirti Narain, *Press, Politics and Society*: *Uttar Pradesh*, 1885-1914, Delhi, 1998, pp. 76-77.

Lionel Carter (ed.), United Provinces Politics, 1936-1937, *Governors' Fortnightly Reports and other Key Documents*, Manohar, New Delhi, 2008, pp. 114, 133.

Marc Galanter, *Competing Equalities: Law and the Backward Classes in India*, Oxford University Press, New Delhi, 1984, p. 28.

Nandini Gooptu, *The Politics cf the Urban Poor in Early Twentieth Century India*, Cambridge University Press, Cambridge, 2001, pp. 149-151, 156-157.

Note on the Depressed Classes by M.C. Rajah, East India (Constitutional Reforms), Report of the Indian Central Committee, 1928-29, London, 1929, pp. 386-87.

Oliver Mendelsohn and Marika Vicziany, *The Untouchables: Subordination, Poverty and the State in Modern India*, Cambridge University Press, New Delhi, 1998, p. 110.

Owen M. Lynch, The *Politics of Untouchability: Social Mobility and Social Change in a City of India*, Columbia University Press, 1969, pp. 68-72; Robert, L. Hardgrave, *The Nadars of Tamilnadu: the Political Culture of a Community in Change*, Berkley, 1969; Gail Omvedt, Cultural Revolt in Colonial Society: The Non-Brahman Movement in Western India, Bombay,1976; Sekhar Bandyopadhyaya, *Caste, Politics and the Raj, Bengal* 1872-1937, K.P. Bagchi & Company, Calcutta, 1990; William R. Pinch, Peasants and Monks in British India, Oxford University Press, Delhi, 1996, Swaraj Basu, *Dynamics of a Caste Movement: The Rajbansis of North Bengal*, 1910-1947, Manohar, Delhi, 2003, etc.

Peter Reeves, *Landlords and Governments in Uttar Pradesh: A Study of Their Relations Until Zamindari Abolition*, Oxford University Press, Delhi, 1991, pp. 2-29.

R.S. Khare, The Untouchable as Himself: Ideology, Identity, and Pragmatism among the Lucknow *Chamars*, Cambridge University Press, Cambridge, 1984, pp. 83-86.

Ram Sahai, representing the depressed classes on the United Provinces Provincial Franchise Committee, Indian Franchise Committee, Vol. II, Government of India, Calcutta, 1932, p. 434.

Reforms Office, Franchise, Proceedings A, July 1920, Nos. 84-114A, NAI, New Delhi.

Report on the Working of the System of Government, United Provinces of Agra and Oudh, 1921-1928 (Allahabad, 1930), p. 560 cited in James Chiriyankandath, "'Democracy' Under the Raj: Elections and Separate Representation in British India", in Niraja Gopal Jayal (ed.), *Democracy in India*, Oxford University Press, New Delhi, 2001, p. 66.

S. Bandyopadhyay, *Caste, Politics and The Raj: Bengal, 1872-1937*, p. 14.

Shashi Bhushan, '*Dalits* and the Ideology of Work in India' in Marcel van der Linden and Prabhu P. Mohapatra (eds.), *Labour Matters: Towards Global Histories*, Tulika Books, New Delhi, 2009, p. 163.

Sudha Pai, *Dalit* Consciousness and Movements in the United Provinces: Colonial Legacies, in R. Basu and S. Dasgupta (eds.), *Narratives of the Excluded: Caste Issues in Colonial India*, Kolkata, 2008, p. 35,

Supplementary Memorandum submitted by Rama Charana to the Statutory Commission, Indian Statutory Commission, Selections from Memoranda and Oral Evidence by Non-officials, Vol. XVI, Calcutta, 1930, p. 350.

The Indian Annual Registrar, January-June, 1928, Reprint, Delhi, 2000, pp. 438-439.

The Indian Annual Registrar, January-June, 1928, Reprint, Delhi, 2000, pp. 92-95.

The Indian Annual Registrar, July-December 1931, Reprint, Delhi, 2000, pp. 325-26.

William R. Pinch, *Peasants and Monks in British India*, Oxford University Press, Delhi, 1996, pp. 92-93.

13
Democracy and Civil Society in India

Rajaram Tolpadi

Needless to say that democracy as a political idea owes its origin to the west. However, the western genesis of the idea of democracy does not necessarily make it Eurocentric as different societies have different ways of articulating or rearticulating democracy in their distinctive cultural and historical pursuits. In India too the chronicle of democratic imagination and pursuit has been historically specific and culturally distinct. Although, the democratic imagination in India might have had its lineages in the historical experience of Western Europe, it cannot be either reduced back to that historical experience or be treated as an unproblematic transposition of an alien idea. In other words, the narrative of the Indian democratic pursuit is by no means a simple and mechanical re-enactment of Western history of democracy.

In India, democracy as a family of ideas emerges and takes shape in the course of events and eventualities associated with her historical encounter with colonialism. The nuanced and fairly long historical relation of India with the west, mediated through the hegemonic rule of colonialism, produced a wide range of ideas, which in due course constituted part and parcel of the Indian idea of democracy. To map out this extremely complex picture of Indian pursuit of democratic imagination, one needs to traverse through the dense historical occurrences of the nineteenth and the twentieth century India. This helps us to understand under what circumstances and responding to which events, ideas were articulated, institutions were envisaged and processes were initiated. The complex history of India's encounter with colonialism could be overviewed in terms of a range of responses of the Indian people from social reform to the nationalist movement; from demand for constitutional rule to the cry for *swaraj* and from efforts of social change to endeavours for social, economic and political transformation. The early response of

Indian society *vis-à-vis* colonialism can be identified in terms of varying kinds of demands for social reform. It varied from the demands of Bengali elites for the abolition of *sati* and for introduction of women education, to the *dalit* demands for self respect and social justice. These different kinds of demands can be identified in a number of movements that emerged in different parts of India and in different contexts of her evolution as a modern society in the larger background of colonial rule. They included movements and struggles against varying kinds of social, political and cultural conditions of oppression as well as injustice. These conditions of oppression and injustice could have been propelled either by native structures of exploitation or by colonial interventions or by both. Different kinds of peasant struggles, working class agitations, *dalit* upsurges, tribal resistances and women struggles are some of the Indian responses to conditions of oppression or non-freedom caused by native or alien forces.

The National Liberation Movement that emerged in India in the early part of the twentieth century is, in fact, a culmination and a combination of all these divergent developments. It should be stated here that the National Liberation Movement did not incorporate into its fold each one of these developments, but provided expressions to quite a few of them.[1] The National Liberation Movement in India, although drew the ideological strength from the constitutional liberal tradition of the west, it radically reconstructed the liberal tradition in accordance with the specific cultural and social needs of Indian society. This was possible precisely due to the fact that the nationalist movement was profoundly and unequivocally anti-colonial in its sensibility. Strong roots of the National Liberation Movement in the Indian cultural traditions enabled the movement to redefine the central values that it sought to achieve and formulate strategies to realize them. For instance, some of the early leaders of Indian nationalism like Gopala Krishna Gokhale or Surendranath Banerjee appeared naïve and straight forward imbibers of English liberal ideology. However, a closer examination of their ideas reveals their striving to domesticate and internalize western influences in the context of India. While, in a different way, other nationalist leaders like Balgangadhar Tilak and M.K. Gandhi exhibited exceptional sensitivity towards the cultural roots of Indian society. Similarly, the nationalist leaders of the subsequent generation like Pandit Jawaharlal Nehru, Jaya Prakash Narayan, Rammanohar Lohia and B.R. Ambedkar were keenly aware of the historical and cultural perplexities of their time.[2] Consequently, the ideas of democracy, secularism, social justice, federalism and decentralization that constituted an integral part of the Indian democratic imagination were subjected to critical scrutiny. This resulted in these ideas being creatively rearticulated keeping in view the cultural and historical context prevalent in India. The nationalist leadership, above other things, intensely recognized that India is a society of diversity and disparity and that the former needs to be strengthened while the latter to be sorted out. Indian democratic imagination, therefore, departs from its western counterpart in as much as it reconstructed the ideological content of democracy in the context of and as a response to the different kinds of differences that existed in India. Thus, Indian democracy theoretically reflects and politically articulates diversity as its normative foundation.

Similarly, the idea of secularism which is integral to the idea of democracy in India has different roots of its own. The secular imagination in India has very little to do with the history of secularism in the west. The history of secularism in the west is always caught up in the Church-State controversy resulting in differentiating the private domain from the public domain. This eventually led to a fairly reasonable distinction between religion and politics in the west. While in India, secularism is a historical product of a multicultural and multi-religious social reality. The nationalist leadership tended to conceive secularism not as a tightly woven theory but as a broadly imagined perspective emerging out of practical necessities. It was envisaged and found necessary to resolve hostility and establish peace among conflicting communities. Secularism in India, therefore, implies on the one hand, the formulation of a state policy that maintains a critical and principled distance from religious communities and on the other, the creation of a civil society consciousness that fosters principles of tolerance, recognition of difference and mutual respect among religious communities. In this context, Rajeev Bhargava aptly characterizes the Indian secularism as a model arising out of religious-strife in India. This "religious-strife" model of secularism, he holds, is fundamentally different from the "Church-State" model.[3]

The idea of social justice is one of the central principles of Indian pursuit of democracy. It is pretty evident that the idea of social justice is inscribed into the core of Indian practice of democracy, as it was widely recognized that democracy in India had to be carried out in a thoroughly unequal and unjust society which is historically disadvantaged partly due to colonial intervention. Social justice is envisaged and incorporated into the corpus of Indian democracy with a great deal of awareness and care towards the prevalence of divergent kinds of differences and disadvantages. What is significant to note here is that, the idea of social justice, institutionalized through the practice of positive discrimination or affirmative action in India was perceived only to wipe out those differences that breed inequality and disadvantage. This is to suggest that Affirmative Action instrumentalized through reservation policy in India is intended only to set right and reorganize unequal social and economic arrangements and to promote cultural diversity. Thus, social justice is an all-pervasive principle that runs all the way through the Indian text of democracy.

The idea of difference and disadvantage take us to another principle or philosophical aspect of Indian democracy—federalism. The Indian idea of federalism also departs from the classical idea of federalism in the west, as it does not rest upon the principle of devolution of power. Instead, it is a distinct idea of distribution of power based on the considerations of regional difference and political disadvantage.

Finally, the idea of decentralization, reflected through the *Panchayati Raj* institutions, constitutes another important aspect of Indian democracy. Although, this idea did not takeoff in the initial years of Indian experiment with democracy, it gained momentum as years passed by.[4] The contemporary cry for decentralization predominantly present in the democratic politics in India is the result of the rise of a new kind of "Demand Politics" seeking greater popular participation in democratic decision making. Peter D'Souza characterizes this new demand as the second wave of Indian democracy.[5] In other words, the increasing demand for decentralization in Indian politics is the beginning of a massive process of democratization of democracy in India.

The democratic Constitution of India is a culmination, institutionalization, and textualization of all the normative aspects enumerated above. The Constitution as a synoptic statement or as a vision document in any given society, enshrines values, establishes institutions and initiates processes. Constitution of India too performs this delicate historical function. In the light of this, the parliamentary form of government, with a certain mechanism of checks and balances and a notion of the supremacy of the parliament, upholds the sovereignty of people. Similarly, the principles of democracy, secularism and social justice strive to hold a diverse citizenry together in harmony. The reasonably independent judiciary enforces and safeguards the Rights of all the citizens and controls the activities of the state. Federalism attempts to ensure regional and cultural identities and the notion of decentralization endeavours to diffuse power and guarantee representation. This is supposed to be the normative frame of the Constitution of India.

Such an identification of normative frame of Constitution of India demands an extremely difficult hermeneutic effort. It meant a careful journey not only into the text of the Constitution but also into the complex context in which the text of the Constitution came to be produced. One can identify at least four contexts as inextricable for an appropriate understanding and interpretation of Constitution of India. They can be identified as follows:

The first among them is the whole context of the British colonial administration during which a large number of constitutional reforms were introduced. Constitutional Reforms of 1909 and 1919 and the Government of India Act of 1935 are the most important among them. The Constitution of India is partly an outgrowth of these various constitutional reforms, which the British introduced from time to time. The parliamentary model that we have evolved in India is entirely attributable to these Reforms. However, this does not mean either that the Constitution of India is a carbon copy of the constitutional reforms the British introduced in India or that the Indian parliament is a replica of the British parliament. What is to be recognized here is the immense historical linkage that modern Indian constitutional democracy has had with British colonial rule. It also needs to be emphasized here that the constitutional reforms that the British introduced in India stands testimony to the liberal side of the British colonial rule. It is remarked by a significant section of scholarship on colonialism that among all the colonial regimes the British colonial dispensation in India happens to be the most generous. In historical retrospect, it can be reasonably maintained that the English educated intelligentsia in India was successful in creatively occupying the liberal space that the British colonialism offered to India.

The National Liberation Movement with its divergent ideological ramifications constitutes another important context that determined the nature and meaning of Constitution of India. Axiomatically, the National Liberation Movement in India is one of the most powerful and popular upsurges that forged a formidable resistance to the ideology of colonialism churning out a wide range of ideas and values. However, among these ideas the liberal democratic ideological strand tended to overpower the course of nationalist movement. It also determined the tone and the tenor of the nationalist discourse and influenced the formation of the Constitution of India. As a result, ideas of democracy, liberty, equality and social justice have become the corner stones of Constitution of India. Significantly, along with the force of ideas the National Liberation Movement produced a wide variety of institutions that played an important role in sustaining democracy as a social phenomenon. In this sense, social organizations like *Brahmo Samaj* and Servants of India Society are institutions responsible to foster democracy as a formidable social philosophy.

Amazingly, the liberal and democratic values that were churned out during the nationalist struggle had a massive impact on the minds of Indian people. In fact, there was a great deal of unanimity and consensus among them in the reiteration and incorporation of these values into the fabric of constitutional and political life of modern India. Consequently, it was resolved without any glimpse of disagreement that India shall be a democracy founded on the principle of Universal Adult Franchise. What a developed democracy like England could achieve over centuries, India could by a single stroke of a pen as it were. Further, the notion of equal right, with due recognition of difference and disadvantage, was also a matter of unanimous acceptance. Although, there was a great deal of heated debate on the issue of reconciling the notion of rights with that of social justice, rights were by and large recognized as sacrosanct.

The live debates in the Constituent Assembly and the kind of problems, perplexities and the challenges that invoked various responses among the framers of the Constitution form another inextricable context to understand and interpret the Constitution of India. Significantly, the Constituent Assembly held its deliberations under the dark shadow of partition. The havoc that the partition caused and the widespread hostility that prevailed among the two dominant religious communities in India, compelled the constituent assembly to go seriously into certain core issues of social harmony and national integration. With enormous violence around and hatred looming large, the Constituent Assembly deliberated on issues of inter-religious harmony and national unity. As a result, the questions as to whether India shall be a federal state or not, if yes what kind of federalism it should be; what is the nature and extent of religious rights, whether religious rights are individual rights or community rights and how does the state intervene and resolve conflicts among religious communities, should India adopt a uniform civil code were the dominant issues deliberated upon.[6] Eventually, India was envisioned as a union of States striking a balance between aspirations of national integration, regional autonomy and a secular political order representing diverse cultural identities and religious tolerance.

Finally, the Indian judiciary, represented by the Apex Court of India, in its historic judgements in the context of democratic politics of independent India, performed the crucial tasks of enumerating, substantiating and interpreting the meaning of the Constitution and the normative values that it represented. The significant judgements that it delivered in cases like, Champakam Dorairajan *versus* State of Madras, Golaknath *versus* State of Punjab, Keshavananda Bharathi *versus* State of Kerala, Minerva Mills *versus* Union of India and Manohar Joshi *versus* State of Maharashtra are some instance in this regard. What is significantly noticeable in these judgements of the Supreme Court is that it did not hang on to any dogmatic view of the Constitution. Its perspective of the Constitution varied in accordance with changing demands and aspirations of the people for whose well-being the Constitution exists. To illustrate this further, one could provide a brisk overview of some of these judgements cited above. In Champakam Dorairajan case the Supreme Court upheld the considerations of social justice while recognizing the fundamental rights of citizens. In Golaknath case it argued that fundamental rights are sacrosanct and that it should be seen as central to Indian democracy. However, in Keshavananda Bharathi case it admitted that the state could impose reasonable restrictions on fundamental rights under certain special conditions. It can do so, the court held, without undermining what it called 'the basic structure' of the Constitution. Similarly in Minerva Mills's case it highlighted the significance of environment and declared it as a right. While delivering its historic verdict on Manohar Joshi case, the Supreme Court unequivocally stated that Secularism is a very important aspect of Indian constitutional democracy. It should be quickly added here that the role of the Supreme Court in enumerating the Constitution and enhancing the prospects of democracy has not always been positive. There are instances where the judgements of the court, instead of strengthening democracy, have proved to be the major setbacks to the onward march of Indian democracy.

Thus, the Constitution of India in terms of a system of values, institutions and mechanisms unfolds clearly laid down chapters on fundamental rights ensuring all its citizens equal rights; zealously enumerated chapters on Directive Principles, cautioning and directing the state of its social responsibilities and a reasonably independent judiciary entrusted with responsibilities of maintaining justice and interpreting the Constitution. It also has a nuanced procedure of Constitutional amendment to ensure on the one hand, the sovereignty of the people and on the other, the need for change according to the requirements of time. Thus, the Constitution of India promises a workable system of democratic politics representing the desires of continuity and change at once. As a vision document, it upholds the principles of democracy, secularism, social justice and diversity as the basis of social and political practice in India.

II

India's reasonable success in evolving a fairly accommodative system of constitutional democracy with a nuanced set of normative principles underpinning it, does not, however, overshadow the appalling problems that Indian society confronts today in terms of democratic governance. Her problems, as a democracy, arises partly out of the intrinsic theoretical limitations of the general character of democracy as a political system and partly due to the historical and cultural modes through which India was grafted into a modern system of democratic politics.

The inadequacies and predicaments of Indian democracy in expanding and radicalizing its contours to reach out to the needs and aspirations of the people are self evident. Even though, critics of Indian democracy have been emphasizing the need to further democratize Indian democracy, nothing substantial has been achieved in this direction. Even after sixty odd years of Indian independence, India remains a mere political democracy vaguely and ambivalently anchored in the philosophy of social justice as the foundational principle. In fact, evidences are frighteningly odd against Indian political democracy evolving into a more vibrant and radical form of democracy. On the contrary, fair deal has been constantly denied to larger sections of the society, who always found themselves in the wrong end of "Indian democracy". Quite sordidly, the story of Indian democracy has been a "meta narrative" of development, under whose heavy shoes the dreams of common people are mercilessly flattened.[7] The gulf between the rich and the poor, the urban and the rural and men and women have been ever on the increase. Poverty, suffering, humiliation, unemployment, malnutrition, disease, displacement and marginalization have become the everyday routine of Indian life. Ethnic and communal violence have increased enormously and have taken despicable proportions over the years. People have been quite often voiceless victims of oppressive structures—modern or traditional, alien or native. In this context we could turn to some of the awful problems that India as a democracy has always confronted.

Critics of Indian democracy have repeatedly point out that part of the perplexities of Indian democracy have emanated out of the historical past in terms of the processes through which India was inducted into a modern, liberal, constitutional democratic political system. This has also been partly due to the specific social, economic and cultural conditions prevalent in India. India's colonial encounter, as well known, restricted her to get exposed to a selective range of ideas and institutions. This was further compounded by India's retarded and unequal socio-economic and cultural conditions that prevented it from becoming a radical democracy. Notwithstanding a few and in between voices of hope and resistance, the overall scenario of Indian democracy is far from being encouraging.

The foremost predicament of Indian democracy has very little to do with its intrinsic inadequacies of democracy as an idea. Instead, it emerges out of its historical compulsions of having to accept and incorporate a paradigm of modernity and development that has its roots elsewhere. It is now well known that the nationalist leadership in India, since independence, carried overboard an agenda of modernization and development, which had little understanding of social and cultural realities in India. Such a close-handed borrowing of the western model of development has, quite often, led to displacement and suffering, particularly to the weaker and disabled sections of Indian society.

Paradoxically, the democratic Constitution in India envisioned an interventionist state to ensure social justice and sustainable development in an unjust and unequal society. However, what turned out is a strong and developmental state which in due course became authoritarian. This is not to suggest either that the Indian state has always been authoritarian or that authoritarianism has always been tolerated without resistance. Instead, whenever Indian state became brazenly authoritarian either at the national level or at the regional level, it always met with massive popular resistance. This is not to indicate that the Indian state has always been strong or insensitive to popular demands. There are instances when it succumbed to the pressures of public opinion mobilized by agitations and democratic politics. At the same time, particularly in the era of globalization, the Indian state has revealed its inherent vulnerability to the ever mounting global pressures of market. As critics point out, like any developmental state, Indian state too exposes its contradictory dimensions of being weak and strong, soft and hard at the same time. Yet, the Indian state has consistently been betraying its immense propensity for violence. The track record of developmental state in India to propel violence and curb popular resistance either in the name of development or national integration is unparallel. One can cite innumerable examples[8] to show how ruthlessly Indian state came down on popular agitations either for regional autonomy or against displacement arising out of the development agenda pursued by the Indian state.

The preceding skepticism towards the dangers of a developmental state turning in to a leviathan state should not be taken as a complete negation of the role of the state in a complex and uneven society like India. It should be recognized that the state in India has a pivotal role to play in the process of achieving justice and equality. Besides, state is the only authority to which people could turn in situations of utter hopelessness and despair. Since the state in India is an institution born out of democratic processes, a hard and fast demarcation line could not be drawn between the state and civil society. Instead, critical enquiry should focus more on establishing a viable relationship between the state and civil society to achieve democratic aspirations. In this context, it is imperative to take a quick glance at the Indian tradition of political thinking with regard to the issue of the relationship between the state and civil society.

One finds a significant strand of radical thinking both in terms of achieving substantive democracy and also in putting reasonable restrictions on state authority to enable and empower a vibrant civil society. This strand of democratic thought in India owes its origin to M.K. Gandhi and ramifies into divergent streams of socialist thought. This Radical Democratic strand exhibit a startling suspicion over the intrinsic possibility of state as an institution becoming the source of violence in the dispensation of political authority. Socialists like Rammanohar Lohia and Jayaprakash Narayan, were foremost among the radical political thinkers in India, who consistently brought to the fore the impending dangers of a centralized political authority endowed with the responsibility of social uplift through development. They recognized the necessity of evolving a vibrant civil society capable of restraining the state from impinging its authoritarian tendencies. In fact, the issues such as the role of state as an agency of change in an unequal society; the appropriate relation between the state and civil society and the ways to bring about those mechanisms and processes that would keep both the state and civil society acting as checks and balances on each other to achieve a genuine democracy, have been the central concerns of the debates on Indian democracy.[9]

The second category of problems that the Indian democracy confronts is a range of constraints and hurdles concerning parliamentary politics and party system. It is self-evident that India's acceptance of parliamentary democracy was due to her acquaintance with parliamentary institutions during the colonial rule. However, the framers of the Constitution of India accepted parliamentary system of politics not only because India was familiar with these institutions but also because they recognized that parliamentary democracy is the most accommodative and representative system that can provide spaces and expressions to divergent interests. The debates in the constituent assembly, the arguments and counter arguments expressed in favour of and against different forms of democracy and the consensus that finally emerged in favour of parliamentary democracy are indicative of the circumstances and considerations upon which India adopted this mode of democracy. Significantly, the parliament in India is not a replica of the British parliament. The point of departure has been that the Parliament in India has to represent not only the people but also the States. The President of India, who represents the nation, is also formally woven into the institution of Parliament. In spite of a nuanced envisioning of the issue of representation in Parliament, Indian democracy suffers from certain inbuilt limitations of the Parliamentary system. A parliamentary system invokes an extremely rigid and hierarchical system of parties and expensive process of elections. The procedures of Parliament and discipline of the party have quite often undermined democracy and reduced elections into a farce game of vote bank politics. This is the reason why critics of Indian democracy have repeatedly pointed out that Indian democracy has succeeded procedurally and not substantially. This is to suggest that India in the last six decades has run the successful course of regular (some times more frequent) elections resulting in shifts in power both at the national and the State levels, formed parliaments and State legislatures from time to time, saw frequent and proactive interventions of judiciary and witnessed effective intercession of the press without actually enhancing substantive arenas of Indian democracy.

Over the last twenty years the milieu of Indian politics in terms of role and impact of political parties has undergone a metamorphosis. This metamorphosis is a shift from, as Rajni Kothari once described, single party dominance system to coalition politics, both at the national as well as regional levels. The preeminence of newly emerged regional as well as national political parties has caused decline of the Congress substantially. Simultaneously, it has brought to the fore new forces and social interests which were hitherto either marginalized or represented in a devious way by Congress and other major political parties. In a nutshell, the emerging scenario of party politics in India has completely wiped out older social equations and strategies to achieve success in electoral politics. This sea change in Indian politics in terms of rearticulating of political interests, Rudolf and Rudolf aptly describe, is a shift from command politics to a new form of demand politics.[10] All these developments in which the hitherto unheard voices being heard, inarticulate interests being articulated, unrepresented interests being represented, do not necessarily mean that Indian democracy is on its historical march forward in exhibiting tendencies of becoming a radical democracy. Still, there is a great deal of parliamentary procedures that come in the way of realization of democratic aspirations. The drudged procedures of parliamentary democracy, extreme authoritarianism exhibited by political parties in the guise of party discipline, conspicuous restriction of freedom of political choice to the citizens and the continued existence of impersonal, corrupt and inefficient bureaucracy have contained India from becoming a more radical democracy.

The third category of problems that Indian democracy confronts is the wide spectrum of issues pertaining to ethnic conflicts, communal politics and regional differences. Historically viewed, these are the products of the contradictory ways in which Indian nationalism came to be articulated and the Indian nation-state came to be established. Even though, the overarching ideology of Indian nationalism was broadly and vaguely anchored in a very accommodative liberal secular nationalism, quite often, it has shown tendencies to fall victim to forms of aggressive and valourized forms of nationalist euphoria. The ambivalent and diffused character of Indian nationalism with recurring and blurred faces of ethno-cultural nationalist outbursts had often produced contradictory situations of ethnic and communal cleavages in a plural and diverse Indian society. Alongside ethnicity and communalism the Indian society has also witnessed various forms of regionalism, partly arising out of the uneven developmental agenda pursued by the Indian state and partly due to certain intrinsic regional/cultural/ethnic variations. Among these varied kinds of problems of ethnicity, communalism and regionalism one ideological strand stands out alarmingly, that is the rise of a Hindu-ethno-cultural nationalism or to use popular shorthand, '*Hindutva*'.

The emergence of *Hindutva* is easily the most striking ideological and political development in India in recent times. Although its origins can be traced back to the first-half of the twentieth century or even earlier, it assumed a formidable political expression only during the 1980s. As an ideology of cultural nationalism, *Hindutva* is ostensibly political in its hermeneutics of Hindu texts, culture and tradition. *Hindutva* is also based on a re-narration of India's past as 'history'—a civilizational history of Indian (Hindu) nation as it were. However, the political prominence that *Hindutva* enjoys today does not necessarily emanate from its theoretical reconstruction of India as a nation and a civilization. Instead, it is a product of the ideological persuasion at the level of civil society carried out by different organizations of *Hindutva*, popularly known as '*Sangh Parivar*'. In a largely heterogeneous society like India, when a dominant religious identity asserts itself valorously, it certainly makes the other weaker' and marginalized religious identities to make similar kinds of assertions for reasons of fear and insecurity. Such assertions and counter assertions over a period of time would result in cascading reactions leading to constant communal tensions and conflicts. In the final analysis these and other concomitant developments lend themselves to a continuum of divergence. The ever increasing and never ending communal divide achieved through ideological persuasions at the level of civil society makes *Hindutva* an alarmingly divisive phenomenon unruffled by electoral political changes. Thus, communalism with all its different and nuanced faces has become an aspect of Indian politics rather than a heterogeneous facet haunting Indian politics.

III

Given the above problems and many more which this chapter does not touch upon, it is imperative for us to return, recover and reconstruct certain intellectual sources within the tradition of radical thinking in India, which can enable us to put these problems in a proper perspective and elicit possible solutions. Democratic socialist tradition in India, with its fairly long and chequered intellectual history, is one such site that we could return to in the light of certain predicaments of Indian democracy highlighted above.

If one of the predicaments of Indian democracy is the historically specific mode in which we imbibed modernity and adopted development, then a critical examination of that form of modernity and development is crucial in any attempt to reconstruct Indian democracy. The democratic socialist tradition, embedded in the cultural and social milieu of Indian society, has something to offer, at least, in the form of critical and reflective insights in this regard. From the very beginning, the democratic socialists, owing to their unequivocal opposition to colonialism and imperialism, have exhibited disbelief towards models of modernity and development that are alien to the cultural and historical context of Indian society. Lohia and JP as the most prolific representatives of this tradition have constantly engaged with the issue of what is the appropriate model of modernity and development that India should pursue. Lohia, in particular, tried to develop a systematic critique of the Nehruvian pursuit of modernity and development.[11] He held that Nehru was duplicating a model of modernity and development which has its roots elsewhere. Such a straight-jacketed model of modernity and development characterized by industrialization, mass production and reckless application of science and technology, he believed, has very little understanding of the historical, cultural and social realities prevalent in India.

Lohia in his larger critique of modernity and development tried to argue that the pursuit of socialism in India should maintain equi-distance both from capitalism and communism. To him, although apparently look two contrasting ideologies, they are, in reality, converge with one another and become two expressions of the same civilizational ethos. Capitalism and communism, Lohia held, share among them astonishing similarities in terms of economic production and political organization. He pointed out that the big machine representing concentrated economic production and leviathan state representing centralized political authority are the hallmarks of capitalism as well as communism. Lohia, therefore, argued that the socialist pursuit in India should break away from notions of concentration and centralization at all levels to achieve a more vibrant and participatory democracy.[12] He tried to conceptualize the idea of economic decentralization in the form of "Small-Unit Machine" and the political decentralization through the notion of "Four-Pillar State".[13]

Lohia's critique of parliamentary democracy and party system also helps a long way in reconstructing the agenda of democracy in India.[14] Characterizing the shortcomings of parliamentary democracy as parliamentarianism, Lohia constantly forewarned the possibilities of democracy being reduced into electoral mimic. He insisted that the political parties in India, more particularly the party that he represented, should seek objectives beyond electoral politics. It is in this light Lohia put forward a number of concrete suggestions and programmes to reorganize political parties and party functioning in India.[15] He believed that parties tend to lose their democratic fervour if they are removed from people and their aspirations. To make sure continuous connection and dialogue between the party and the people, Lohia envisioned a good number of subsidiary organizations to transform political parties into active agencies of popular will. Further, he persistently saw the intrinsic connection between movement and the party. Lohia was unwavering in his resolution that the parties should either be the outcomes of the movements or be the initiators of the movements. Only then, he held, the parties could become the real vehicles of democratic transformation.[16]

The significance of Lohia in radicalizing Indian democracy also emanates out of his efforts to bring the backward classes into the fore of Indian politics. This was possible for him through the astoundingly sharp critique of caste system in India. He initiated a wide variety of struggles and agitations that empowered the backward classes and enabled them to take decisive roles in the processes of democratic politics in India. In fact, Lohia's contributions are immense in envisioning agitations as effective forms of democratic politics. His insistence on sixty per cent reservation in government employment and education for *dalits*, *adivasis*, minorities and other backward classes; his concerted demand for drastic agrarian reforms in India and finally, his recognition of caste as a great force of political mobilization have, in a nutshell, expanded the frontiers of democratic politics in India. Lohia should also be remembered for his keenness to anchor democracy in the cultural fabric of Indian society. The movement that he launched against the domination of English and his insistence on using vernacular in the public sphere; his radical interpretation of texts, sites and symbols of Indian cultural life and the fervour with which he engaged in reconstructing India's past on radical lines are some indicators of his zeal to provide a cultural basis for Indian democracy.[17]

JP too did not lag behind in proposing drastic modifications to help Indian democracy overcome its theoretical as well as political impasse.[18] During his long, strenuous and eventful journey into the realms of ideologies, from Marxism to *Sarvodaya* and from *Sarvodaya* to "Total Revolution," JP was singularly engaged with the question of democracy in which people mattered. He recognized in terms of his interrupted political career, above other things, that democracy survives only when people are activated and organized. Together with Lohia he also believed that the centralized political authority has also proven to be the greatest enemy of democracy. He shared with Lohia deep-seated conviction that state as a political institution is intrinsically strong, and slides into authoritarianism and violence, while civil society, on the other, with its diversity and contradictions is intrinsically weak. Lohia argued that the political parties should be transformed into agencies of civil society with wide social networking. However, JP saw political parties as major hurdles in achieving genuine democracy. Consequently, JP conceived a party-less democracy based on organized popular will expressed through *Janasangharsha Samitis*. Thus, both Lohia and JP, in spite of their less significant differences of opinion, represent that part of radical democratic aspirations in India articulated through the ideas of economic and political decentralization, agitational politics and active and participatory civil society.

The preceding discussion on the significance and contributions of democratic socialists in radicalizing Indian democracy is not to suggest that the solutions to the problems that the Indian democracy confronts are readily available in the Indian socialist discourse. Instead, what is emphasized in the paper is the need to return, recover and reconstruct those aspects of Indian democratic socialist tradition, which would facilitate the general task of rebuilding Indian democracy. It has already been pointed out in the paper that certain aspects of democratic socialist concerns are already present in the contemporary sequence of events of Indian democracy. The contemporary cry for *Panchayati Raj* experiments; the demand of backward classes for greater representation and the impact of *dalit bahujan politics* are a few instances of the socialist presence in the practices and processes of Indian democracy. However, one strongly feels that the democratic socialist aspirations in India are either not adequately represented or some times even dubiously represented in the instances cited above. One main reason for this is that most of these representations are always almost caught up either in electoral arithmetic or in vote bank politics. The need, therefore, is to get down into the serious endeavour of retrieving some of those socialist aspirations, and re-root them in the vibrant civil society activism. Such an activity of anchoring radical aspirations and values in the terrain of civil society would probably result in the achievement of those radical values enshrined in the Constitution of India. This, in turn, facilitates Indian democracy to achieve its substantive objectives. To achieve this, we need to wrench democracy out of the predominant interpretation of it merely as a political arrangement. By this, we are able to visualize democracy as a set of foundational principles necessary for a meaningful collective life.

REFERENCES

1. India witnessed a wide variety of struggles and agitations during the later half of the nineteenth century and early part of twentieth century. These developments have played a determining role in shaping India as a modern society and a nation. See, Sankar Ghose, *Political Ideas and Movements in Modern India*, Calcutta: Alied Publishers, 1975.
2. See, A. Appadorai, *Documents on Political Thought in Modern India*, Volumes I and II, New Delhi: Oxford University Press, 1976.
3. Rajeeva Bhargava, (Ed.), *Secularism and its Critics*, New Delhi: Oxford University Press, Delhi, 2001.

4. The idea of decentralization did not figure in during the debates in the Constituent Assembly as well as during the first three decades of independence. One major reason for this is that the leaders who sphere-headed the framing of the Indian constitution and formation of the modern Indian state were not favourably disposed to the idea of decentralization. See, Austin, Granville. *The Indian Constitution—The Corner Stone of a Nation*, New Delhi: Oxford University Press, 1972.
5. D'Souza, Peter. "Sociological Imagination and Institutional Vision," paper presented in the international seminar on the Philosophy of the Indian Constitution held in Goa, September 2001.
6. Shefali Jha discusses in detail the debate on religious rights in the Constituent Assembly in her paper, "Secularism in the Constituent Assembly Debates 1946-50," presented in National Seminar on Secularism held in Simla, 1995.
7. There are many instances in which the disadvantaged sections of Indian Society become voiceless victims of developmental agenda pursued by the Indian state. Narmada river valley project is one such instance in this regard where thousands of people are displaced without even a promise of fair compensation. See for more vivid description of distortions of development, Sainath, P., *Everybody Loves a Good Drought*, Penguin Books India (P) Ltd., 1996.
8. Ethnic and communal violence have increased stupendously causing unimaginable proportions of death, suffering, and loss of property and livelihood. It has been pointed out by these studies that, on the one hand, there has been conspicuous civil society disengagement on the issues of ethnicity and communalism, and on the other the active participation of the State and bureaucracy in instances of communal violence. See, G. Rajashekhar, *Surathkal Komu Galabhegalu* (Communal Violence in Surathkal), Bangalore: Navakarnataka Publications, 2002.
9. Rajni Kothari discusses in detail how the state in India has become an enemy of democracy in India in his book, *State Against Democracy*, New Delhi: Ajantha Publications, 1988.
10. Rudolph, L. and Rudolph, S., *In Pursuit of Laxmi*, Chicago: The University of Chicago Press, 1978.
11. See for a detailed study on modernization and socialist interventions in India, Tolpadi, R. "Ram Manohar Lohia—A Study", unpublished Ph.D. thesis, Mangalore University, India, 2000.
12. Rammanohar Lohia, *Marx, Gandhi and Socialism*, Hyderabad: Rammanohar Lohia Samata Vidyalaya Nyas, 1963, pp. 320-363.
13. *Ibid.*, pp. 242-257.
14. Rammanohar Lohia, *Notes and Comments*, Vols. I and II, Hyderabad: Rammanohar Lohia Samata Vidyalaya Nyas, 1973.
15. Rammanohar Lohia, *The Caste System*, Hyderabad: Rammanohar Lohia Samata Vidyalaya Nyas, 1964.

16. Rammanohar Lohia, *Language,* Hyderabad: Rammanohar Lohia Samata Vidyalaya Nyas, 1956 and *Interval during Politics*, Hyderabad: Rammanohar Lohia Samata Vidyalaya Nyas, 1972.
17. N.C. Mehrotra, (1978) *Lohia: A Study*, New Delhi: Atma Ram & Sons.
18. Prasad, Bimal (ed.) *Jayaprakash Narayan: Essential Writings* (1929-1979), New Delhi: Manohar, 2002.

NOTE

1. The democratic socialist tradition in India owes its origin during the Nationalist Movement by way of the establishment of the Congress Socialist Party (CSP). The CSP was a left wing group, with in the Indian National Congress, established to intensify the nationalist movement by turning it unequivocally anti-colonial and anti-imperialist. It also intended to radicalize the agenda of the nationalist struggle by incorporating into it the aspirations of socio-economic transformation of Indian society. After independence, the CSP severed its relation with the Congress and ramified into a number of splintered groups and parties over a period of time. See, John Patrick Haithcox, *Nationalism and Communalism in India*, Princeton: Princeton University Press, 1968.

14

Safe India, Insecured Citizens: Challenges of Military and Terrorism

Gopalji Malviya

India's crisis of peace and security has been a phenomenal issue and concern since its emergence as sovereign, democratic, secular republic. The major task of state and nation building have been accomplished in the most peaceful, stable and democratic process. The formidable task of nation building has also been resolved with the great degree of devotion, skill and resilience. India as an emerging power stands at a vital threshold of six decades of its existence with no relent in the challenges, pressures and the crisis of its internal security. India's experience and encounter with the multiple threats of insurgencies terrorism, leftwing extremism, narco-trafficking, religious fundamentalism are as old as the republic, however, the magnitude, complexity and the virulence of such threat has increased in manifold ways resulting in severe and serious complications in India's internal security.

India's current challenge of peace and security has been a major concern particularly since December 2001. When terrorist assaulted Parliament, they struck at India's nerve centre; a qualitatively different target; and at variance with India's previous experience with India's multiple threats of insurgencies, terrorism, left wing extremism, narcotic trafficking, religious fundamentalism and sub-nationalism. The unending acts of terror blasts continue to take toll and security apparatus continues to fail and this has aggravated to new levels of crisis, resulting in paralysis of the security governance. The number and the magnitude of the operational success of terrorist entities are pointer to the radicalization of Islamic militants. These radicals, with resources, technology and networking, have acquired the capability to inflict their asymmetric means of offensive with assured capacity of destruction at any place of their choice. The question that arise whether Islamic militants in India are grown and transformed into formidable groups that could challenge the very pillars of the nation? The new levels of crisis escalations resulting in the chaos in society and confusion in the minds of Indian decision makers. The stage looks set where "collective violence" may emerge a reality with each instance of breakdown in law and order preparing the ground and justification for the next round. Various efforts of innovative reconciliation have not seen the desired results; the other precedence is the Indian States have highly developed capacity to accommodate those practitioners of violence and crime who commit this against the innocent people and security forces.

The Jammu & Kashmir is under fire, North-East is burning, West Bengal and Telangana is simmering. While the crime rate is ever growing in the country, the abduction and extortions has almost become an industry for criminal *mafia*, *Rangdari* and *Supari* culture is fast emerging as a new brand of threats to Indian citizens. Various forms of economic crimes including Money laundering, *Hawala* transaction, small arms proliferation and human trafficking are on rise. Regular train hijacking, arson, sabotage, damaging government property and assault on security personnel are new form of tactics adopted by the militants. The debate on countering these internal threats however at different occasions has been overwhelmed by politics, rather than deterrent actions. Question thus arises in a mighty India with large armed forces backed by nuclear weapons, strong economy and technological base, while India seems to be safe whether Indians are secured? Whether India is heading for a functional anarchy? Whether distrust citizens are demoralized?

It has become an increasingly recurrent strategy for insurgent movements as well as identity-based groups to make their voice heard through armed attacks and bomb blast in place of public dialogue. Independent India is no stranger to the problem of tackling armed terrorists and has faced long-running insurgencies as well as sporadic attacks in many parts of the country. Adherence to the constitutional provision of "substantive due processes" must be an essential part of our collective response to terrorism. Any dilution of the right to a fair trial for all individuals, however heinous their crimes may be, will be a moral loss against those who preach hatred and violence.

"India in the twenty-first century has turned out to be the confluence of every kind of violence: insurrection or insurgency in order to carve out sovereign states; armed liberation struggle motivated by a rejected ideology; and terrorism driven by religious fanaticism. Never before has the Indian state faced such a formidable challenge." India is in the grip of variety of structured violence prevalent and known in the different name tag. There is a basic difference in left wing extremist violence and terrorism. While terrorist actions are planned and executed in total secrecy by a small group, the Naxals commit violent act with the mass co-operation of local people in large numbers. They prefer to attack in broad daylight to show that they and not the Government agencies are in command. According to a recent report of the Union Home Ministry, the Naxals are now active in 23 of the 28 States in the country. Their aim is to "liberate and control State and administrative machinery of India after two or three decades". The report says there are 39 left extremist groups in India with a combined armed wing of over 1 lakh, over 175 districts are affected. The ruling elite and leadership is unanimous that left wing extremism is greatest danger to peace and security in India.

There have been two major views on the reasons for the increasing intensity of terrorist activities in India. The first view points out that the presence of foreign terrorist groups particularly in Jammu & Kashmir has significantly raised the level of violence not only in the State but also in other theatres of conflict in India. This has happened not only through the support extended through materials and logistics and to local militant groups but also by export of terrorism to other parts of the country. Secondly, the consistence effort to render communal overtones to the conflict in Kashmir may also be understood in this light. These foreign terrorist groups have also played the most destabilizing the role of inciting the local militants to take up arms through inducement, coercion or threat.

Indian security apparatus and elite are largely indifferent or have shied away from formulating an internal security doctrine. Since independence there is no serious attempt to institutionalize mechanism, direction or assertive policy to deal with "internal threats", interim, *ad hoc* and incremental means have been favourite methods adopted by the successive governments since independence. There is virtually no means to define coherently "the enemy within" the sources of threats, the appropriate instruments that are required to deal with the perceived enemy and political will to thwart enemies design. Since the last decade there has been continuous assault on Indian citizens and their psyche. Pakistan's strategy of "bleed India with thousand cuts" seems to be working well. In absence of any well-defined and coherent internal security doctrine, India's security apparatus has failed to plug the reoccurrence of terrorist attacks. Intelligence fraternity too is groping in dark about the actual strengths, source, capacity and logistics of enemy's next plan.

This indicates that something is seriously wrong with our domestic security apparatus that we almost never apprehend those killers of innocent citizens. Is it lack of political will or lack of governance in the security establishment? The politicians and the bureaucracy are already pontificating about the need to reinvigorate security measures to counter these terror attacks. There is need to underscore the fact that even after nearly sixty years of our independence there is no clear understanding among our leaders, political class, bureaucracy, business establishment and media about the nature of the security problems and challenges that India faces. The problem has been compounded by the trend of security acquiring a far more comprehensive connotation.

Unfortunately in India these terror attacks and militancy is seen as mere a 'law order' concern and treated as subject of provincial State, whenever, political violence in a massive scale breaks out in a State, the police become the first responders. Police in India are trained, equipped and mentally conditioned to deal with civil disorders only. When confronted with serious threats to internal security like terrorism, insurgency and other proxy war situations, they find it difficult to respond effectively. In such a situation, State seeks the expert assistance of Para-military forces. As Para-military forces other than Central Reserve Police Force (CRPF) are raised, trained and equipped to meet a specific need of national security, when deputed to deal with large scale disorders and proxy war situation, they are required to a quickly modify and reorient their operational doctrines to meet the situation at hand. State police need better training and modern equipments to achieve high level of professionalism. Creation of Federal Police or National Militia would constitute and appropriate step to meet the challenge. Frequent alerts and advisory by the Central agencies to State governments needs a fresh look for a meaningful action. Advancement in technology, communications, and transport has lent a new dimension to terrorism. India has learnt the hard way that terrorist activity has ramifications—international and inter-State that require special expertise and resource not always available with an already overstrained State police. The idea of a Central agency to investigate terrorism and related offensives has been mooted by many committees and experts, the latest being the Administrative Reforms Commission in June 2008.

Most of the security reforms that are conceived after recent terrorist attacks would take months and perhaps years to implement. Even if India's covert services are research and analysis wing and intelligence bureau begin to enhance their language skill areas of specialization and enhance their technological resources it will take long time to realize the desired results. Even the expansion of National Security Guard would take a long time to be operationalized against sophisticated terror. The local police forces are the first responders to terrorist attacks require modern equipments, advanced training and effective policing. Creating and enhancement of coastal defence, setting up State level marine police and its infrastructure would require effective coordination and foresight. Overall what is lacking in Indian security force is 'Professionalism' that needs to be addressed. In India, coordination between different States police system and Central agencies on terrorism is woefully inadequate. This situation could have been avoided if Kargil Review Committee recommendations to create central counter terrorist exchange centre was implemented.

The Constitutional status of internal security is itself amorphous. The Constitution assigned specific responsibilities for safeguarding and preserving the security of the country to different levels of government, with external security allotted to the centre and domestic security to the States. Public Order (i.e., maintenance of law and order) has accordingly been incorporated as the first item in List II (State List) of the Seventh Schedule. But events since 1947 have demonstrated that a major function of security exists at an intermediate level somewhere between military defences against external enemies and police maintenance of law and order, and involves many features of both. This is the area of internal security, which Constitution of India does not specifically address perhaps even people as farsighted are founding fathers could not envisage a situation of proxy war, where hostile external powers could foment instability inside the country by providing covert encouragement, sustenance and encouragement to separatists organizations operating internally.

The politico-administrative lethargy has led to decline of vital institutions. Vitiation of electoral process rampant corruption at every levels of authority, ever-growing violence in the society, criminalization of politics and politicization of criminals, creation of vote banks and lack of accountability raises the important question whether governance is the core issue for ensuring India's peace and security. If one peeps through the corridors of post-independent history of India, it would be seen that following issues have gradually emerged and transformed into major source of internal security. Over a period these crises also raised a question of governance and security and also put a question mark on federal structure of India.

1. Militancy in Kashmir.
2. Khalistan movement in Punjab.
3. Ethno-political movements in North-East.
4. Naxalite movements; Left wing extremism.
5. Tamils sub-nationalism blend with LTTE sponsored violence.
6. Regional aspiration for Bodoland, Jharkhand further fuelled, similar cry for Uttaranchal, Vidarbha, Poorvanchal, Ladakh, Jammu, Haritpradesh, Telangana and Gorkhaland.
7. Caste-based violence seeking to change societal hierarchies.
8. Communal violence in certain parts of the country.
9. Intra-State conflicts.
10. Proliferation of small arms.
11. Narrow Nationalism, Fundamentalism and linguistic dictates by political party and organized groups.
12. Undermining of secular structure of the Constitution of India by different fundamental outfits.
13. Religious fundamentalist organization rooted in religious obscurantism have long been prone to sudden bursts of irrational violence at the slightest provocation.

Genesis of these could be seen through 1950s but now it has gained political overturns. These micro-level crises have been visible since independence however either they were taken very lightly or they were not paid adequate attention. Some of these were political aspirations and dissatisfactions later converted as the mass movements. External actors fuelled some of these insecurities, in accordance to suit their agenda to destabilize India. Thus, clearly identified as externally fostered internal threats.

Most important and active onlookers are our political leaders who have cynically sought to use these internal disorders and violence to advance their electoral agendas. The politicians belonging to "coalition *dharma*" find an opportunity in each of these events. Concern in the name of minorities and vote bank obviously takes the front seat and internal security concerns have become the causality in the fragile security governance for quite some time. There is hardly any hope for change in the priority in the near future. It is not clear whether government has any political will to invent any coherent policy response to meet the challenges of internal disorder accept the rhetoric statement "that we will not allow enemy to succeed in its design", well, enemy has been succeeding most of the times! Situation demands the attentions of our ministers and politicians towards realization that on issue of national importance and public politics, a degree of professional conduct and etiquette is required of them and also to avoid blame game.

The focus is not on the political class alone. The rest of the internal management system and the civil society have to make changes in their ways of handling such problems to nourish and safeguard the polity. To begin with, citizen and politician can explore new ways of conducting our public discourse. There has to be moratorium on the culture of controversy, which puts a premium on converting every debate into confrontation; media will have to dewean itself from its grand conceit that its biases and prejudices are more representatives than those of the democratic classes. Much of the media is given to manufacturing "Public Opinion" spuriously, often unwittingly but also often knowingly playing favourites among political parties and leaders. These traits were at work much before "Mumbai 2008" and because large sections of the media continue to suffer from institutional arrogance, it was only natural that the coverage of the terrorist assault should have become a matter of public concerns.

Also civil society does not exist in India because of prevailing socio-economic and political environment does not permit this. Our country lacks any political culture suitably needed for a civil society. Deliberate attempts have been made to weaken the civil structure by the forces of *status quo* and power hungry ruling elite. The fragile societal force also provides the ruling class to exploit them these are primarily variety of hurdles for a viable civil society in India. There are lack of political culture, lack of accountability, religious fundamentalism, element of militancy/terrorism, state sponsored terrorism, controlled media, class differences, economic fragility, poor governance, and rampant corruption.

Regrettably, the compulsions of electoral policies dictate the use of communal, caste and class divisions by the political masters to consolidate their respective vote banks. This is bound to generate social conflicts and violence in society. The electoral politics lies at the roots of governance and security. Money and muscle power obviously become the important ingredients for this phenomena. The problem is also perceived to be with the politics and politicians who have reduced the agenda of governance in pursuit of power. The dilemma before the state is that it can reform itself while remaining party to its sustained misgovernance.

Evolving and strengthening appropriate legislation and streamlining the process of judicial conviction of the fugitives is another area that needs some priority and attention. Creation of fast tract courts to avoid judicial delay and enactment cf a deterrent anti-terror law would constitute an essential step forward. The need of the hour is to institutionalize, develop procedure and process that would boost inter institutional co-ordination, facilitate professional conduct of operations on a thorough professional policy analysis. Lack of professional mindset for informed debates, fierce expression of spite, bitterness and mutual political acrimony take place instead of constructive policy discussions. Indian politicians are known for rhetoric penchant without substantive action or operation; this has eroded the credibility of such oft repeated statement.

Terrorism and militancy cannot be seen as a monolithic projection of threat, this need to be analyzed from various angles like religious, ethnic, ideological, psychological, political, economic, military and larger security canvas. Questions thus arise whether this could be eliminated or contained without addressing the root cause? It looks as if India is engaged in a "war without front" there is a subtle low intensity conflict spreading in different parts of India without any tangible solutions on horizon. Mere deployment of security forces may not bring desired results. Multiplicity of security force is also not an answer to the complex situation. Military and security force can only contain the militancy to some extent; they will not be able to eliminate it. In a resolution adopted on December 2008, Indian Parliament vowed not to rest "until the terrorist and those who have trained, funded and abetted them are exposed and brought to justice" and proclaimed that India "will be victorious in its fight against the barbaric menace of terrorism." Roots of all evil "need to be addressed" by political consensus, robust and assertive decision making through democratic governance. Augmentation of socio-economic standard and preservation of pluralistic culture would be in India's interest.

15

Four Studies in Non-State Experiments with Peace Making in Contemporary India

Samir Kumar Das

Nuclear wars or for that matter conflicts threatening to turn into such wars seem almost avoidable today. The real threat comes from the growing number and ferocity of internal wars being fought in vast parts particularly of Asia, Africa and Latin America on an everyday basis. More than two-third of violent conflicts today falls under this category. States have killed their own citizens more than their enemies. As Cold War came to an end and the threat of nuclear wars becomes distant, local wars fought within nations, localities and regions are taking their toll on us. Groups and communities, hitherto lying dormant under strong states or the threat of local wars eventually spiralling into full scale nuclear war, are up in arms on the basis of their ethnic and religious identities or various other forms of affiliation and are settling their scores by spilling each other's blood. Millions are displaced from their homes and are constantly on the move. The states and other political agencies are found to be increasingly inadequate to meet this threat. Simple military solutions—whether by state or other multilateral institutions, have already turned ineffective, at times counterproductive. With the proliferation of cheap and light weaponry across the globe, none of us feels safe and secure. While we are facing newer threats, our responses bear the legacy of Cold War. Newer threats call for newer responses.

Such issues as rights, justice and democracy were always left to the sovereign states for decisions. And now with the disintegration or at least the loosening grip of states in many parts of the world, these issues have acquired certain measures of autonomy from them. Thus, the state is no longer viewed as the sovereign agency for deciding on the demands for homeland, rights of the indigenous peoples to justice and albeit contentious claims over resources and environmental protection, etc. While issues of rights and justice refuse to be settled within the confines of predominantly state-centric 'democratic' institutions already in place, we are yet to evolve appropriate institutions in this regard. Civil society institutions are often offered as solution. These institutions – as some of the great liberal philosophers would have us believe, were required to keep the State under a leash—perhaps not to replace it.

This chapter highlights (a) the issues underlying some of the major conflicts in contemporary India; (b) four of the non-state initiatives and experiments with conflict resolution, which to my mind are important; and finally (c) some of the challenges they face while trying to manage and resolve the conflicts. The four studies assembled here are only a preliminary attempt at appreciating the complexities involved in the non-state experiments with peacemaking and conflict resolution in India. The chapter does not intend to go into the controversy of whether this entire plethora of initiatives undertaken by some of the non-state actors while seeking to resolve the conflicts can as well be designated as civil society initiatives. Experiments being what they are, are met with varying degree of success and there is hardly any scope for valourizing or celebrating them. Nor should our portrayal of these initiatives give one a sense that state's role as an actor in conflicts—whether by generating and abetting or by mitigating and resolving them has in any way diminished. But it is important to note that the decade of the nineties has witnessed a rising intensity and incidence of conflicts on the one hand and an amazing proliferation of civil-society or more broadly non-state groups intent on resolving conflicts of some sorts.

I

The report submitted very recently by the Administrative Reforms Commission describes "Maoist violence" as the single most potent source of conflict in contemporary India—potentially much more threatening than even the conflicts centering on secessionist and independentist demands. Prime Minister Manmohan Singh has described it as "the single biggest internal security challenge" confronting the country. Maoism in India has travelled from an unknown village of Naxalbari in West Bengal in late 1960s to reach by 2006, 509 police stations comprising 7,000 villages of as many as 14 States of the Indian Union covering the heart of India. This accounts for almost 26 per cent of the country's geographical area. About 35 per cent of the country's total population is now affected by Maoist violence. Approximately 6,000 persons have lost their lives as a direct result of this conflict in the last 20 years, with an estimated 4,000 killings occurring in the last decade. According to Government estimates, 4,666 persons have fallen prey to Maoist violence during 2002-2006. Overall 3,674 people have died in 3,032 insurgency-related incidents in Jammu & Kashmir, North-East and Maoist violence alone between January 2004 and March 2007—making it the second deadly region in the world after Iraq. Although insurgent attacks are specific to particular regions, Islamist militants strike all over the country.

Table 15.1: Number of Deaths by Different Kinds of Violence (January 2004-March 2007)

Islamic Terrorist[1]	1878
Left Extremists	974
North-East terrorists	751
Others	16
Unknown	55

Source: *The Times of India* (Kolkata), 1 September, 2007, p. 8.

It has been estimated that about 41 per cent of the fatalities have occurred in Jammu & Kashmir alone while 27 per cent resulted from Maoist violence affecting 14 States—particularly Chhattisgarh, Andhra Pradesh, Jharkhand, Bihar, Maharashtra, Orissa, West Bengal, Uttar Pradesh and Karnataka. About 20 per cent of all fatalities were the result of the multiple insurgencies of India's North-East. More than 40,000 persons lost their lives in the J & K conflict since 1989 with an average of 100 persons per month. While 715 people died in 2005 in the North-East, 627 were killed in militant violence in 2006.

The "Maoist violence"—now 40 years old, differs from other insurrectionary movements at least in three respects: First, instead of aiming at secession from the Indian State, it intends to change the political system of the country and transform its socio-economic structure. Second, because of this wider all-India perspective, it has been able to avoid inter-ethnic and communal or religious feuds, which mar many other insurrections (like, Naga-Kuki, Bodo-Santhal, Karbi-Dimasa, Hindu-Muslim, and Hindu-Sikh conflicts). Third, as for its tactics, unlike other conflicts, it has generally avoided indiscriminate terrorist attacks that kill ordinary citizens on a mass scale—although in some areas it has destroyed public property and indulged in extortions from the common people.[2]

This does not, however, mean that the ethnic and communal conflicts are on the wane. As we enter global times, these old conflicts have undergone substantial changes as much as newer conflicts have emerged making the task of resolution all the more complex and difficult. At one level, state's control over people's world of identities—not just in India but everywhere—has loosened—thanks to globalization and our national identity is only one of many identities—and not necessarily the most dominant one, that we have today. At another level and as a corollary to it, globalization has made it possible for the otherwise locally and regionally based identities to bypass and cut across the national boundaries and become part of global and transnational networks. Most of the ethnic and communal groups today have their global links. The global has impinged on the local and *vice versa*—thanks to globalization. The process has offered to the locally-based ethnic groups the opportunity of being in league with the global actors and multilateral bodies. This has contributed to a certain sharpening of these identity-based conflicts. Globalization has transformed these conflicts into what in official circles is known as 'terrorism'. 47,371 persons according to Government figures have died to terrorist violence during 1994-2005.

As India turns into what USAID has recently designated as, a "transforming economy", newer conflicts have surfaced. The GDP is growing by about 9 per cent, while corporate sector is growing furiously at a little over 12 per cent. Sensex has already crossed the 20,000 mark. Savings rate is increasingly gaining in percentage terms and now stands at an impressive 33 per cent mark. Yet, agriculture is lagging behind with only 2-3 per cent rate of annual growth. Starvation deaths in the countryside are not uncommon. Agriculture is stagnating and the fragmentation of land due to disintegration of families and overcrowding has apparently made land unproductive and trapped it in some form of low employment equilibrium. Economic planning now focuses more on industry and the industrial strategy of acquiring mainly agricultural land and giving it to the private investors for setting up industries and Special Economic Zones (SEZ) has already become a new source of conflict in many parts of India. SEZs are set up with the objective of attracting private investments by way of offering tax cuts and other infrastructural support. The Central Government has so far cleared 237 SEZs scattered over such States as Maharashtra, Andhra Pradesh, Karnataka, Tamil Nadu, Punjab, Haryana, Uttar Pradesh, and West Bengal after the passage of SEZ Act in 2005. According to newspaper reports, in West Bengal alone, over 200,000 acres of land are supposed to be acquired by the government. In many parts of India, conflicts are taking place on the issue of government's takeover of cultivable land. About a million small and medium-sized landowners and perhaps a few millions more earning their livelihood from agriculture whether as sharecroppers or landless agricultural labourers plus their families, are going to be affected by it. The signs of discontent are particularly visible in the States of Punjab, Maharashtra, Orissa, Andhra Pradesh and West Bengal. New and hitherto unknown political organizations and alignments have come into being—cutting across ethnic and party lines. The conventional political parties do not seem to be in the forefront any longer. In many cases as in the cases of Bhumi Uchchhed Pratirodh Committee (or the Committee for Resisting Eviction from Land) or Krishi Jami Raksha Committee (Committee for the Protection of Agricultural Land) active in Nandigram and Singur of West Bengal, the new organizations that have come into being represent diverse forces at times in opposition to each other. In many cases, established political parties have also witnessed mass desertions at local level resulting often in a certain swelling of ranks of the newly set up organizations. While all this shows a perceptible depreciation of established political organizations and parliamentary forces, one wonders whether these changes might translate into electoral reverses or not. Besides, many of these conflicts, we mentioned, are of overlapping nature.

II

Although different types of conflicts call for different forms and strategies of solution, there is growing realization even in government circles that simple law-and-order approach to the conflicts mentioned above will not be enough. After a close reading of the memoirs and interviews, Ashis Nandy for example notes that fatigue has already set in, particularly in the ranks of the security forces and a certain realization has dawned upon the policy makers that strong arm tactics will not pay in the long run.[3] The role of civil society groups and initiatives in managing conflicts and eventually settling and resolving them can hardly be underestimated. Although in recent years, the surfacing of conflicts is often seen to be accompanied by a certain disintegration of civil society groups and initiatives, all is certainly not lost. In the context of the recent carnage in Gujarat, such civil society groups as Sabaramati Ashram—that could have played a crucial role in mending fences between communities had Gandhi been alive—were shut while protecting their auspices from the threat of vandalization by the communal forces. As Teesta Setalvad of Communalism Combat reports:

> Where also amidst the savagery, injustice and human suffering is the 'civil society', the Gandhians, the development workers, the NGOs, the fabled spontaneous Gujarati philanthropy which was so much in evidence in the earthquake in Kutch and Ahmedabad! The newspapers reported that at the peak of the pogrom, the gates of Sabarmati Ashram were closed to protect its properties; it should instead have been city's major sanctuary. Which Gandhian leaders, or NGO managers, staked their lives to halt the death-dealing throngs? It is one more shame that we as citizens of this country must carry on our already burdened backs that the camps for the Muslim riot victims in Ahmedabad are being run almost exclusively by Muslim organizations. It is as though the monumental pain, loss, betrayal and injustice suffered by the Muslim people are the concern only of other Muslim people, and the rest of us have no share in the responsibility to assuage, to heal and rebuild.[4]

The ethnic and communal conflicts in other words do not spare the so-called civil society organizations so much so that these organizations provide the sites where the same conflicts are reenacted, played out. Yet some of the rather unconventional non-State organizations are seen to be playing an active role in mitigating if not resolving these conflicts. In this connection, I propose to refer to four of what I consider as major non-State experiments with conflict resolution in contemporary India.

First of all, we may refer to the "Hoped pattern" named after the famous police officer—Suresh Hoped who introduced it in Brigand—a medium-sized town of Maharashtra visited by frequent cycles of communal violence till the early 1990s. He learnt from his experience as a police officer that Hindu-Muslim conflicts in Bhiwandi occur almost as regular cycles precisely because there is an acute lack of information flow across communities. While the Hindus do not have any live interaction with their Muslim counterparts, the Muslims similarly do not have any kind of live interaction with the Hindus. The result is: Both these communities continue to harbour and be guided by certain stereotypes about their other transmitted to them by their respective processes of socialization. In the absence of any live interaction and information exchange, these stereotypes do not stand the test of verification. Besides, he also learnt from his experience as a police officer dealing with communal riots that such mechanisms (as Peace Committees) of information exchange otherwise put in place to preempt eruptions of communal violence crumble precisely at the height of communal violence and do not survive them.[5] More than the mere presence of these mechanisms and the sense of false satisfaction that we often derive from it, what is most needed are their stability and the ability of these mechanisms to withstand the outbreak of communal violence and conflicts. As a solution he experimented with the idea of establishing *mohalla* (or neighbourhood) committees consisting of an equal number of members drawn from each of the conflicting communities, headed preferably by a police officer and to ensure that they regularly meet and discuss issues amongst themselves without divulging its content to the outsiders. The equal representation of the Hindus and the Muslims with these committees will prevent the minority Muslims from being swamped by the Hindus while taking crucial decisions. In matters of mitigating communal conflicts and mending fences, the principle one should adopt is to treat the minority not as a minority but as a partner placed on an even platform. The police officer attached to the local police station will not offer any solution, but will help the members in finding a solution. His duty is to facilitate and certainly not, to dictate. The task of facilitation ranges from holding regular meetings and bring the rivaling parties together to provide protection to them during frenzied times. The model worked wonders. While neighbouring Mumbai was a standing witness to the worst ever orgy of communal violence in 1992-93, Bhiwandi was evidently spared of it.[6]

III

The first experiment requires government mediation. The *mohalla* committees are not left to fend for themselves but each is kept under a police officer attached to the local police station, having a sense of the locality and the social milieu within which it functions. The policeman serves as the living bridge between communities at the peak of communal riots. This obviously makes a great demand on the will and integrity of the police officer for making these committees function effectively and take an active role in keeping communal riots at bay. But, the second experiment is conducted by the conflicting parties themselves—at times though, at the instance of Church or any other civil society group. The Naga-Kuki conflict in the hills of Manipur that took its toll of over 600 human lives in early 1990s came to an end almost by that time precisely because the two militant organizations spearheading the conflict reached a mutually hurting stalemate. Although the Church urged them to reach an agreement, they eventually came to realize themselves that the politics of vendetta would not be beneficial to either of them. At a time when the rivalling militant organizations are evenly keeled, neither is powerful enough to obliterate the other and the violence between them does not show signs of subsidence. Continuation of violence gradually becomes a mutually losing game. As a result, the militants reportedly sat together at the instance of the Church and demarcated and distributed the villages between themselves for the purpose of exercising control over them. The idea was to isolate the parties and reducing if not completely preempting any interaction between the communities. Virtual partition or segregation of the areas of influence is held as the key to the resolution of conflicts. While in the first experiment, the avoidance of conflicts is assumed to be predicated on the frequency and regularity of interaction and information flow between them, the second experiment is based on the opposite assumption that the interactions and information exchanges are responsible for the outbreak of conflicts between communities. The *raison d' ētre* behind the partition of the subcontinent was also the same: the best way to resolve the conflicts is to keep the communities separate and erect a rigid wall between them. Many peacemaking efforts actually take on such lines. The temporary truce that was brokered between the Liberation tigers of Tamil Eelam and the State of Sri Lanka at the Norwegian initiative was firmly embedded in the idea of partitioning the space and keeping the army and the LTTE separate so that the contacts and encounters between them might be kept at the minimum, if not completely ruled out. That the complaints of violation finally made the truce unworkable and a complete breach is a different matter. The Indo-Naga ceasefire that is continuing between the Government of India and the National Socialist Council of Nagalim (I-M) since 1997 is also based on the same assumption of quarantining the army from the militants and *vice-versa*. Complaints and accusations of ceasefire violation are freely traded between the rivaling parties. This does not of course leave room for any interaction between the conflicting communities and, therefore, hardly generate any civility between them. Although peace is sought to be made through non-State initiatives, one still remains unclear whether such initiatives qualify as civic initiatives. In the theoretical literature developed on the subject, civil society is defined primarily as a space where people inhabiting it treat others civilly, that is to say, as individuals or groups with equal entitlements to rights, equality and livelihood like theirs and the two modalities of treating individuals and groups civilly and treating them as members of one or the other ethnic community are not only distinct but distinguishable. While the distinction between 'us' and 'them' is central to the formation of ethnic communities, a certain kind of non-dualistic ethics characterizes the coming into being of civil societies.[7] Partition reenacts the same dualistic logic while setting peacemaking initiatives in motion: The duality of either/or replaces both/and neither/nor from the peace process.[8] While Naga-Kuki agreement mentioned above has provided for reasonably stable peace in the hills of Manipur largely since 1993, historically partitions have ignited more conflicts than have solved them.

IV

While in the second experiment, third party mediation plays only a cosmetic mediating role (because the realization of the futility of conflicts emerges from amongst the parties); the third experiment aims at making peace possible only through third party mediation. It is interesting to note that in times of heightened ethnic and intercommunity conflicts when communal lines are hardened, it is mostly the women who are seen to cross the ethnic lines. Men being what they are often find it beneath their honour to mend fences with the members of another community. In fact *Athwass* (a Kashmiri word which means handshake or holding of hands as an extension of solidarity or trust) is the name of an initiative conceptualized at the Women in Security, Conflict Management and Peace (WISCOMP) roundtable held in 2000 that brought together women from Kashmiri Pundit, Muslim and Sikh communities for the first time in almost a decade since the conflict in its renewed form broke out in the Valley. Its main objective is to familiarize them with "contrasting realities and narratives", they hold and harbour toward each other and this is expected to ensure transparency in their dealings with others and dissolve the boundaries. Such interventions by women in conflict situations are by no means unique to Kashmir.[9] CRG keeps organizing a series of dialogues amongst the representatives from eastern India and the North-East with a view to mutually appreciate the respective positions and differences that keep the conflicting parties apart. While elaborating on the objective, the report on the first dialogue held in Kolkata in 2001 points out:

> We, the members of Calcutta Research Group feel that Bengal is not just adjacent to the States of the North-East but is also

> related to the region through social, economic and political networks of human rights and peace. Therefore, as members of a young peace research group we have decided to hold this dialogue in Kolkata hoping that such a dialogue may bring out saner voices of peace in the region. It is in this spirit that CRG felt the necessity of organizing a civil society dialogue where all possible shades of opinion could be represented and rearticulated, organized and reshuffled in a manner that guarantees against privileging of any one of them.[10]

Its strategic location in Kolkata gives it a relative distance and most importantly a vantage point to bring representatives from different communities otherwise at war with each other to feel relieved and repose confidence in the organizers who are otherwise not involved as parties to the conflicts in the region. At the heyday of conflicts when rivalling parties have virtually broken all normal channels o communication between them, the third parties play a critical role in serving as a vehicle of communication between them. North East Peoples' Initiative (NEPI) based in Guwahati working from within the region seeks "to bring together experts and academics that (*sic*) can analyze the peace pacts of the past, and activists who would attempt to share their experiences of some of these processes—their conditions for success and failure—in order to define the conditions for justice and peace in the region in the coming days". The first seminar organized by NEPI in September 2005 was successful in drawing together organizations that were partisan and involved in mutual hostility and even conflicts.

V

Besides, there have been *secular* experiments with mitigating conflicts and violence by non-State actors. These experiments may be secular in either of the two ways: One, when the members of one community come to the rescue of another in a particular locality or neighbourhood at a time when both of them are otherwise involved in a fierce conflict between them. Such examples of Hindus protecting mosques and Muslims protecting temples of their respective neighbours within the same locality are by no means rare. Sometimes political parties are instrumental in cross-mobilizing people to stop violence and arson during communal riots. The Tram Workers' Union affiliated to the Communist Party of India for example while deploying their cadres followed the same logic during the 'Great Calcutta killing' of 16 August, 1946 with the expectation that members of the same religious community are unlikely to attack each other.[11] Two, the joint resistance by the Hindus and the Muslims (or whatever be the rivalling communities) form resistance groups and committees together on their own and seek to mitigate conflicts. Such groups and committees can function effectively to the extent that their members are able to transcend their narrow ethnic and communal interests. If they are unable to do so, they seek to use them as sites for promoting their interests. Such examples of counter-use are also not rare. For instance, if the Muslims feel compelled to make compromises and thereby peace with the Hindus, then peace achieved in this manner can only be fragile and unstable. The civil-society argument in this context will be that "public reasons" (*a la Rawls* for instance) must replace narrow ethnic and communal interests. Insofar as people are informed by "public reasons", that is to say, reasons that are understandable to their other, and by a common concern, they can be parts of the same political undertaking that can alleviate ethnic and communal divisions that otherwise exist between them. The civil society should not be made a part of the slinging power game between the groups and communities.

Beyond this point, the argument of common experiment with peacemaking has little agreement between its proponents. One section of proponents following the Gandhian tradition tends to argue that such secular forms of resistance must also be of non-violent nature. Violence being of self-spiralling nature cannot be an answer to violence. Moreover, the exercise of violence *per se* is immoral and unethical. A softer version of this argument is that violence against interethnic violence must be strong enough to overpower it. Given that the State still wields the monopoly over the legitimate instruments of violence, non-State agencies are not supposed to have such means of superior counter-violence at their disposal. In its absence, what resistance can do is to change the rules of the game and pit non-violence against violence. Not violence but the moral strength of having transcended the narrow ethnic and communal barriers could be the response to such ethnic conflicts. While this is an essentially moral argument, we have examples of people falling prey to violence because of their moral convictions. Nepaldeb Bhattacharya, an eminent Left leader from 24-Parganas (North)—close to Calcutta—was seriously injured when he stood between two irate mobs and tried to reconcile between them. Moral strength may add to one's physical vulnerability in times of riots and violence.

This leads another section of proponents to make an advocacy for secular and armed resistance to ethnic and communal conflicts. At one level this contests the State's theoretical monopoly over the legitimate instruments of violence. No State can approve of the presence of armed groups within its territory taking up law in their own hands and punishing those guilty of spreading communal frenzy. Viewed in this sense, there is a necessary antinomy between the two. But at another level, it also makes good the State's lacuna of enforcing law and order and its inability to put a stop to ethnic and communal conflicts. In that sense, the armed groups only supplement and do not supplant the State.

Like many other insurgent groups, the United Liberation Front of Assam (ULFA) based mainly in Assam too believes that the people retain their right to violence only as a means of self-defence at a time when violence by the State only helps "the enemies of the people". The riots that broke out in Nagaon in the wake of the demolition of the historic Babari mosque in December 1992 could have by newspapers accounts gone out of control—thanks to the inadequacy of the police forces and the weapons at their disposal—had ULFA cadres not intervened in time and launched an armed campaign against the perpetrators of violence. As one report puts it, most of junior and medium-level officers too wanted heart and soul that in the absence of adequate security preparations, ULFA cadres should take charge of the situation and keep the situation under control.[12] One must keep in mind that ULFA was already declared a banned organization by that time. ULFA was committed to the task of punishing those who took part in the violence against the Bengali-speaking Muslims in 1983.

Besides organized interventions, there are many other interventions, which because of their unorganized nature escape our notice. In this connection, I may refer to the individual interventions as an example. Since these interventions are made essentially by individuals—whether as medical practitioners or otherwise, they fear reprisals from the communities they belong to and grant interviews only on conditions of anonymity. Thus, a gynecologist, who had supervised the birth of baby born of an allegedly Bangladeshi woman held in Raiganj prison lockup in 2004, was subjected to severe forms of social ostracization. As the anti-immigrant sentiment runs high, he and his family are denied almost all the essential social services including those of barbers and washermen and even the vendors in the local market refuse to sell vegetables to them. Daily life becomes unusually difficult for this family. He has to move all the way to the distant markets to stock the provisions. The children of his locality refuse to play with his three daughters. The doctor on condition of anonymity told me: "I have done whatever I thought was necessary for me to do at that time; let others think of the nation. I have no regrets." As a matter of fact, he has to suffer all this because of his personal convictions. He is nobody in the political world—neither a member of any political group nor an enthusiastic voter; nor is he known for his consistently radical political views. Yet he dared to cross the frontiers of the nation at the risk of being branded as anti-national while responding to his professional calling. A local doctor, an ordinary mortal—a devil in the locality, yet an ethical being! It is the ethicality of the ordinary that enables one to transcend the boundaries despite all the ambiguities and ambivalences involved in such initiatives. These examples are by no means rare.[13] Although such interventions prove to be very effective in cases of interethnic and communal conflicts, civil society groups based primarily in urban and metropolitan centres are only slowly responding to the Maoist and land-based conflicts. This obviously speaks a lot about the nature of our civil society groups and institutions.

VI

We do not know whether it is possible to characterize these experiments as *civil society* experiments. The mainstream notion of civil society heavily influenced by Western thinkers, views the latter as a space that is only pitted against the State, but is *civil* in more positive terms. Any non-State space is not necessarily civil unless that treats all individuals and groups belonging to it as equal and full rights-bearing citizens. In that sense ethnicity based on an ineradicable dualism between 'us' and 'them' is antithetical to the very idea of civil society. But, such non-dualistic ethic characterizing the mainstream notion of civil society may also emerge from within the ethnic groups and communities.[14] In simple terms, one does not have necessarily to stick to the otherwise commonplace ethnicity-civil society dichotomy in order to appreciate the role of civil society in a country like India. Indeed, the assumed dichotomy has inspired many reformulations of civil society particularly the newly emerged concept of "political society". Our studies are intended to throw insights into the possibility of reimagining civil society in the non-Western context. It demands an altogether different reading of our history and society. These studies also show that there is no civil society existing as a given space in a society shot with conflicts. The articulation of this space depends on the politically expedient character of the negotiations by the non-State actors with the conflicts. The problem with the dichotomized view of civil society is that it seeks to define civil society as a space and not as a process whereby such a space gets articulated or does not get articulated or even articulated in different manners. That is the reason why I have avoided the term "civil society" and used a politically less controversial term "non-State actors". The involvement of non-State groups and initiatives in the peace process may not help infusing peace with the principles of rights, democracy and justice. Civil society initiatives attempt to bring these principles to bear on it. We must keep in mind that peace process unleashed by the non-State actors may often culminate in the production of a very 'illiberal' society.

REFERENCES

1. The data assembled here are Government estimates and such terms as 'terror' and 'terrorists' are freely used in Government circles. The use of such terms in this Table does not necessarily mean that we too subscribe to them.
2. The point was mentioned by Sumanta Banerjee in his presentation to a seminar on "Remaking the State: Conflicts and Peace processes in South Asia" organized by the Nelson Mandela Centre for Peace and Conflict Resolution, Jamia Millia Islamia, New Delhi on 9-10 March, 2007.
3. Ashis Nandy (1989): "The political culture of the Indian State" in *Daedalus*, Fall, 1989.
4. Teesta Setalvad, "Cry the Beloved Country: Reflections on the Gujarat Massacre" in *The Other Voice*, March, 2002, pp. 222-23.
5. Even established and organized political parties are unable survive communal flare-ups. See, Samir Kumar Das, "Dangar Dawai Naki Munider Matibhram?" (in Bengali) ['Solution to Communal Riots or the Muddle of the Wise?'] in *Shubhashree*, 37, Annual Number, 1998. pp. 3334.
6. See, Suresh Khopade, *Bhivandi Riots 1984* (Mumbai; Granthali, 1998).
7. Christopher G.A. Bryant (1995): "Civic Nation, Civil Society and Civil Religion." In John A. Hall ed., *Civil Society: Theory, History, Comparison* (Cambridge: Polity, 1995), p. 147.
8. Varshny however does not take into account the role of segregation and partition in mitigating ethnic conflicts. See. Ashutosh Varshney, *Ethnic Conflict and Civic Life: Hindus and Muslims in India* (New Delhi: OUP, 2001).
9. Urvasi Butalia, ed., *Speaking Peace: Women's Voices from Kashmir* (London: Zed Books 2002).
10. Samir Kumar Das & Paula Banerjee, eds. (2001), *Civil Society Dialogue on Human Rights and Peace in the Northeast* (Calcutta, Calcutta Research Group, 2001), p. 1.

11. Sadhan Banerjee, *Asamanya Birgatha* (Calcutta: National Book Agency, 2003).
12. Subir Bhaumik, "Sena-Police Nai, Nagaonke Banchalo ULFA Jangirai" (in Bengali) [Not the Army, Nor the Police, the ULFA militants saved Nagaon] in *The Ananda Bazaar Patrika*, 15 December, 1992.
13. For a theoretical analysis of democracy cutting across borders, see, Samir Kumar Das, "Democracy Beyond Borders: Indian democracy in the Age of Globalization" in Bhupinder Brar *et al.*, *Globalization and the Politics of Identity in India* (New Delhi: Pearson Longman, 2008).
14. J.P.S. Uberoi for instance, seeks to find out the traces of such non-dualistic ethic in the religious traditions of Sikhism and Shiite Islam and regards them as the basis of civil society. Such non-dualism makes us appreciate our differences from others and *vice versa* without being hostile towards them. See, J.P.S. Uberoi, *Religion, Civil Society and the State: A Study of Sikhism* (Delhi, OUP, 1996).

16

Dalits and the Ideology of Work in India: In Comparative Perspectives

Shashi Bhushan Upadhyay Shashi

In this chapter we will try to explore the place and role of the *dalits*[1] in the work regimes which emerged and developed in India over centuries. We will attempt to see how the Indian tradition perceives work in general, as well as in the context of what have been traditionally associated with the notion of lowly/degraded work. The notion of work is analyzed in comparison with the socio-economic and cultural thinking in Post-Reformation Europe where there was a deep shift in the meaning of work. Manual work acquired a central place in the post-Reformation thinking in Europe where it was put on par, if not above, other kinds of work. From there it was transported to North America where it acquired greater poignancy due to relative absence of feudal notion about manual labour. The crucial role played by various Protestant, particularly 'ascetic' sects in this process has been analyzed in detail by various scholars, most prominently by Max Weber who linked it with the development of capitalism. It is with this comparative perspective that this chapter tries to explore the notions associated with work in precolonial and colonial India to see how the ideology of work in India affected the *dalits* and how *Dalit* thinking on this issue was shaped.

According to the Census of 2001, the scheduled castes, which are largely coterminous with the *dalits*, number 166 million and comprise about 16.2 per cent of the population. Only about 16 per cent of them live in urban areas while 84 per cent of them live in rural areas. In the rural areas, they form about 18-20 per cent of rural population, while in urban areas their share of population is 12-14 per cent. They are found in most Indian States, but are mostly concentrated in Uttar Pradesh, Bihar, Bengal, Tamil Nadu, Andhra Pradesh, Rajasthan and Maharashtra. There are hundreds of castes among them which speak various languages and follow different life styles.[2] The *dalit* workers, particularly in the traditional rural society, performed two types of functions: (1) their **caste** work or the ritual functions which were associated either with organic waste or with death and which defined their castes, and which were supposedly responsible for their untouchability; and (2) the work which marked the great majority of them as a labouring **class** in the production process. These two roles were not strictly separate, but influenced each other. Thus, because of the stigma attached to untouchability and the traditional injunction against holding land, the untouchables could be coerced and mobilized as low-paid workers. On the other hand, due to their poverty and their subordinate position, they were compelled to undertake ritually demeaning labour either in the villages or in urban areas. It is this caste-class continuum as well as differentiation which serve as a background to assess the *dalit* response to the meaning of work in India.

WORK IN WESTERN TRADITION

In hunting-gathering societies work was an indivisible part of life and the distinction between work and leisure did not exist. There is no distinctive term for work in the language of the hunters and gatherers.[3] In agricultural societies class divisions started emerging and were accompanied by separation of work and leisure. Moreover, for the subordinate people the amount of work increased. With the onset of civilization the hierarchical arrangement of societies almost became a norm. The creation of sufficient surplus gave rise to classes of people who could be increasingly free from manual work and specialize in spiritual and military matters. These classes developed vested interests in leisure and tried to control the working classes through various ideological and military means. Various justifications were given by the philosophers and thinkers to create and maintain hierarchies. In most pre-modern societies the prevailing view considered manual work as degrading.

The dominant ideology in the Greek society despised manual work and considered it demeaning. The Greek word for work was *ascholia* which had a negative meaning as absence of leisure (*schole*).[4] The manual work was considered suitable only for slaves who were regarded more as instruments of production than human beings. As Aristotle said, "A slave is an animated instrument".[5] The free people were asked not to soil their hands from labour. They could pursue warfare, large-scale commerce and arts, particularly architecture and sculpture which were considered honourable occupations.[6] Plato and Aristotle considered leisure as a source of happiness, of spiritual enlightenment and pursuit for higher truth. It was, however, fully realized that the pursuit of leisure was dependent on regular manual labour involved in production of goods and services. Thus slavery was considered natural and it was proposed that while some people were born to pursue a life of leisure, there were others who were born to toil hard. The slaves, who were not Greek citizens, supported the edifice of upper-class leisure. The Greek philosophers argued for maintaining such division of labour which would allow the higher classes of Greek citizens to lead a comfortable life.

The Romans derived from the Greeks the negative notions about work. They also considered work (*negotium*) as the absence of leisure (*otium*). They believed that certain kinds of labour were degrading and that they should be done only by the slaves. The free men were to be engaged in military matters, commercial pursuits and state affairs. Even poor free people who, due to poverty, were forced to work were held in contempt.[7] In the religious culture of the western world, however, there was a contradiction in its attitude towards work. In the Hebrew thinking the work seems to have originated from a curse when Adam was evicted from the Garden of Eden for disobeying God's command. Thus work was regarded as a curse by God to punish the disobedience by Adam and Eve.[8] At the same time, however, work was viewed as necessary not only to prevent poverty and misery but also as a means of atonement for sin.

In Christianity, work was still considered as God's punishment for the original sin. However, on the positive side, work was also regarded as necessary to remain self-sufficient and not be dependent upon charity of others. In addition, the surplus earnings could be shared with needy persons. In this way, Christianity and the Church "elevated work and the worker from the base position accorded to him by Aristotle".[9] Manual work was not despised, but considered as an instrument of self-purification. Thus, even though the medieval aristocracy still regarded work as ignoble, the religious system gave work a high place. But there was no intrinsic value in it. Work was basically a morally neutral activity necessary to maintain life.[10]

PROTESTANTISM AND THE NEW WORK ETHIC

It is generally recognized that Protestantism changed the cultural environment in several regions of Europe. It not only intervened in religious matters and endeavoured to pose a challenge to Catholicism but also introduced various changes in what may be said to belong to the secular life of people. What Max Weber called the Protestant ethic is one such profound intervention in moulding the course of development in Western Europe and North America. According to Weber, it was Martin Luther who first introduced the idea of 'calling' in the religious discourse which meant that for each individual God had set a "life-task, a definite field in which to work". This idea was new because although some "positive valuation of routine activity in the world" existed earlier in the religious culture of Western world, it had now acquired an altogether new significance. The emphasis on worldly duties, the assertion that this was "the only way to live acceptably to God", and, even more importantly, the notion that "every legitimate calling has exactly the same worth in the sight of God" radically altered the hitherto existing ideas about work in general and manual labour in particular.[11] Luther, therefore, pioneered this worldly attitude to work, but it was ascetic Protestantism or the Puritanism which gave tremendous push to this idea and imbued the work with an intrinsic meaning. Calvinism, Methodism, Pietism and Baptism were the sects which, through constant indoctrination, changed the meaning of work in the Western world for good and created a powerful ideology of work which is now commonplace.

Protestant ethic freed work from various constraints and changed the attitude towards work in a fundamental manner. It brought work to the centre of human experience and desire. Only God was above work, and work was considered the way to reach God. The hierarchical division of work was declared null and void. All work was said to be of equal value. The derogatory attitude related to manual work was slowly undermined. It was now considered ennobling and capable of rinsing the soul of people. In fact, it was the life of leisure which was declared to be a sin in the eyes of God. At yet another level, Protestant ethic, particularly in its Calvinist form, differed from other systems of religious thoughts, such as Islam, which also had a positive attitude towards work in that it released work from all moral and community constraints. It was the individual who could become a member of the elect by working and could enter into communion with God. Secondly, it lifted the religious sanction against profit-making and accumulation of wealth. In fact, these were considered desirable. Thirdly, Calvinism justified social and economic inequality as long as it was the result of work and accumulation through work. It promoted and justified the unbridled quest for accumulation of wealth. However, a spendthrift and ostentatious life was considered morally incorrect, and frugal existence was advocated. This ideology found strong support among the bourgeoisie and self-employed artisans who, by working hard, hoped to advance in life.

However, such an espousal of work ethic did not come so naturally to the factory workers stripped of the means of production and working for others. With industrialization work became monotonous and invasive, covering longer time and larger spaces than was hitherto the case. In such a situation it became imperative that work should be imbued with some value. It would come only with intense preaching and indoctrination. According to Christopher Hill, in England, the "Protestant preachers in the late sixteenth and early seventeenth century undertook a cultural revolution, an exercise in indoctrination, in brainwashing, on a hitherto unprecedented scale."[12] Through constant religious and secular preaching it was made into an established fact that work was the centre of all human activities. The difference between the humans and the animals was work. It was the key to human progress and it carried its own rewards. In the late eighteenth and early nineteenth century England, Methodism enforced strict work-discipline among its followers through preaching in the Church and the Sunday schools. Its promise of benefits from hard work and the threat of divine punishment if one did not work were also used to persuade people to follow the industrial work-discipline.[13]

Manual labour moved to the centre to such an extent that a large part of modern economic thinking laid stress on the production of goods and on the labour required to do it. Labour became a matter of central concern with the development of classical political economy. With Marxism, labour became the all-important phenomenon.

Protestant ethic played a great role in the development of capitalism which led to an intensification and exploitation of labour. It does not mean that Protestantism was the only route through which societies were ushered into capitalism. A study of the industrialization in South Korea in recent times points out that the Confucian ethics supplied the ground for promoting a work ethic which stressed labour harmony and subordination to authority. Such an application of Confucianism was in sharp contrast to its traditional role which was responsible for social stagnation. However, in the modern period it has been used in East Asian and South-East Asian countries to promote a work ethic which has played a big role in economic dynamism.[14] It has also been argued that, despite belief to the contrary, the non-Protestant cultures also have shown a very strong commitment to work ethic. Thus, in a comparative study of the work ethic in Australia and Sri Lanka, it is asserted that work ethic is a universal phenomenon and "Sri Lankans seem equally, if not even more committed to hard work". In Sri Lanka, Buddhism has played a great role in inculcating a work ethic. The study concludes that "most religions and most cultures seem to have a common concept of a work ethic when it is defined as a commitment to hard work and excellence. Hard work is seen as an end in itself and even as morally right".[15] Many other countries with different belief systems have also moved on the road to economic development of various kinds.

What is more difficult to assert, however, is that whether such societies have been able to abolish the hierarchy of work and have imparted dignity to all kinds of work, as Protestantism has done in the areas of its influence. And this is of crucial importance because this particular dimension of Protestantism generated several radical ideologies of equality which were subversive to the system. If all work is equal, it was argued then all humans are equal. And, therefore, it was asserted that nobody has the right to exploit or rule over others.[16]

Thus, while the official Calvinist ideology stressed hard work in one's calling, emphasized thrift, encouraged accumulation of capital and induced capitalist development, the radical ideologies could utilize the arguments for different ends. Some Puritan preachers were already denouncing the nobles because they "live in no calling". One writer "argued that gentlemen were the real vagabonds, who do not labour in a calling: by their own and by God's law they should be punished". Gerald Winstanley, the leader of a radical sect, the Diggers, stated that "No man can be rich but … either by his own labours or by the labours of other men helping him…. Rich men receive all they have from the labourer's hand, and what they give, they give away other men's labours, not their own".[17] Thus, the nobility was committing theft, because the "property was justified by work and was not justified without it, so that idleness should be followed by expropriation".[18]

Thus while the Protestant ethic, by emphasizing on hard work in a calling, increasingly created a conservative condition for subjugating the workers; it also, through its stress on the dignity of all kinds of work, created the ideological condition for the growth of radical doctrines which challenged amassing of wealth by some created by the labour of others.

IDEOLOGY OF WORK IN PRE-COLONIAL INDIA

In the early Vedic period, there was a three-fold division envisaged among the Vedic people consisting of the warrior nobility, priests and the commoners. But these positions were neither endogamous nor hereditary. There was a certain division of labour in this period, but there is no reference to any four-fold *varna* system nor is there any mention of untouchability in the *Rig Veda*. Although the *Rig Veda* uses the term *varna* (colour) to distinguish the Aryans from the *Dasas*, its connotations were not racial but linguistic and cultural.

Three fundamental changes were taking place in the later Vedic society—emergence of a clearly discernible social stratification, urbanization and acceptance of the increasing authority of the State.[19] *Varna* system now took shape as a distinct marker of social stratification. Theoretically, according to various texts, the Indian society was divided into four *varnas*—the Brahmans (priests), the Kshatriyas (warriors and nobles), the Vaishyas (cultivators, traders and commoners) and the Shudras (labourers). The three upper *Varnas* were given the status of twice-born or *dwija* which was denied to the Shudras. The mythical origin of this system was sought in the ritual sacrifice of the mythical being *Purusha* (the Man) as provided in a late hymn of the *Rig Veda*. These positions slowly became hereditary accompanied by a broad division of labour. This provided the basis for an elaborate division of castes and sub-castes, closely associated with occupations and following the taboo on commensality and inter-marriage.[20]

The *Dasas* were subjugated and reduced to the level of labourers, the word *dasa* acquiring the meaning of a slave. In *Rig Veda* as well as in the later Vedic texts there is no mention of untouchability, although two groups—the *Chandala* and *Paukasa*—are mentioned as "objects of spite and abhorrence and exist at the lowest ritual and social level".[21] Gradually, the divisions became theoretically more rigid. The *Dharma Sutras* (fifth to second centuries BC) and the *Dharma Shastras* almost invariably mention the four-fold divisions in a hierarchical sequence with Brahmans at the top and the Shudras at the bottom. The most important text formulating and justifying this division in society was Manu's *Dharmashastra* (Laws of Manu), popularly known as *Manu Smriti*.

Composed some time during the first-two centuries A.D., Manu's *Dharmashastra* laid down rigid codes for observance by members of particular *varna* in all walks of life. It assigned supreme position to Brahmans and declared that the Brahman "is the Lord of this whole creation… because he was born of the highest part of the body, because he is the eldest, and because he maintains the *Veda*". Thus, "All of this belongs to the priest [i.e., Brahman], whatever there is in the universe", he "deserves all of this because of his excellence and his high birth".[22]

On the other end, the Shudra owns nothing and is not allowed to do so. His duty is to remain in service of the three upper *varnas*. As Manu ordains: "The Lord assigned only one activity to a servant [i.e., Shudra]: serving these (other) classes without resentment".[23] For this service, "They should assign him a livelihood out of their own family property according to his assets, taking into account his ability, his skill, and the number of his dependants". Moreover, "They should give him the leftovers of their food, their old clothes, the spoiled parts of their grain, and their wornout household utensils". He further declared that a Shudra "should not amass wealth, even if he has the ability, for a servant [i.e., Shudra] who has amassed wealth annoys priests [i.e., Brahmans]".[24] This hierarchy of *varnas* was expected to be maintained in all spheres of life and law. Manu was particularly harsh on the Shudras and women. There was no equality envisaged in work, in society, before law, or even before God.

Viewed in secular terms, the significance of these injunctions was to provide the three upper *varnas* with abundant cheap labour.[25] The application of these laws would provide the dominant classes the "strategies for combining land surplus with unfree labour", a reserve pool of labour which even maintained itself so as to be available for peak demands.[26]

Although the *varna* order provided the broad division, it was the caste system which became more relevant for the functioning of society. The caste with its hereditary and endogamous character and with its association with particular occupations restricted the vertical mobility among its individual members. Such mobility was possible only if the caste group decided to move elsewhere and took up another work. Gradually, the association between occupation and caste became more marked, particularly at the lower levels.[27]

There was another development taking place during the Gupta and the post-Gupta periods. It was the further degradation of all forms of manual labour. The cultivators, who until now had formed part of the Vaishya *varna*, now became *shudras*. In fact, now almost all castes working with hands occupied the bottom ladder of the society and were assigned the ritual rank of the *shudras*.[28] This, in turn, pushed down those engaged in manual as well as ritually impure labour. Starting with *Vishnusmriti*, where the term was first used, there are increasing references to the untouchables (*asprishya*), and the rules about untouchability became stricter.[29] At the level of work, we now find a broad three-fold division in the society:

1. the *dwija* or twice-born castes, consisting of the Brahmans, the Kshatriyas and the Vaishyas, who were generally involved in non-manual work;
2. the Shudras who formed part of the *varna* system at the bottom and who were engaged in various kinds of manual work, particularly agricultural and artisan work; and
3. the untouchables who were engaged in ritually impure manual work, but also supplied the bulk of agricultural labour.

It is difficult for any society to be so rigid in practice and the Indian society was anything but stagnant. Various economic, social and political developments were taking place and different ideological and material influences were evident. In fact, in Indian society the tradition of dissent and protest was evident right since the dominant tradition was being formulated. It was in the *Upanishads* that we find the earliest expressions of questioning the hereditary basis of social stratification and the relevance of rituals and sacrifices as the means of propitiating the gods. There were other forms of dissent and protests expressed in the tradition of the renouncers and the materialists such as *Ajivikas*, *Charvakas* and *Lokayatas*. But more organized religious traditions like Jainism and Buddhism, which differed from Brahmanism in a comprehensive manner, provided strong alternatives for the non-Brahman groups. Jainism spread in various regions of Indian subcontinent, but it was Buddhism which became the dominant religion in India for many centuries. These creeds did not believe in the caste system even though they did not attack it directly. Their egalitarian and non-caste approach and much less expensive worship attracted a lot of followers from the poor and discriminated groups.

These religions were monastic and placed great emphasis on renunciation. Thus Buddhist doctrine emphasised different roles for the *bhikkhus* (monks) and the *gahapatis* (householders) and outlined "separate methods of each in the search for liberation from rebirth".[30] In the monasteries, caste rules were not observed and special measures like interdining, taking on a new name and shaving of hair were taken to emphasise the egalitarian and other worldly character of the monasteries. Even in the society Jainism and Buddhism promoted a non-caste creed. However, there were limits to their radical role in the society. Buddhism also maintained a distinction between high and low on the basis of caste (*jati*), family (*kula*), work (*kamma*) and craft (*sippa*). Some occupations were considered high whereas certain others were termed low. The non-manual professions such as counting, accounting and writing are generally considered high, while occupations such as carriage-building, carpentry, basket-making, pottery, leatherwork, weaving, etc., were considered low.[31] The elite groups in the Buddhist texts do not perform manual work. Even *gahapatis*, who were in near exclusive control of agriculture and who were a very respectable group in society, did not work with their own hands.[32] Certain groups were considered untouchable even in the Jain and Buddhist text on the basis of their occupations. Thus hunters, fishermen, tailors and acrobats are described as untouchables by birth in Jain texts.[33] And in a Buddhist text the flute-makers are reckoned as a group "in which a Bodhisatta is not re-born".[34] It appears that although the new and heterodox faiths did shake the Brahmanical order, they could not uproot it. It is also possible that many beliefs and practices in the society had trans-religious significance and following.

Islam was another very important influence on the Indian society in the pre-colonial period. It is generally conceived as an egalitarian religion which has a positive attitude towards work. According to *Qur'an*, work is an obligatory activity and necessary for a balanced individual and social life.[35] But when Islam spread outside the less stratified Arab world to more complex and hierarchically organized societies, the Muslim society acquired a complex and hierarchical character. Various justifications were given for the hierarchical arrangement of the society. The notions of social hierarchy, which were not part of the *Qur'an* and early Muslim community, were now slowly incorporated in the emerging schools of Islamic law and jurisprudence. In India, the situation became even more complex when Islam encountered a society segregated on the basis of hereditary castes. The conversion to Islam from various strata of Indian society added to the complexity because the new converts brought their old beliefs and practices to the new fold. Scholars have pointed out that the Indian Muslim society could be broadly divided into three social strata—*ashraf* (noble born) which included the victorious Muslim nobility and the high-caste Hindu converts; the *ajlaf* (mean and lowly) which included the Muslim commoners either migrants or converts; and *arzal* (excluded) which comprised the people engaged in occupations which were considered very low and untouchable in Indian society. It is a well-recognized fact that in India the Muslim society is stratified on the basis of castes, and these castes follow restrictive rules on endogamy and commensality. Thus, even with Islam in India the attitude to work remained confined to a hierarchical framework which related birth to occupation.[36]

Bhakti movement, deriving from various sources, offered an anti-caste ideology on the whole. In the process, it also opposed the hierarchical ordering of work and its justification in terms of purity and pollution. It pleaded for equality of work as it did for equality of human beings. But *Bhakti* movement was not monolithic and it encompassed a variety of people and ideologies. In its radical variant, represented by Basav, Kabir, Nanak, Ravidas, Dadu, Tukaram and many others, its attack on social inequality was more thorough going. In the process, it also attacked the inequality related to the ritual rendering of work in a hierarchical manner. However, several other *Bhakti* saints, such as Tulsidas, Ramdas, etc., did not attack the *varna* order and justified the hierarchy of work. But even they believed that work of any kind was good enough to attain God provided one was devoted to the Lord. In this way, there was certain democratization in religious thinking set in motion by the *Bhakti* movement. But it did not go very far in practical terms and the caste society was able to dominate and dilute the radical slant of the *Bhakti* ideology. Thus, even the radical variant of *Bhakti* movement could not succeed in transforming the work culture in traditional India.[37]

It does not mean, however, that all people in pre-colonial India lived according to these codes. There was a lot of variations at the ground level. There were also various instances of changes in the traditional caste occupations. Thus we find that in the Mithila region of present-day Bihar a majority of Brahmans were engaged in cultivation while only about 12 per cent worked as priests. A large number of Brahmans were working as coolies in the factories in Surat.[38] Studies point out that in South India "the economy was highly diversified in comparison to its late nineteenth century successor", and only about 60 per cent of the workforce was directly engaged in agriculture.[39] There was a lot of mobility and the labour enjoyed a number of rights. The untouchables could cultivate lands and become sharecroppers. In certain hazardous areas, the untouchables were the sole occupants of land as they were ready to take risks.[40] Moreover, the formation of various regional states in the eighteenth century and incessant warfare among them offered several opportunities to the groups at the bottom of the society. There was an increased demand of labourers as construction workers, tank diggers, servants, transport workers, etc. Besides, the fighting armies needed ever increasing numbers of soldiers. All these developments were indicative of the fact that at the ground level the reality did not quite follow the dictates of the written laws and the situation varied from place to place.

COLONIALISM AND THE DEVELOPMENT OF DUAL LABOUR REGIME

The British colonial project in India was beset by a deep dilemma. The imperial interests demanded that hierarchies of various kinds should be observed with the British Crown at the top. Moreover, in a country where they formed a hopeless minority, the British wanted powerful allies and, in return, were ready to justify and reinforce what was perceived as the traditional social organization. On the other hand, as the inheritors of the Protestant ideology and the Enlightenment, they also swore by the Protestant work ethic, and equality and freedom for all.

The colonial rule tried to reduce the complexity present in the pre-colonial society, particularly in the late pre-colonial period and relied too heavily on high-caste, particularly Brahmanical, sources for understanding and codification. The colonial identification of caste and occupation pushed several *Dalit* castes, often against their wishes, into such jobs, like sweeping and scavenging, which were considered customary and appropriate for them. Thus, the *Chuhras* from Punjab were forced to work as sweepers in Delhi and other cities, despite the fact that they did not work earlier as such. Moreover, the Chief Commissioner of Delhi refused to accept the nationalist demand for education for the *Chuhras* and other *Dalit* castes on the ground that a lot of work was available for the "hereditary calling of the sweeper".[41] The competition for jobs also added its weight in favour of this caste-occupation identification. The massive Census operations sought to justify this thinking by supposedly providing a numerical basis for this.

In matters of actual policies, during the nineteenth century, the colonial rule allied itself with the dominant classes in the countryside. It led to the restriction on the rights of the labouring classes who had gained some ground during the regional autonomy of the previous century. The untouchable pariahs in the Madras presidency, who during the eighteenth century had formed a significant part of several local armies, were now debarred from the military services on the basis of 'custom'. The *Mahars* and *Mangs* from Western India faced similar fate in the latter half of the nineteenth century. The newly emerging theories about the so-called martial races deprived the *Dalits* from finding respectable jobs in the army thereby forcing them into odd urban jobs or ritually demeaning rural work as Cohen says the *Dalits* became the "unwilling victims of the theory of 'martial races' ".[42]

Untouchable labourers were ejected from the cities in the South on various pretexts. Thus, the *pariahs*, who might have been one-third of the population of Madras city in eighteenth century, constituted barely 10 per cent of the urban population of Madras Presidency in late nineteenth century. In this way the untouchables were forced back into agriculture in a servile position with their rights severely curtailed.[43]

The early colonialists also viewed the position of labour in terms of "kin, land, village communities, and ascriptive identities as the ligaments of the sub-continental political economy".[44] With the introduction of private property in land the marginal groups with certain customary rights in land became dependent labourers. The influx of machine-made goods from England drove the self-employed artisans into the ranks of agricultural labourers.[45] To meet the contingencies of production and the demands of metropolitan capitalism, the colonial state allowed and promoted various forms of bondages, despite the law about the abolition of slavery. Forced labour became almost a law demanded by both the colonial officials and the landlords. Such instances of forced and unpaid labour are to be found throughout the colonial period and are reflected in various literary works of the twentieth century. Laws were formulated for recruitment of "statute labour" to perform public works. Low-paid workers were recruited as personal servants of colonial officials. Coercive labour was common in the times of military urgency or natural calamity. Penal labour was used for the construction of roads and railways. The Madras Compulsory Labour Act of 1858 formulated that "any person bound by ... [local] custom to contribute labour" would have to pay compensation if he refuses to work. Thus, the colonial law validated the caste-based organization of labour in the name of custom and tradition. It further justified bonded servitude, even slavery, on the ground that there were complementarities between master and slave, and the latter were provided with material security in return for labour.[46] Various itinerant groups such as the Yerukulas, Bhantus, Banjaras, Budhuks, Sansis and Bowarias who were engaged in legitimate professions earlier and who lost their work when the colonial rule stabilized were declared criminal tribes and faced police oppression quite often. A relationship between caste and crime was sought to be established, thereby relegating such groups to the margins of the society. Many of them were also forced to perform low-paid or even servile work.[47]

At another level, however, the colonial state observed the law of equality and freedom in the domains it considered to be outside the customary social sphere. Thus, the Indian Contract Act of 1872 was based on the notion that there should be contractual relationship between the employers and employees. Various statutes were formulated to promote the written contracts in matters of employment. Government services, large mills and other undertakings, and the plantations were governed by this ideology. It is different matter that in actual practice the written contracts became another tool for enforcement of the employers' authority which, particularly in the plantations, forced the workers to servility. The workers were not in a position to take advantage of the principle of freedom enshrined in such laws.[48] Nevertheless, at the theoretical level, it confirmed the idea of equality and freedom and allowed the workers, particularly in the urban areas, to take advantage of law if they were in a position to do so.

Thus colonialism created a dual labour regime for the Davits. In the countryside, they became subject to the traditional control in an even more intense form, while in the cities they could claim equality with others. Even though in actual practice there was a lot of discrimination even in the urban areas, the relative anonymity of existence, the absence of upper caste social control and the notion of legal equality provided the Dali workers certain parity with the non-Dali workers. Thus the contradiction between the existence of the Davits in the villages and in the cities became much sharper than ever before. This is one of the important factors which influenced the Dali thinking in the process of developing a broader identity.

DALI THINKING AND THE MEANING OF LABOUR

Urban life, however, did not offer immediate relief. Even in urban areas, the Davits were mostly in low-paid and those jobs associated with their castes such as working with leather, sweeping and scavenging. Even in the case of the well-to-do sections of the urban Davits, such as the Chimers in Punjab, the Jotas in Agra and the Khakis in Kaptur in U.P., the link between caste and occupation remained. It is mostly in their supposedly traditional jobs such as leatherwork and pig rearing that they did well and acquired some amount of wealth. However, even the prosperous Davits faced a lot of discrimination in the urban society. They were not allowed in the temples, schools, restaurants, and clubs, not to speak of the upper caste private spaces. Therefore, even in the cities, there was a contradiction inherent in the social existence of the Davits. Whereas the direct caste oppression had ceased both at work and at home, there was a general discrimination in the labour market and in the society as such. This hiatus between the newly acquired freedom and occasional wealth, on the one hand, and the low social status on the other, created conditions for the emergence of powerful protest movements which attacked the social division of labour based on caste and ritual status. The Adi Dharma movement in Punjab, the Adi Dravidic movement in Tamil Nadir, Adi Karnataka, Adi Andhra movements and the Adi Hindu movement in U.P. were some of the important movements in the early twentieth century which were socially based on the urban Davits and derived their sustenance from the resentment and anger generated by these contradictory experiences.[49]

The leaders of these protest movements challenged the notion that the so-called low and untouchable castes had inherited the menial occupations and were suited for them. They asserted that they were the past rulers of India and their status was undermined through victory and fraud. Ram Charan, one of the Adi Hindu movement leaders, said in a speech in 1927:

> "They [the untouchables] were made to do the most insulting and demeaning jobs, such as cleaning excreta and dirty clothes. They were repeatedly told that you are *shudras* and your only work is to serve. Those who were thus made to serve were then called untouchables."[50]

Although these *Dalit* movements attacked the notion of caste-based division of labour and desired freedom in the choice of jobs, they did not question the very notion of purity and pollution involved in the work, nor did they question the idea of work as inherited. Their assertion was that they were not the ones who inherited these jobs, as they were earlier the rulers of the land and were later forced to undertake such low and polluting work.

It is true that the *Dalit* view of work was not straight and simple. It was quite complex emerging from pre-modern work environment with its ritual and social stigma, but also from a need to find dignity of being in the modern work situation which, although largely devoid of any ritualistic meaning, had class exploitation in its structure. In a society where untouchability was associated with ritually polluting work and manual work in general was held in contempt, the *Dalit* ideologues sought identity in a putative glorious past.

There were some who were proud of a life of labour. Hira Dom, generally considered to be the first *Dalit* poet in Hindi, wrote a poem entitled "The Complaints of an Untouchable" ('*Ek Achhoot ki Shikayat*') which was published in September 1914 in a famous Hindi literary magazine, *Saraswati*, then edited by one of the most important Hindi journalists of his times, Mahavir Prasad Dwivedi. In this, he asserts the worth of the *Dalits vis-à-vis* upper castes:

> We don't beg like Brahmans
> Don't oppress others by wielding sticks like Kshatriyas
> Don't cheat like Baniyas
> ...
> We earn our bread by sweating
> And the whole family eats
> By equally sharing it.

B.R. Ambedkar, a *Dalit* leader from Maharashtra, who was soon to become the most respected leader of the *Dalits* in India in the post-independence period, gave the matter a serious thought. He emphasized the nature of the villages as most oppressive place for the untouchables and considered them as 'the working plant of Hindu social order'. According to him, the Indian village was divided into two sections—touchable and untouchable. The touchables formed the majority who lived inside the village while the untouchables comprise a minority which stayed outside the village. The former were economically strong and independent while the latter were poor and dependent. The untouchables had to perform several duties in the village which no one else was prepared to do and for this they might or might not receive any remuneration. In other ways also the existence of the untouchables was sub-human and at the mercy of the touchables. The "only secure source of livelihood open to the untouchables in some parts of the country" was "the right to beg food from the Hindu farmers of the village".[51] Thus, the entire structure of work in the rural areas was forced, demeaning and unremunerative for the *Dalits*. He, therefore, advised his followers and all the untouchables to move out of the villages whenever they found an opportunity.

He further argued that caste system was not merely a division of labour. If it had been so, there was no harm in it because "Civilized society undoubtedly needs division of labour". The problem starts when this division of labour is "accompanied by this unnatural division of labourers into water-tight compartments". Thus caste system also divides labourers. Furthermore, it is a hierarchical division of labourers in which one category of labourers is graded above the other and so on. In addition, these categories are also hereditary. Thus caste system is a peculiar division of labour where the labourers are divided and graded one above the other and the work is inherited. Ambedkar thinks that "this stratification of occupations which is the result of the Caste System is positively pernicious". This division of labour is not based on choice and individual's interest. Instead, its basis is "the dogma of predestination". According to him, the problem with the industrial system in the West is not so much the poverty and suffering of the labourers as the fact that so many people are involved in the jobs which hold no interest for them. "Such callings," he says, "constantly provoke one to aversion, ill-will and the desire to evade". In India this system prevails in much more intensified form:

> There are many occupations in India which on account of the fact that they are regarded as degraded by the Hindus provoke those who are engaged in them to aversion. There is a constant desire to evade and escape from such occupations which arises solely because of the blighting effect which they produce upon those who follow them owing to the slight and stigma cast upon them by the Hindu religion. What efficiency can there be in a system under which neither men's heart nor their minds are in their work? As an economic organization Caste is, therefore, a harmful institution, inasmuch as, it involves the subordination of man's natural powers and inclinations to the exigencies of social rules.[52]

In his opinion, therefore, it was the negative social and cultural attitude related to certain kinds of work which made these works abhorrent. As long as such conditions existed, he thought that it would be better for the *Dalits* engaged in such work to move away from it.

CONCLUSION

The dominant thinking in pre-modern world regarded manual work as degrading. In India, the situation became even more complex because of the *varna* order and the castes which grouped people according to their birth and occupation. The long tradition of dissent and protest in pre-colonial India mitigated these conditions, but was unable to make any fundamental change in the dominant ideology of work. The colonial rule, with its ambivalent stance towards work and Indian social hierarchy, created a dual labour regime for the subordinate castes which made them vulnerable in the rural areas but provided them relatively more ideological and economic strength in the cities. This gave impetus to the emergence of powerful protest movements of the lower castes in colonial India. But, while these movements radically criticized the hierarchies of the caste system, their contribution in questioning the dominant ideology of work was less pronounced.

The *Dalits*, on the whole, resent caste-related work. About other types of work, their response may be comparable to non-*Dalit* workers, or they may even show more commitment. But the experiences of untouchability related to caste work turn them against it. The traditional cultural code about work seems to have an overbearing meaning even for those who have rebelled against tradition. Thus, work acquires its meaning in the social and cultural experience of the people.

REFERENCES

1. The term '*Dalit*', literally meaning 'crushed' or 'ground down' has been discursively adopted by and for those groups in society which have faced social and economic discrimination in terms of untouchability and difficulty to possess land, and who suffer from various levels of religious discrimination.
2. Ghanshyam Shah, "*Dalit* Movements and the Search for Identity", in Ghanshyam Shah (ed.), *Dalit Identity and Politics*, (New Delhi: Sage, 2001), p. 196; and Ghanshyam Shah, Harsh Mander, Sukhadeo Thorat, Satish Deshpande and Amita Baviskar, *Untouchability in Rural India*, (New Delhi: Sage, 2006), p. 37.
3. Esin Can Mutlu and Ozen Asik, "A Look Over the Concepts of Work and Leisure Throughout Important Historical Periods", *Journal of American Academy of Business*, Cambridge, 2:1, 2002, p. 13.
4. *Ibid*., p. 14.
5. P.D. Anthony, *The Ideology of Work,* (London: Tavistock, 1977), p. 20.
6. Michael Rose, *Re-Working the Work Ethic: Economic Values and Socio-Cultural Politics* (London: Schocken, 1985), p. 28.
7. *Ibid*., pp. 27-28.
8. *Ibid*., p. 28.
9. Anthony, *The Ideology of Work*, p. 37.
10. *Ibid*., pp. 37-38.
11. Max Weber, *The Protestant Ethic and the Spirit of Capitalism,* (London: Routledge Classics, 2001), pp. 40-41.
12. Christopher Hill, *The World Turned Upside Down: Radical Ideas during the English Revolution* (Harmondsworth: Penguin, 1975), p. 324.
13. E.P. Thompson, *The Making of the English Working Class* (Harmondsworth: Penguin,1980), pp. 391-411.

14. Robert Westwood and Peter Lok, "The Meaning of Work in Chinese Contexts: A Comparative Study", *International Journal of Cross Cultural Management: CCM*, August, 2003, Vol. 3, No. 2; and Andrew Eungi Kim and Gil-sung Park, "Nationalism, Confucianism, Work Ethic and Industrialization in South Korea", *Journal of Contemporary Asia*, 2003, Vol. 33, No. 1.
15. F.S. Niles, "Towards a Cross-Cultural Understanding of Work-Related Beliefs", *Human Relations*, 1999, Vol. 2, No. 7, pp. 865-66.
16. Anthony, *The Ideology of Work*, p. 44.
17. Hill, *The World Turned Upside Down,* pp. 331-32.
18. Anthony, *The Ideology of Work*, p. 45.
19. Romila Thapar, *Cultural Pasts: Essays in Early Indian History* (New Delhi: OUP, 2000), p. 216.
20. Kumkum Roy ["Some Problems in Constructing *Varna* Identities in Early North India", in Dev Nathan (ed.), *From Tribe to Caste*, Shimla: Indian Institute of Advanced Studies, 1997] has argued for "a more fluid understanding of *varna* categories" [176]. According to her the *varna* order could be changeable occasionally. Even more important was the existence of alternative non-*varna* identities. Thus, there was "a continuous probably increasingly complex process of creating and maintaining such an identity rather than the imposition of a hierarchical order once and for all" [193]. Even while agreeing with her, it may be emphasized that within the *varna* system or even within the Buddhist social order the top positions were occupied by the Brahmans and the Kshatriyas whereas the manual workers were generally assigned a low social position and those performing manual as well as ritually impure work were pushed to the very bottom at various levels of untouchability.
21. Vivekanand Jha, "Stages in the History of Untouchables", *The Indian Historical Review*, 1975, 2:1, p. 14.
22. Wendy Doniger and Brian K. Smith, *The Laws of Manu* (New Delhi: Penguin, 1991), p. 13.
23. *Ibid*., p. 13.
24. *Ibid*., pp. 249-50.
25. For a general survey on the economic significance of caste for the dominant classes in Indian history, see Irfan Habib, "Caste in Indian History", in Irfan Habib, *Essays in Indian History* (New Delhi: Tulika, 1995).
26. Peter Robb, "Meanings of Labour in Indian Social Context", in Peter Robb (ed.), *Dalit Movements and the Meaning of Labour in India*, (Delhi: OUP, 1993), p. 12.
27. Vivekanand Jha, "Stages in the History of Untouchables", *op. cit.,* p. 19.
28. Suvira Jaiswal (*Caste: Origin, Function and Dimensions of Change*, Delhi: Manohar, 2005) emphasises the downward mobility in contrast to R.S. Sharma and Romila Thapar who stress the upward mobility of the *Shudras*. According to Jaiswal, "the status of communities involved in manual work

in agriculture and crafts declined in a feudal economy which developed a hierarchy of intermediaries deriving their income from land tilled by the primary producers. The ruling class developed a contempt towards manual labour and exploited those engaged in it" [70-72.]

29. Vivekanand Jha, "Stages in the History of Untouchables", *op. cit.*, pp. 24-31. Even in South India, similar processes were in work and by the middle of the first millennium AD there were *varna* and caste hierarchies in place, and occupation was one of the major criteria to assign rank. See, Rajan Gurukkal, "From Clan and Lineage to Hereditary Occupations and Caste in Early South India", in Dev Nathan (ed.), *From Tribe to Caste* (Shimla: Indian Institute of Advanced Studies, 1997).
30. Thapar, *Cultural Pasts,* p. 222.
31. Uma Chakravarti, *The Social Dimensions of Early Buddhism* (Delhi: OUP, 1987), pp. 101-13; and Richard Fick, "The Despised Castes: North-East India in Buddha's Time", in Aloka Parasher-Sen (ed.), *Subordinate and Marginal Groups in Early India* (Delhi: OUP, 2004).
32. Uma Chakravarti, "Of Dasas and Karmakaras", in Utsa Patnaik and Manjari Dingwaney (eds.), *Chains of Servitudes: Bondage and Slavery in India* (Madras: Sangam Books, 1985), p. 47.
33. K.R. Hanumanthan, "Evolution of Untouchability in Tamil Nadu up to AD 1600", in Aloka Parasher-Sen (ed.), *Subordinate and Marginal Groups in Early India*, (Delhi: OUP, 2004), p. 127.
34. Fick, "The Despised Castes", p. 90.
35. Abbas Ali, "Scaling an Islamic Work Ethic", *The Journal of Social Psychology*, 128:5, 1987, and Darwish A. Yousef, "Islamic Work Ethic: A Moderator between Organization Commitment and Job Satisfaction in a Cross-cultural Context", *Personnel Review*, 2001, 30:2.
36. Imtiaz Ahmad (ed.), *Caste and Social Stratification among Muslims in India* (Delhi: Manohar, 1978); and Syed Ali, "Collective and Elective Ethnicity: Caste Among Urban Muslims in India", *Sociological Forum*, 17, 2002.
37. Karine Schomer and W.H. McLeod (eds.), *The Sants: Studies in Devotional Tradition of India* (Delhi: Motilal Banarsidass, 1987); and David N. Lorenzen, *Religious Movements in South Asia*, New Delhi: OUP, 2005.
38. K.N. Panikkar, Culture, Ideology, Hegemony: Intellectuals and Social Consciousness in Colonial India, (New Delhi: Tulika 1998, first published 1995), pp. 4-7.
39. David Washbrook, "Land and Labour in Late Eighteenth Century South India: The Golden Age of the Pariah?" in Robb (ed.), *Dalit Movements and the Meaning of Labour*, p. 71.
40. *Ibid.*, pp. 72-73.
41. Vijay Prasad, *Untouchable Freedom: A Social History of a Dalit Community* (New Delhi: OUP, 2000), p. 44.
42. Philip Constable, "The Marginalization of a *Dalit* Martial Race in Late

Nineteenth and Early Twentieth Century India", *The Journal of Asian Studies*, 2001, 60:2; and Stephen P. Cohen, "The Untouchable Soldier: Caste, Politics, and the Indian Army", *The Journal of Asian Studies*, 1969, 28:3, p. 456.

43. Washbrook, "*Land and Labour in Late Eighteenth Century in South India*", pp. 83-85.
44. M.R. Anderson, "Work Construed: Ideological Origins of Labour Law in British India to 1918", in Robb (ed.), *Dalit Movements and the Meaning of Labour*, p. 91.
45. *Ibid*., pp. 96-97.
46. *Ibid*., pp. 101-102.
47. Meena Radhakrishna, "Colonial Construction of a 'Criminal' Tribe: Yerukulas of Madras Presidency", *Economic and Political Weekly*, July 8-15, 2000; and Mukul Kumar, "Relationship of Caste and Crime in Colonial India: A Discourse Analysis", *Economic and Political Weekly*, March 6, 2004.
48. Anderson, "Work Construed", pp. 107-110.
49. Owen Lynch, *The Politics of Untouchability: Social Mobility and Social Change in a City of India,* New York: Colombia University Press, 1969, Mark Juergensmeyer, *Religion as Social Vision: The Movement against Untouchability in Twentieth Century Punjab* (California: University of California Press, 1982); Nandini Gooptu, "Caste and Labour: Untouchable Social Movements in Urban Uttar Pradesh in the Early Twentieth Century", in Peter Robb (ed.), *Dalit Movements and the Meaning of Labour in India* (Delhi: OUP, 1993); and Gail Omvedt, *Dalits and the Democratic Revolution: Dr. Ambedkar and the Dalit Movement in Colonial India* (Delhi: Sage, 1994).
50. Gooptu, Nandini, "Caste and Labour", p. 291.
51. Babasaheb Ambedkar, *Writings and Speeches* (compiled by Vasant Moon), (Education Department, Government of Maharashtra, 1987-89), Vol. 5, pp. 19-24.
52. Ambedkar, B.R., *Writings and Speeches,* Vol. 1, p. 48.

17

Politics of Representation: *Dalit* Mobilization in the United Provinces, 1927-1937

Swaraj Basu

Mobilization along caste and community lines parallel to the mobilization under the Congress leadership in the formative phase of electoral battle for political power very well reflect on the patterns of political socialization. In case of United Provinces (UP) it has been observed that in the 1920s almost 93 per cent of the MLCs belonged to upper-caste Brahmins, Thakurs, Vaishyas, and Kayasthas although they comprised only about a fifth of the Hindu population in the province.[1] Introducing the provision for separate electorate for the Muslims by the Reforms Act of 1909 the British government succeeded in projecting itself as the custodian of interests of the minorities. By deciding to identify the disadvantaged groups and making provisions to empower them the colonial government encouraged '*Dalits*' and other minorities to demand for political representation in order to protect their interests by themselves.[2] The Government of India Act of 1919 introduced direct election for representations in national and local bodies. Though the franchise was limited to mainly propertied males but the spirit of elected representatives aroused aspirations among people to put forth their demands for legitimate share in the representative bodies. Particularly *Dalits* became assertive for getting their representation in legislative bodies in order to protect their rights which they were denied for long. The Indian National Congress which was considered as the representative body of Indians cutting across community and caste however failed to impress upon various sections of Indian society, particularly minorities and *Dalits* were vocal for reservation of seats for them in the representative bodies. This resulted in mobilization of *Dalits* to assert for legitimate share in the decision making bodies. The period 1927 to 1937 holds significant importance in the process of constitutional reforms in India and also witnessed major initiatives taken by the Indian National Congress and other political as well as social groups to impress upon the colonial government their views on the representation in the legislatures. This chapter makes an attempt to understand how *Dalits* in UP mobilized themselves to assert for separate identity and made efforts to establish their claims for political power. I like to argue that marginalization and denial of legitimate socio-political rights of *Dalits* by the upper caste Hindus is a historical reality, but since early twentieth century *Dalits* reacted to this in divergent voices. Along with the consolidation of *Dalit* identity for political power, the divergence of interests within *Dalits* and how the *Dalit* mobilization failed to address grievances of majority of *Dalit* masses, particularly *Dalits* in villages, need to be looked into. This chapter is an attempt to explore the complexities around *Dalit* political representation in 1920s and in 1930s in UP.

POLITICAL REPRESENTATION OF *DALITS*

The Secretary to the Government of India, Reforms office wrote to the Chief Secretary, Government of UP on 20 January, 1920 on the representation of the depressed classes in the proposed provincial legislative council under the Government of India Act 1919. In the opinion of the government, "in the UP the population which could fairly be regarded as in any real sense 'depressed' is not important". However, if the State government desires to have one or two more nominated seats the Government of India does not have any objection to such reservation.[3] In his letter to the Secretary, Government of India, Reforms Office, Kunwar Jagdish Prasad, OSD (Reforms), UP wrote that *Dhobi*, *Nai*, *Kori* and *Khatik* who are included in the so-called depressed classes cannot be regarded as depressed. "The majority of the depressed classes in this province like the *Pasis*, *Doms* and *Bhangis* are criminal tribes or people who could produce no satisfactory representative." The Lt. Governor was not inclined to increase the representation of the depressed classes and the non-official members are also against the increase of depressed classes' member from the present number of one nominated member.[4] Mr. J.M. Holms, Chief Secretary, UP wrote to the Secretary, Government of India, Home Department on March 1908 that in the district boards and municipal boards "the representation of a few castes is no doubt out of all proportion to their numbers, but it must be remembered that the mass of the Hindu population is to be found in the lower castes—*Chamars*,

Ahirs, Pasis and the like—the separate representation of which is not within the range of practical politics, and the Lt. Governor doubts whether any system of caste representation is either necessary or workable."[5] These references on the question of *Dalit* representation in legislative bodies in UP show that the government in the beginning of the twentieth century was not yet convinced of making increased representation of *Dalits*. But the government was very much convinced of using *Dalits* as its support base by making some provision for *Dalits* in education and services.

The Census authority acknowledged the difficulties in defining the "depressed classes", still the Census of 1931 provides a long list of untouchable and depressed classes and numerically most dominant among them in UP were *Ahirs, Bhars, Koris, Chamars, Dusadhs, Pasis*, etc.[6] William Crooke's book, *Tribes and Castes of the North West Province and Oudh*, published in 1896 and then the Census Reports since 1901 provide significant details on the caste system in UP and the changes that were taking place in the caste system. E.A.H. Blunt in his book, *The Caste System of Northern India* observed that "the caste system is not rigid, but mutable, and that its evolution is still proceeding: new castes and sub-castes come into existence, old customs fall into abeyance. One result of this is that no account of caste, however complete and accurate it was at the time when it was written, remains so for long".[7] This observation of Blunt may be considered as the outcome of the growing representations made by various middle and lower castes to the Census authorities to get enumerated as one of the twice born castes. It is argued that the policy of the colonial government as well as the political and economic changes brought about by the government greatly influenced the mobilization along caste lines for socio-political rights of *Dalits*.

Analyzing the problem of untouchability existing in India Marc Galanter observes that two approaches are visible, 'evangelical' and 'secular'. "The 'evangelical' approach stresses the uplift of untouchables to higher Hindu standards and the penance of caste Hindus for the injustices of untouchability, which is seen not as an integral part of Hinduism but as some external impurity. Uplifted untouchables and repentant Hindus will join together in a purified and redeemed Hinduism. At the other extreme, the secular approach stresses the denial of civil rights and economic opportunities and seeks to combat them by vigorous government intervention, and political action to obtain it.... "In the 'evangelical' approach, the emphasis is on moral regeneration and philanthropic uplift; in the secular approach, it is on civic and economic improvement under government auspices'.[8] The British government attitude may be explained as 'secular'."

Although the colonial government initiated the process for popular representation in the legislatures in the late nineteenth century, but it was the Montagu-Chelmsford Reforms of 1919 which for the first time made statutory provisions for the representation of *Dalits* and directed the local governments to nominate them in the Legislative Councils. In the Central Legislature for the first time in 1927 M.C. Raja from Madras province was nominated as representative of *Dalits*. Since the late nineteenth century various castes and sub-castes in UP formed associations like *Kurmi Sabha, Jatav Mahasabha,* and *Nishad Mahasabha*, etc. to protect the interests of their respective caste groups. Most of these castes besides taking up measures to improve their social condition gave representations to the government for education, employment and special representation. The Government of India Act 1909 accorded separate electorate to the Muslims. Acceptance of communal representation by the government aroused hope among *Dalits* to press for similar provision for *Dalits*. In 1917 when Edwin S. Montagu, the Secretary of State for India, announced to accede to the demands of Indians for right to self-government the leadership of *Dalit* movement claimed representation of *Dalits* in the government on communal basis. The *Dalit* leaders demanded reservation of a fixed number of seats for them in various representative bodies because they were of the opinion that the representatives of other communities would not protect their interests. Although Montagu and Chelmsford in their report acknowledged the need to protect the interests of *Dalits* by the government but they did not recommend any special provision for ensuring representation of *Dalits*. But a beginning was made by making provision for representation of *Dalits* by nomination in the Provincial Legislative Councils and the Central Legislative Assembly. Majority of *Dalits* were denied of voting right because of property qualifications and even few who had the voting right could not exercise the right because of the dominance of the upper castes. *Dalits* were not happy with the concession given to them and decided to put pressure on the British government for larger share in the legislative bodies. Apart from mobilization at regional levels *Dalits* held an all India conference at Nagpur in 1920. This was the time when Gandhi emerged as the leader of the Indian National Congress and appealed to *Dalits* to support the movement for *Swaraj* and assured them his support in their movement against oppression. But the leadership of *Dalits* was not very convinced with the assurance given by Gandhi and some upper caste Hindu leaders.

They were apprehensive that the upper castes might use them for their own benefits. Rather they were pinning hope on the British government to accede to their demands that *Dalits* must be represented by their elected members in order to protect their own interests. The *Dalits* in a conference organized at Allahabad in 1926 expressed their gratitude to the British for protecting their political interests and giving them the rights which the Hindus had never given. They demanded complete separation from the Hindus in order to safeguard their interests.

Then in 1927 the British government announced the appointment of the Indian Statutory Commission under the chairmanship of Sir John Simon for reviewing the Government of India Act 1919 and to suggest further constitutional amendment. As the commission did not have any Indian representative so the Indian National Congress decided to boycott the commission. *Dalit* associations however hold different opinion and the All India Adi Hindu Conference, All India Depressed Classes Association and other *Dalit* groups welcomed the appointment of the commission and decided to put forward their demands to the commission. The various *Dalit* groups who appealed to the commission were as follows:

Bahiskrit Hitakarini Sabha of Bombay, Depressed India Association of Bombay, All India Shri Jatav Mahasabha of Agra, Adi Hindu Sabha of the United Provinces, All India Adi Hindu Mahasabha, Kahar Sudharak Mahasabha of Cawnpore, All Bengal Namasudra Association, Bengal Depressed Classes Association, and All India Depressed Classes Association, etc.[9] In the presidential address of the Adi Hindu Conference held at Lucknow on 29 January, 1928 Rama Charan (MLC, UP), said, "All the leading institutions, the Congress, the Liberal Federation, the Hindu Mahasabha and the Calcutta Muslim League have passed resolutions in favour of boycott of the Commission. But our Associations and leaders have advised us to desist from such suicidal act…we cannot raise ourselves without outside help and if we boycott the only outside help of the British Government, we shall be doomed to everlasting slavery. Therefore, with all the defects that may be in the Commission we cannot but welcome it."[10] The *Dalits* were united on the question of reservation of seats but they had differences over the modalities of representation. The appointment of Simon Commission further aroused the aspirations of *Dalits* to voice for their demands and the period from 1927 to 1937 witnessed dramatic developments on the issue of the representation of *Dalits* in different representative bodies. Before we take up the *Dalit* mobilization around the Simon Commission for greater representation in legislative bodies let us have a look at the caste dynamics of UP at that time and how the different *Dalit* groups mobilized themselves. Response from the Indian National Congress and the Hindu Mahasabha towards the mobilization of *Dalits* in UP also needs to be analyzed in order to understand the diverse strands on the issue of *Dalit* representation.

DALIT MOBILIZATION IN UP IN 1920s

Caste being the most important determinant of one's social status in the Hindu society a deliberate attempt was made by the colonial government to gather information in the census on caste ranking based on the claims made by various castes. The Census Commissioner of the United Provinces of Agra and Oudh observed that caste and nothing else determines one's estimation in society and no reform initiative succeeded in changing this mind set.

"To a Hindu his caste is the determining factor in his life and beside it his age, civil condition, birth-place and even his occupation are matters of comparative indifference. It was, therefore, difficult for the individual to appreciate that the object of the enquiry was merely to ascertain the numbers of each caste; and the ancient tradition that the King or the Government was the ultimate authority in determining questions of caste probably helped the popular feeling that the effect of the census record, so far as the individual was concerned, would be to fix his particular position in the social scale. The opportunity of the census was, therefore, seized by all, but the highest castes to press for recognition of social claims and to secure, if possible, a step upwards in the social ladder. This attitude has been strengthened by the recent development of the caste *sabhas*, or societies, whose purpose is to advance the position and welfare of the caste."[11]

The studies on caste mobilization in the late nineteenth and early twentieth centuries in different parts of India show that how centering around the census different caste groups, particularly middle and lower castes, made representation to the census authorities to enumerate them as one of the three twice born castes—Brahmin, Vaishya and Kshatriya.[12] In the United Provinces the same trend was visible and the Census Reports of 1921 and 1931show how a large number of castes under the banner of their respective caste *sabhas* and *mahasabhas* tried to establish their claims to be recorded as one of the twice born castes. It would be interesting to refer here the observations made by A.C. Turner in justifying the decision of the caste return in the Census.

"...I venture to suggest that the Census Reports in dealing with caste have done a positive good by bringing to the light of day some undoubted evils of the caste system. Would untouchability and child-marriage have received the attention they have but for the publicity they initially gained through the Census returns? Again, take the increasing number of caste claims. Each of these represents an effort on the part of some members of the caste or community concerned towards social uplift, stimulated by the census return.... If the caste system is dead how can the retention of the caste return perpetuate the system? As regards this province the truth is that although a progressive few have broken through caste restrictions, caste is still "the foundation of the Indian social fabric...So long as, the Caste System is such an important factor classification by caste can scarcely be abandoned..."[13]

In UP compared to southern and western India mobilization of *Dalits* for new social identity was not much visible before the early twentieth century. Although the nineteenth century reform movement did not have much impact in UP, the Arya Samaj succeeded in influencing a sizeable section in society. The Arya Samaj in UP made special efforts to bring the *Chamars* under its reform initiative and it is argued that most Jatav leaders who were earlier *Chamars* but later on claimed to be descendants of Kshatriyas were under the influence of the Arya Samaj.[14] Although the Arya Samajists practiced *shuddhi* movement through moral reform, vegetarianism, teetotallerism, etc. to remove the social stigma of lower castes but in practice the Arya Samaj movement failed to bring the desired change in the upper caste attitude towards the lower castes.[15] A study of the Jatavs of Agra by Owen M. Lynch shows that in the early twentieth century an advanced section within the Jatavs by bringing social reforms among their caste members asserted their claim to Kshatriya status. To establish their Kshatriya identity a book *Jatav Life* was written in 1924 and in support of their claim they referred the Lomash Ramayana and with the help of the legend of the Parasuram they explained their present identity as *Chamars*.[16] The move towards upward mobility by the advanced section of the Jatavs points towards the acceptance of the caste system. While the Jatavs claim to Kshatriyahood was not acceptable to other upper castes, the Jatavas themselves rejected the claim of *Guliyas* to be *Jatavas* and *Kshatriyas*.[17] According to Lynch "the Jatavs freely chose, in fact fought, to be included on the list of Scheduled Castes. This option brought them concrete benefits from the government, but it also continued to identify them as an Untouchable caste, a position quite inconsistent with their claim to Kshatriya status".[18] William R. Pinch has talked about the *Kurmis*, *Yadavas*, *Kushavahas*' movement for

Kshatriya status with the help of *Vaishnava* mythology in the early twentieth century in UP. "A popular verse of the time, attributed to one Bharat Bharati ...urged its audience to reflect,

> Who were we, what has happened, and where are we going now?
> Gather round everyone and ponder these questions together.
> If we fail to appreciate the entirety of our past,
> We may never realize who we really are.

Jati reformers of the early twentieth century took this poetic counsel particularly seriously and spent endless hours reconstructing, indeed reinventing the pasts of their communities.'[19] Badri Narayan has explained the Pasis' attempt to prove their Kshatriya identity in terms of the legend of Parashurama. He points to the fact that not only the scholars of lower castes but the Arya Samaj activists and scholars also published number of books to give the middle and lower castes honourable position within the existing caste system. The *Kshatriya Varg Kosh*, translated in Hindi by Pandit Hardayal Sharma of Meerut in 1899, *The Nishad Vanshavali* written by Shri Devi Prasad in 1907, *Maha Lodhi Vivechana* by Mathura Prasad Sharma in 1912, *Ahir Itihas Ki Jhalak* by Dileep Singh Yadav in 1914, *Kurmi Kshatriya Itihas* by Abhayananda Saraswati in 1927, etc., are some such examples.[20]

Another dominant trend of *Dalit* mobilization in the early twentieth century in UP was the Adi-Hindu movement launched by Swami Achhutananda. Swami Achhutananda (1879-1933) was born in a *Dalit* family in a village in Farukhabad district in UP. Initially he was with the Arya Samaj movement but later on left the Arya Samaj and said that "This sect has been constructed in order to save the Brahmin religion from the attacks of the Christians and Muslims. [...] Its profession of purification is a fraud and a clever verbal gimmick of the *varna* system".[21] Swami Achhutananda developed the Adi-Hindu philosophy and started the Adi-Hindu movement to unite all the untouchables against the caste system. Nandini Gooptu has stated that in the early twentieth century *bhakti* (devotionalism) was practiced extensively by urban untouchable poor in UP and lower-caste *sants* (saints) like Kabir, Ravidas became very popular. "For the untouchable poor in the towns, the message of caste equality and the denial of ritual hierarchy in *bhakti* gave them a means to question the discriminations, disabilities and deprivation that they continued to face. This was in contrast to those upwardly mobile sections of untouchables who, as counter-elite aspirants, sought to find a niche in caste Hindu society, and claimed higher status and respectability through sanskritisation within the caste hierarchy rather than stepping outside it."[22] Through the Adi-Hindu movement Swami Achhutananda tried to develop a radical cultural alternative focusing on individual equality and justice and at the same time he stressed on the importance of having say in the political process. R.S. Khare has observed that "The cultural ideology of Achchutananda...is actually given varied social reception among the Lucknow *Chamars*. It might still be too radical for some, too mild for others, and even irrelevant for some others." In his opinion there was visible division within the untouchables, one group wanted to improve them within the Hindu social system and the other, more radical, wanted to leave the Hindu social system.[23] To counter Swami Achhutananda's campaign the Arya Samaj started an All India Shraddhananda Dalitoddhara Sabha. G.D. Birla and M.M. Malaviya started an All India Achhutoddhara Sabha which later on merged with the Congress-backed All India Dalit Varga Sabha.[24] The Adi-Hindu movement failed to develop sound organizational base and practically remained confined to Agra and Kanpur. Leaders of the movement became more active in getting share in the local power structure. Later on in the early 1930s a break-away faction formed the Depressed Classes League with the support of the Congress.[25] The mobilization of *Dalits* suffered setback because of some of their leaders sided with the Congress. Participation of the Adi-Hindu movement in the deliberations of the Simon Commission was opposed in a meeting of the United Provinces Depressed Classes Conference in Agra on April 1928. Dharam Prakash who was one of the chief architects of the Depressed Classes League opposed Ambedkar's strategy in favour of conversion.

An important point to be noted in the Census Report of 1931, United Provinces is the notes on untouchables, depressed classes and backward classes given in the Appendix. Explaining the origin of untouchable and depressed classes the note refers to the initiatives taken by the advanced section of *Dalits* to bring new social and political consciousness among their members through their caste associations. They also tried to change their social habits and customs and adopted new caste names to prove themselves as descendants of the twice-born castes. Some tried to dissociate them from Brahmanic Hinduism by embracing the Arya Samaj creed while some started calling themselves Adi-Hindus meaning by the original inhabitants of Hindustan. However, the report says that as only 3 per cent of the depressed classes are literate so the initiatives taken by the leaders of the depressed classes are yet to influence the masses.[26]

Although the reform initiatives made by *Dalits* or others for *Dalits* had limited appeal among the less advanced section of *Dalits*, a beginning definitely was made to challenge the given identity in the name of the caste system.

It would be pertinent here to point out that in the early twentieth century in UP the Arya Samaj through various initiatives tried to bring change in orthodox Hinduism and opposed the prevalent form of caste system particularly untouchability. The Arya Samaj opened schools in UP for education of the children of untouchables and succeeded in bringing many of such children, both boys and girls, in their schools.[27] The Hindu Mahasabha was equally concerned of the growing alienation of *Dalits* from the upper caste Hindus and its socio-political implications. Efforts were being made to retain them within the Hindu fold by appealing to the members of the upper castes for change of heart by removing social and ritualistic barriers. Politically, Mahatma Gandhi in particular along with some other leaders of the Indian National Congress realized the importance of winning over the *Dalits* so that they do not respond to the appeasing strategy of the colonial government. In a note submitted to the committee on Indian constitutional reforms in the 1920s M.C. Rajah, an all India leader of *Dalits* wrote that individual social reformers raised their voice against caste prejudices in India only after Mahatma Gandhi appealed for the removal of untouchability the Congress as well as other political parties put the removal of untouchability in an agenda of political programme. Leaders like Lala Lajpat Rai, Pandit Madan Mohan Malviya, Pandit Motilal Nehru, Tej Bahadur Sapru urged for solving the problems of *Dalits*. The Hindu Mahasabha at its Jabalpur session in 1928 adopted the following resolutions:

> "…Hindu Maha Sabha declares that the so-called Untouchables have equal rights with other Hindus to study in public schools, to take water from public wells and other sources of drinking water, to sit with others in public meetings and to walk on public roads. The Maha Sabha calls upon all Hindus to remove such restrictions as may be existing anywhere at present in the way of the so-called Untouchable Hindus exercising these rights…"

This Hindu Maha Sabha is of opinion that every Hindu to whatever caste he may belong has equal social and political rights…

This Maha Sabha looks upon the practice of nomination of the representatives of the Depressed Classes by the Government to the Local

Bodies, Provincial Councils and the Assembly as most harmful and injurious to the true interests of the country and considers that this practice will become a source of creating a great gulf in the near future between other Hindus and the so-called Untouchable Classes. In the opinion of the Maha Sabha the right course to stop this practice is to put forward and back proper candidates belonging to the so-called Untouchable Classes to the elected bodies named above."[28]

Importance of *Dalits* in the battle for political power was not only realized by various political groups in India alone, the British officials were equally aware of socio-political reality. The Census Report of 1931 observes,

> "If Hindus wish to include these millions in their community for political reasons they cannot logically exclude them socially, and what is more, if they persist in excluding them socially, the depressed classes will completely throw over Hinduism. In these days of growing democracy (growing in India, firmly established in almost every other country in the world), the millions comprising the depressed classes will not be content to endure the lot of outcastes in the present life in the hope of finding themselves in a higher social plane at their next reincarnation. Educated Hindus realize this, and hence the uplift of the untouchable and depressed classes figures prominently in the programmes of Hindu political leaders and social reformers."[29]

All these directly contributed towards the formation of a number of caste associations by *Dalits* like Jatava Maha Sabha of the *Chamars*, Kshatriya Sabha of the *Ahirs*, Kahar Sudharak Maha Sabha representing *Malas, Dhuriyas,* Lodhi Rajput Association of the *Lodhs*, Kurmi Kshatriya Association of the *Kurmis*, etc., to protect the interests of their respective caste groups in the early twentieth century in UP. There were also organizations like Adi-Hindu Sabha, All India Shraddhananda Dalitoddhara Sabha, the Depressed Classes Association to voice for the demands of *Dalits*.[30] All the individual caste associations were primarily engaged in tracing history of the origin of their castes and to establish their claims as one of the twice born castes by emulating ritual and cultural practices of the upper castes. They also published journals/newspapers like *Nishad Samachar* by Ram Charan, *Vishwamitra* by Ramnarayan Yadavendu, *Jivan* by Manikchand, *Adhikar* and *Manav Kalyan* by Dharam Prakash.[31] Initiatives in this direction came mainly from the advanced section of the marginalized castes. Leaders of these caste associations were mainly concerned about improvement of material conditions of their members by demanding provisions for education and reservation of government jobs for members of their castes. The *Dalits*, particularly the advanced section within them, being conscious of their marginalization socially, economically and politically over the years wanted to make use of the opportunity created by the British government in their favour so that they can establish their legitimate political right in the decision making process Nandini Gooptu has shown how the second generation of urban untouchables after getting education with the help of the Arya Samaj and the Christian Missionaries took initiatives for the uplift of the untouchables. Most prominent among the untouchable leaders in UP were Swami Acchutananda (1879-1933) and Ram Charan (1888-1938). "The untouchable leaders associated with the Arya Samaj gradually became convinced that the Samaj acted as the army of high caste Hindus, whose only intention was to rally the Hindu community against the Muslims, and the Samaj's attempt to uplift the lower castes was merely a part of this strategy. They argued that the Samaj did not aim to eradicate untouchability and that *shuddhi* was a cunning ploy to perpetuate the hold of the higher castes over the untouchables".[32] In the early 1930s over the issue of supporting the Congress there was a division within the Adi Hindu Movement and the break away group formed the Depressed Classes League. Gandhian organizations and institutions could not generate much interest among the untouchable poor by offering vocational training or making provision for education of children. "The elements of social control and discipline of the lower castes, as well as the imposition of a higher-caste value system that these approaches implicitly harboured or explicitly advanced, inevitably rendered the relation between the nationalist reformers and the untouchables increasingly tension-ridden from the 1920s. This contradiction was further accentuated against a background of Adi Hindu social reforms which sought precisely to reverse the tendencies of the upper castes to impose their own values and practices."[33] In the following section we would try to explain the initiatives taken by *Dalits* in UP to have their representatives in various legislative bodies.

THE SIMON COMMISSION AND *DALIT* REPRESENTATION

All India Depressed Classes' conference held in New Delhi on 26th February, 1928 adopted resolution expressing loyalty to the British and appreciating its decision to appoint the Simon Commission. The conference appealed to the Commission to consider the representation of *Dalits* and urged upon its members from various provinces to collect materials and put up their demands before the commission. M.C. Raja in his presidential address said "Unless the depressed classes, who formed one-sixth of the population, were given the fullest opportunity for development, physical, mental, moral and spiritual, India would never get *swaraj*". Apart from asking the government for separate electorate and more representatives from *Dalits* the conference also urged upon the government for appointing members of *Dalits* to represent labour in various legislatures and also banning the practice of employing poor *Dalit* tenants by the landlords in United Provinces, Punjab and Central Provinces.[34]

In December 1928 an all parties convention was called in Calcutta in which along with the members of the Congress, the Hindu Mahasabha, the Muslim League, Trade Union and Peasant Organizations, Women's Organization, there were representatives from Achhut Uddhar Committee, Shardhanand Dalit Uddhar Sabha, and Dayanand Dalitoddhar Mandal, etc. In the convention Mr. J.M. Sengupta welcoming the delegates told that the purpose of the convention was to draw up a constitution overcoming the internal differences in order to stand as one body against the common enemy. "We are here to discover a formula which will substitute our divergences and enable us to carry on the struggle against the foreign government. The Simon Commission, I firmly believe, is in the nature of an offensive launched by the British people to scatter our forces, to expose our differences and, if possible, to make it difficult for us to fight them as one united nation".[35] There was a deputation from *Dalits* of UP consisting of Rama Charana, MLC; Khem Chand, Ex-MLC; President, Jatav Mahasabha; Nanak Chand Dhusya, President, Adi-Hindu Sabha, U.P.; Bhagat Mulluram, Member, District Board, Fatehpur, representative of All India Adi-Hindu (Aboriginals) Mahasabha, Raja Ram of Kahar Sudharak Mahasabha, Cawnpore, etc., to the Indian Statutory Commission. Major demand from *Dalits* was that according to their population in the province which was about one-third of Hindu population they should have proportionate representation. At that time there was only one nominated member from *Dalits* by the governor in the legislative council of UP. In the Commission when it was pointed out that some castes like *Ahirs* who wear sacred thread how they can be considered as depressed. In response Rama Charana said, "it is one thing to claim to wear a sacred cord; it is another thing that he is recognized as being entitled to wear a sacred cord." The *Ahirs*, the *Malas*, the *Jatavas* (a sect of *Chamars*) many of them do claim to be twice-born as the Brahmins, the Kshatriyas and the Vaishyas, but they are never recognized. When the deputationists were asked about the prospect of elected representatives of *Dalits* in UP Ram Prasad Ahir said that "I think the time has not yet come when we can seek election because there is in the villages the landlord who is generally of the higher caste. He has got all the influence over these lower castes and if he sets up somebody who is of his calibre, he can carry the day and our own candidate cannot be elected. So, for the time being we should be given representation by nomination". Other members from *Dalits* did not support the opinion of Ram Prasad Ahir and demanded for separate election. Members also argued that *Ahirs, Malis*, etc., are not considered as *Dalits*, they are considered as backward classes. In reply to the question who are considered as *Dalits* in U.P. Khem Chand said that *Dhobis*, *Chamars*, *Koris, Bhangis, Pasis*, etc., in reply to the question about number of educated members from *Dalits* Rama Charana said that there were at least twenty four to thirty six graduates and 12 practicing lawyers.[36]

In the Supplementary Memorandum submitted to the Statutory Commission Rama Charana stated that "It is true that some selfish persons instigated by the like of the higher class, have started Sabhas wherein some of these castes claim to be 'Kshatriyas'....If these castes were acknowledged to be Kshatriyas, the Kshatriya Sabha would have absorbed their Sabha, and they would exist no more. On the contrary in the Kshatriya Sabha, no *Ahir, Gadariya, Kurmi* or any member of the lower class was ever invited. There is a proverb running:

> "Ahir, Gadaria, Pasi,
> Tinon Satya Nasi".
>
> Born and brought up with these ideas, how can the higher classes have any sympathy with the lower classes?"[37]

In a conference of the All India Adi-Hindu (Depressed Classes) held at Allahabad on December 1927 it was stated that the movement of Adi Hindus was for their elevation in Hindu society. The following resolutions were passed in the conference:

"This conference respectfully conveys to His Majesty the King Emperor the loyal feelings of the Adi-Hindus (Depressed Classes) and expresses a sense of deep debt of gratitude for all that is being done for the uplift and betterment of the said Adi-Hindus.

This conference accords a hearty welcome to the forthcoming Statutory Commission and expresses its full confidence in the European Members of the said Commission, for if Indians had been appointed the grievances of the Adi-Hindus would have been totally ignored.

This Conference appoints the following gentlemen to prepare evidence for production before the Royal Commission on our behalf—M.C. Rajah, B.R. Ambedkar, G.A. Gavai, and Swami Achhutanand, etc."[38]

At the special session of the Adi-Hindu (Aborigines) conference held at Lucknow on 29th January, 1928 Rama Charana in his presidential address stated that members of the Adi-Hindus have created their genealogies to prove the Rajput lineage and started wearing sacred thread. However, members of upper castes are forcing to remove the threads. He said that "All the leading institutions, the Congress, the Liberal Federation, the Hindu Mahasabha and the Calcutta Muslim League have passed resolutions in favour of boycott of the Commission. But our Associations and leaders have advised us to desist from such suicidal act…We cannot raise ourselves without outside help and if we boycott the only outside help, the British government, we shall be doomed to everlasting slavery. Therefore with all the defects that may be in the Commission we cannot but welcome it." On behalf of the Adi-Hindus, Rama Charana put forward the following demands:

"1. Separate communal representation for the Adi-Hindus according to population in local bodies and in the local and central legislature as well as in the Council of State.
2. Appointment of at least one minister from amongst us in each province.
3. Share according to our population in public services.
4. Special facilities for the education of our children, etc."[39]

The memorandum submitted by the United Provinces Addharam (Aborigines) Sabha, Dehradun claimed that "We do not wish to call ourselves Hindus but we all untouchables of different classes wish to be called 'Addharmies' and in the next coming census we should write 'Addharmies'. We do not want Swaraj in India under present condition as it will mean practically a monopoly of the caste Hindus".[40]

All India Adi Hindu (Aborigines) Mahasabha, Cawnpore which claimed to represent *Dalits* of UP and Punjab held its executive meeting on 25th May, 1928 and nominated Swami Achhutananda, President, Adi-Hindu Mahasabha, Cawnpore and Vice-President, All India Depressed Classes

Association, Nagpore along with B. Jham Lal, B. Nanak Chand Dhusia, and B. Badriprasad, etc. to appear before the Simon Commission and to put their demands. In their demands they asked for greater representation in representative bodies, voting right to all Adi-Hindus, taking over by the British of the native States and *zamindari* estates in order to save *Dalits* from the begar system. *Swaraj* should not be given unless *Dalits* are given equal right and opportunities with the upper castes.[41]

In a meeting of the Adi-Hindu depressed classes of UP under the presidentship of Mr. Janki Prasad Dhanuk held on 25th November, 1931 in the district of Farukhabad representing *Dalits* like *Kori, Chamar, Dhobi, Dhanuk*, etc., resolution was passed congratulating the British government for providing rights to *Dalits*. They expressed confidence in the government nomination of B.R. Ambedkar and Srinivasan as delegates to the Round Table Conference to represent the interests of *Dalits*. The meeting also expressed no confidence in the leadership of Mahatma Gandhi and the Congress.[42]

In a letter addressed to the Private Secretary of the Viceroy, Government of India, Dharam Prakash, Secretary, the UP Depressed Classes Association wrote that majority of *Dalits*, particularly of UP and Punjab, feel strongly against the Poona Pact. "My Association beg to bring to His Excellency's kind consideration that the Depressed Classes of Northern India were not represented in the previous conferences with the result that the views and aims of the Depressed Classes of Northern India were not expressed and as such they request His Excellency to choose a representative from UP to the Committee that will shortly be formed."[43] In addressing the 9th session of All India Depressed Classes Conference at Gurgaon on 31st October, 1931 M.C. Rajah, President, said that out of the 37 associations that placed before the Simon Commission, 35 demanded Separate Electorates. "We need hardly say that we want separate Electorates for our Community. Our men elected directly by us can alone communicate faithfully to Government our thoughts and feelings, our grievances and suggestions for our improvement."[44] Rama Charana representing the depressed and backward classes was one of the seven members of the Provincial Committee of UP constituted by the government to submit recommendations before the Simon Commission for the proposed constitutional reforms in India. As per the report Rama Charana "agreed to 15 seats being reserved in the Lower House out of a total strength of 182 and five out of a total strength of 60 in the Upper House". Rama Charana accepted the system of nominations as only a temporary measure and after ten years this would be reconsidered. The report further stated,

> "the Depressed and Backward Classes deserve encouragement and we have no objection to the Public Service Commission being instructed to bear the claims of these classes in mind when making appointments, and we recommend accordingly....We are also convinced that as advancement and education proceed the present classification of the Depressed and Backward Classes will change. A great many castes which may at present be included within the definition of "Backward" classes would, once they are high up in the social and educational ladder, refuse to be so defined and would probably resent to be relegated to that category."[45]

The Dalit Jat Sudharak Sabha, Gorakhpur in a memorandum submitted to the Indian Franchise Committee on March 1932 stated that "it would not be in the interest of the depressed classes to have separate electorates even if they are possible. This Sabha would prefer reserved seats in joint electorate on the population basis....This Sabha is very grateful to the efforts of Arya Samaj and Indian National Congress in general and to Mahatma Gandhi and Swami Shraddhananda in particular as they have practically vanished the stigma of untouchability from these provinces, the result is that the only caste that can now be regarded as untouchable is *Bhangi*."[46]

The United Provinces Hindu Backward Classes League, Lucknow in its memorandum stated that "Our league considers that the depressed classes are not likely to secure representatives of their own choice in the general electorate in these provinces even if adult franchise could be introduced. The reasons are that there is no fixity of tenure nor fixity of rent and the depressed classes are considered socially too low to become members of Legislatures, by the landlord, money-lender, and other influential high class Hindus....Taunting remarks are dinning in our ears, "Let any number of voters be increased, they are after all under our control"."[47]

"In the last election a few persons from amongst the depressed classes were sent to the Provincial Council by the hoodwinking of the Congress committees and the caste Hindus as their dummies, not on account of any sympathy for them. They were sent up with proclamation in the streets that the Council had become such a contemptible institution that it was only fit for the depressed classes. This is the real value the caste Hindus attach to these classes."[48]

There were leaders like Gandhi and Tej Bahadur Sapru within the

Congress who strongly advocated for the inclusion of *Dalits* although many *Dalit* leaders were not convinced with their concern. Sapru observed, "I do say what is my most sincere conviction, that unless you are able to solve your own social problems about the depressed classes and the untouchables, I do not see any real prospect for real genuine constitutional advance, and any constitution that you may get will certainly not arouse any interest in me, because I do feel, howsoever good, howsoever perfect, howsoever ideal your constitution may be unless you have got the support of the minorities and unless you command the confidence of those whom in your vanity you may describe as depressed classes, your constitution will not be worth a day's purchase."[49] *Dalits* lack of confidence on the Congress leadership was chiefly because of the upper caste domination within the Congress and its inability to accommodate the *Dalit* voices.

"The Report on the Working of the System of Government, United Provinces, January 19th, 1928, Volume III, submitted to the Indian Statutory Commission says at page 2:

> "In the province as a whole the four leading castes, Brahman, Thakur, Vaishya and Kayastha, form 21.1 per cent of the total Hindu population, but these five castes have supplied no less than 93 per cent of the Hindu members of the Council. The Jat, with 1.8 per cent of the population, have contributed another 5 per cent to the Hindu membership; and all the millions included in the multitude of other Hindu castes including the real agricultural castes, though they amount to over 76 per cent of the Hindu population have only succeeded in supplying 2 per cent of the representation."[50]

The Simon Commission admits that most of the associations representing *Dalits* which appeared before the Commission favoured separate electorates with seats allocated on the basis of population. However in spite of its agreement for reservation of seats for *Dalits* the Commission did not agree to the demand for separate electorate thinking that this may hamper the political amalgamation of *Dalits* with others. The number of seats proposed to be reserved for *Dalits* was increased and in case of United Provinces it was enhanced from 1 to 10. Swami Achhutananda and Nanak Chand Dhusiya as representatives of *Dalits* from U.P. attended the All India Depressed Classes Association meeting at Simla on July 1930 which refused to accept the Commission's recommendation unless separate electorate is granted. Ambedkar refused to be part of the deliberations of All India Depressed Classes Association.[51] When Lord Irwin, Governor General of India, announced to hold Round Table Conference in London to resolve the issue of representation in legislative bodies, the Adi-Hindu Depressed Classes Society in UP reiterated its demand for separate electorate.[52] However, M.C. Rajah, President of the All India Depressed Classes Association, changing from his earlier position decided to support joint electorate and signed an agreement to this effect with Dr. B.S. Moonje, President of the All India Hindu Mahasabha. Dr. Ambedkar opposed this pact and put up forceful demand for separate electorate. Division within *Dalits* was clear on the issue of representation. The government on its part invited Dr. Ambedkar and Sri Srinivasan to represent *Dalits* in the Round Table Conference to decide on *Dalit* representation to legislative bodies. This was followed by hard bargaining between Ambedkar and Gandhi on political representation of *Dalits* and after prolonged deliberations and heart burning the Poona Pact was signed by Gandhi and Ambedkar. The Poona Pact ensured 148 reserved seats for *Dalits* but the *Dalit* leadership had to give up their claim for separate electorate. There were sharp reactions from *Dalits* to the Poona Pact in different provinces and in UP the UP Depressed Classes Association wrote to the Viceroy stating that how the Poona Pact was against the interests of *Dalits*.[53] The Government of India Act 1935 adopted the recommendations of the Poona Pact, but the reserved seats were enhanced from 148 to 151, the reserved seats for UP however remained at 20 out of total 228 seats. In 1937 when the general election was held under the provisions of the Government of India Act 1935 the Congress won majority of the Scheduled Castes seats. In terms of electoral gain *Dalits* succeeded in raising their number from 1 in 1919 to 20 in the UP Provincial Legislature and the result shows different affiliations of *Dalits*. The Congress won fifty nine out of sixty five reserved seats in the election of 1937 in UP, Bihar and Madras. *Dalits* failed to put up an all India organization to fight the election against *Dalit* candidates backed by the Congress. However, Dr. Ambedkar analyzing the election of 1937 concluded that the Congress had won only 18 per cent of the vote in the reserved seats but because of splitting of votes among non-Congress candidates and other factors the Congress won majority seats in reserved constituencies.[54] A.C. Pradhan noted that the Congress put up candidates in most of the reserved seats and won absolute majority in the reserved seats whereas no *Dalit* leader except Dr. B.R. Ambedkar could successfully organize *Dalits* under one political organization even at the regional level.[55] Oliver Mendelsohn and Marika

Vicziany observed that "the Congress had greater national support from Untouchable voters than did any other organization in the 1930s".[56] Although the success of the Congress in the electoral battle proved its hold over power politics, *Dalits*' success was in forcing their way into decision making bodies which so far was out of their reach.

CONCLUSION: ONE IDENTITY DIVERGENT VOICES

Importance of caste identity in contemporary electoral politics of India is prominently displayed but in no way it was less important in colonial India. The only difference is in context. The way religious identity was used to sharpen the division in Indian society along religious lines, in the same fashion the existing division along caste lines was exploited for meeting political ends. The process of consolidation of caste identity began immediately after the Revolt of 1857 by the colonial government, then the classification and enumeration of caste in the census and other government records, followed by the colonial policy of "protective discrimination" and then creation of seats reserved for the Scheduled Castes and the Scheduled Tribes in the Government of India Act of 1935. The government initiative to identify the deprived social groups may be interpreted as a device to counter the movements under the Congress leadership and at the same time it may appear to many as welfare measures to protect the interests of *Dalits*. Efforts made by the colonial government to introduce electoral reforms in India by making provision for representation of socially oppressed groups accelerated the process of mobilization along caste lines, particularly the marginalized groups. In spite of its regional variations *Dalits* all over India by late nineteenth and early twentieth century succeeded in creating a new identity to press for their demands to be addressed by the government. This mobilization not only assured the government the success of its divisive politics, but alarmed the Congress as well as the Hindu Mahasabha with the prospect of loosing the support of a vast section of indigenous society. Studies on the social mobility of *Chamars, Pasis,* and *Kurmis,* etc., in UP and the Adi-Hindu movement in the province in the early twentieth century clearly suggest the growing consolidation of *Dalit* voices for the rights which they were denied of in the name of caste hierarchy. The Simon Commission further consolidated *Dalit* voices by arousing aspirations of *Dalit* leaders to share political power which so far remained the prerogative of the upper castes. The consolidation of *Dalit* identity which can be largely attributed to the policies of the colonial government has important ramifications within the indigenous society. In UP the Congress, the Hindu Mahasabha and the Arya Samaj in their own way adopted the policy to integrate *Dalits* within the mainstream, but *Dalit* leadership was skeptical towards the maneuvers of the upper castes. To *Dalits* the immediate concern was not only upward social mobility but to get its legitimate share in the various policy making bodies. Thus, along with the efforts made by the upwardly mobile castes to enumerate themselves as one of the three higher *varna* category they also became vocal for their representation in legislative bodies. Different associations cutting across various *Dalit* groups emerged to fight for the interests of *Dalits*. As our study shows in UP *Dalits* were members of Adi-Hindu organization as well as All India Depressed Classes Association and also there were All India Shraddhanand Dalitoddhar Sabha started by the Arya Samaj and All India Achhutoddhar Sabha started by M.M. Malaviya which later on merged with the Congress-backed All India Dalit Varg Sabha. Realizing the importance of the emerging *Dalit* voices mainstream political parties like the Congress and the Hindu Mahasabha felt the urgency to integrate the issues concerning *Dalits* in their agenda of political action. This political mobilization along *Dalit* identity was in no way much different from such mobilization in other provinces in India. Writing on the development of caste politics in Bengal during the late nineteenth and early twentieth century Sekhar Bandyopadhyaya observed that by appealing to caste identity many caste associations, particularly *Dalits*, in Bengal succeeded in mobilizing the community, but failed to use the protest mentality of the masses for any radical movement against caste system. Leaders of *Dalits* got 'embroiled more in council politics or faction-fighting".[57] The situation was not much different in other regions also. As the consolidation of *Dalit* identity in the 1920s and 1930s in UP was a much visible reality so was the failure of *Dalit* leadership as well as of the government to address the plight of rural *Dalits* who formed the bulk of rural peasantry.

What emerges from our analysis of political mobilization of *Dalits* in UP are that the articulate and advanced section among *Dalits* in UP became conscious of the importance of rallying the masses of their community along the caste lines. As in other province in UP also *Dalit* leaders failed to form one single party articulating the common interests of *Dalits*. More importantly beyond the caste identity *Dalit* organizations failed to take up the economic issues affecting lives of *Dalit* masses. *Dalits* in urban areas and villages were living in two different realities. Bulk of rural agricultural labour force belonged to *Dalits* and on the contrary the British were supporting talukdari system against the interests of *Dalit* agricultural labourers. The entire *Dalit* mobilization was in the hands of articulated urban *Dalits* and none of government action was in the interests of majority of *Dalit* masses. *Dalit* identity had more symbolic value rather than any real term gains for common *Dalits*. The colonial rule did not take measures to remove the traditional controls over *Dalit* work force in the countryside, although in urban areas as a result of colonization *Dalit* workers were not subjected to the upper caste social control. Shashi Bhushan argues that "the contradiction between the existence of the *Dalits* in the villages and in the cities became much sharper than before'.[58] In the villages *Dalits* comprised the poor peasants and agricultural labourers working in the lands of *zamindars* and *talukdars* who mostly belonged to the upper castes. *Zamindars* and *talukdars* control over lands and his higher social status forced *Dalits* to live on the mercy of *zamindars* and *talukdars* which the movements spearheaded by *Dalit* leaders in urban areas failed to change. Peter Reeves in his study of landlords and governments in UP has shown the correlation between economic power and *jati* and how the economic control was used to suppress *Dalit* voices in village society.[59] Kapil Kumar's study of '*Tenants, Landlords, Congress and the Raj in Oudh 1886-1922*' also refers to the economic and social exploitation of *Dalits* at the village level who constituted the bulk of the rural proletariat. Narrating the form of exploitation Kapil Kumar writes, "Belonging to the "low caste" the *Chamars* were socially the most exploited people. They were very often subjected to do *begar* and they never had the guts to ask for remuneration. The *nais* (barbers), *dhobis* (washermen) and *bhangis* (sweepers) rendered free services to these "barons". The pots prepared by *kumhars* (potters) were forcibly taken away by the *zamindari karindas* and the peons of the touring government officials, free of cost."[60] The British government was well aware of the exploitation of the agricultural labourers by the landlords. But the landlords were dearer to the British so the government left the poor peasants at the mercy of the landlords. The urban *Dalit* leadership also failed to take up the issue of *Dalit* oppression by the landlords at the village level. Even at the time of formation of provincial government in UP after the election of 1937 on the question of inclusion of a *Dalit* in the ministry the fortnightly report states that apart from the financial viability "the difficulty of finding a reliable man and one who would bring any kind of strength to the cabinet is considerable".[61] This report is a testimony to the fact that the real concern of the government was how to retain its control over the Indian Empire rather than breaking the existing chain which has tied *Dalits* over the years. However one cannot overlook the spirit of poor *Dalits* to stand together cutting across caste identity against the landlords and the British. In the 1920s peasant mobilization in UP caste and class combined together but the mobilization was derailed because of encouragement of urban upper caste domination in the Congress leadership. Eka movement under the leadership of Madari Pasi had massive *Dalit* participation. Kapil Kumar in an article on "Rural Women in Oudh 1917-47" has shown that how women from poor peasant families cutting across caste lines mobilized themselves against talukdars, small zamindars and capitalists which the upper caste leaders did not appreciate.[62] Similarly, caste identity was missing among the peasants when they stood against the landlords. At various kisan sabha meetings and centres of peasant upsurge members belonging to various castes came together. "To oppose their exploitation the tenants-at-will looked beyond their caste and kinship relations, making it a combined effort of the exploited."[63]

On the contrary in urban areas the entry to political power became so competitive even among *Dalit* leaders that they forgot the need of a united *Dalit* voice. In the fortnightly confidential report on political condition in UP in the beginning of 1937 Harry Haig wrote to Lord Linlithgow on 23rd April, 1937 that "The Scheduled Castes representatives are mostly at loggerheads with each other, and each potential leader is looking to his own advantage".[64] Due to limited franchise majority of *Dalits* were not having voting rights and, therefore, by making provision for reservation of seats in legislative bodies the government might have earned the goodwill of an articulate section of *Dalits* but in real terms this was more of a tokenism rather than bringing major changes in the lives of *Dalit* masses. Divergent interests and divergent voices weakened the possibilities of *Dalits* to put up united challenge against the social, economic and political exploitation that they were subjected to. Further, *Dalit* voices raised under the period of study though peripherally touched social and political issues as far as the sufferings of rural *Dalits* were concerned the voices were yet to take a shape.[65]

REFERENCES

1. Report on the Working of the System of Government, United Provinces of Agra and Oudh, 1921-1928 (Allahabad,1930), p. 560 cited in James Chiriyankandath, " 'Democracy' Under the Raj: Elections and Separate

Representation in British India", in Niraja Gopal Jayal (ed.), *Democracy in India*, Oxford University Press, New Delhi, 2001, p. 66.

2. In the Indian caste system people belonging to the lowest social order were referred by various names such as 'Untouchables', 'Depressed Classes', '*Harijans*', and 'Scheduled Castes', etc. The reference to the term '*Dalit*' describing the lower castes is found in the 1920s. Although Sudha Pai writes that "The word *Dalit* has been used in Uttar Pradesh only since the late 1980s", we find the references of 'Shraddhanand Dalit Udhar Sabha' in Delhi in 1920s, 'Dalit Jat Sudharak Sabha' in United Provinces in 1920s and also a weekly '*Dalit Bandhu*' started in 1928 by P.N. Rajbhoj. (Sudha Pai, *Dalit* Consciousness and Movements in the United Provinces: Colonial Legacies, in R. Basu and S. Dasgupta (eds.), *Narratives of the Excluded: Caste Issues in Colonial India*, Kolkata, 2008, pp. 45-46). AICC Paper, File-AP-9,10,16,17/1928, NMML, New Delhi, Indian Franchise Committee, Vol. II, Government of India, Calcutta, 1932, p. 415, R.K. Kshirsagar, Dalit Movement in India and its Leaders, M.D. Publications, New Delhi, 1994, p. 135). But the usage of the term *Dalit* got momentum in the early 1970s following the *Dalit* Panther movement in Maharashtra. (S.M. Michael, Introduction, in S.M. Michael (ed.), *Dalits in Modern India: Vision and Values*, second edition, Sage Publications, New Delhi, 2007, p. 16). In this paper I have used the word '*Dalit*' in place of words like 'Untouchables', 'Depressed Classes' to refer the lower castes in caste hierarchy.]
3. Reforms Office, Franchise, Proceedings A, July, 1920, Nos.84-114A, NAI, New Delhi.
4. *Ibid*.
5. Correspondence Regarding Council Reforms, Vol. I, Part-I, Calcutta 1908.
6. *Census of India*, 1931, pp. 631-638.
7. E.A.H. Blunt, *The Caste System of Northern India* (April, 1931), Reprint, New Delhi, 1968, p. 208.
8. Marc Galanter, *Competing Equalities: Law and the Backward Classes in India*, Oxford University Press, New Delhi, 1984, p. 28.
9. A.C. Pradhan, *The Emergence of the Depressed Classes*, Bookland International, Bhubaneswar, 1986, pp. 115-116.
10. Indian Statutory Commission, Written Evidence, United Provinces, Vol. I, Calcutta, 1930.
11. Census of India, Report, 1921, cited in Census of India, 1931, United Provinces of Agra and Oudh, Vol. XVIII, Part-I, Report, A.C. Turner, Allahabad, 1933, pp. 528-529.
12. Owen M. Lynch, *The Politics of Untouchability: Social Mobility and Social Change in a City of India*, Columbia University Press, 1969.
13. Robert, L. Hardgrave, *The Nadars of Tamilnad: The Political Culture of a Community in Change*, Berkley, 1969; Gail Omvedt, *Cultural Revolt in Colonial Society: The Non-Brahman Movement in Western India,* Bombay,

1976; Sekhar Bandyopadhyaya, *Caste, Politics and the Raj, Bengal 1872-1937*, K.P. Bagchi, & Company, Calcutta, 1990; William R. Pinch, *Peasants and Monks in British India,* Oxford University Press, Delhi, 1996, Swaraj Basu, *Dynamics of a Caste Movement: The Rajbansis of North Bengal, 1910-1947*, Manohar, Delhi, 2003, etc.

14. Census of India, 1931, United Provinces of Agra and Oudh, Vol. XVIII, Part-I, Report, Allahabad, 1933, p. 533.
15. Christophe Jaffrelot, *India's Silent Revolution: The Rise of the Low Castes in North Indian Politics*, Permanent Black, New Delhi, 2003, pp. 199-200.
16. Kirti Narain, *Press, Politics and Society: Uttar Pradesh, 1885-1914,* Delhi, 1998, pp. 76-77.
17. Owen M. Lynch, *The Politics of Untouchability: Social Mobility and Social Change in a City of India*, pp. 68-72.
18. *Ibid.*, pp. 74-75.
19. *Ibid.*, p. 84.
20. William R. Pinch, *Peasants and Monks in British India*, Oxford University Press, Delhi, 1996, pp. 92-93.
21. Badri Narayan, *Inventing Caste History:* Dalit *Mobilisation and Nationalist Past*, in Dipankar Gupta (ed.), *Caste in Question-Identity or Hierarchy*? Sage Publications, Delhi, 2004, pp. 195-198.
22. Chandrika Prasad Jigyansu, Swami Achhutanand, Lucknow, Bahujan Kalyan Prakashak, 1960, p. 100, cited in Christophe Jaffrelot, *India's Silent Revolution: The Rise of the Low Castes in North Indian Politics*, Permanent Black, New Delhi, 2003, p. 201.
23. Nandini Gooptu, *The Politics of the Urban Poor in Early Twentieth Century India,* Cambridge University Press, Cambridge, 2001, pp. 149-151.
24. R.S. Khare, *The Untouchable as Himself: Ideology, Identity, and Pragmatism among the Lucknow Chamars*, Cambridge University Press, Cambridge, 1984, pp. 83-86.
25. Christophe Jaffrelot, *India's Silent Revolution: The Rise of the Low Castes in North Indian Politics*, pp. 202-3.
26. *Ibid.*, p. 205.
27. *Census of India*, 1931, pp. 626-628.
28. A Note on the progress and activities of the Arya Samaj based on the materials provided by Pandit Rahas Behari Tewari, Secretary of the Arya Pratinidhi Sabha, United Provinces, Census of India, 1931, pp. 505-508.
29. Note on the Depressed Classes by M.C. Rajah, East India (Constitutional Reforms), Report of the Indian Central Committee, 1928-29, London, 1929, pp. 386-387.
30. Census of India, UP, 1931, p. 630.
31. Indian Statutory Commission, Vol. XVI, Selections from Memoranda and Oral Evidence, Calcutta, 1930, pp. 347-363.
32. Sudha Pai, Dalit Consciousness and Movements in the United Provinces:

Colonial Legacies, in R. Basu and S. Dasgupta (eds.), *Narratives of the Excluded: Caste Issues in Colonial India*, Kolkata, 2008, p. 35.

33. Nandini Gooptu, *The Politics of the Urban Poor in Early Twentieth Century India*, Cambridge University Press, 2001, pp. 156-157.
34. *Ibid.*, pp. 177, 182.
35. The Indian Annual Registrar, January-June, 1928, Reprint, Delhi, 2000, pp. 438-439.
36. The Indian Annual Registrar, January-June, 1928, Reprint, Delhi. 2000, pp. 92-95.
37. Indian Statutory Commission, Oral Evidence-United Provinces, Vol. II. Supplementary Memorandum submitted.by Rama Charana to the Statutory Commission, Indian Statutory Commission, Selections from Memoranda and Oral Evidence by Non-officials, Vol. XVI, Calcutta, 1930, p. 350.
38. Indian Statutory Commission, Written Evidences, Vol. I.
39. *Ibid.*
40. *Ibid.*
41. *Ibid.*
42. Government of India, Reforms Office, File No. 111/32-R, NAI, New Delhi.
43. Government of India, Reforms Office, File No. 199/19032, NAI, New Delhi.
44. The Indian Annual Registrar, July-Dec.1931, Reprint, Delhi, 2000, pp. 325-26.
45. Indian Statutory Commission, Vol. III, Reports of Provincial Committees, Calcutta, 1930, pp. 241-243.
46. Indian Franchise Committee, Vol. IV, Government of India, 1932, pp. 823-824.
47. *Ibid.*
48. Ram Sahai, representing the depressed classes on the United Provinces.
49. Provincial Franchise Committee, Indian Franchise Committee, Vol. II, Government of India, Calcutta, 1932, p. 434.
50. Indian Franchise Committee, Vol. II, Government of India, Calcutta, 1932, p. 429.
51. Indian Franchise Committee, Vol. II, Government of India, Calcutta, 1932, pp. 412-420.
52. File No. 163/III/30-R, Reforms Office, NAI.
53. *Ibid.*
54. File No. 199/32-R, Reforms Office, NAI.
55. B.R. Ambedkar, *What Congress and Gandhi Have Done to the Untouchables*, 1945, (Reprint) 1991, p. 156.
56. A.C. Pradhan, *The Emergence of the Depressed Classes*, Bookland International, Bhubeneswar, 1986, p. 204.
57. Oliver Mendelsohn and Marika Vicziany, *The Untouchables: Subordination, Poverty and the State in Modern India*, Cambridge University Press, New Delhi,1998, p. 110.

58. S. Bandyopadhyaya, *Caste, Politics and The Raj: Bengal 1872-1937*, p. 14.
59. Shashi Bhushan, "*Dalits* and the Ideology of Work in India" in Marcel van der Linden and Prabhu P. Mohapatra (eds.), *Labour Matters: Towards Global Histories,* Tulika Books, New Delhi, 2009, p. 163.
60. Peter Reeves, *Landlords and Governments in Uttar Pradesh: A Study of Their Relations Until Zamindari Abolition*, Oxford University Press, Delhi, 1991, pp. 2-29.
61. Kapil Kumar, *Peasants in Revolt: Tenants, Landlords, Congress and the Raj in Oudh*, Manohar, New Delhi, 1994, pp. 47, 66.
62. Lionel Carter (ed.), *United Provinces Politics, 1936-1937,* Governors' Fortnightly Reports and other Key Documents, Manohar, New Delhi, 2008, p. 133.
63. Kapil Kumar, Rural Women in Oudh 1917-47 in Kumkum Sangari and Sudesh Vaid (eds.), *Recasting Women: Essays in Indian Colonial History*, Rutgers University Press, New Jersey, 1990, pp. 362-363.
64. Kapil Kumar, *Peasants in Revolt: Tenants, Landlords, Congress and the Raj in Oudh*, pp. 224-225.
65. Lionel Carter (ed.) *United Provinces Politics, 1936-1937,* Governors' Fortnightly Reports and other Key Documents, p. 114.

18
Sri Lanka: Ethnic Conflict and Its Management

Prashant Amrutkar

South Asia is the region of conflicts in various manners. Ethnic Conflict is one of the important forms of conflict which affects peace and stability of the region.

The complexity and magnitude of the Sri Lankan conflict have grown over the last five decades, making it one of the most protracted and devastating conflicts in the world today. With the prolongation of conflict, the chances for establishing peace have become distant, the gap between two communities (Sinhalese and Tamils) has widened and new elements have been introduced to the conflict.

The case of Ethnic Conflict in Sri Lanka is much more complex business than a simple straight forward confrontation between a once well entrenched minority the Tamils and powerful but insecure majority thc Sinhalese. It is a classic case of a sense of relative deprivation.

The exploration of the failure of the peace process in the island points to a combination of internal and external factors that impede the establishment of a liberal democratic political structure. Despite its reputation as a Third World democracy, the Sri Lankan polity has, since independence, increasingly developed into an illiberal democracy. Although possessing nominal features of a democracy, the Sri Lankan political system is saturated with highly undemocratic elements. Amongst these elements, the *ethnocisation* of the society, confrontational politics and violence are specifically addressed by this study.

The 1983 black July riots in Sri Lanka (The riots which began in the night of July 24, 1983) converted it into one of the most notorious killing fields in the world. There are two conflicting parties named Sri Lankan government (represents the Sinhalese) and the LTTE (represents Tamil community). The conflict was stopped at the end of Velupillai Prabhakaran (LTTE leader) by the Sri Lankan army on May 19, 2009. But there is a question about the peace management process adopted by the Sri Lankan government.

This chapter tries to criticize so called peace process through military action against LTTE. There is a need to study this problem from the psychological, developmental and humanitarian point of view. This chapter analyzed the deep rooted seeds of the problem, its historical background, its various domestic and international angles and perceptions, and International angles as well as regional implications of the Sri Lankan Tamil insurgency. The nature of the problem, the effect of Ethnic Conflict in Sri Lanka on regional security, the militarily *remediation* of the problem by Sri Lankan government and its result is focused here.

Finally, the study identifies the contemporary role of *diaspora* communities as a severe hindrance to a lasting peace in the country. Thus, the analysis concludes that lasting peace in the island is possible only through the promotion of genuine liberal democracy, both from within and outside.

At last suggestions for future peace, stability and development have been put forward.

If the discrimination, *terrorization* and *marginalization* of the Tamil people continue, it won't be long before a Prabhakaran clone surfaces. The challenge before the "victor" is to display humility, large-heartedness and justice.[1]

As the news of the end of LTTE supremo Velupillai Prabhakaran sank in, one's mind thinks that the beautiful island nation of Sri Lanka is shaken by the flames of ethnic conflict during last thirty years and the number of times the government and people of Sri Lanka hoped that the ethnic conflict would end and peace is possible in the tiny nation savaged by violence, terrorism and fear.

Now this is better time to look back at the Sri Lankan government's conflict management process and to suggest some remedies for future peace building process.

NATURE OF ETHNIC CONFLICTS

An ethnic conflict or ethnic war is a war between ethnic groups often as a result of ethnic nationalism. They have become quite apparent since the Cold War; they often lead to various war crimes including genocide. Academic explanations of ethnic conflict generally fall into one of three schools of thought: primordialist, instrumentalist and constructivist. Intellectual debate has been focused on devising ways of managing conflicts, through instruments such as consociationalism and federalism.[2]

Primordialist Accounts

Proponents of primordialist accounts of ethnic conflict argue that "ethnic groups and nationalities exist because there are traditions of belief and action towards primordial objects such as biological features and especially territorial location."[3] The primordialist account relies on a concept of kinship between members of an ethnic group. Donald Horowitz argues that this kinship makes it possible for ethnic groups to think in terms of family resemblances.

There are a number of political scientists who refer to the concept of ethnic wars as a myth because they argue that the root causes of ethnic conflict do not involve ethnicity but rather institutional, political, and economic factors. These political scientists argue that the concept of ethnic war is misleading because it leads to an essentialist conclusion that certain groups are doomed to fight each other when in fact the wars between them are the result of political decisions. Opposing groups may substitute ethnicity for the underlying factors to simplify identification of friend and foe.

Ethnic Conflict in the Post-Cold War World

Although the study of ethnic conflict has a long history, genuine interest in ethnic conflict beyond the comparative political science subfield dates from the collapse of the Soviet Union and Yugoslavia, both of which were followed by ethnic conflicts that escalated to violence and civil war.

One of the most debated issues relating to ethnic conflict is whether it has become more or less prevalent in the post-Cold War period. At the end of the Cold War, academics including Samuel P. Huntington and Robert D. Kaplan predicted a proliferation of conflicts fuelled by civilizational clashes, tribalism, resource scarcity and overpopulation.

Ethnic Conflict Regulation

A number of scholars have attempted to synthesize the methods available for the resolution, management or transformation of ethnic conflict. John

Coakley, for example, has developed a typology of the methods of conflict resolution that have been employed by states, which he lists as: *indigenization*, accommodation, assimilation, acculturation, population transfer, boundary alteration, genocide and ethnic suicide.[4] John McGarry and Brendan O'Leary have developed taxonomy of eight macro-political ethnic conflict regulation methods, which they note are often employed by states in combination with each other.[5]

They include a number of methods which are clearly morally unacceptable.

- Methods for eliminating differences: 1. Genocide, 2. Forced mass-population transfers, 3. Partition and/or secession (self-determination), and 4. Integration and/or assimilation.
- Methods for managing differences: 1. Hegemonic control, 2. Arbitration (third-party intervention), 3. *Canonization* and/ or federalization, and 4. *Consociationalism* or power-sharing.

In the light of this discussion the case of Sri Lankan ethnic conflict can be studied.

ETHNIC CONFLICT IN SRI LANKA

The Sri Lankan Civil War was a war fought on the island of Sri Lanka. Beginning on July 23, 1983, there was an on-and-off insurgency against the government by the Liberation Tigers of Tamil Eelam (the LTTE, also known as the Tamil Tigers), a separatist militant organization which fought to create an independent Tamil state named "Tamil Eelam" in the north and the east of the island. After a 30-month-long military campaign, the Sri Lankan military defeated the Tamil Tigers in May 2009.[6]

For over 25 years, the insurgency caused significant hardships for the population, environment and the economy of the country, with over 80,000 people officially listed as killed during its course.[7] The tactics employed by the Liberation Tigers of Tamil Eelam resulted in them being branded as a terrorist organization in 32 countries, including the United States, India, Australia, Canada and the member nations of the European Union.

After two decades of fighting and three failed attempts at peace talks, including the unsuccessful deployment of the Indian Army, (the Indian Peace Keeping Force from 1987 to 1990) a lasting negotiated settlement to the conflict appeared possible when a cease-fire was declared in

December 2001, and a ceasefire agreement signed with international mediation in 2002.[8] However, limited hostilities renewed in late 2005 and the conflict began to escalate until the government launched a number of major military offensives against the LTTE beginning in July 2006, driving the LTTE out of the entire Eastern Province of the island. The LTTE then declared they would "resume their freedom struggle to achieve statehood".[9, 10, 11]

In 2007, the government shifted its offensive to the north of the country, and formally announced its withdrawal from the ceasefire agreement on January 2, 2008, alleging that the LTTE violated the agreement over 10,000 times.[12]

Since then, aided by the destruction of a number of large arms smuggling vessels that belonged to the LTTE,[13] and an international crackdown on the funding for the Tamil Tigers, the government took control of the entire area previously controlled by the Tamil Tigers, including their *de facto* capital Kilinochchi, main military base Mullaitivu and the entire A9 highway,[14] leading the LTTE to finally admit defeat on May 17, 2009.[15]

THE BEGINNINGS OF THE ETHNIC CONFLICT

The Pre-Colonial Situation

The peopling of Sri Lanka has been a continuous process of migrants from India with indigenous and other earlier migrant groups. The Sinhala or Sinhalese (74%) constitute the major ethnic group; the Sri Lankan Tamils, who inhabit the north and east form 12.6 per cent and the group known as Indian Tamils (nineteenth century migrants for work on plantations) 5.6 per cent of the population. While Muslims constitute the third largest ethnic group (7.4%), there are also small minorities such as Burghers (people of mixed decent), and Malays. All the major groups in Sri Lanka belong to a similar ethnic mix of migrants from various parts of India, especially South India, to which there have been South-East Asian, Arab and European admixtures. In spite of this, each ethnic group today has a distinct identity with strongly held myths of origin; the Sinhala believe that they are Aryans from Bengal, the Tamils claim pure Dravidian origin, and the Muslims aspire to decent from Arabs.

The history of ethnic conflict in Sri Lanka is the history of emergence of consciousness among the majority community, the Sinhala, which defined the Sri Lanka society as Sinhala-Buddhist, thus denying its multi-ethnic character. The growth of this consciousness impinged on the minorities in Sri Lanka to the extent that internal resolution of the problems becomes impossible.

The Sinhala dominated the country from about fifth century BC and succeeded in establishing a kingdom with its centre in the North Central Province of the island. The term 'Sinhala' was first used to indicate the royal family of the island, then extended to cover the royal retinue and then further extended to include the people; this social process dating to about the 6th century AD is simultaneously the process of the ethnic consolidation of the Sinhala people.[16] The Sinhala kingdom which controlled the entire island most of the time entered into relations both of alliance and hostility at various periods with the Chola, Pandiya and Chera Kingdoms of South India. There were frequent invasions from these kingdoms, and also frequent alliances and intermarriage of the four royal families. There were thus strong links with India, especially South India. This long history of links with South India is still present in popular Sinhala consciousness, with perhaps the aggressive acts being best remembered.

In the twelfth and thirteenth centuries, certain developments in Sri Lanka determined its ethnic demography in a decisive way with effects that have continued to the present[1]. The demographic distribution lays down a territorial basis for the major ethnic groups; in the case of the Tamils, the territorial concentration grew into a concept of a "traditional Tamil Homeland". This did not arise for Muslims since they were scattered over the whole island, with a majority presence in only a part of the Eastern Province.

Religion also played a dominant ideological role in ethnic consolidation. Buddhism, introduced from India in the third century BC, became the religion of the Sinhala as well as the state religion. Hinduism remained the religion of the Tamils. Apart from the conversion of a section of both Sinhalese and Tamils to Christianity during the colonial period, the incongruence between Sinhala and Buddhist on the one hand, and Tamil and Hindu on the other increased.

The Colonial Period

Social and economic developments during the early colonial period under the Portuguese and then the Dutch—commercialization of agriculture, the registration of title to land, registration of births and deaths, *proselytisation*—contributed towards a freezing of ethnic boundaries[2].

This meant in effect the consolidation of the Sinhala community in the central and south-western parts of the island and of the Tamil community in the north and on the eastern seaboard. Economic developments during the occupation of the island by the British gave rise to two other phenomena which made the ethnic picture in Sri Lanka even more complex.

1. The coffee plantations established by the British in the nineteenth century brought to Sri Lanka, as plantation labour, a population of over one million Tamil workers from South India. These were at first seasonal migrants but with the development of tea plantations the majority became permanently domiciled on the plantations. The question of their citizenship rights became an issue that subsequently sored relationships between India and Sri Lanka.
2. Economic developments during this period were mainly in the central and western areas of the island. This left the Tamil community in a disadvantaged position. They sought to overcome this by moving in large numbers to employment in the State services, in the private sector and by entering the learned professions. This process was helped by the growth of educational facilities in English in the Tamil regions, particularly the Jaffna peninsula. This meant not only that large number of Tamils migrated to the southern and central regions for purposes of employment but also that Tamil traders established themselves in these regions. The local bourgeois thus created multi-ethnic, but predominantly Sinhalese. With Burghers and Tamils too enter the various professions and the State services. The Sinhala bourgeois found its expansion constrained in various areas. The main import and export trade was dominated by the British and Indians and retail trade throughout the country by Muslim and Chettiar traders. Sinhala traders could not break into these areas because of a lack of access to finance which was controlled by British bankers or South Indian Chettiars. The Sinhala professionals and the educated "petit-bourgeois" also felt this competition in so far as they had to vie with Burghers and Tamils for State and private employment. Workers at their own level found themselves confronted with migrant workers from Kerala and Tamilnadu as well as with workers of indigenous minority groups.[17]

These barriers to their advancement were perceived by the Sinhala at all levels as being caused by the non-Sinhala elements. To understand why economic *antagonisms* should be perceived in ethnic terms, one must examine the way in which the Sinhala asserted a sense of national identity as the basis for winning political reforms which would give them more power.

Sinhala Buddhist Identity

In asserting a Sinhala identity and in legitimatizing Sinhala control of the country's polity, the leaders of the Sinhala revivalist movement reconstructed an image of the Sinhala past using many elements of the 'origin' mythology like Sri Lanka becomes the land of Sinhala and the land of *Dharma*—the Buddhist doctrine. The belief was that the survival of the Buddhist religion was dependent on the survival of the Sinhala people; the people surviving as long as they espoused the doctrine and controlled the land consecrated to the religion. Thus the religion, the people and the land were bound together in an indissoluble unity.

Such a revivalist ideology attempted to establish a Sinhala-Buddhist hegemony of the island antagonistic to non-Sinhala, non-Buddhist groups. It is this Sinhala-Buddhist consciousness that has resulted in the denial of the multi-ethnic and multi-religious character of Sri Lankan society and in a refusal to accept the collective rights of other minority groups. This Sinhala Buddhist identity is against all foreigners and minorities. Over the last 100 years, it has been asserted against Muslims, Christians, Tamil plantation workers, Malayalis and Sri Lankan Tamils.[18]

POLITICAL REFORMS AND REASONS FOR CONFLICT

The agitation spearheaded by the political reformers of the early twentieth century.

1. Unsolved Question of Citizenship

The question of citizenship of migrant plantation labour from south India was not been solved by the government.

2. Divide and Rule Policy

The British Governor (following the old stratagem of divide and rule) had nominated members to the legislature on the basis of ethnicity.

3. Ethnic Representation

The unity of bourgeois broke down over the question of ethnic representation. These reforms of 1931 did not meet with the favour of minority ethnic groups. The constitution would ensure the dominance of the Sinhala majority.

4. Unequal Economic Development

The development was mainly in the central and western areas of the island. The Tamil community was in a disadvantaged position. The government refuses to allocate certain scarce resources to Tamil areas and some times even shelved internationally sponsored development projects in these regions.

5. Sinhala Control over the Countries Polity

The Constitution was enacted in the face of minority protests and minority fears were realized in 1936 when a totally Sinhala Board of Ministers was chosen.

6. The Emergence of Ethnic based Organizations

This was justified by the Sinhala "Maha Sabha's leader, S.W.R.D. Bandaranaike.

7. Minority Rights Denied

The revivalist ideology amongst Sinhala-Buddhist hegemony was not accepted to the rights of minority groups.

8. Sinhala-Buddhist Resurgence

The Sinhala-educated *intelligentsia* reiterated the ideals of Sinhala-Buddhist resurgence which are against the English speaking members of the upper class which wielded economic and political power.

9. Promotion of Buddhism

The promotion of Buddhism as the national religion stirred a wave of anti-Tamil feeling.

10. Replacement of English by Sinhala

In 1956 Bandaranaike replaced English by Sinhala as the only official language. It had the unfortunate effect of alienating the Tamil-speaking part of the Sri Lankan society.

11. Removal of Tamils from Civil Services

The enactment of new language policy as a means not only to reduce the number of Tamils in State services. Tamils were underrepresented in terms of ethnic percentages in the State Services.[19]

12. Ethnic Sinhala Hegemony in the Field of Education

In the 1970s by the system of 'standardization' for science students, whereby "the minimum entry requirements for a Tamil student were higher than for a Sinhala medium student."[20] This was clearly discriminatory and created the impression that the government deliberately reduced the opportunities available to Tamil youth in government service. This was an explosive grievance in a community that had long looked on education as the main means of social and economic advancement[3].

13. State-aided Colonization

After 1930 and soon Sinhala settlements began to appear in the predominantly Tamil eastern province as well. This led to a shift in demographic patterns. (for example, in the Trincomalee district there was an increase of the Sinhala population from 20.7% to 33.6% between 1946 and 1981.) This process of State-aided colonization was seen not only as a thereat to the political status of Tamils in the affected areas, but also as a threat to existence of the Tamils as a community with its own linguistic and cultural identity.

14. Radicalizing the Tamils

Ethnic outbidding had contributed to anti-Tamil action, and the next wave of anti-Tamil riots in 1958, again saw Sinhalese hoodlums operating with utter impunity. In many cases, the police failed to move against the rioters, a clear sign that the minority could no longer trust Sri Lanka's institutions to operate impartially. Sinhalese radicals retaliated by staging large anti-

Tamil riots in 1977 and 1981. Shockingly, official security forces and government supporters played a major role in these. In July 1983, orgiastic anti-Tamil riots spread like wildfire across the country, killing thousands of Tamils.

15. Institutionalized Sinhala Political Hegemony

The republican Constitution of 1972, while proclaiming Sinhala as the official language, declared that Buddhism had the 'foremost place' in Sri Lanka, thus almost affirming a Sinhala Buddhist state. It is precisely the history that persuaded the Tamils that co-existence with the Sinhala in a single polity was no longer possible.

16. Illiberal Governance

The 1978 Constitution gave the presidency near-dictatorial powers, which both President Jayewardene and Ranasinghe Premadasa (1988-93), used freely against the separatists.

These are the main reasons for ethnic conflict or civil war in Sri Lanka.

THE TAMIL FACTOR IN POLITICS

The Tamil ethnic group sought to counter this growing discrimination by demands at a political level.

1. Demand of Balanced Representation

Before independence, the Tamil Congress unsuccessfully demanded balanced representation—50 per cent seats for the Sinhala and 50 per cent for the combined minority ethnic groups.

2. Federal Political Structure and Autonomy

Later, in the face of continuing discrimination, a Federal Party emerged which asked for a federal political structure that would give Tamils a degree of autonomy in the areas inhabited by them, as well as adequate representation at the centre.

3. Separate State

It was in this period of accelerated demands and rejection that Tamil political leaders concluded in 1976 that only a separate state could ensure the security and welfare of the Tamil people, a state carved out of the northern and eastern provinces of Sri Lanka to be called "Tamil Eelam".

4. Use of Parliamentary Democratic Process

While the established political party of the Tamils—the 'Tamil United Liberation Front' (TULF)—was demanding a separate State and using parliamentary democratic processes towards obtaining it.

5. Adoption of blood shade

Some Tamil youths, dissatisfied with the non-violent policies of the TULF, formed groups which took up arms in the same cause[4].

It is only necessary to state that it led to a protracted and bitter war in the northern and eastern parts of Sri Lanka during the course of which the state security forces were guilty of severe excesses, attacks on civilians and serious violations of human rights of the Sri Lankan citizens, while the armed groups in turn resorted to brutal killings of both the Sinhala civilians and those Tamils thought of as 'informers'. The number of deaths has been estimated at 6,000 by the government and 15,000 by Tamil groups; damage to property is incalculable.

MAIN PHASES OF CONFLICT

In the Ethnic Conflict in Sri Lanka there are six phases of conflict named Eelam War-1, 2, 3 and 4. India's military intervention through IPKF (Indian peace keeping forces) is also a part of conflict. The last and concluding phase of conflict was 2007 onwards.

Eelam War I – (1976 to 1987)

In this initial phase of civil war, the process of politicization of Tamil youths in the North and the East started to form militant groups. The most prominent of these groups was the TNT, which changed its name to the Liberation Tigers of Tamil Eelam or the LTTE in 1976. The LTTE initially carried out a campaign of violence against the state.

Indian Involvement (1980 to 1990)

India became involved in the conflict in the 1980s for a number of reasons, including its leaders' desire to project India as the regional power in the area and worries about India's own Tamils seeking independence. India became more actively involved in the late 1980s; the Indo-Sri Lanka Peace Accord was signed on July 29, 1987, by Indian Prime Minister Rajiv Gandhi and Sri Lankan President Jayewardene. Under this accord, the Sri Lankan Government made a number of concessions to Tamil demands, including a devolution of power to the provinces, a merger—subject to later referendum—of the Northern and the Eastern provinces into the single province, and official status for the Tamil language (this was enacted as the 13th Amendment to the Constitution of Sri Lanka). India agreed to establish order in the North and East through a force dubbed the Indian Peace Keeping Force (IPKF), and to cease assisting Tamil insurgents. Militant groups including the LTTE, although initially reluctant, agreed to surrender their arms to the IPKF, which initially oversaw a cease-fire and a modest disarmament of the militant groups.

The signing of the Indo-Lanka Accord, so soon after JR Jayawardene's declaration that he would fight the Indians to the last bullet and there was a question on India's peace mission. While most Tamil militant groups laid down their weapons and agreed to seek a peaceful solution to the conflict, the LTTE refused to disarm its fighters.[21] The IPKF then tried to demobilize the LTTE by force and ended up in three years long full-scale conflict with them.

The IPKF also soon met stiff opposition from the Tamils. Simultaneously, nationalist sentiment led many Sinhalese to oppose the continued Indian presence in Sri Lanka. The calls for the withdrawal of the IPKF from both sides of the Sri Lankan conflict grew. This was the failure of the Indian peace mission.

Support for the LTTE in India dropped considerably in 1991, after the assassination of ex-Prime Minister Rajiv Gandhi by LTTE. India remains an outside observer to the ongoing peace process, with frequent demands by many groups for an extradition of Velupillai Prabhakaran.[22]

Eelam War II – (1990 to 1993)
Eelam War III – (1994 to 2005)
Eelam War IV – (2006 to 2008)

The 1990-2008 phases were full of conflict and bloodshed. This included LTTE's attack on Sri Lankan arm forces, suicide bombing on political leaders, army officers and crowded places and civilian areas, in the southern and western part of government controlled areas in Sri Lanka. The struggle between LTTE and Arm forces for capturing and maintaining control over the North and Eastern part of Sri Lanka was the continuous chain of struggle in this era.

The Last Phase of Conflict (2008-2009)

In the last phase of conflict arm forces capture LTTEs stronghold area like Parappakandal in Mannar District, the town of Mallavi,[23] troops had captured Kilinochchi, which the rebels had used for over a decade as their *de facto* administrative capital.[24] The entire Jaffna peninsula was captured by the Sri Lanka Army by January 14, 2009,[25] On January 25, 2009, SLA troops captured Mullaittivu town,[26] on February 5, 2009, the military captured the last Sea Tiger base in Chalai [27] The Sri Lanka Air Force openly vowed to destroy the entire leadership of the LTTE.[28] On January 2, 2008, the Sri Lankan government officially pulled out of the Ceasefire Agreement.[29]

This stage of the war has been marked by increased brutality against civilians and rapidly mounting civilian casualties. On March 26, 2009, the military claimed that there was only one square km left in Tamil Tiger control outside the no-fire zone. Less than three years ago, the LTTE controlled 15,000 km^2. On April 21, 2009, Sri Lankan troops reportedly launched a 'final assault' against the LTTE, especially targeting its leader Vellupillai Prabhakaran.

May 16, 2009: President Declares Victory

Sri Lankan President, Mahinda Rajapaksa declared victory on May 16, 2009. However, the war did not end until the following day. Sri Lankan troops raced to clear the last LTTE pockets of resistance. As the last LTTE strongpoint crumbled, Sri Lankan troops killed 70 rebels attempting to escape by boat. The whereabouts of LTTE leader Vellupillai Prabhakaran and other major rebel leaders were not certain, however, Sri Lanka's government announced that Prabhakaran was dead on May 17, 2009.[30] Several other important LTTE commanders committed suicide. Upon hearing news of the Sri Lankan victory, people celebrated in Colombo.

There are two ways to see the victory of Sri Lankan Government in the conflict:

1. First, the failure of peace process by government; and
2. Second, the failure of maintaining the liberal democratic structure in Sri Lanka.

FAILURE OF PEACE PROCESS AND LIBERAL DEMOCRATIC POLITICAL STRUCTURE

The exploration of the failure of the peace process in the island points to a combination of internal and external factors that impede the establishment of a liberal democratic political structure. Despite its reputation as a Third World democracy, the Sri Lankan polity has, since independence, increasingly developed into an illiberal democracy. Although possessing nominal features of a democracy, the Sri Lankan political system is saturated with highly undemocratic elements. Amongst these elements, the ethnocisation of the society, confrontational politics and violence are specifically highlighted in this case.

There were some diplomatic steps forwarded by Sri Lankan government and LTTE during conflicting period, which are supported to create and maintain positive atmosphere for peace talk.

1. **Bandaranaike-Chelvanayakam Pact of 1958:** S.W.R.D. Bandaranaike, Prime Minister and leader of the SLFP (Sri Lanka Freedom Party) arrived at an understanding with the leader of the Federal Party (the Bandaranaike-Chelvanayakam Pact of 1958) which gave Tamils a degree of regional autonomy, including control of the land settlement in their areas. However, Bandaranaike had to abandon the pact in the face of opposition from the United National Party (UNP) and was killed by a monk in 1959.
2. **Peace Talks in Thimphu:** Peace talks between the LTTE and the government began in Thimphu in 1985, but they soon failed, and the war continued.
3. **Indo-Sri Lanka Peace Accord:** This accord was signed on July 29, 1987, by Indian Prime Minister Rajiv Gandhi and Sri Lankan President Jayewardene. Under this accord, the Sri Lankan Government made a number of concessions to Tamil demands, including a devolution of power to the provinces, a merger—

subject to later referendum—of the Northern and the Eastern provinces into the single province, and official status for the Tamil language (this was enacted as the 13th Amendment to the Constitution of Sri Lanka). India agreed to establish order in the North and East through a force dubbed the Indian Peace Keeping Force (IPKF), and to cease assisting Tamil insurgents. Militant groups including the LTTE, although initially reluctant, agreed to surrender their arms to the IPKF, which initially oversaw a cease-fire and a modest disarmament of the militant groups. But after stiff opposition of Sri Lankan people and LTTE, IPKF unable to do its job and the problem still continues.

4. **Legislative Initiatives:** In the 1980s and 1990s, successive governments enacted a number of official acts to appease the Tamil community, including recognizing Tamil as an official language and merging the Northern and the Eastern Provinces of the country.
5. **Cease Fire:** A tentative ceasefire held in 1990 as the LTTE occupied itself with destroying rival Tamil groups.
6. A ceasefire was agreed in January 1995, but the ensuing negotiations proved fruitless.
7. **Peace Movements:** By mid-2000, human rights groups estimated that more than one million people in Sri Lanka were internally displaced persons, living in camps, homeless and struggling for survival. As a result, a significant peace movement developed in the late 1990s.
8. **Norway's Mediation:** February 2000, Norway was asked to mediate by both sides, and initial international diplomatic moves began to find a negotiated settlement to the conflict.[31]
9. **Unilateral Ceasefire:** Hopes for peace gained ground as the LTTE declared a unilateral ceasefire in December 2000, but they cancelled it on April 24, 2001, and launched another offensive against the government.
10. **Growing Desire for Peaceful Settlement:** Towards the end of 2001, however, following the attacks of 9/11, the LTTE began to declare their willingness to explore measures for a peaceful settlement to the conflict.
11. **Another Cease Fire:** On December 19, amidst efforts by Norway to bring the government and the Tamil Tigers to the negotiating table, the LTTE announced a 30-day ceasefire with the Sri Lankan government and pledged to halt all attacks against

government forces.[32] The new government welcomed the move, and reciprocated it two days later, announcing a month long ceasefire and agreeing to lift a long standing economic embargo on rebel-held territory.[33]

12. **Signing of Memorandum of Understanding:** The two sides formalized a Memorandum of Understanding (MoU) on February 22, 2002, and signed a permanent ceasefire agreement (CFA). Norway was named mediator.
13. **Peace Talks in Phuket:** The much-anticipated peace talks began in Phuket, Thailand on September 16, 2002 and 5 further rounds followed in Phuket, Norway and Berlin, Germany. During the talks, both sides agreed to the principle of a federal solution and the Tigers dropped their long-standing demand for separate state. This was a key compromise from the LTTE, which had always insisted on an independent Tamil state and it also represented a compromise from the government, which had seldom agreed to more than minimal devolution. Both sides also exchanged prisoners of war for first time.[34]
14. **Peace Talks in Geneva:** The Norwegians continued efforts produced a breakthrough when both parties agreed on February 7, 2006, that new talks could be held in Geneva, Switzerland on February 22 and February 23, 2006. These talks were reported to have gone "above expectations", with both the government and the LTTE agreeing to curb the violence and to hold further talks on April 19-21, 2006.[35]
15. **Breakdown of Peace Talks:** Both parties agreed to unconditionally attend peace talks in Geneva, Switzerland on October 28-29, 2006.[36] However, the peace talks broke down due to disagreements over the reopening of the key A9 highway, which is the link between Jaffna and government controlled areas in the south.
16. **Search for Political Solution:** Political pressure was placed on Mahinda Rajapaksa to find a political solution to the conflict and he called for a meeting with parliamentarians allied with the Tigers in March 2009, but they refused until the government resolved the humanitarian crisis faced by civilians trapped in the fighting.[37]
17. **UN Human Rights Council Initiative:** On May 8, 2009, a group of independent United Nations experts called on the Human Rights Council to urgently set up an international inquiry to

address the "critical" situation in Sri Lanka amid fighting between the Army and Tamil rebels.[38]

All these and other events show that government of Sri Lanka as well as LTTE was stepping forward for peace in the region but the result was not positive.

SOME SUGGESTIONS FOR PEACE BUILDING

Peace and stability in Sri Lanka is possible through some positive steps which are as follows.

1. **Dialogue:** The government of Sri Lanka should seriously have dialogue with the Tamils.
2. **Healing Touch:** The government must concentrate on healing the wounds in relationship between the Sinhalese and Tamils in the State.
3. **Economic Development:** The government should work on economic development and solving unemployment problem of Tamils because massive numbers of poor unemployed youths are being easily allured by the insurgent groups.
4. **Civil Society's Initiatives:** The civil society especially every sane person, the NGOs and the community associations should come forward and work for peace.
5. **Decentralization and Devolution:** Issues of decentralization and devolution of power lie at the core of the solution of ethnic conflict.
6. **Equality:** Equal status and equal opportunities to all communities will maintain the brotherhood in the society.
7. **Assimilation:** Absorb and incorporate people and ideas into a wider society or culture.
8. **Diplomatic Ways:** In future Sri Lankan government should adopt diplomatic ways to solve confrontation.
9. **Arbitration (Third Party Intervention):** There are various pattern mainly conflict waging, mediatory, intervention to care for human rights, etc.
10. **Canonization:** A political or administrative subdivision of a country. In this case of conflict federal political structure and autonomy is the solution.

To sum up, with what Bhupinder Brar has argued that South Asia should be looked as a 'region of nations' rather than as a "region of states".[39] The suggestion followed from my belief that 'regions' are culturally and socially more natural and historically more deeply entrenched in South Asia than are the states.

Finally, the study identifies the contemporary role of diaspora communities as a severe hindrance to a lasting peace in the country. Thus, the analysis concludes that lasting peace in the island is possible only through the promotion of genuine liberal democracy, both from within and outside.

CONCLUSION

The tortured history of Sri Lanka's peace process *versus* its ethnic minority is well known. Various aspects are behind it like the colonial history, ethnic outbidding, ethnic hatred, gap of development between two communities, development of illiberal democracy, the *ethnocisation* of the society, unfaith upon diplomatic ways and failure of democratic process.

Not only the domestic elements but some times the ethnic disturbances in a country are exploited by a neighbouring state India. Any active involvement of India in this highly violated issue is a part of India's dominant hegemonic role in the South Asian continent. India worries about her own Tamils seeking independence. The latter was particularly strong in the Indian State of Tamil Nadu, where ethnic kinship led to strong support for independence for Sri Lankan Tamils. India, through its intelligence agency Research and Analysis Wing (R&AW), provided arms, training and monetary support to a number of Sri Lankan Tamil militant groups, including the LTTE. The LTTE's rise is widely attributed to the initial backing it received from R&AW. In this manner Indian involvement is a big factor for this conflict.

The contemporary role of diaspora communities as a serve hindrance to a lasting peace in the country, the revivalist ideology amongst Sinhala-Buddhist hegemony was not accepted to the rights of minority groups. The promotion of Buddhism as the national religion stirred a wave of anti Tamil feeling. All anti Tamil policies of Sri Lankan government widen the gap between two communities. And radicalizing the Tamils and anti Tamil riots in 1958, 1977, 1981 and July 1983 (Black July) was done a job as oil in the fire.

There was a peace process adopted by Sri Lanka government and LTTE, like peace talk in Thimphu in 1985, Indo-Sri Lanka Peace Accord on July 29, 1987, peace talk in Phuket, Thailand on September 16, 2002, peace talk in Geneva, Switzerland in February 7, 2006,. Both conflicting sides agreed to ceasefire many times but there was no permanent ceasefire agreement among them. Norway was asked to mediate by both sides, and initial international diplomatic moves began to find a negotiated settlement to the conflict. But unfortunately it was helpless and the problem becomes unsolved. The unsuccessful deployment of the Indian Army and the Indian Peace Keeping Force from 1987 to 1990 was also the step forward for peace keeping.

But at last government of Sri Lanka used its ultimate force and gave full stop to the diplomatic way of peace process. There arises a question of the peace management process of Sri Lankan government, in which the international community became just a spectator, the international organization like UNO which did nothing to protect rights of Tamils in Sri Lanka.

NOTES

1. When the hydraulic economy and civilization that had flourished in the north-central plains came to an end, the Sinhala people migrated to the rain-fed areas in the central and south-western regions of the island. The north-central plains reverted to jungle with a few scattered villages. With little control from the Sinhala kingdom, the Tamil people became concentrated in the northern and eastern coastal regions that were closest to that part of the Indian mainland also populated by Tamil speaking people; eventually Tamils of northern region established the Jaffna Kingdom at the end of the thirteenth century.
2. The Portuguese arrived in Sri Lanka in 1505 and occupied the south-western littoral of the island and in due time, the northern and eastern coastal regions. The Dutch succeeded them in 1658 and, as did Portuguese, ruled the Sinhala and Tamil areas as separate regions. During this period, the Sinhala Kingdom continued to exist, first in the south-west and then in the hill country in Kandy. The British succeeded the Dutch in 1796 and eventually subdued the Kandiyan Kingdom in 1815. In 1833 they brought the whole island, i.e., the areas occupied by the Sinhala and Tamils, within one administrative unit.
3. This system was replaced in 1978 by a system of 'standardization' that was designed to give equal opportunities to students from educationally disadvantaged areas. However, since Jaffna was classified as an educationally-advanced area, the net effect was very much the same.
4. These include, among others, the LTTE (Liberation Tigers of Tamil Eelam), PLOT (Peoples Libration Organization of Tamil Eelam), EPRLF (Eelam Peoples Revolutionary Libration Front), and EROS (Eelam Revolutionary Organization of Students).

REFERENCES

1. Edirippulige, Sisira, *Ethnic Conflict in Sri Lanka: Obstacles to the Peace Process*, http://hdl.handle.net.
2. Ethnic Conflict, http://en.wikipedia.org/wiki/Ethnic_conflict.
3. Steven Grosby, "The verdict of history: The inexpungeable tie of primordiality — A response to Eller and Coughlan", *Ethnic and Racial Studies* 17(1), 1994, pp. 164-171.
4. John Coakley, The resolution of ethnic conflict: Towards a typology, *International Political Science Review,* 13(4), 1992, pp. 343-358.
5. John McGarry and Brendan O'Leary "Introduction: The macro-political regulation of ethnic conflict", in John McGarry and Brendan O'Leary (eds.) *The Politics of Ethnic Conflict Regulation: Case Studies of Protracted Ethnic Conflicts*, London: Routledge, 1993, pp. 1-40.
6. Adele Balasingham, *The Will to Freedom — An Inside View of Tamil Resistance*. Fairmax Publishing Ltd., 2nd ed. 2003.
7. Sri Lanka military, rebels trade death toll claims Reuters India, http://in.reuters.com. 1 March, 2008.
8. Guardian, Ceasefire raises Sri Lankan peace hopes, http://www.guardian.co.uk, 22 February, 2002.
9. Dillip Ganguly (Fox News), Monitors Say 4,000 Dead in Sri Lanka, http://www.foxnews.com, 23 February, 2007.
10. Amal Jayasinghe (AGENCE FRANCE-PRESSE), Sri Lanka's war seen far from over, http://washingtontimes.com, 14 July, 2007.
11. Somini Sengupta (*The New York Times*), Sri Lankan Government Finds Support From Buddhist Monks, http://www.nytimes.com, 25 February, 2007.
12. Ministry of Defence, Government takes policy decision to abrogate failed CFA, http://www.defence.lk, 2 January, 2008.
13. Sri Lanka Navy, Sri Lanka Navy destroys the 10th LTTE arms ship 1700 km off Dondra, http://www.navy.lk, 08 October, 2007.
14. Bloomberg, Sri Lankan Forces Capture Last Major Rebel Base in Northeast, http://www.bloomberg.com
15. From correspondents in Colombo, Tamil Tigers admit defeat in civil war after 37-year battle, http://www.news.com.au, Retrieved 17 May, 2009.
16. R.A.L.H. Gunawardena, "The People of the Lion" Sinhala Consciousness in History and Histography in *Ethnicity and Social Change*, Colombo, 1985, pp. 55-107.
17. Kumari Jayawardena, *Ethnic and Class Conflicts in Sri Lanka*, Colombo, 1986. (chapter 3 and 5).
18. Kumari Jayawardena, 1986, p. 14.
19. C. Abeysekera, "Ethnic Representation in Higher State Services" in *Ethnicity and Social Change*, Colombo, 1985, p. 243.
20. Sunil Bastian, "University Admission and the National Question", in *Ethnicity and Social Change*, Colombo, 1985, p. 220.

21. Associated Press, Sri Lankan military says, Tamil rebels abduct 2 rivals, http://www.chinapost.com.tw, 12 December, 2006.
22. BBC, Tamil Nadu demands Tiger extradition, http://news.bbc.co.uk, 16 April, 2006.
23. Gamini Gunaratna, Sri Lankan troops enter Tigers final frontier, http://www.colombopage.com
24. Hindu.com, Kilinochchi captured in devastating blow to LTTE, http://www.hindu.com,
25. Bloomberg.com, Sri Lankan Military Seizes Last Rebel Base on Jaffna Peninsula, http://www.bloomberg.com, 14 January, 2009.
26. Somini Sengupta, Sri Lankan Troops Take Last Rebel Stronghold, *New York Times*. http://www.nytimes.com, 26 January, 2009.
27. Ministry of Defence, Army captures last sea tiger base and clears entire Visuamadu area, http://www.defence.lk, 5 February, 2009.
28. BBC News, Senior Tamil Tiger leader killed, http://news.bbc.co.uk, 2 November, 2007.
29. Agency France Press, Government ends ceasefire with Tamil Tigers, http://www.france24.com, 2 January, 2008.
30. Is LTTE chief Prabhakaran dead? Yes, says Lanka govt, http://news.in.msn.com, 17 May, 2009.
31. Susannah Price (BBC News), Norway role in Sri Lanka peace plan, http://news.bbc.co.uk, 1 February, 2000.
32. BBC News, Sri Lanka rebels announce truce, http://news.bbc.co.uk, 19 December, 2001.
33. BBC News, Sri Lanka enters truce with rebels, http://news.bbc.co.uk, 21 December, 2001.
34. BBC News, Upbeat opening for Sri Lanka talks, http://news.bbc.co.uk, 16 September, 2002.
35. BBC News, Sri Lanka foes to 'curb violence', http://news.bbc.co.uk, 24 February, 2006.
36. Bharatha Mallawarachi (Conflict and Religion), Sri Lanka – Tamil Tigers OK Talks with Sri Lanka: Tamil Tigers Agree to Unconditional Talks with Sri Lankan Government, http://conflict-religion.boker.tv, 3 October, 2006.
37. Sri Lanka says final standoff with Tigers approaches, http://ca.news.yahoo.com
38. UN, Urgent international scrutiny needed in Sri Lanka, say UN rights experts, http://www.un.org, 8 May, 2009.
39. Bhupinder Brar, SAARC: If Functionalism has Failed, Will Realism Work?, *South Asian Survey*, Vol. 10, No. 1, 2003, p. 40.

19

Shifting Context and Focus: UNHCR's Role in Peace-Building in East Timor

K. Savitri

Ever since the United Nations mounted its first multi-dimensional peacekeeping force in Namibia in 1989, second generation peacekeeping operations have become the mainstay of international conflict resolution. Post-1989 phase has also been characterized by the rapidity with which some of the international agencies have been invited to douse the flames after agreement to cease-fire and deployment of international forces has been reached. While multifaceted missions have endeavoured to search for solutions to conflicts through a holistic approach, they have come to subsume humanitarian mandate in their fold. The ambitious nature of these operations has necessitated the involvement of those agencies that had hitherto remained insulated from strictly peace and security functions. UNHCR has been one such office that has been repeatedly asked to fulfil the humanitarian mandate as a partner in the peacekeeping operations. Since 1990s, therefore, there has been a predominant shift in UNHCR's role from protection of refugees to providing humanitarian aid. These changes in context and sudden demand on efficacy of UNHCR have been immediately followed by regular frequency and pervasiveness of crises that have almost choked the responsive capacity of the agency.

This article attempts to assess the shift in the nature and efficacy of the functions of UNHCR with particular reference to its role in resolving the refugee crisis in East Timor. This article revolves around three main foci—the international **context** in which the crisis in East Timor surfaced, the **shift** in the role of UNHCR as a result of that changed international context, and the overall **impact** of the context and shift on the functioning of UNHCR. This essay is divided into three parts. The first part looks at the changed context, followed by the East Timor crisis in the second part and the last section offers a broad set of critical comments.

THE CONTEXT: CHANGING ROLE OF THE UNHCR

The 1990s have typically given rise to intra-state conflicts exacerbating the refugee crises in many parts of the world. Intra-state conflicts inhere fluid political situation making it difficult to establish responsibility of state protection for refugees. People fleeing from violent regions are unsure of the conditions in their home country and are easily overwhelmed by the attendant problems of survival. A growing number of refugees in the world are those fleeing the violence associated with political instability (including political transition), the denial of human rights and general lack of governmental protection in their country. The UNHCR has been called on to be a participating member of complex peacekeeping operations. Refugee population fleeing from conflict-ridden societies has placed unreasonable demands on the systemic capacities of UNHCR. Lack of internal security, overbearing militia groups, language barriers, inaccessible terrain, and the general intensity and urgency of problems have overwhelmed the organization. Lack of security has often caught UNHCR in a catch-22 situation—whether to go ahead and help the needy risking its personnel's safety or to retract and abandon those in urgent need of humanitarian relief to save the personnel from attacks. A significant feature of some of these conflicts is the political-military role played by the refugees themselves and the difficulty encountered in separating the warring groups from refugees in the camps.

The decade of 1990s has witnessed two divergent, and some times, opposite trends. On the one hand, increasing number of refugees are ending up either in the cross-border camps, or at the doorstep of other countries owing to uncertain situation at home; on the other hand, countries in North and South are manifestly displaying protectionist tendencies in their refusal to host refugees. The reasons for this trend are not far to seek. Most states find it difficult to cope with social and economic problems occasioned by the refugee influx. The developing countries in particular are already overstressed due to resource constraints; the prospect of handling a large number of refugees simply makes it difficult for them to withstand. Sometimes, shared cultural affinities of refugees from neighbouring countries can destabilize the precarious social balance and demographic composition in a host country leading to social conflicts. The developed countries' reluctance to host refugees emanates from the geographical, strategic and social agenda in these countries.[1] The host countries are increasingly seeking to return refugees. The refugees on their part are in a dilemma. They would like to return home to escape from the miserable conditions in camps, inordinately uncertain life, lack of access to social services in host countries, intimidation, extortion and, some times, eventual deportation. Therefore, both from the standpoint of host countries of North and South and the refugees themselves, return and repatriation seems to be the most preferred option.

Pressure has been brought on the UNHCR in the last decade to facilitate repatriation of refugees as a permanent, lasting solution to the refugee problem. The temptation to repatriate the refugees as quickly as possible and declare the camps as closed is high because of Political pressure by the host country and donor fatigue of agencies. UNHCR's traditional agenda of protecting refugees needs to be revitalized with a new zeal if its humanitarian agenda in post-conflict societies is to be of relevance. Unfortunately, protection of refugees is a shrinking area of UNHCR's current engagement.[2] A better coordination among the various aspects of peace building is essential (including aspects like development aid) if post-conflict peace building has to be made meaningful. Herein lies the problem—UNHCR's involvement in post-conflict nation building with other agencies having a political outlook has considerably reduced its autonomy and independence.[3]

In the post cold war era, humanitarianism and humanitarian assistance is a powerful political weapon to score victories over adversaries. The refugee camps in one's territory helps the states to project their image as serving a noble cause to attract foreign assistance besides influencing the outcome of a conflict. The refugees can be used the refugees to act according to host country's agenda in conflict areas.[4] There is also a problem of "phantom soldiers", i.e., quoting to the humanitarian agencies an inflated as buffer zones between a state and the humanitarian agencies. Blockade of humanitarian aid is used to compel number of refugees in order to procure more food supplies for armed groups in the camps or to stock pile the food supplies for future use in case of prolonged fighting. This problem has been witnessed in many places including Cambodia Rwanda and East Timor. Often, UNHCR is unable to even ascertain an accurate number of refugees in camps to plan their repatriation or resettlement.

The agencies face intimidation, harassment and expulsion, because they are seen as furthering the cause of the refugee producing state.[5] Thus, Indonesian army and its armed supporters saw UNHCR and other agencies seeking to help the refugees as cutting at the roots of their movement. Refugees are increasingly being denied access to social services like education and health in the host country since "decisions on asylum and treatment remain the prerogative of individual states"[6] UNHCR, therefore, faces difficulties in protecting refugees when states are intransigent.

Ever since the UNHCR moved into delivering humanitarian assistance, its traditional role as a protector of refugees has been diluted. Increasing emphasis on 'emergency' action has undermined the organization's focus on long term solutions to the refugee problems. Repatriation has not always been voluntary and the conditions under which they have been carried out less than satisfactory. The organization has been too overwhelmed by the severe nature of civil conflicts that renders any humanitarian activity impossible.

THE BACKGROUND: REFUGEE CRISIS IN EAST TIMOR

East Timor had been a Portuguese colony that was invaded in 1975 by Indonesia. International community had not really recognized Indonesia's invasion (except Australia) but continued to treat East Timor as an occupied territory. Australia and other countries brought pressure on Indonesia to test domestic consent to its continued rule over East Timor. Under pressure from the US, UN and some international financial institutions, Indonesia agreed to hold a referendum in East Timor under the UN aegis. The UN Advanced Mission in East Timor, that oversaw the referendum process, was deployed in limited strength to East Timor in 1999. In the referendum, the people of East Timor voted overwhelmingly for independence, much against the wishes of Indonesia but in line with its expectation.

The referendum in East Timor was delayed twice by the UN because of the terror campaign run by the pro-independence militia. Stockpiling of ammunition to be used in the event of vote for independence option was widely reported in the Australian media. The limited UN personnel sent to East Timor to oversee the referendum too had an inkling of impending violence and it is likely that they had made it known to their headquarters in New York. Several members of the Timorese population were held captive in mountains to work on coffee plantations to prevent them from voting in the referendum. As part of the terror campaign, even people sheltering in churches were killed in April 1999.[7]

The referendum took place on 30th August, 1999. Ignoring the threats, the East Timorese overwhelmingly (98%) voted for independence. Soon after, the locally organized militias supported by TNI (Tentara Nasional Indonesia—Indonesian Armed Forces) and police ran on a rampage in the capital Dili and other major towns systematically destroying every trace of property and infrastructure. Schools, houses, offices, equipments, and everything else was burnt, looted or destroyed. It is appalling to see how an entire country can be destroyed systematically in a few days' time. Within a period of three-weeks, hundreds were killed, houses torched and thousands rendered homeless. The militia killed indiscriminately while moving some of the population forcibly to West Timor. Rest of the population fled either into the hills or across the border to West Timor. It is yet difficult to ascertain the number of people killed but almost one-third of the country's 8,90,000 population were displaced and forcibly removed to West Timor at gun point or made to flee into inaccessible hills and jungles of the interior.[8] The shock and apathy of the international community was evident in that despite knowing well that TNI had made elaborate arrangements for mounting violence to prevent independence of East Timor, it did nothing to preempt the situation from erupting into the worst kind of systematic loot. In fact, the multi national force—International Forces in East Timor (INTERFET)—was authorized by the United Nations on 15th September, 1999,[9] a fortnight after the referendum, after Australia[10] brought pressure on the United Nations and offered to lead the force. On 25 October, the UN authorized the deployment of United Nations Transitional Administration in East Timor (UNTAET) to replace INTERFET.[11] It will be nearly impossible to rebuild a country's human skills for at least a generation. The UN and other agencies had their hands full in restoring basic infrastructure and services like education and health.

The UNSC Resolution 1272 of 25th October, 1999 mandated the UN Transition Administration in East Timor (UNTAET), among other things:

1. to exercise all "legislative and executive authority including the administration of justice"; and
2. to coordinate humanitarian and reconstruction assistance and help create democratic institutions.

THE MANDATE OF THE UNHCR

The overall range of the mandate was very broad. It included everything from providing emergency humanitarian assistance to repatriation, rehabilitation, reconstruction, and reconciliation. In the immediate aftermath of violence, some 270,000 persons were forced to flee to West Timor and other areas of Indonesia. The initial mandate of the UNHCR was to protect and assist the East Timorese refugees in West Timor, to promote voluntary repatriation, rehabilitation and reintegration of refugees. The main concern of the organization was, therefore, refugees outside East Timor although it did try to cater to the needs of the internally displaced persons.

Repatriation, Rehabilitation and Reconciliation

The UNHCR remained a partner of other international agencies in the field of humanitarian assistance. It coordinated the repatriation programme with IOM and worked with nine implementing partners in West Timor and 14 national and international NGOs in East Timor.[12] The UNHCR and the International Organization for Migration (IOM) organized flights and ferries from West Timor to help those willing to repatriate in October 1999. The initial repatriation was impressive but the refugees had to be literally "extracted" some times in difficult and perilous circumstances. Repatriation by land for those camps far from the seacoast remained particularly challenging. The convoys were stoned; people were too frightened to leave.[13] By December 2001, more than 1, 90,000 refugees had voluntarily returned though up to 70,000 persons still remained in West Timor refugee camps. The Secretary General reported that between September and January 2000, the World Food Programme and its implementing partners (CARE, World Vision and CARITAS) distributed food to 610,000 displaced persons. In addition, the relief organizations were to sponsor food-for-work schemes in support of schools, hospitals and clinics, and community rehabilitation and development.[14] Most refugees were provided with assistance to survive the first few months if they decided to return to East Timor. The assistance included rice, utensils, plastic sheets, and nails, etc., to make temporary shelters until habitable houses were ready. Those refugees who did not wish to repatriate were given the option of staying on in West Timor to be relocated there or elsewhere. They mostly consisted of former militia groups who feared reprisals would be exacted from them for having participated in the anti independence carnage. A minority of those who did not wish to be repatriated had economic interests as retired civil servants of the Indonesian government in East Timor. They feared denial of pensionary benefits in addition to uncertain conditions in East Timor.

The situation in the refugee camp in West Timor remained grim. The militia basically had three strategies: physical intimidation, misinformation and diversion of funds meant for refugees. The refugees constantly suffered physical intimidation and psychological stress at the hands of militia despite an agreement between the Indonesian army and INTERFET on 22 November, 1999 to facilitate movement across the border, and another agreement with UNHCR to separate civilians from armed militias in the camps. The Indonesian authorities blew to the wind both the agreements: Neither the refugee movement was facilitated nor the militias separated from civilians although international standards stipulate host states' obligation to allow UNHCR and other humanitarian personnel free and unimpeded access to all refugee camps and settlements.[15] The militia spread false information and rumours that East Timor was unsafe, that the returnees will be attacked by the Australian troops and that their women would be violated by the INTERFET soldiers. UNHCR and IOM disseminated information on safe conditions in East Timor but it came to naught, as their access to the refugee camps was severely limited.

Security Conditions

Security conditions were treacherous and deteriorated drastically as the mission progressed. Ironically, the UNHCR depended mainly on the local police in West Timor and the Indonesian army for security of its personnel. The refugees were literally held hostage by the militia in the camps. On 22 September, Mrs. Sadako Ogata visited East Timor and during the visit, the Indonesian authorities gave assurance that full "security and access to all the people in need of assistance" in West Timor will be provided. On 20 October, 1999, the TNI ordered the militia to open the gates of one camp in West Timor. Tens of thousands of refugees rushed to the UNHCR camp in East Timor for food, water shelter and medical help.[16] In reality, militiamen were reported to be rounding up youth, training them and killing them if they refused to obey the orders. Women were forced into subjugation, and abducted, never to be returned to their families. In November, the UN Special Rapporteur on violence against women, Mrs. Radhika Coomaraswamy, was refused permission by the Indonesian government to visit West Timor to investigate reports of sexual abuse in the camps.

The fragile nature of cease-fire in post-conflict societies has hit UNHCR time and again. In East Timor, UNHCR staff has been physically discouraged from entering the camps, subject to stone throwing, and guns fired into the air as warnings. UNHCR was forced to mount commando-style snatch-and-run "operations while parking its trucks outside a camp and moving in as quickly as possible to" extract refugees before militia members could act.[17] The entire operation (both humanitarian assistance and repatriation) had to be suspended and the personnel retreated after 6 September, 2000 when three UNHCR personnel were brutally beaten and killed and their bodies burnt by the militia in Atambua in West Timor. In view of the tragedy, the United Nations Security Coordinator (UNSECOORD) declared Phase-V, signifying the withdrawal of all international staff from the area.

The Atambua tragedy was the height of the security problem. Prior to the tragedy, some UNHCR personnel were attacked in the refugee camps leading to Phase-IV security declaration by the UNSECOORD, which prohibited all but emergency humanitarian activities in West Timor.[18] After the Atambua tragedy, the operation was put on hold until early 2001. The Security Council repeatedly urged the Indonesian government to take effective steps to restore law and order in refugee camps but to no avail. It also expressed concern[19] over the presence of a large number of militia in the camps and their intimidation of international staff. UNHCR had to postpone indefinitely its activities including registration process to ascertain the wishes of refugees to return to East Timor and to provide them with accurate information about the situation in East Timor. The Security Council asked the Indonesian government to honour and implement its MOU signed with UNHCR on 14 October, 1999 and a later security agreement concluded between the local authorities and the UNHCR. The Security Council further passed a resolution[20] calling on the Indonesian authorities to provide security but proved little effective. After the withdrawal of its personnel, UNHCR depended on the Indonesian government to coordinate its activities but supervision of refugee camps and maintaining relations with local leaders became that much more difficult. Later on, pressure was brought on Indonesian government by donor countries led by the United States that unless it disbanded the militias, separated armed groups from refugee population, provided security to international staff and conducted registration of refugees, its international reputation would be seriously damaged.

The Indonesian government conducted refugee registration programme in June 2001. The entire process lacked credibility due to several irregularities. There were only 12 international observers for 507 registration centres and insufficient number of interpreters to translate the registration form from Bahasa to Tetum for the refugees. Many local residents registered as refugees and then expressed the willingness to stay back in Indonesia. This served the government's position well. Unfortunately, UNHCR declared that the camps would be closed after 1

September, 2001 based on the flawed registration process.[21] There were still about 50,000 refugees living in the camps and they constituted high risk groups as they had endured the camps for over two years and, as a result, had greater physical, social and psychological needs.

Beyond repatriation, effort was also made to rehabilitate refugees to the extent possible in their own communities or regions so that the refugees felt secure and did not suffer alienation from their pre-crisis community affiliation. Rehabilitation and reintegration programmes in East Timor included short-term programmes such as shelter programme and reconstruction of East Timor through Quick Impact Projects (QIPS). The transition to long-term rehabilitation included development of the country's basic infrastructure and social reconciliation programmes. Support was extended to national and local level peace and reconciliation programmes.

The emphasis on reintegration included a two-pronged approach of providing basic physical, material support and psychological support for healing the wounds. The material support was in the form of providing employment to the immediate returnees, clearing areas for safe rehabilitation, and relocating the returnees in their own communities. The UNHCR also conducted reconciliation meetings, civic education programmes and psychosocial sessions for traumatized persons. However, reconciliation programme had been hampered by lack of facilities for investigation and prosecution of the guilty owing to human, financial, technical and logistical resources.[22] A Commission for Reception, Truth and Reconciliation was later established to bring the guilty to book in accordance with law. The most serious problem was violence against women. Women and girls had been taken away as war prizes and such women continued to experience trauma and it was more difficult to reintegrate them on return.

A CRITICAL APPRAISAL

The international community relied heavily on the co-operation of the Indonesian government. Much of the initiative was lost there. How could the country that reluctantly granted independence to its former colony turn around and help the repatriation of refugees or disband the militia that had acted on its order? The UN was clearly indulging in wishful thinking. UNTAET and UNHCR proceeded with the conclusion of an MOU with the government of Indonesia on various aspects of the mission, even as a New Zealand soldier was murdered on 24 July, 2000 and violence continued unabated in refugee camps. Obviously, promise and performance were at variance with each other. The international community did not demand adherence to the principles of international co-operation from the Indonesian government prior to signing the documents and it is still difficult to say that they expected it to honour the commitments. As it turned out later, the government dumped the MOUs soon after. Barely a month before the Atambua tragedy, and around the time when the New Zealand worker was killed, the Security Council took note of the Secretary-General's proposal to reduce the size of UNTAET in view of the situation on ground.[23] The forces could have been easily redeployed to facilitate the humanitarian mandate of the mission rather than to prune the international presence. In the East Timor enclave in West Timor (at Oecussi), for example, there was no presence of either INTERFET or UNTAET, making delivery of aid and prevention of rape and killings in the camps impossible. This town was surrounded by West Timor and was connected to East Timor by an 80 km road. Moreover, the mission had the requisite mandate from the Security Council to respond appropriately to the situation.[24]

Early warning system has often been suggested as a solution to preempt the refugee crisis from occurring in the first place. However, the United Nations has time and again ignored the early warning given by its personnel. The Organization acts only after a crisis has struck. In Rwanda, the UN special rapporteur on extrajudicial, summary, or arbitrary executions strongly warned the international community of potential genocide in Rwanda but the UN member-states took little notice of it.[25] Similar instances can be replicated in East Timor. Refugee flow could have been considerably contained had early warning been heeded. The UNHCR had it relatively easy in helping the IDPs who returned to Dili after the INTERFET had been deployed, but it was almost excluded from the makeshift camps in West Timor. Monsoon rains brought in their spell threat of disease in overcrowded, muddy camps.

Some form of international accountability needs to be ensured. "The UNHCR today is not held responsible when it 'incorrectly' declares that a source state as safe for return, closes a camp and facilitates the repatriation of the refugee population who suffer persecution on return."[26] In spite of less than ideal conditions in East Timor for returnees, UNHCR, jointly with the Indonesian government, declared all camps as closed on 1 September, 2001 in the face of protest from several NGOs and other agencies working in the area. The Indonesian government refused to provide assistance or security to the refugees after this closure. Such declaration clearly amounted to abandoning international responsibility by the organization. There were still about 50,000 refugees living in the camps and their status had not been decided. Such precarious decisions will put the refugees increasingly at risk. The premature closure of camps has also resulted in repatriations that cannot be called entirely "voluntary". Many a time, refugees are left with no option but to return unwillingly to their place of origin even when the situation in the home country is far from conducive to accepting a sudden increase in inhabitants. Besides, the UNHCR has largely been concentrating on repatriating and reintegrating refugees in a short term without giving thought to long-term sustainability of refugees in their country of origin.

Most states today recoil in horror when confronted with receiving refugee population. Sometimes, the post-conflict societies are among the poorest that are in no position to cater to the needs of returnees. Development aid will have to focus on reintegration of returnees rather than merely provide handouts in the initial phase. UNHCR-run QIPs have been very helpful for two reasons: they have helped the reconstruction and reintegration process and provided immediate source of livelihood and employment to the returnees. However, QIPs are emergency development projects that are not meant to address long-term issues of sustainability.

The UNHCR will have to pay more attention to procuring, compiling and disseminating critical information beyond the promotional material if it wishes its activities to be seen in right perspective. More often than not, one has to depend on NGOs for critical information about the plight of the refugees, the problems encountered by them since such information is not forthcoming from UNHCR. Critical material can sensitize the world and some times, international opinion can have a sobering effect on the intransigence of the host country. In case of East Timor, the outside world knew little, besides what was included in the Security Council documents, about the problems faced by the refugees and the UNHCR alike during the mission until the NGOs like Human Rights Watch, Amnesty International and the East Timor Action Network (ETAN) came up with reports on the basis of independent field visits. The Organization's own assessment of the ground realities will have far reaching credibility in countering rumours and misinformation. Stock taking after each operation and "lessons learnt" studies are essential if the UNHCR has to equip itself well for its future tasks. Some UNHCR staff has off record given a very realistic account of the difficulties encountered in East Timor. If they can be encouraged to put down those reviews for the Office's own future reference, it will have developed a very impressive information base.

CONCLUSION

In summing up one may say that there are areas that need urgent improvements to enhance the systemic capacity of UNHCR and greater attention paid to the specifics of mandate in future. The policy of providing refugee aid will have to take into account the economic conditions of the region where refugee camps are situated in the host country before planning disbursement of aid. Local conditions can foment extreme reaction to international help for the refugees. In West Timor, for example, the refugee crisis had placed a large burden on this border district since it was one of the poorest provinces of Indonesia. At one point of time refugees outnumbered the local population leading to social tension.[27] Added to it refugee influx had deteriorated the sanitation and significantly reduced employment opportunities for the locals in the area. Many locals were lured into registering themselves as refugees in exchange for food and blankets.

The role of UNHCR in East Timor brings in sharp relief the problems faced by the agency in implementing the mandate. The drawbacks are as much due to the nature of the mandate and prevailing circumstances on ground as the institutional inadequacies. UNHCR encountered difficulties pertaining to fragile nature of cease-fire, lack of security and no co-operation from the host country, as enumerated above. The need, however, is for the agency to put in place a strategy to circumscribe such limitations in future operations if they are to be successfully completed on time with least human and material loss. The suggestions put forth in the section on critical assessment point towards this.

REFERENCES

1. B.S. Chimni, 'Recovering from Civil Conflict', *International Peace-keeping*, Vol. 10, 2002, p. 163.
2. R. Black and K. Koser, ed., *Refugee Repatriation and Reconstruction,* Berghahn Books, 1999, pp. 11-12.
3. B.S. Chimni, 'Globalization, Humanitarianism and the Erosion of Refugee Protection', RSC Working Paper No. 3, Oxford University: Refugee Studies Centre, 2000, p. 14.<URL: http://www.rsc.ox.ac.uk/chimni3.pdf>
4. Gil Loescher, *Beyond Charity: International Cooperation and the Global Refugee Crisis,* Oxford University Press, 1996, p. 28.
5. *Ibid*., p. 29.
6. *Ibid*., p. 30.
7. Suai Church massacre in April 1999. See, Noam Chomsky, 'Comment on

East Timor', URL<www.motherjones.com/east_timor/comment/chomsky.html>

8. James Traub, 'Inventing East Timor', *Foreign Affairs,* Vol. 79, 2000, pp. 78-79; Jarat Chopra, 'The UN's Kingdom of East Timor', *Survival,* Vol. 42, 2000, p. 27.
9. UNSC Resolution S/RES/1264(1999), 15 September, 1999.
10. James Cotton, 'Against the Grain: The East Timor Intervention', *Survival,* Vol. 43, 2001, p. 127.
11. UNSC Resolution S/RES/1272(1999), 25 October, 1999.
12. UNHCR, *Global Report 2000*, p. 335.
13. *IOM News,* [1999] pp. 1-4.
14. UN Security Council, *Report of the Secretary-General on the United Nations Transitional Administration in East Timor,* UN Doc. S/2000/53 of 26 January, 2000, at p. 8.
15. Human Rights Watch, *Indonesia/East Timor: Forced Expulsions to West Timor and the Refugee Crisis*, Vol. 11, No. 7(c), December, 1999.<URL: http://www.hrw.org/reports/1999/wtimor/>
16. BBC Special Report<www.news.bbc.co.uk/1/hi/world/asia-pacific/480351.stm>
17. See ref. no. 15 above.
18. UNHCR, *Global Report 2000,* p. 332.
19. UN Doc. S/6905, 3 August, 2000.
20. UNSC Resolution S/Res/1319(2000), 8 September, 2000. The resolution, stressed "that those responsible for the attacks on international personnel… must be brought to book", called on the "Indonesian authorities to take immediate and effective measures to ensure the safe return of refugees", that "UNHCR workers cannot return to West Timor until there is a credible security guarantee" and underlined that UNTAET should respond robustly to the militia threat in East Timor, consistent with resolution 1272(1999) of 22 October, 1999 [emphasis added].
21. East Timor *Action* Network, an NGO working in East Timor. <www.etan.org/news/>
22. UNHCR, *Mid-Year Progress Report 2001*, p. 176.
23. UN Doc. S/6905, 3 August, 2000.
24. See the wordings of the UNSC Resolution 1319 (2000) above.
25. Gil Loescher, *The UNHCR and World Politics: A Perilous Path*, Oxford University Press, 2001, p. 306.
26. G. Gilbert, 'Rights, Legitimate Expectations, Needs and Responsibilities: UNHCR and the New World Order', International *Journal of Refugee Law*, Vol. 10, 1998, p. 382.
27. Programme on Humanitarian Policy and Conflict Research, Harvard University<www.preventconflict.org/portal/main/maps_wtimor_refugees.php>

20

Getting Over International Economic Crises: Relevance of Gandhian Approach

S.K.G. Sundaram

Globalization refers to the process of integration of the economies of the world through free movement of goods, services and capital. Financial globalization is prominent since it is considered to be the life blood of trade and development. The process began to gather momentum after the Second World War, during 1950s and 1960s. As trade began to expand rapidly, financial globalization also became more prominent with governments of the advanced countries deregulating the financial sector and promoting investment. Financial sector reforms gradually integrated the economies of the world by stimulating the flow of funds and encouraging foreign investment. As a result world exports increased from \$61 billion in 1950 to \$3447 billion in 1990 and to \$10,393 billion in 2005. The global foreign direct investment (FDI) rose from \$202.5 billion in 1990 to \$1463.6 billion in 2000.

Technological innovation and faster information flow, aided by a sharp increase in total savings being channelled into financial investments across borders, have fostered the dramatic globalization of capital flows—defined as the flow of capital across borders. These flows—including debt, portfolio, equity and direct investment based financing—increased from \$1.5 trillion in 1995 to \$6 trillion in 2005.[1] (*Finance & Development*, March 07, p. 14.) In developing countries like China and India such rise in financial globalization leads to larger exports and rising incomes that further lead to a rise in consumption of what in India has come to be known as "fast moving consumption goods".

This globalization boom continued till 2007 with all round global growth. The growth rate of advanced countries more than doubled from 1.2 per cent in 2001 to 3.1 per cent in 2006 and estimates for 2007 and

2008 were lower but still more than double of growth rate in 2001. The emerging market economies and developing countries were performing still better. (see Table 20.1 below for more details)

However, this rising tide of financial globalization, expanding level of incomes and consumption suddenly turned sour in 2008-09 when the US economy fell in an unwarranted recession precipitating a global recession and crisis.

In contrast to the estimates of 4.9 per cent (see Table 20.1) in the growth of world GDP in 2008, the World Bank slashed the estimates of growth to 2.5 per cent, and still worse in 2009, it slashed the growth estimate to less than 1 per cent, at 0.9 per cent! However, subsequently the performance of the US economy improved. In the third quarter of 2009 the US economy grew at 3.5 per cent which has raised the hopes of an early end of the recession. But though the duration period of the global recession has remained short, its intensity has been quite high[2] (*Hindustan Times*, 11-12-2008). This will be discussed later. The focus in the next section will be on the factors that contributed to the emergence of the global recession.

Table 20.1: GDP Growth Rates during 2001-08

Region	*2001*	*2002*	*2003*	*2004*	*2005*	*2006*	*2007 PE*	*2008 PE*
World	2.5	3.1	4.0	5.3	4.9	5.4	4.9	4.9
USA	0.8	1.6	2.5	3.9	3.2	3.3	2.2	2.8
Euro Area	1.9	0.9	0.8	2.0	1.4	2.6	2.3	2.3
U.K.	2.4	2.1	2.7	3.3	1.9	2.7	2.9	2.7
Japan	0.2	0.3	1.4	2.7	1.9	2.2	2.3	1.9
Korea	3.8	7.0	3.1	4.7	4.2	5.0	4.4	4.4
China	8.3	9.1	10.0	10.1	10.4	10.7	10.0	9.5
India	4.1	4.3	7.3	7.8	9.2	9.2	8.4	7.8
Advanced Economies	1.2	1.6	1.9	3.3	2.5	3.1	2.5	2.7
Other Asian Economies	1.7	3.2	2.4	4.1	3.2	3.6	3.3	3.4
Emerging Markets & Developing Countries	4.3	5.0	6.7	7.7	7.5	7.9	7.5	7.1

Source: World Economic Outlook, 2007, IMF (Quoted in Investor's Guide, *Economic Times*, 16-4-2007.
PE = Provisional Estimates

As discussed above, it can be seen from the Table 20.1 that the sterling performance of China followed by India.

FACTORS THAT LED TO THE RECESSION

The financial crisis that led to recession appeared to be due to the emergence and prevalence of unsustainable and hazardous financial transactions in which high returns were offered to "entice new investors to lend and invest" which are not realized in the market by borrowers. Thus "greed for quick and big money" replaced 'need'. In course of time this led to erosion of business confidence. Further, since the financial market remained highly deregulated various innovative derivatives were created which contributed to expansion of financial market transactions. The crisis emerged when loans were given to borrowers at sub-prime rates and the borrowers did not honour their obligations. Earlier when financial crisis hit the hedge fund "Long Term Capital Market" (LTCM) in September 1998, it was rescued by the Fed by injecting $3.6 billion.[3] (Sunanda Sen, 2008). Later in March 2008 another large bank "Bear Sterns" also failed marking the beginning of the financial crisis, giving an indication of the shape of things to come. Rumours started spreading of an impending collapse of the financial system.

The financial crisis reached a climax around September 2008, when two major investment banks, the Fannie Fae and Fredie Mac dealing with mortgage loans were taken over by the U.S. Treasury. Another major investment bank AIG, a large insurance bank whose assets were spread over 130 countries, was recapitalized by the Treasury with an injection of $85 billion against 80 per cent equity stake with AIG. By September 11, 2008 funds injected by the Fed in the financial market were around $900 billion and the amount kept rising. Around this period another major investment bank, the Lehman Brothers went bankrupt on September 12, 2008. Further, around the same period more institutions Merryl Lynch, Goldman Sachs and Stanley Morgan Investment also failed.

Merril Lynch was taken over by the Bank of America and the other two were converted into holding companies. Another major bank Washington Mutual, biggest bank accepting deposits from and lending to ordinary clients also failed and was nationalized[4] (P.R. Dubhasi, 2008). All these institutions thus fell prey to wild speculations aimed at making quick money instead of logical thinking and sensible business.

The crisis had an international impact and continued till the second quarter of 2009 when the intensity of the recession began to show abatement, thanks to the stimulus measures announced and implemented all over the world. A positive indication was reported with the announcement of earnings of $1.8 billion by Goldman Sachs in the first quarter of 2009[5] (*Economic Times*, 15-4-09).

GLOBAL IMPACT OF FINANCIAL CRISIS

The impact of financial crisis which led to the fall of so many financial institutions, created a panic situation all over the global financial and economic system. The banking system came under severe strain. There was a loss of confidence in the financial system, financial institutions and in the ability of the government to deal with the situation. Fear of recessions turned into reality.

The congressional research service report for Congress (July 10, 2009) titled "The Global Financial Crisis: An Analysis and Policy Implications" (CRS Report) has the following to say in its summary:

> "The world has entered a global recession that is causing widespread business contraction, increases in unemployment, and shrinking of government revenues. Some of the largest and most venerable banks, investment houses and insurance companies have either declared bankruptcy or have to be rescued financially. Nearly all industrialized countries and many emerging and developing nations have announced economic stimulus and/or financial sector rescue packages, such as the American Recovery and Reinvestment Act of 2009 (P.L. III-5). Several countries have resorted to borrowing from the international Monetary Fund as a last resort. The crisis has exposed fundamental weaknesses in financial systems worldwide, demonstrated how inter-connected and interdependent economies are today, and has posed vexing policy dilemmas."[6]

As the above report points out, the recession was truly global. Almost all countries were affected and it was clear that remedies and recovery measures had to be globally coordinated.

Roger Altman (Altman Roger C., 2009) has narrated effectively the impact of the crisis on the U.S. economy on the one hand and globally on the other.[7]

As regards impact on the U.S. economy, Altman has pointed out that the global recession has put the "U.S. model of free market capitalism out of favour". The US will now be focused inward and constrained by unemployment and fiscal pressures. The US households lost 20 per cent of their net worth in just 18 months during mid-2007-end 2008. The US is also strongly criticized all over the world for its inability to take effective action that led to the global recession. Americans in general are also criticized for spending beyond their means.

Coming to the global impact, it is Altman's contention that the crisis will be deep and prolonged. "The long standing wisdom that everyone wins in a single world market has been undermined." He has also pointed out that global trade, capital flows and immigration are declining. He has also brought out the structural and significant changes that are taking place in the global economy. Firstly, the era of *laissez faire* has ended, and the role of state has been expanding, together with re-regulation of markets. Secondly globalization is in retreat both in concept and practice. Thirdly, the world may be entering a new global phase marked by less leadership, less coordination and less coherence. (Emerging powers are not still capable of full leadership). And fourthly, the crisis likely will increase geopolitical stability. It is to be seen how the world emerges after the crisis.

Europe has exhibited a lack of unity on how to deal with the situation. Japan is expected to become weaker. It was also felt that the developing countries have also been hard hit. Some of them have resorted to emergency loans from the IMF. Africa has also been experiencing a decline in capital flows.

The CRS report referred earlier has explained that the global recession of 2008-09, next only to the Great Depression of 1930s, has been dealt with in four phases. "The first has been intervention to contain the contagion and restore confidence in the system....The second one has been coping with the secondary effects of the crisis, particularly the global recession and flight of capital from countries and from emerging markets and elsewhere that have been affected by the crisis. The third phase of this process is to make changes in the financial system to reduce risk and prevent future crises....The fourth phase of the process is dealing with political, social, and security effects of the financial turmoil. One such effect is the strengthened role of China in financial markets".[8]

One IMF estimate of the total cost of global financial crisis puts it at $11.9 trillion[9] (*Free Press Journal*, 10-8-09). Further, the developing countries now face tightening of external financial conditions, declining commodity prices, contraction of export markets, sharp decline in Overseas Development Assistance (ODA), low private capital inflows, big reduction in remittances from abroad and the return of migrants to home countries.[10] (Muchkund Dubey, 2009). The global stock markets were worst affected. A record $14 trillion was wiped off the world share values in 2008. The world market value over the years rose from $30.5 trillion in 2003 to $60.9 trillion in 2007, but fell steeply to $31.9 trillion in 2008, a fall of 47.6 per cent, reflecting the magnitude of the crisis. 94 out of 116 developing countries experienced economic downturn in economic growth. Among these 43 countries were very poor.

CASES OF CHINA AND INDIA

China and India were among the few countries that escaped much of the severity experienced by the USA and other countries. Both had a small deceleration in their growth rates, but that is all. As Altman has pointed out that "it has also not gone unnoticed that nations with insulated financial systems, such as China and India, have suffered the least economic change".

China

China is considered to be a clear winner, whose unique political-economic model has come through unscathed. China continues to grow at 'enviable' rates. It is now the world's wealthiest country measured by financial reserves and it is making strategic investments that others cannot make.[11] (Altman Roger C., 2009).

But the CRS Report while conceding that China's loss may be relatively less has pointed out that China has not been immune to the effects of financial crisis because of its heavy reliance on trade and foreign direct investment (FDI). The Report points to the slow down in construction in several cities fall in prices and growing levels of unoccupied buildings. Exports and FDI have shown a declining trend and there have been production and job losses. Besides, China's GDP growth may be less in 2009. There are also numerous restrictions on capital flows and individuals and lack of transparency, as a result the impact may not be fully clear, but still it cannot be denied that China has not been much affected by the global recession.

India

India is perhaps next only to China in its economic performance during the recession period. While India's foreign trade has been affected to some extent, and its growth has fallen marginally, its FDI has continued to rise, as the Table 20.2 illustrates.

Table 20.2: India: Growth Rate of GDP and FDI

Year	*GDP Growth Rate (%)*	*FDI in Billion US$*
2003-04	8.6	2.2
2004-05	7.5	3.2
2005-06	9.4	5.5
2006-07	9.7	15.7
2007-08	9.0	24.6
2008-09	6.7	27.3
2009-10	7.7(E)	19.8(+)

Source: Various estimates of GDP and *Hindustan Times* 25-4-2009 for FDI
E = estimates + = April-November, 2009 only.

Table 20.2 highlights the facts of rising FDI and impressive growth rates. The forecast for 2009-10 has been at a higher level of 7.7 per cent and some estimates have projected that India will reach the growth level of over 9 per cent from 2010-11 onwards.

The important reasons for India's positive performance include its domestic demand based economy and its resilient service sector. Further the regulatory system was in place and scope for large capital convertibility was limited. Therefore, India was expected to face the recession without much adverse consequences (Manoj Pant, *Economic Times*, 2008). The World Bank also has a similar view.

However, this does not mean that India faced no adverse effects. There have been production and job losses and widening inequalities. Industries most affected by weakening demand were airlines, hotels and real estate. Export sector also suffered setbacks. Information Technology and BPO sectors were also adversely affected. (Ruddar Datt). India came out with a fiscal stimulus three times during December 2008 and February, 2009 estimated to be amounting to Rs.138,000 crores constituting approximately 3.5 per cent of the GDP.[12] (Free Press Journal, 2009).

MEASURES TO COPE WITH THE CRISIS

There has been no doubt that, since the origin of the Great Recession has been in the USA, the lead to deal with the crisis should also emerge from there. And so it has been, but the USA sought and received support from other countries. The details are given below.

As stated earlier, the USA made it clear that by itself it cannot be a "regulatory island" in an international market place where there are multinational corporations, independent and instant transfer of wealth, lightning fast communication and globalized trading system for equities and securities. Hence some coordination was needed. This was agreed. The vehicle for forming an international consensus on measures to be taken by different countries was the G-20, with IMF and the newly formed Financial Stability Board consisting of 25 member countries and major international institutions like IMF, OECD and World Bank. The mandate of the Board included providing early warning on macro-economic and financial risks and measures to cover them and also advise and act on issues that needed to be tackled.

In the USA, the Department of the Treasury on June 17, 2009, released the Obama Administration proposal for financial regulatory reform. The proposal focused on five areas and included establishing the Federal Reserve as a systemic risk regulator, creating a Council of Regulators, regulating all financial derivatives, creating a Consumer Financial Protection Agency, improving coordination and oversight of international financial markets, and other provisions. Legislation in Congress also would address these issues.

At the April 2009 G-20 Summit at London, the G-20 leaders decided to add $1.1 trillion to the resources of international financial institutions ($750 billion to IMF, $250 billion to boost global trade and $100 billion for multilateral development banks). During the period of November 2008 to April 2009, all leading countries announced their own stimulus measures. These included all major developed and advanced countries including (figures in brackets indicate amounts in billion US dollars): the USA (787); China (586); Japan (350); European Union (256); Mexico (54); South Korea (37.87); Australia (35); Canada (32); and Russia (20). General stimulus measures included lowering of interest, easing of credit, subsidies for export, and incentive for more output and higher growth and employment. (As stated in the earlier section, India contributed Rs.138,000 crores).

RELEVANCE OF GANDHI IN HANDLING FINANCIAL CRISIS

The economic and financial crisis was addressed at the international level by many countries announcing stimulus measures. However, the root causes that brought about such a severe recession are still being analyzed.

Here comes the relevance of Gandhi. While many factors contributed to the recession, their significance can be subjected to Gandhian analysis.

It is pointed out that "Americans spent beyond their means" aided by a credit card based economy. This consumerism could not be sustained. The crisis stared on their faces, and their consumption fell by record rates. In Gandhian perspective this is irrational and unjustified because Gandhian philosophy is based on stable and equitable spending and simple living with contentment. It is based on the belief that need can and must be satisfied but greed can never be satisfied. In the crisis situation erratic and panic driven consumer behaviour was witnessed which accentuated the crisis.

Another reason for financial crisis has been the recklessness of the banking and financial institutions in giving loans and credit to sub-prime borrowers including those with "dodgy credit backgrounds". Gandhian system would never have accepted such recklessness on the part of business. On the contrary the Gandhian system would demand the bank management act under Ghandhiji's Trusteeship principles.

The role of government also deserves to be examined more critically. Gandhiji believed in a decentralized set-up, but advocated State role in important sectors like key industries. Banking and financial institutions constitute another important sector in the economy. It is obvious that the governmental agencies were not vigilant and did not effectively regulate the behaviour of the institutions in the financial sector. But there is also a view that "it was not the lack of regulation that led to this cataclysm but sheer recklessness on the part of key players in the financial sector". It should be noted that the US government took over several bankrupt institutions in the financial sector in order to avoid further damage. But it was considered to be a little too less and too late, resulting in heavy damage. In this context, the Government of India's role has come in for appreciation. Regulation to prevent recklessness helped the Indian government while lack of such a role in America resulted in the collapse of the financial sector.

Excessively speculative transactions that are highly risky in relation to their returns, often termed as 'ponzi' deals would never have been permitted under the Gandhian system. It can ruin the investor's financial position and create instabilities in the financial markets as well as investors' homes. Such deals were significant in the prevailing financial crisis.

Apart from the "spending beyond the means" in a credit card dominated economy, there was also the psychology of "American dream" for luxurious homes. This was also associated with an "addiction to high consumption", again thanks to cashless credit prone economy. This resulted in a combination of greed supported by easy credit and lower interest rates. This ultimately led to "the country itself living beyond its means". Hence budget deficits and external deficits due to vigorous export promotion by China led to spiralling national debt. All such behaviour is unthinkable under the Gandhian system wherein need is to be met and greed has to be discouraged.

It should be noted that many of the crises, involve 'human' factors. Collapse of macro-level economic activity has happened several times in the history and the 'human' causes like greed have been repeated in such crises. One prominent view that exposes this 'human' element in the present crisis is given below:

> "The CEOs of these financial institutions were the new 'moghals' whose insatiable greed led to reckless financial operations in complete disregard of the productivity in the real economy. The goal was "maximization of profits" in the short run and not sound long term development. Concepts like honesty, loyalty to an institution and sound business became old fashioned and discarded. The greed of the CEOs soon turned into personal acquisition in an unscrupulous fashion. They awarded to themselves hefty compensations in various forms including salaries, perks, bonuses and stock options. The CEOs deserted the investors they were serving at the first opportunity after making a fast buck. They did not hesitate to indulge in fraud in which they were joined by reputed accounting firms; as was brought out in the Enron case whose fabulous boss, Kenneth Lay, a favourite of President Bush, had to end his last days in jail undergoing a sentence after the scandal came into the open and the firm collapsed. The FBI disclosed that CEOs of some of the financial institutions which recently collapsed are under investigation for deliberately misleading the investors. While giving them assurances regarding the bright prospects of their companies in their private communications on the internet to each other, they were talking of impending financial collapse....As a result of the greed of the CEOs of the American corporations, the gap between the top and bottom of the society in financial wealth and income has reached astronomical proportions."[13] (P.R. Dubhashi, 2008)

Gandhian system would have expected the CEOs to behave as trustees with a high sense of responsibility and a deep sense of commitment to the well-being of investors. But instead, self-aggrandizement overtook 'trusteeship' approach and brought ruin for all.

What is shocking is that no significant attempt seems to have been made to investigate the role of those whose behaviour has contributed to the building up of the financial crisis. J.K. Galbraith in his recent book (2004) has analyzed such behaviour and crises and laments that there has been no check on the big business and such things keep happening as if a matter of course. He says that "the world of finance is a well recognized area of innocent fraud". In such a world "prediction of the unknown is a cherished and often a well rewarded occupation". He points out that those employed or self-employed who predict future financial performance of an industry or firm, given the unpredictable but controlling influence of the large economy, do not know and normally do not know that they do not know.[14] The result is "elegant escape from the reality". In all these, the false and favourable reputation of Fed has a strong foundation. Bankers/experts build it, advocate lower interest rate and more spending for increasing income, output and employment. But this is not real life. In other words, every crisis is taken for granted and we move from crisis to crisis, affecting poor and common investors.

The above analysis brings out the importance of immediate and long term relevance of Gandhian philosophy and approach to deal with national and international problems. Some such approaches are presented below.

One of the important reasons for the current financial crisis reducing its intensity and moving towards stability and progress has been the international co-operation and dialogue. Gandhiji believed in dialogue which he expresses comprehensively while discussing industrial relations or labour-management co-operation. Gandhism believes in class harmony and not class conflicts. This has also relevance to international relations where Gandhism advocates solution of problems through dialogue. For this purpose the suggestion of institutionalizing the global capital market dialogue through an appropriate form of organization like a group or forum is worth considering.[15] (James Turley, *Economic Times*, 20.6.08)

The role of Gandhism has been important in all crises and problems. While Gandhiji believed in minimum government, he was also aware of the strategic significance of state or government. According to him if people and government act as trustees there is no problem. But, said Gandhiji, "if people fail, I believe we shall have to deprive them of their possession through the state with minimum exercise of violence". In case of the USA, the government entered only when the financial system was on the verge of collapse. But in India the state was wise enough to keep control over financial system even under reforms. The Government of India decided to retain the dominance of the public sector banks and also strengthened the banking system by offering $5 billion in capital, which has paid off in the present crisis where India's financial system is still fine and fettle. Internationally every country must be encouraged to lay down an effective monitoring system.

At the international level during the times of crisis, ideological or political considerations must not come in the way of coordinated action. The problems of developing countries where people are relatively much poorer should be attended to expeditiously and sympathetically. Gandhian philosophy advocates that poor people's basic needs should receive top priority. "I hate privilege and monopoly. Whatever cannot be shared with masses is taboo for me"[16] said Gandhiji.

It should also be kept in view that the crisis emerged out of failure of regulatory bodies, auditors, rating agencies and CEOs of the financial institutions who were not vigilant in their jobs. Once the crisis became serious, the Government arranged for large bailouts. Policy makers should be aware that such bailouts can some times encourage more risky behaviour in the market. It is reported that market earlier looked out for a bailout of Lehman Brothers, but when this did not happen within the time they had anticipated, Lehman Brothers came under pressure and had to declare its bankruptcy. Whenever such crises emerge in the future, the policymakers should intervene appropriately and swiftly. Monitoring, remedial and reinforcing actions must be taken effectively and quickly. This approach would also be consistent with a Gandhian approach. Gandhiji was not against harsh measures if there was no better alternative.

The UN Commission of Experts on the Reform of the International Monetary and Financial system, has made valuable recommendations including a balanced response to global recession; a new global reserve system with SDR as its anchor; a global reserve currency; Regional Monetary arrangements; strengthening the lending capacity of multilateral development banks; creation of a global financial regulating authority and a global competition authority; and coordination of global macro-economic policies.[17] Such recommendations under the aegis of the UN are consistent with Gandhian approach as he was a firm believer of absolute oneness of God and Humanity. These recommendations, if implemented with international coordination and co-operation, are bound to promote a stable international order, economy and society, in short, a Gandhian society.

REFERENCES

1. Articles relevant to *Finance & Development* (March 2007, December 2008, September 2009 issues, IMF, Washington DC.
2. *Hindustan Times* "Is it Great Depression?" December 11, 2008; see also "That Shrinking Feeling", March 10, 2009.
3. Sen, Sunanda (2008) "Global Financial Crisis: A Classic 'Ponzi' Affair?" *Mainstream,* (New Delhi, 2008) October 24-30, pp. 11-14.
4. Dubhashi, P.R. Collapse of the Financial Institutions of American Capitalism, *Mainstream*, New Delhi: October 24-30, 2008, pp. 7-10.
5. *Economic Times*, "Goldman Numbers Spread Global Cheer", April 15, 2009.
6. CRS Report for Congress, The Global Financial Crisis: Analysis and Policy Implications, Coordinator-Dick K. Nanto, Congressional Research Service, www.crs.gov (Washington: 2009).
7. Altman Roger C., "Globalization in Retreat—Further Geopolitical Consequences of the Financial Crisis", *Foreign Affairs*, July-August, 2009.
8. CRS Report, *op. cit.*
9. Total Cost of Global Financial Crisis, *Free Press Journal*, August 10, 2009.
10. Dubey, Muchkund, Towards a New International Monetary & Financial Architecture, *Mainstream* (New Delhi: 2009), April 17-23, pp. 7-12.
11. Altman Roger C., *op. cit.*
12. *Free Press Journal*, Total cost of global financial crisis, August 10, 2009.
13. Dubhashi, P.R., Collapse of the Financial Institutions of American Capitalism, *Mainstream* (New Delhi: 2008), October 24-30, pp. 7-10.
14. Galbraith, J.K. *The Economics of Innocent Fraud—Truth for Our Time*, Houghton Mufflin & Co. (USA: 2004).
15. James Turley, *Economic Times*, "Global Capital Market Dialogue Vital", June 16, 2008.
16. Prabhu R.K. and Rao U.R., *The Mind of Mahatma Gandhi*, Navjivan Publishing House (Ahmedabad: 1967); Pasricha, Ashu, "Hind Swaraj: Retrieving the Sacred in the Globalized World", *Journal of Gandhian Studies*, Vol. VII, No. 1, 2009.
17. Report of the Commission of Experts of the President of the United Nations General Assembly on Reforms in International Monetary and Financial System (21 September, 2009).

Index